GW00862522

The Politics of Decline

Also by Geoffrey K. Fry

STATESMEN IN DISGUISE

THE GROWTH OF GOVERNMENT

THE ADMINISTRATIVE 'REVOLUTION' IN WHITEHALL

THE CHANGING CIVIL SERVICE

REFORMING THE CIVIL SERVICE

POLICY AND MANAGEMENT IN THE BRITISH CIVIL SERVICE

THE POLITICS OF CRISIS

The Politics of Decline

An Interpretation of British Politics from the 1940s to the 1970s

Geoffrey K. Fry
Emeritus Professor of British Government and Administration
University of Leeds, UK

First published 2005 by
PALGRAVE MACMILLAN
Houndmills, Basingstoke, Hampshire RG21 6XS and
175 Fifth Avenue, New York, N. Y. 10010
Companies and representatives throughout the world

PALGRAVE MACMILLAN is the global academic imprint of the Palgrave Macmillan division of St. Martin's Press, LLC and of Palgrave Macmillan Ltd. Macmillan® is a registered trademark in the United States, United Kingdom and other countries. Palgrave is a registered trademark in the European Union and other countries.

ISBN 0–333–72622–7

This book is printed on paper suitable for recycling and made from fully managed and sustained forest sources.

A catalogue record for this book is available from the British Library.

Library of Congress Cataloging-in-Publication Data
Fry, Geoffrey Kingdon.
  The politics of decline : an interpretation of British politics from the 1940s to the 1950s / Geoffrey K. Fry.
     p. cm.
  Includes bibliographical references and index.
  ISBN 0-333-72622-7 (cloth)
     1. Great Britain–Politics and government–1945-1964. 2. Great Britain–Politics and government–1964-1979. 3. Political parties–Great Britain–History–20th century. I. Title.
DA588.F79 2005
320.941′09′044–dc22

2004053452

10   9   8   7   6   5   4   3   2   1
14   13   12   11   10   09   08   07   06   05

Printed and bound in Great Britain by
Antony Rowe Ltd, Chippenham and Eastbourne

To S. E. Ayling

Contents

Preface

This book is an interpretation of British politics from the 1940s down to the resolution of the IMF Crisis of 1976. Like its predecessor volume, *The Politics of Crisis*, which dealt with the period between 1931 and 1945, this is not the work of a writer who is a political animal in the Aristotelian sense. The criticism that all this means is that I am a residual or reluctant Conservative has some basis, but it was not until near the end of the period considered in this book that I voted with any consistency, or, indeed, at all. Of the two ideologies that were to contest the future – socialism and economic liberalism – it always seemed to me that the latter would prevail. As I have written about economic liberalism, there are those who count me as a believer, but all I believed in was that it was the winning side. Then again, that I was taught political philosophy by Michael Oakeshott has been said by some to have converted me to Conservatism, but it was negative influences that mattered most: my working class parents tired of the Labour Party ignoring their views and those of people like them; Aneurin Bevan expounded his unappealing views of what a future socialist Britain would look like at a public meeting in my youthful presence. At the time of Suez, I shared the contempt that all but one of my fellow low ranking servicemen had for Hugh Gaitskell's behaviour. I managed to attract universal condemnation from the same audience for my argument that Britain could not act without American support, which was not going to be forthcoming anyway. After much consideration, this argument is also advanced in Chapter 7 in much safer circumstances. So is my contemporary argument that the Soviet Union had no choice about crushing the Hungarian Uprising because to do otherwise would signal the end of its Empire. This led to me being condemned as a Communist. Spending my youth in the Armed Forces confirmed what would be best described as a *Lord of the Flies* view of the masses, reinforced since on a very regular basis by my addiction to attending football matches. So, I have no taste for populism and in this book there will be no display of the *bien pensant* views that have come to dominate the British political class and the literature.

Though, as was the case with *The Politics of Crisis*, in some ways the author has spent all his adult life preparing for the writing of this book, and he takes responsibility for its content, the book's completion owes a lot to the encouragement of others. As with my seven previous books, many of my serving and former colleagues at the University of Leeds have encouraged me in this venture, led by Owen Hartley, James Macdonald, Richard Whiting, Edward Spiers, David Murdoch, David Bell, Alan Deacon, Kevin Theakston, David Seawright, Patrick Bell, Christopher Lord, Neil Winn, and Clive Jones. As before too, I am indebted to the staff of the Brotherton Library at Leeds, especially Susan Grayson, Lindsay Scutchings, and Lynne Thompson. I also thank Rodney Lowe of the University of Bristol for his help. As is evident from several references, Edward Boyle was generous to me with his time when he was Vice Chancellor of the University of Leeds. This had to be from a sense of duty on his part because he knew very well what I thought of his *bien pensant* views. My friends on the explicit Left have been very generous to me too, and so have my many other friends, especially Richard Dickason. I thank my wife for her tolerance once more during the research and writing of this book. I am grateful to the archivists who helped me when dealing with private papers and those of the Conservative and Labour parties, and in those instances in which copyright holders are involved I also record my gratitude to them. While, in writing this book, the author has found invaluable the intellectual background provided by the many hours that he has spent over the years reading Cabinet and departmental papers in the then Public Record Office, this book is not full of specific citations. The materials used are cited in the Bibliography, and, as can be seen there, they mostly comprise primary sources, including those that have been published, Hansard, and official reports. As I wrote about British domestic politics during the Second World War in *The Politics of Crisis*, I have not done so in this book, concentrating instead on the building of the post-war world. That so much attention is given to the Attlee Governments follows from the reality that they did so much more than the others. I add that, unlike many academics and journalists who write about British politics, I do not believe that I would have done better if I had held office. The contempt for politicians that has become fashionable seems to me to have been taken to excess. Few of us would impress if our failings were on display on a public stage.

If God gives me the time, and my health holds up, I hope to write a further book about the Thatcher era. In a happy life, I have owed so much to others. I dedicate this book to S.E. Ayling, my history master at the local grammar school that I attended, whom I tracked down with some difficulty just before he died to thank him for all he did for me. I take this opportunity to thank him again.

GEOFFREY K. FRY

1

'A Period of National Humiliation and Decline'

'Thus, then, on the night of the tenth of May, at the outset of this mighty battle, I acquired the chief power in the State, which henceforth I wielded in ever growing measure for five years and three months of world war, at the end of which time, all our enemies having surrendered unconditionally or being about to do so, I was immediately dismissed by the British electorate from all further conduct of their affairs.'[1] So wrote Winston Churchill retrospectively of his appointment as British Prime Minister in 1940, and of his dismissal from that office as a consequence of the defeat of the Conservative Party that he led in the General Election of 1945. 'This is not necessarily the end', Churchill said of his defeat at the time,[2] and this more immediate judgement proved to be the sounder one in the sense that he was to be Prime Minister once more as soon afterwards as 1951, and Conservative Governments then ruled until 1964. Churchill was not to leave the centre of the British political stage until 1955, and he was not to die until 1965, but in or out of office, alive or dead, Churchill was a Ghost in the Machine of British politics, a reminder of the country's Finest Hour in 1940, and a symbol of Britain's continuing aspiration to be a Great Power, which, of course, he articulated better than anybody else. It may well be that relatively few electors would have shared Churchill's feeling of being 'very lonely without a war' in 1945,[3] and his love of war was a source of widespread distrust of him as a peacetime political leader: but one 'lesson of history' drawn from his behaviour in the 1930s that Churchill could be said to have handed down which did command wide support thereafter was of the importance of provision for defence and that Appeasement never pays in foreign policy. The other 'lesson of history' that the electorate seemed to draw from the 1930s

1

was that there was neither any need for the high levels of unemployment that had scarred British society during that decade, nor for the constraints then placed on the scale of State social provision. By the latter part of the Second World War, Treasury officials believed that the prevailing mood in British politics was to anticipate and plan for a Brave New World rather than a Cruel Real World,[4] and, if this interpretation did not quite capture what many, possibly most, electors seemed to be seeking, it did recognize that, in terms of domestic policy, 'sound finance' and the other tenets of economic liberalism were redundant for the then foreseeable future, and that those of Keynesian full employment and the Welfare State of the Beveridge Report were the orthodoxy.

This was the 'lesson' of the result of the General Election of 1945, which remained a Ghost in the Machine of British politics for long afterwards along with the Keynesian dispensation itself. Despite the association of that economic and social order with the decline of the British economy compared with those of its main rivals, it was to take thirty years before sufficient political momentum built up in favour of the politics of the Cruel Real World. Reflecting on a political career that had then spanned the period from the 1940s to the 1970s, the Conservative, Lord Hailsham commented that 'it has been a matter of supreme regret to me that my public life has taken place in a period of national humiliation and decline, the like of which I do not know that the British nation has ever experienced in recent history ... one can well ask oneself whether by greater sagacity, insight, courage, or virtue one could not have achieved more or at least allowed less that was of value to be sacrificed.'[5] The British political elite or class or nation provides an inviting target for blame, not least the 'liberal' intelligentsia of whom one of their number was too kind when he wrote that 'their greatest mistake was to neglect – and some even to despise – the need for their country to become more efficient, more productive in business and industry'.[6] The record of the 'liberals' encouraged the observation that even conscious traitors would have to have been especially well placed to do as much damage to their country. The 'liberals' and those who deferred to them have to take the blame for making changes in public policy in the sphere of law and order that offended against popular opinion, but the broad mass of the electorate had no quarrel with the comforts of the Keynesian dispensation. There were consequences that the electorate came to dislike, not least in relation to Britain's ambitions to remain a Great Power, which was, of course, in a country with a system of representative government, a role that could only be sustained by a successful internationally competitive economy. As early as 1952, Churchill, bemused by Britain's already evident continuing relative economic decline, lamented that 'when I came to America before it has been as an equal … They have become so great and we are now so small. Poor England! We threw away so much in 1945.'[7] If a pyrrhic victory had been obtained then, this was better than none at all. Even in his seventies, Churchill had addressed the question of what Britain should do next. The answers he came up with inevitably showed him in part to be a prisoner of the past, and in one respect the victim of a romantic delusion, but he did identify the brutal realities of the immediate future in Europe and the way forward.

2
Ghost in the Machine: Britain as a Great Power

'We are the only unbroken nation that fought against Hitler's tyranny in the war from start to finish', Churchill said of Britain's role in the defeat of Nazi Germany in the Second World War a year after that event. 'We sought no material gains ... We, and with us the whole Empire and Commonwealth ... drew the sword against the mighty antagonist at the call of honour and in defence of the rights of weaker nations, according to our plighted word, according to the fair play of the world. We did not fight only in the sacred cause of self defence like the Russian[s] ... No one attacked *us*. We fought for a higher and broader theme. We fought against tyranny, aggression, and broken faith, and in order to establish that rule of law among the nations which alone can be the shield of freedom and progress.'[1] There could be no nobler crusade than the one that Britain waged against Nazi Germany, given that the Soviet Communist system, its moral equivalent and one time ally, was the less immediate threat in geopolitical terms. There could be no more glorious way to mark the end of Britain as a Great Power than to lead by example in defiance of the Nazi regime, and then to play her full part in the coalition with the Americans and with Stalin's Russia that destroyed Hitler's regime and its Axis allies. This Unholy Alliance had served its purpose so admirably that, for a time, there were those in the West, mainly Americans, who believed that it could persist and form the cornerstone of the United Nations Organization and, thus, of a lasting peace. There were some in the West who wanted the Soviet Union to become the predominant power in the world in the name of socialism, and who worked to achieve that goal. The ideological divide between Soviet Communism and Western liberal democracy, though, was of an order that guaranteed conflict, which the development of nuclear weapons ensured took the form of the Cold War, the continuation of the Second World War by other means with, once more, Britain heavily engaged from the outset.

'There are three circles which are linked together: the circle of the British Empire and Commonwealth, the circle of the English speaking world, and the circle of united Europe', Churchill declared on 20 April 1949,[2] thus defining the context within which he believed British post war foreign policy should be conducted. This Churchillian vision had the attraction for those conducting that foreign policy that Britain was perceived as having a crucial role to play in each of the interrelated circles that comprised the Western world, and such was Churchill's stature as a world statesman that his views commanded attention in international politics even when he was not the British Prime Minister. Churchill's 'three circles' declaration represented a synthesis of his most important previous post war pronouncements, especially his Fulton Speech of 5 March 1946 about the Sinews of Peace and his Zurich Speech of 19 September 1946 about the Tragedy of Europe. In his Fulton Speech, on the basis that 'last time I saw it all coming and cried aloud to my fellow countrymen and to the world, but no one paid any attention', Churchill had led the way in warning the West that Soviet Communism constituted 'a growing challenge and peril to Christian civilization', and, unlike the mealy mouthed, he did not hesitate to draw the parallel with the rise of Nazi Germany. 'From Stettin in the Baltic to Trieste in the Adriatic, an Iron Curtain has descended across the Continent', Churchill declared. 'Behind that line lie all the capitals of the ancient states of Central and Eastern Europe. Warsaw, Berlin, Prague, Vienna, Budapest, Belgrade, Bucharest and Sofia, all these famous cities and the populations around them lie in what I must call the Soviet sphere, and all are subject in one form or another, not only to Soviet influence but to a very high and, in many cases, increasing measure of control from Moscow ... The Communist parties, which were very small in all these Eastern States of Europe, have been raised to pre-eminence and power far beyond their numbers and are seeking everywhere to obtain totalitarian control. Police governments are prevailing in nearly every case, and so far, except in Czechoslovakia, there is no true democracy ... this is not the liberated Europe we fought to build up. Nor is it one which contains the essentials of permanent peace.'

Churchill argued that, since it was from 'the quarrels of the strong parent races in Europe that the World Wars ... have sprung', it followed that 'the safety of the world requires a new unity in Europe',[3] and in his Zurich Speech he developed this theme. 'The first step in the

European family must be a partnership between France and Germany', Churchill stated in the belief that 'there can be no revival of Europe without a spiritually great France and a spiritually great Germany ... I shall not try to make a detailed programme for hundreds of millions of people ... . But I must give you a warning. Time may be short ... . If we are to form the United States of Europe or whatever name or form it may take, we must begin now.'[4] In this urgent work, Churchill said, 'France and Germany must take the lead together', with Britain and the British Commonwealth of Nations in the role of 'friends and sponsors of the new Europe' championing 'its right to live and shine'.[5] Three years later, Churchill spelt out his country's position: 'Britain is an integral part of Europe, and we mean to play our part in the revival of her prosperity and greatness. But Britain cannot be thought of as a single State in isolation. She is the founder and centre of a world wide Empire and Commonwealth. We will never do anything to weaken the ties of blood, of sentiment and tradition and common interest which unite us with the other members of the British family of nations.' Churchill believed that a reconciliation of interests was possible between Britain's role at the head of both the Commonwealth and the European Movement,[6] though he was unable to say what form it would take. Churchill's view of Britain's role in the post war world had a further dimension, which he spelt out in the Fulton Speech. 'Neither the sure prevention of war nor the continuous rise of world organization will be gained without what I have called the fraternal association of the English speaking peoples', Churchill declared. 'This means a special relationship between the British Commonwealth and Empire and the United States ... I will venture to be precise ... . Eventually there may come – I feel eventually there will come – the principle of common citizenship, but that we may leave to destiny, whose outstretched arm many of us already clearly see.'[7]

Churchill used the term 'English speaking peoples' because 'there is no other that applies both to the inhabitants of the British Isles and to those independent nations who derive their beginnings, their speech, and many of their institutions from England, and who now preserve, nourish, and develop them in their own ways'.[8] No less than four volumes of *A History of the English Speaking Peoples* were eventually devoted to developing Churchill's thesis on this subject. 'The break between Britain and America made by the American Revolution was neither complete nor final', Churchill wrote[9] in terms that recalled the thinking of the late nineteenth-century Liberal imperialists such as Lord Rosebery, who saw the Americans as being part of the British or Anglo Saxon political culture.[10] It may well be that the course of world history would have been different if the Founding Fathers of the American Constitution had decided to adopt, say, German as an official language. As it was, and contrary to persistent legend, the Constitution made no provision at all for an official language, and the English language continued to predominate because it always had done so. This did not mean that the American Revolution represented anything other than a final political break with the British Empire as far as the revolutionaries were concerned. Moreover, though Churchill stressed the closeness of Anglo-American ties, as he would be expected to with an American mother and the making of frequent trips to, and of much money in, the USA, there never was much doubt about the antipathy that many Americans displayed towards the very existence of the British Empire-Commonwealth. This was more than a matter of disputes over the border with Canada, and as late as 1896, the then Prime Minister and Foreign Secretary, Lord Salisbury, who did not subscribe to the 'special relationship' idea, contemplated the possibility of war with the USA.[11] In his Fulton Speech, Churchill said of the two World Wars that 'twice in our own lifetime we have seen the United States, against their wishes and their traditions, against arguments, the force of which it is impossible not to comprehend, drawn ... into these wars in time to secure the victory of the good cause'.[12] If these 'wishes' and 'traditions,' which really amounted to isolationism, meant that the USA could not only stand aside while Britain fought a total war but obtain a profit from it, this behaviour had to have implications for the 'relationship', and if what turned out to be the First World War could be perceived as having so markedly a European conflict that the Americans could maintain until 1917 that it was not a matter for them, there never was any realistic prospect of the Second World War having a similar geopolitical character.

For the early part of this second total war, the 'special relationship' was largely sustained by the close personal and political friendship between Churchill in his Former Naval Person role and President Franklin Delano Roosevelt. This did not mean, however, that Roosevelt did not continue to subscribe to the perfidious Albion interpretation of British behaviour, and, at times, to act accordingly, and the American President never disguised his determination to play his part in the abolition of the British Empire as, for many, though not Churchill, was made evident in the Atlantic Charter. Early in 1941, when Britain had exhausted her supply of dollars, the Americans responded with the

Lend Lease arrangements, which transformed the situation, though, as an official historian remarked, these never covered all Britain's dollar requirements, and the Americans saw to it that no more dollars were forthcoming than were necessitated by genuinely austere standards, and, in addition, Britain had been required to commit herself to non-discrimination policies in post-war trade,[13] which meant, of course, the undermining of Imperial Preference. By contrast, when, following the German invasion of that country, Lend Lease arrangements were also made with the Soviet Union, the American authorities operated on the principle, in the words of Averell Harriman, later to be the US Ambassador in Moscow, of 'give and give and give, with no expectation of any return, with no thought of a *quid pro quo*'.[14] The dramatic nature of Churchill's appeal to the Americans to 'give us the tools and we will finish the job'[15] did not hide Britain's desperate need for the USA to move beyond a form of benevolent neutrality towards her to actually fighting at her side, which the Americans never did until forced to do so.

Hitler built the Unholy Alliance that eventually destroyed his regime by invading the Soviet Union and declaring war on the USA. Fortunately, for Britain, it was a later historian and not Hitler who dreamt up the ploy of the dictator declaring war on Japan after her attack on Pearl Harbour,[16] thus thwarting Roosevelt's plans for America to join the fight against Nazi Germany, always assuming that he meant to intervene. Indeed, fortune did favour the brave in Britain's case, though, of course, the Big Three had become the Big Two and a Half by 1944, and this political reality, which Churchill later publicly acknowledged,[17] meant that the post war world was not one that Britain led the way in shaping.

'Let no man underrate the abiding power of the British Empire and Commonwealth', Churchill told the American audience that attended his Fulton Speech in 1946. 'Do not suppose ... that half a century from now you will not see 70 or 80 million of Britons spread about the world and united in defence of our traditions, our way of life, and of the world causes which we and you espouse.'[18] This was no more than brave talk in a world dominated by two countries that were antipathetic to the continuance of the British Empire-Commonwealth, if for different reasons. The ambition of Communism always was to conquer the world, and the addition of more possessions in Eastern and Central Europe to the Russian Empire as a form of reward for defeating Nazi Germany on the Eastern Front only served to emphasize the imperialistic nature of the Soviet system, much as the callous use of manpower to obtain that victory exemplified the cruelty of the regime that Lenin and

Stalin had built. Without doubt, the Soviet Empire was a formidable prospective foe, but, of the Big Two and a Half, the more immediate threat to British interests proved to be Britain's fellow liberal democracy. For the Americans acted as if they were resolved to teach Britain that the virtue that she had displayed in being the only country to have fought Nazi Germany from 1939 all the way down to 1945 was literally going to have to be its own reward. The Americans were in a position to impose their will for, in the immediate aftermath of the war, the American economy accounted for 50 per cent of global industrial output,[19] and the USA was in a position of military, economic and financial dominance in international affairs that was comparable with that Britain had established in 1815, and which she had maintained for much of the rest of the nineteenth century.

The opportunity was there for what remained of the twentieth century to be, as Henry Luce had anticipated, 'the American century', and, in 1942, Vice President Henry Wallace translated this into 'the Century of the Common Man',[20] taking forward 'the March of Freedom of the past 150 years', as supposedly represented by the American Revolution, the French Revolution, and the Russian Revolution.[21] Though Wallace never actually said that he wanted 'to give a quart of milk to every Hottentot' as had been reported to Roosevelt,[22] the President replaced him by Harry S. Truman as running mate on the Democratic ticket for the 1944 Election, which meant, of course, that when Roosevelt died early in his fourth term, it was Truman as Vice President who succeeded him and not Wallace. In this way, the Western world narrowly escaped having an American President who really did merit being described as a Communist dupe, though it had been Roosevelt himself who had acted on the belief that he could 'personally handle Stalin' on the basis, as he told Churchill, that Stalin 'likes me better' than 'either your Foreign Office or my State Department'.[23] Stalin could be expected to carry on 'liking' the President as long as Roosevelt continued to act on the principle in dealing with the Soviet dictator that 'if I give him everything I possibly can and ask nothing from him in return, *noblesse oblige*, he won't try to annex anything and will work with me for a world of democracy and peace'.[24]

By 1944, to judge from statements made by Roosevelt's Chief of Staff, William Leahy, and the State Department, American foreign policy was predicated on the basis that the main danger to peace was the Soviet Union and Britain contesting the future of Europe, and the best way to prevent conflict was for the USA to play the role of an honest broker rather than joining with Britain in making initiatives since that would convince the Russians that the Western powers were 'ganging up' on them. The British thought that this approach was naïve, and, on the way to the Teheran Conference in late 1943, Churchill observed to Harold Macmillan: 'Germany is finished ... The real problem now is Russia. I can't get the Americans to see it.'[25] British behaviour in confronting Communist activity in Greece and Italy met with American disapproval, [26] and it took blatant Soviet behaviour in Poland as well as in other areas that the Red Army 'liberated', for Roosevelt to heed the advice that Churchill and now Harriman were giving him. 'Averell is right; we can't do business with Stalin', Roosevelt belatedly recognized. 'He has broken every one of the promises he made at [the] Yalta [Conference].'[27] Within a few days of taking office in April 1945, President Truman was told by Vyacheslav Molotov, Stalin's Foreign Minister, how he could co-operate with the Soviet Union 'by doing what Russia wanted'. Truman recalled: 'I explained to him in words of one syllable and in language he could understand that co-operation required agreement and concessions on both sides and that co-operation is not a one way street.'[28] By early 1946, Truman was to write that 'I'm tired [of] babying the Soviets'. He had come to believe that 'unless Russia is faced with an iron fist and strong language another war is in the making. Only one language do they understand – "How many divisions have you?" I do not think we should play compromise any longer.'[29]

The Americans had not played compromise from the beginning in dealing with the form of international economic order that they wanted for the post-war world, with the economic preponderance of the USA ensuring that they would get their way, and that the preferred arrangements would be to the disadvantage of Britain and undermining of her economic relationship with her Empire-Commonwealth. In the main negotiations about Lend Lease as well as, more specifically, the form that the peacetime international monetary system would take, the British Government had the services of John Maynard Keynes in the role of plenipotentiary. Even the economist, Lionel Robbins, who had come to be an admirer, did not consider that Keynes was the equal of Churchill, but did detect 'pure genius' in the man, and portrayed the Americans 'sitting entranced' in the presence of this 'God like visitor'.[30] The various British delegations lacked neither talent nor social confidence, which explains the verse:

> In Washington Lord Halifax
> Once whispered to Lord Keynes:

'It's true *they* have the money bags
But *we* have all the brains.'[31]

Lord Halifax certainly had 'brains' in one sense, being a Fellow of All Souls, Oxford, but that, as a failed Foreign Secretary and an Appeaser, he was even considered as a possible successor to Neville Chamberlain as Prime Minister in May 1940, notably by the Labour Party, has to be a curiosity, though Halifax deserved credit for standing aside for Churchill, recognizing his own unsuitability for the role. Halifax had been later effectively expelled to Washington as British Ambassador, and, as Churchill and Roosevelt commonly dealt directly with each other, it was not surprising that Halifax's role was reduced to being, as he said, 'not much more than a Post Office'.[32] As for Keynes, Dean Acheson, later to be Secretary of State in the Truman Administration, wrote that he was 'not only one of the most delightful and engaging men I have ever known but also ... one of the most brilliant. His multi faceted and highly polished mind sparkled and danced with light. But not all felt his charm; to some he appeared arrogant'.[33] Politics commonly has the character of a minority interest, as does economics, so often the hard part, and among those who concerned themselves with such matters, Keynes had been internationally famous, or if one prefers, notorious, ever since he had written *The Economic Consequences of the Peace*, denouncing the supposed iniquities of the Versailles Treaty of 1919. *Punch* celebrated Keynes's fame with a poem of ten verses, the first of which ran as follows:

There was a superior young person called Keynes,
Who possessed an extensive equipment of brains,
And, being elected a Fellow of King's,
He taught Economics and similar things.[34]

Keynes was well able to deal with international prominence both then and later, given that he shared the opinion that he was a polymath. That Keynes was the leading economist of his generation was commonly conceded even outside his native Cambridge, and his achievements in the sphere of government and politics, business, and in the world of the arts were testimony to the range of his talents. Keynes's style, though, remained that of an academic. One biographer remarked that to the end of his life there was an unsparing quality about his brilliance, that he was often fiercely confrontational in discussion, being a wounding opponent in argument, and that words like lunatic were only too easily used against adversaries.[35] This was scarcely unusual behaviour in university life, to be found, for example, in the kinder-garten level of much of the book reviewing. Familiar, too, was the use of intellectual gifts in the service of a preferred point of view whatever the evidence, and this was present in Keynes's book, *The Economic Consequences of the Peace.*

The facts were that the reparations demanded of Germany under the Treaty of Versailles amounted to about 6–7 per cent of her national income, which sums were not of a different order than the 5.6 per cent of French national income that Prussia had demanded and received over a five year period after her victory in the Franco-Prussian War of 1870–71,[36] and Keynes must have known this. Being in the Norman Angell tradition, Keynes acted as if he believed that wars should not pay, especially, it seemed, for the victors, and wrote accordingly. Those who, like Georges Clemenceau, took the pes-simistic view that 'human nature ... is always the same',[37] meaning that it never improved, and who, hence, maintained that there was 'no place for "sentimentality" in international relations'[38] were condemned for cynicism.[39] Not surprisingly, the last verse of the poem in *Punch* had the following observation:

> Still we feel, as he zealously damns the Allies,
> For grudging the Germans the means to arise,
> That possibly some of the Ultimate Things,
> May even be hidden from Fellows of King's.[40]

Certainly those in the peculiar Bloomsbury Group who deplored Keynes's 'worldliness'[41] had little basis for their concerns.

'If the Americans wish to take over the tin and rubber resources of the British Empire, they must be prepared to take over at the same time the responsibility for the territories in which they are situated', Keynes wrote in the autumn of 1940 about British investments in Malaya, and, with those in South America also in mind, he warned against 'the present emergency being used as an opportunity for picking the eyes out of the British Empire, and seizing its assets without taking over its liabilities'.[42] Keynes added that 'when in the game of Beggar My Neighbour all the cards belong to one player, that is the signal for the game to come to an end'.[43] This depended on what sort of 'game' the Americans were playing, and in what manner they were playing it. When Roosevelt said in 1942 that 'we will have more trouble with Great Britain after the war than we are having with Germany now',[44] what he said only made sense in terms of a remarkable level of distrust of British intentions and a fear of her ability to fool the Americans into doing what she wanted, with the suspicion that the Americans would have to pay for the privilege. Keynes recognized some differences between the British and American political cultures, notably in his observation that when the Mayflower left Plymouth it must have been full of lawyers,[45] but he neither seemed to understand how the American political system worked nor that Anglophilia was less than universal in Washington.[46] Whatever Keynes's qualities as an envoy, as Robbins observed, he was not much of a negotiator.[47]

'Maynard thinks we are a great [and] independent nation, which on the financial side is patently not true', a senior British Treasury official observed of Keynes in May 1941. 'I think he is inclined to ask as of right what [the Americans] are only prepared to give us as a favour. It seems to me very important to keep moral indignation out of these discussions if we are to get anywhere.'[48] The gulf in intellect between Keynes and leading figures in the US Treasury such as Henry Morgenthau and Harry Dexter White was not necessarily likely to be conducive to harmonious relations, though, in White's case, there was an additional factor at work, namely that he was a Soviet agent. Roosevelt was given information about White's treachery as early as 1939, as, indeed he was about Lauchlin Currie, one of his own administrative aides, but the President chose not to believe it, presumably in much the same spirit that, in 1944, he insisted on a KGB codebook that had fallen into American hands being given back to the probably surprised Russians.[49] White and Currie may well have derived a great deal of private pleasure from fooling Keynes, their intellectual superior, about their real allegiance. As White's views could be interpreted as predicating the eventual emergence of a world social democratic order involving both the USA and the Soviet Union,[50] he was also fooling himself, not least about the character of Stalin's regime. At the time, White made no secret of his antipathy towards Britain,[51] and Keynes was also well aware that Currie was 'very anti-British'.[52] This would have also served as a good description of Henry Morgenthau, Roosevelt's Secretary to the Treasury to 1945, who was well described as determined to reduce Britain to the political and economic status of an American satellite in the post-war world.[53] As for the State Department, Cordell Hull, the Secretary of State down to 1944, devoted a chapter of his memoirs to emphasizing that he was not an enemy of Britain.[54] This was true in an explicit sense, though, just to give one example, Hull's ideas on the form that international economic arrangements should take, which were in essence those of multilateralism, were plainly antagonistic to Britain's imperial interests, and meant to be.

When commending the Bretton Woods international arrangements to the House of Lords in May 1944, Lord Keynes paid tribute to the work of the US Treasury, the State Department, and the Federal Reserve Board in Washington in constructing the relevant Agreement,[55] which he described as the product of 'a mixed marriage of ideas'. Of his own proposals, Keynes said that 'there were certain features of elegance, clarity and logic in the Clearing Union plan which have disappeared. And this, by me at least, is to be much regretted. As a result, however, there is no longer any need for a new fangled international monetary unit ... bancor, unitas, dolphin, bezant, daric, and heaven knows what.'[56] Keynes had previously said of his own proposals and those of White that 'neither plan conceals a selfish motive',[57] and, of course, the Americans wanted the dollar to be king. With the American economy dominant, their favoured system of multilateralism in world trade served their national interest too, and, as one friendly observer commented, the USA pressed for non-discrimination in season and out of season, and adopted an unbecoming evangelism in its assault upon the sterling area and Imperial Preference.[58] Like some other forms of evangelism, though, there was an idealistic dimension to the American commitment to multilateral trade, and, certainly, its advocates could not be accused of undue attention to practical details in the absence of an adequate mechanism for adjustments between creditor and debtor nations involving means that ensured that they would be made with the minimum of economic disruption.[59] As Keynes said at the Savannah Conference in early 1946, he had been 'intimately connected with what will ... always be known as the Bretton Woods plan', and he celebrated the birth of 'the lusty twins' of 'mixed and collective parentage' whom 'we have decided to call Master Fund and Miss Bank'. As to how the new international institutions would work, Keynes noted the risk that the 'two brats shall grow up politicians', but he detected 'no malicious fairy' at work.[60] Morgenthau's replacement as Secretary to the Treasury, Fred Vinson, took this oratorical flourish as a personal slight, remarking, 'I don't mind being called malicious, but I do mind being called a fairy!'[61] As Judge Vinson had been earlier informed by Keynes that American proposals for dealing with international cartels seemed 'principally designed to make a paradise for lawyers',[62] it can be seen that Keynes's diplomatic skills had not improved. Whether this made any difference can be doubted, since Keynes and the British could only expect to be one parent of the International Monetary Fund and the World Bank – the two 'twins' he identified – and ones which were still alive at the end of the twentieth century. The Bretton Woods system was one of fixed exchange rates with controls on capital movements surviving the cull of wartime measures that the Americans intended, becoming an international economic order with a bias towards expansion that survived into the 1970s.

Once Nazi Germany had been defeated in May 1945, the future of Lend Lease became an issue, with President Truman being advised that the level of provision should be reduced, and when the relevant order was presented, Truman recollected that when his advisers 'asked me to sign it, I reached for my pen, and, without reading the document, I signed it'. The order was interpreted literally, with an embargo being placed on all shipments to the Soviet Union and to other European nations, even to the extent of some of the ships being turned around and brought back to American ports for unloading. Truman recalled that 'the British were the hardest hit, but the Russians interpreted the move as especially aimed at them. ... The result was that I rescinded the order'.[63] One of Truman's biographers suggested that the President was less ignorant about the content of the relevant order and its likely immediate effects than he cared to remember, being well aware that Congress was tired of financially supporting argumentative Allies.[64] Whether this was so or not, on 21 August 1945, before Imperial Japan had formally, and thus finally, surrendered, Truman further directed that all Lend Lease operations should be discontinued and the foreign governments concerned notified accordingly. Dean Acheson, who was not involved in this decision, recalled that in later years President Truman had told him that this action was 'a grave mistake'.[65]

The response of the British Prime Minister, Clement Attlee that 'the sudden cessation of a support on which our war organization has so largely depended puts us in a very serious financial position'[66] put the matter mildly. Churchill said that 'I cannot believe that it is the last word of the United States',[67] in which belief he was to be more than justified within two years, as by then events had forced the Americans to come to terms with the political and economic realities of the post-war world, not the least of which was that Britain was no longer a rival that needed to be humbled. More immediately, Britain needed an American loan. 'Keynes, in his talks with Ministers just before leaving for Washington, was almost starry eyed', Hugh Dalton, the Chancellor of the Exchequer, recalled. 'He was very confident that, in the coming negotiations, he could obtain American aid that would be ample in amount, and on most satisfactory conditions. He told us that he could get ... a free gift ... . There would be no question of a loan to be repaid, or of a rate of interest on a loan. Nor did he, at any stage, say much to us about ... conditions to be attached by the Americans to any aid from them.' Dalton recorded that 'as the talks went on, we retreated, slowly and with a bad grace and with increasing irritation, from a free gift to an interest-free loan, and from this again to a loan bearing interest; from a larger to a smaller total of aid; and from the prospect of loose strings, some of which would be only general declarations of intention, to the unwilling acceptance of strings so tight that they might strangle our trade and, indeed, our whole economic life'.[68]

Keynes reported to the House of Lords in December 1945 that 'we soon discovered ... that it was not our past performance but our future prospects of recovery and our intention to face the world boldly that we had to demonstrate. Our American friends were interested not in our wounds, though incurred in the common cause, but in our convalescence. They wanted to understand the size of our immediate financial difficulties, to be convinced that they were temporary and manageable and to be told that we intended to walk without bandages as soon as possible. In every circle in which I moved in Washington, it was when I was able to enlarge on the strength of our future competitive position, if only we were allowed a breather, that I won most sympathy. What the United States needs and desires is a strong Britain, endowed with renewed strength and facing the world on the equal or more than equal terms that we were wont to do. To help that forward interests them much more than to comfort a war victim'.[69] This was an optimistic interpretation of American attitudes towards Britain at this time, and *The Economist*, for one, preferred bitterness, observing that 'it is for the Americans to say what pleasure they take in a bargaining victory won over their best friends at such a price ... . It would be hard to find an Englishman who did not think that advantage had been taken of his country's honourable extremity to drive a very hard bargain ... . Nor is Britain's present need for dollars anything for which shame need be felt. Our present needs are the direct consequences of the fact that we fought earliest, that we fought longest and we fought hardest. In moral terms we are creditors; and for that we shall pay

$140 million a year for the rest of the twentieth century. It may be unavoidable; but it is not right.'[70] For all the pleasure, presumably born of inferiority, that Dalton seemed to take in his former Cambridge tutor's difficulties with the Americans, Dalton was still convinced that Keynes was 'the best chief negotiator' that Britain could have had in dealing with 'this most complicated subject', despite the dislike that characterized relations between Keynes and Vinson.[71] 'Please remember that you are dealing with Kentucky' was the advice Keynes got from an associate about negotiations with Vinson. 'Well, Kentucky will have to like it', replied Keynes, who proceeded to deliberately enrage Vinson.[72] As before, it seems doubtful if this behaviour made that much difference. Harry White 'should be accorded an honourable place in British annals', according to Harrod,[73] but what was not a secret about White was his opposition to a loan for Britain, and, though he failed to achieve that objective, White did ensure that those who favoured Britain having a loan of the size she wanted were excluded from the US Treasury committee that advised Vinson.[74]

'We shall emerge from this war, having won a more solid victory over our enemies, a more enduring friendship from our Allies, and a deeper respect from the world at large, than perhaps at any time in our history', Keynes declared in the House of Lords in May 1944. 'The victory, the friendship, and the respect will have been won, because, in spite of faint-hearted preparations, we have sacrificed every precaution for the future in the interests of immediate strength with a fanatical single-mindedness which has few parallels. But the full price of this still has to be paid. I wish that this was more generally appreciated in the country than it is.'[75] Privately, four months later, Keynes stated that 'we cannot police half the world at our own expense when we have already gone into pawn to the other half. We cannot run for long a great programme of social amelioration on money lent from overseas. Unless we are willing to put ourselves financially at the mercy of America and then borrow from her on her own terms and conditions sums which we cannot hope to repay, what are we expecting? Are we looking forward to a spectacular bankruptcy (not, altogether, a bad idea) from which we shall rise the next morning without a care in the world? Or are we following some star at present invisible to me?'[76] Keynes was not just of his generation in his desire that Britain should 'remain a Great Power',[77] though this aspiration was incompatible not only with the relative economic weakness that he had identified, but also with the American Sense of Mission that envisaged a world in which there was no place for the British Empire-Commonwealth as a political force of importance.

The origins of the belief that America herself had a Manifest Destiny followed from its sense of geographical predestination allied to the belief that the country had a special form of government and the duty of spreading this. When the moving frontier closed in the 1890s, America had to look elsewhere for economic expansion, notably, but by no means exclusively, China, and if Woodrow Wilson's maxim that trade flourished best when there was a stable world order savoured of the obvious, he added to it the belief that the world should evolve towards the American form of democracy because democracies did not make wars with each other. The USA declared war on Imperial Germany in 1917, though of the German Constitution of 1871 as amended in 1888, Wilson himself had written that 'the members of the Reichstag were elected for a term of five years by universal suffrage and secret ballot'.[78] Initially, the Reichstag may well have been a 'fig leaf covering the nakedness of absolutism', as Karl Liebknecht once commented, but after 1890, even though its influence was mainly negative, the Reichstag seems well described as having become the focal point of the German political system.[79] If, however, in some way Imperial Germany was not allowed to count, the war that the Americans waged with Spain in 1898 could not be ignored. Under the Constitution of 1876, Spain had an elected Cortes.[80] Of course, that Germany and Spain were monarchies and colonial powers offended against the American model, but Wilson had not specifically taken up the Kantian position that perpetual peace predicated a world of republics,[81] and contemporary Belgium and Holland were monarchies and imperial powers too, and without them being counted the number of democracies would be few. Of course, if what was wanted was a stable world order for its own sake and not one designed primarily to serve American interests, then colonial empires provided a form of political stability, as, to give an obvious example, the consequences of the decline and fall of the Ottoman Empire illustrated. In its nineteenth-century isolation, 'the United States has stood for something unique and grand in the history of mankind', the American conservative thinker, William Sumner, observed in 1899, but, he added, in the previous year 'it had knocked to pieces a poor, decrepit, bankrupt old state like Spain', and in waging this war, he believed, the Americans had gone over to 'the standards of which Spain is a representative'.[82]

Isolationism most certainly did not die as a political force in American politics, but the USA had become an imperial power just like any other, with the cant used to justify its actions resembling that which had been conventionally advanced by British imperialists in their own cause, and, as was inevitable, with behaviour aimed at promoting a stable world only too often having the opposite effect. As if to confound their critics and even their enemies, the Americans were to prove capable of acts of remarkable statesmanship and generosity not just of word but also of deed, though, naturally, it was as well for others not to count on this. Making 'the world safe for democracy' meant, of course, making it safe for American capitalism, and, though one notes that Richard Nixon chose to say Wilson had provided 'the greatest vision of America's world role',[83] it would be more realistic to describe Wilson as the most influential architect of twentieth-century American foreign policy because he eloquently clothed the bleak skeleton of American self-interest in the attractive clothes of idealism.[84] Nonetheless, they were see-through clothes. The alleged moral superiority of dollar imperialism compared with the sins of colonialism supposedly only practised by others was a notion that few outsiders were likely to take seriously, any more than they would believe that, as we have seen, the enthusiasm for freer trade on the part of the Americans at Bretton Woods was unrelated to their country's contemporary economic self-interest or the damage to be done to a trading rival, the British Empire-Commonwealth. Similarly, the principle of national self-determination was portrayed as being noble, but that its implementation would be undermining of the British Empire was surely appreciated. It seemed to be simply assumed by at least some Americans that the new rulers of the former colonies of the European powers would behave like President George Washington and step aside at the end of a term of office and not vote themselves President for life, or until that life was taken. The American desire for new nation states, all of them supposed to be democracies, of course, did not stop them from coming to encourage a United States of Europe, imitation of oneself being the sincerest form of flattery, and another supposed development promoting a stable world order. General Dwight David Eisenhower said of a United States of Europe in 1951 that 'a step by step gradual approach' was not good enough because its establishment would 'instantly ... solve the real and bitter problems of today'. Churchill applauded the speech,[85] as, indeed, he always welcomed American engagement with European matters. That closer

British involvement with the rest of Western Europe did not take place in the immediate post-war period was later to be widely regretted, not least on economic grounds, although it has to be doubted if such a development then would have rescued the British economy, in the domestic management of which it was Keynes's 'star' that was to be followed, down.

3
Ghost in the Machine: The Keynesian Full Employment Welfare State

'A Welfare State is a State in which organized power is deliberately used (through politics and administration) in an effort to modify the play of market forces in at least three directions', wrote one of its historians. 'First, by guaranteeing individuals and families a minimum income irrespective of the market value of their work or property; second, by narrowing the extent of insecurity by enabling individuals and families to meet certain "social contingencies" (for example, sickness, old age and unemployment) which lead otherwise to individual and family crises; and, third, by ensuring that all citizens without distinction of status or class are offered the best standards available in relation to a certain agreed range of social services.' The same historian observed that 'the first and second of these objects may be accomplished, in part at least, by what used to be called a Social Service State, a State in which communal resources are employed to abate poverty and to assist those in distress. The third objective, however, goes beyond the aims of a Social Service State. It brings in the idea of the "optimum" rather than the older idea of the "minimum". It is concerned not merely with abatement of class differences or the needs of scheduled groups but with equality of treatment and the aspirations of citizens as voters with equal shares of electoral power.'[1] The Butler Education Act of 1944 represented an advance of educational opportunities compared with previous State provision, but it was the Beveridge Report that came to be seen as encapsulating the philosophy of the Welfare State, and, to give that State paper its proper title, *Social Insurance and Allied Services*, may well have been the only official publication in the history of British government that most of the electorate had heard of, let alone possibly read, if only in summary. In the months following the Report's appearance in November 1942, its effective author and sole signatory, Sir William Beveridge, enjoyed public fame in which he gloried, recalling in his memoirs that 'my name and features became known to everybody through illustrated papers and films ... more than once I caught young women surreptitiously sketching me as they sat opposite me in the train between Oxford and Paddington; if I liked the looks of the young woman, as I generally did, I asked to be shown the result and autographed it for her'. Taxi drivers told him that they wanted him to be the next Prime Minister, Beveridge wrote, as indeed they well might do in search of a tip, and he recorded a contemporary opinion that 'Sir William, possibly next to Mr Churchill, is the most popular figure in Britain today', and even that he had been mistaken for the then Prime Minister, adding that, 'no doubt ... I was looking important'.[2]

Keynes was much more important than Beveridge in laying the intellectual foundations of the economic and social order that was to dominate British domestic politics from the 1940s to the 1970s, though it seems likely that the overwhelming majority of the population had never heard of him, or, in any specific sense, Keynes's *General Theory of Employment, Interest and Money*. The political significance of Keynes's masterpiece was that he could be believed to have provided the answer to the standard response of those versed in the liberal economics of the Classical and Neo-Classical Schools to proposals for increased State activity outside of the boundaries of the Night Watchman and even within those limits: 'where will the money come from?' In the immediate aftermath of the Beveridge Report, one socialist writer rejoiced in the order of change that she believed Keynes had wrought: 'Any discussion of what we can afford is bound to reflect the astonishing revolution which has taken place in reputable economic thought since the publication ... of Lord Keynes's *General Theory of Employment* turned heresy into orthodoxy. This revolution goes right to the bottom of what is meant by "affording" anything. In the old days the parallel between the individual and the State was simple and unchallenged. The upright, the responsible, the prudent, lived within their incomes; while the unbalanced budget was the sign of the spendthrift, the waster, and the bankrupt – upon whom judgement would promptly descend. Now ... everything is turned upside down ... the more the Chancellor spends, the more he gets, for spending creates employment, and employment creates income and income creates income tax.'[3]

Ten years before, Keynes had come to ask himself whether all economists were mad except for Richard Kahn and himself,[4] and the prime reason for the self-effacing Kahn's exclusion from the ranks of the insane seems to have been that he was prepared to play an invaluable supporting role in the intended Keynesian Revolution in economic theory. When Keynes's two volumes of *A Treatise on Money* did not change the world of economics in 1930, Keynes seemed to resolve not only to rework his economic thinking by embracing such concepts as Kahn's theory of the multiplier, but also to kill off the existing orthodoxy by unfair means if necessary. Scholarship having failed, it was back to the combative approach that had worked so well in *The Economic Consequences of the Peace*. When the successor volume to *A Treatise on Money* was published in 1936, Keynes was on the attack from the beginning: 'I have called this book *The General Theory of Employment, Interest and Money*, placing the emphasis on the prefix *general*. The object of the title is to contrast the character of my conclusions with those of the Classical theory of the subject, upon which I was brought up and which dominates the economic thought, both practical and theoretical, of the governing and academic classes of this generation, as it has for a hundred years past. I shall argue that the postulates of the Classical theory are applicable to a special case only and not to the general case, the situation which it assumes being a limiting point of the possible positions of equilibrium. Moreover, the characteristics of the special case assumed by the Classical theory happen not to be those of the economic society in which we actually live, with the result that its teaching is misleading and disastrous if we attempt to apply it to the facts of experience'. Keynes added that 'the Classical Economists was a name invented by Marx to cover Ricardo and James Mill and their predecessors, that is to say for the founders of the theory which culminated in the Ricardian economics. I have become accustomed ... to include in the Classical School the followers of Ricardo, those, that is to say, who adopted and perfected the theory of the Ricardian economics, including (for example) J.S. Mill, [Alfred] Marshall, [F.Y.] Edgeworth, and Professor [A.C.] Pigou'. Keynes wrote that he was 'perhaps perpetrating a solecism'[5] in treating the history of economic thought in this cavalier manner. 'It will be admitted by the least charitable reader that the entertainment value of Mr Keynes's *General Theory of Employment* is considerably enhanced by its satiric aspect', J.R. Hicks commented. 'Even if they are convinced by Mr Keynes's arguments and humbly acknowledge themselves to have been "classical economists" in the past, they find it hard to remember that they believed in their unregenerate days the things Mr Keynes says they believed.'[6] Keynes said of *The General Theory* that 'this book is chiefly addressed to my fellow economists', with 'its main purpose' being 'to deal with difficult questions of theory, and only in the second place with the applications of this theory to practice'. Keynes asked for 'forgiveness, if, in the pursuit of sharp distinctions, my controversy is itself too keen'.[7] This appeal was entirely unconvincing, since Keynes's undeclared ambition was to displace Alfred Marshall, his intellectual mentor, as Authority in economics, and if Hicks found it hard to understand why a recent and not widely known book by Pigou called *The Theory of Unemployment* was treated as typifying the failings of the supposed Classical Economists,[8] the answer was that Pigou was the keeper of the Marshallian flame, which made him a prime target, and the idea was to engage him in controversy, and, thus, to maximize publicity for Keynes's ideas within the academic community.

Retrospectively, an unbeliever, Harry Johnson, thought that 'in directing his attack at the Neo-Classical concept of an economic system equilibrating at full employment and presenting a general theory of underemployment equilibrium of which the Neo-Classical theory was a special case, Keynes's polemical instinct was surely right, both because Neo-Classical ways of thinking were then a major obstacle to sensible anti-Depression policy and, because, for professional economists, the concept of equilibrium has always had far more intellectual appeal as an analytical companion than its opposite'.[9] Those not caught up in the world of economic theory might wonder at the utility of a Keynesian macroeconomic model resting on the assumption of 'a closed system',[10] which was not of obvious relevance to a British economy dependent on international trade, and a model that also assumed perfect competition at microeconomic level,[11] which seems to have been an unknown market form since, possibly, the mid-Victorian Manchester Cotton Exchange, and one which made no allowance for trade union activity. It is at least open to doubt whether *The General Theory* would have been a theory at all without the additional 'little apparatus' that Hicks swiftly supplied.[12] 'The old ideas were never repudiated or rooted out of the basic assumptions of his thought', Keynes wrote of Marshall,[13] and, though treating Marshallian School, along with others, as an Aunt Sally[14] was meant as a repudiation, Keynes's 'struggle of escape from habitual modes of thought' was, as he seemed to fear,[15] incomplete. Even the admiring Harrod judged that 'Keynes has not affected a revolution in fundamental economic theory but a readjustment and a shift of emphasis',[16] though Hicks's 'skeleton apparatus'[17] was the practical means of reconciliation with traditional economics. While it was difficult to believe that its author did not intend to settle matters in *The General Theory*, the difficulty of establishing at times what 'Keynes really meant' promoted both debate and a succession of interpretative texts, which kept 'the new economics' to the fore. Keynes had exempted himself from the threat of intellectual redundancy for the then foreseeable future by devaluing the knowledge and experience of the older economists, and thus handing an advantage to those of the younger generation who elected to become followers, even providing them with new terminology of impressive difficulty to master in the form of the propensity to consume, liquidity preference, and the marginal efficiency of capital.[18]

'What Keynes supplied was the excitement of a new beginning as the residue of Classical economics was swept away', Lorie Tarshis, one of the new Keynesians, was to write. 'He supplied too that measure of impatience the situation called for and the opportunity for all of us to be a part of a great adventure ... what Keynes supplied was *hope* ... that prosperity could be restored and maintained without the support of prison camps, executions and bestial interrogations. In those years many of us felt that by following Keynes ... each one of us could become a doctor to the whole world.'[19] Keynes had declared in *The General Theory* that 'the authoritarian state systems of today seem to solve the problem of unemployment at the expense of efficiency and of freedom. It is certain that the world will not much longer tolerate the unemployment which, apart from brief periods of excitement is ... in my opinion inevitably associated with present day capitalist individualism. But it may be possible by a right analysis of the problem to cure the disease whilst preserving efficiency and freedom'.[20] Keynes had come to the view before that 'capitalism, wisely managed, can probably be made more efficient for attaining economic ends than any alternative system in sight',[21] and having identified the need 'to invent new wisdom for a new age',[22] in the opinion of himself and his followers and the converted, he had now done this. So, for the Britain of the 1930s, Keynes had seemed to provide the means of escape from the straitjacket of Neville Chamberlain-type economic policy. From now on, Governments could be seen to be doing things, and those things would work, or so the 'new economics' said.

Roosevelt's Governments did engage in a lot of economic activity under the New Deal, and this seemed to impress enough American voters to sustain an electoral coalition that ensured that for the twenty years after 1933 there was a Democratic President in the White House. Ironically, in terms of promoting economic recovery, and in fact, the

Chamberlain approach in Britain proved relatively more effective than the New Deal did in the USA, and if Roosevelt saved American capitalism, it was acting as the 'arsenal of democracy' in the Second World War that worked the economic miracle.[23]

One of his biographers found it easy to imagine Keynes in the Conservative Party of Harold Macmillan and R.A. Butler, with whom he had become personally friendly, which was not the case with any of the Labour leaders.[24] By that stage, though, that wing of the Tory Party, at least, could be classified as being part of 'the progressive forces of the country' with whom Keynes had explicitly aligned himself.[25] Keynes had disliked the inter-war Conservative Party because he deemed it to be intellectually barren,[26] and associated with illiberal attitudes towards what he called 'sex questions'.[27] Keynes took his opposition to the Tory-dominated National Government to the extent of voting Labour for the only time in his life in 1935,[28] though he was soon to commend Stanley Baldwin to Beatrice Webb as a model statesman, and express to her an unmitigated contempt for the official Labour Party.[29] Keynes personally and financially supported Sir Stafford Cripps's call for a Popular Front in 1939.[30] When Keynes wrote then that 'there is no one in politics today worth sixpence outside of the ranks of liberals except the post-war generation of intellectual Communists under thirty five', and praised the Left Book Club,[31] he was not only electing to forget earlier contempt for young Communists,[32] but also that he had dismissed Marxian socialism as 'illogical and so dull'.[33] Keynes was engaging in irreverence for its own sake, always a risk for those unwise enough to take the writings of G.E. Moore seriously, and he badly needed things to do. When he was elevated to the peerage in 1942, Keynes recognized that he was 'in truth ... still a Liberal'.[34]

The coming of war gave Keynes another chance to excel, as we have seen in the sphere of international economic relations, even if one colleague exaggerated Keynes's influence when he wrote that 'he was the strangest civil servant Whitehall has ever seen, less the servant and more the master of those he served'.[35] Like its predecessor, the Churchill Coalition Government did not have to defer to Keynes when, for instance, he wrote *How To Pay For The War* in 1940, though, such was his prominence in the political nation that, in the context of total war, and casting around for ideas about such problems of public finance, it would be natural for the Chancellor of the Exchequer, Sir Kingsley Wood, to seek his advice. *How To Pay For The War* was a masterpiece in the use of English to present complex ideas, and intellectual appeasement of the Labour Party in the form of proposals for the taxation of capital[36] did not disguise Keynes's objective which was 'to devise a means of adapting the distributive system of a free community to the limitations of war'.[37] This was to advocate the fiscal theory of war control,[38] whereas, in a situation of total war, time was bound to be more important than money, being the one priority that was virtually absolute.[39] So, the war economy was run along lines that Keynes had categorized as 'totalitarian',[40] and, as one biographer recorded, *How To Pay For The War* did not provide a blueprint for what followed, though Keynes's idea of deferred pay was adopted in the form of post war credits, the prices of basic necessities were maintained at a stable level by subsidies as he had recommended, and family allowances were eventually introduced. Keynes was in favour of rationing basic necessities in short supply, but not more widespread rationing and price controls because this would lead to shortages and queues. It was the latter approach that was adopted.[41]

Nonetheless, though others had also made their contribution in the form of providing the admittedly still crude underlying and necessary national accounting framework that was used, there was evidence of Keynes's influence in the Budget was that presented by Sir Kingsley Wood on 7 April 1941, which departed from the traditional emphasis on the Government's own financial housekeeping and no direct concern with its macroeconomic consequences to involve a consideration of the prospective inflationary gap, thus marking an acceptance of the Government's responsibility for the management of aggregate demand. Keynes himself believed that 'a revolution in public finance' had taken place,[42] and Sir Edward Bridges of the Treasury wrote that '1941 [was] the date when a new theme was introduced into the making of the Budget, namely the inflationary-deflationary theme, a conscious attempt to use fiscal measures to hold the balance between the money in people's pockets and what they could buy with it'.[43] The arrangements for Treasury control of public expenditure, though, still had the feel of their Gladstonian origins more than a quarter of a century later. From the Budget of 1941 to the White Paper on Employment Policy of 1944 tends to be portrayed as a short step,[44] but it was not that straightforward. There were Keynesian converts among the economists in the War Cabinet Office, notably James Meade,[45] but there were senior Treasury officials, notably Sir Richard Hopkins, whom Keynes had found a formidable opponent in the 1930s, who were not.[46] Hopkins chaired the committee whose report[47] formed the main basis of the White Paper. Keynes had been largely uninvolved, but elected to describe the report concerned as 'an outstanding State Paper which, if one casts one's mind back ten years or so, represents a revolution in official opinion', before making detailed criticisms of its content.[48] The eventual White Paper famously declared at the outset that 'the Government accept as one of their primary aims and responsibilities of a high and stable level of employment after the war'.[49] Keynes commented on the White Paper that '[it] is better to have got something, even if it is wrong in detail, because I believe the Civil Service has infinite power of making things work once it is clear that it intends to work it. My own feeling is that the first sentence is more valuable than the rest.'[50]

Whether or not, except implicitly, Beveridge was on the long list of those whom Keynes defined as mad at various times because they had disagreed with him seems not to be recorded, but others must have wondered about Beveridge's behaviour when he experienced difficulties dealing with the fame that he avidly sought as the main author of *Social Insurance and Allied Services*, published in late 1942. 'This is the greatest advance in our history', he said of the Beveridge Report to the future Prime Minister, Harold Wilson. 'There can be no turning back. From now on Beveridge is not the name of a man: it is the name of a way of life and not only for Britain, but for the whole civilized world.'[51] Beatrice Webb recognized that 'Beveridge has had a great personal triumph ... . It is a queer result of this strange and horrible war that Beveridge, whose career as a civil servant and as Director of the [London] School of Economics was more or less a failure, should have risen suddenly into the limelight as an accepted designer of a New World Order.'[52] What the Beveridge Committee had been asked to do was 'to undertake, with special reference to the inter-relation of the schemes, a survey of the existing national schemes of social insurance and allied services, including workmen's compensation, and to make recommendations'.[53]

The Treasury representative expected merely 'a tidying up operation',[54] and this seemed to be what the Government wanted,[55] but Beveridge believed that 'the time has come to consider social insurance as a whole, as a contribution to a better world after the war'.[56] Thus, the Plan for Social Security contained in the Beveridge Report was nothing less than part of 'an attack upon five great evils: upon the physical Want with which it is directly concerned, upon Disease which often causes that Want and brings many other troubles in its train, upon Ignorance which no democracy can afford in its citizens, upon the Squalor which arises mainly through haphazard distribution of industry and population, and upon the Idleness which destroys wealth and corrupts men, whether they are well fed or not, when they are idle'.[57] Beveridge exceeded his remit in the grand manner when he went on to make declarations of the kind that 'the happiness of the common man' was 'the object of government in peace and in war',[58] a statement that would be news to the mass of the population from the ranks of which, predictably, the socially privileged Beveridge was not drawn.[59] When he addressed his actual subject matter, Beveridge was clarity itself in setting out the 23 main changes that constituted his recommendations, and what they represented. 'What is proposed today for unified social security springs out of what has been accomplished in building up security piece by piece', Beveridge wrote. 'It retains the contributory principle of sharing the cost of security between three parties – the insured person, his employer, if he has an employer, and the State. It retains and extends the principle that compulsory insurance should provide a flat rate of benefit, irrespective of earnings, in return for a flat contribution from all. It retains as the best method of contribution the system of insurance documents and insurance stamps. It builds upon the experience gained in the administration of unemployment insurance and later of unemployment assistance … . It provides for retaining … national health insurance. It provides for retaining within the general framework of a unified scheme … workmen's compensation … . While completing the transfer from local to national government of assistance by cash payments, it retains a vital place for local authorities in the provision of institutions and in the organization and maintenance of services connected with social welfare. The scheme proposed here is in some ways a revolution, but in more important ways it is a natural development from the past. It is a British revolution.'[60]

In other words, it was not a revolution at all, but a necessary rationalization of the existing arrangements, with one addition to a comprehensive national insurance scheme dealing with sickness, unemployment and old age, being what Beveridge called 'children's allowances … provided wholly out of taxation'.[61] Beveridge emphasized that his Plan for Social Security assumed 'the maintenance of employment and the prevention of mass unemployment', not least on grounds of cost,[62] but such financial considerations did not stop Beveridge from anticipating the establishment of 'a comprehensive national health service'.[63] Keynes told Beveridge that his Report was 'a grand document, although you can scarcely expect [that] it will be adopted just as it stands',[64] and Keynes added that, though he was concerned about the Budgetary situation in the early peacetime period, 'for these years there is no cheaper scheme on the map'.[65] The Coalition Government was cautious about committing its successors to the scale of public expenditure involved, but popular support for the Beveridge Plan was of an order that in 1944, in addition to the White Paper on *Employment Policy* already noted, further White Papers were issued on *A National Health Service*, which Service it was proposed would be 'free to all',[66] and on *Social Insurance*, one White Paper on this subject being about the scheme generally and what were now to be called family allowances,[67] and the other being about the Government's proposals for replacing the existing system of workmen's compensation by a new scheme of industrial injury insurance.[68]

When the White Paper on *Employment Policy* came before the War Cabinet in May 1944, Churchill said that he understood it on the basis that 'what is proposed for public authorities is the exact opposite of what would be generally done by private persons, that when things look bad, they should not draw in their horns but push them out and launch forth into all sorts of new expenditures'. The Minister of Reconstruction, Lord Woolton, replied that 'this is exactly so, and that it will be necessary to do a good deal of education of the public mind upon it'.[69] It seemed likely that two total wars within a generation had educated the public, or at least large segments of the electorate, into the view that the State could be the Universal Provider, not least of full employment, if the politicians chose. The familiar piece of conventional wisdom that Governments could find the money for wars and they could do so in peacetime to promote housing and other forms of State social provision if only the political will existed, had been endorsed by Beveridge in his famous Report when he had written that 'the abolition of want just before this war was easily within the economic resources of the community', and that this had not been done had been 'a needless scandal'.[70] In fact, it was the demands of total war that made the mass of the electorate familiar with the necessary high level of taxation. As the classic study of the subject stated, 'in [the] 1937–38 [financial year] the burden of the income tax was still very light for the lowest income groups: almost no working class family with children was affected', but by the financial year of 1941–42 the income tax base had dramatically expanded.[71] The introduction of PAYE made for more efficient income tax gathering arrangements than before,[72] and purchase tax extended the range of indirect taxation as well.[73]

In 1945, Colin Clark, already on his intellectual journey to the Right, argued '25 per cent of the national income is about the limit for taxation in any non-totalitarian community',[74] which view Keynes endorsed,[75] believing that otherwise an escape would be sought by means of inflation.[76] Keynes had also believed that once 'full employment as nearly as practicable' had been attained 'the classical theory comes into its own again from this point onwards',[77] though the notion that politicians would practise abstinence in this way was fanciful. *Employment Policy* had said of manpower that 'it is not enough that it should be employed', it should be 'employed efficiently',[78] but when Ernest Bevin, the Minister of Labour, commended the White Paper to the House of Commons it was in terms of the prospective abolition of the 'social disease' of unemployment, and of any political parties who wished to survive at the next General Election having to endorse 'the principle of full employment'.[79] What was full employment? Beveridge had the answer. He had described Keynes as 'a quack in economics' in 1931,[80] and he had been dismissive of *The General Theory* in 1936,[81] but by 1944, when he published an unofficial Beveridge Report called *Full Employment in a Free Society*, Beveridge had all the enthusiasm of the Keynesian convert, feeling able to say that '3 per cent appears as a conservative, rather than an unduly hopeful, aim to set for the average unemployment rate of the future under conditions of full employment'.[82] Keynes said to Beveridge that there was 'no harm in aiming at 3 per cent, but I shall be surprised if we succeed'.[83] Keynes himself seemed to think in terms of a level of 5 per cent of unemployment as representing full employment, 'chiefly on the ground that it seemed ... that this is the highest that the public would stand in post-war conditions without demanding something very drastic to be done about it'.[84]

Keynes believed that 'the ordinary Budget should be balanced at all times', considering that 'the more socialized we become, the more important it is to associate as closely as possible the cost of particular services with the sources out of which they are provided ... . This is the only way by which to preserve sound accounting, to measure efficiency, to maintain economy and to keep the public properly aware of what things cost'. It was 'the capital Budget which should fluctuate with the demand for employment', and Keynes thought that 'the social security budget should be one section of [this] long-term Budget'.[85] Quite how this would work Keynes never explained, and the Treasury's Sir Richard Hopkins was unconvinced.[86] Keynes described the National Insurance Fund element in the Beveridge Plan as 'a valuable fiction,'[87] but he was soon critical of 'lavishness on pensions', observing that 'what amounts to the abandonment of the contributory principle leads us into uncharted seas'.[88] Beveridge had sternly stated in his Report that 'citizens ... should not be taught to regard the State as the dispenser of gifts for which no one needs to pay',[89] and that 'in establishing a national minimum, it should leave room and encouragement for voluntary action by each individual to provide more than that minimum for himself and his family'.[90] In 1948, Beveridge published a book called *Voluntary Action* extolling the virtues of such activity. By then, it was too late, not least because the Beveridge Report had said earlier that there was plenty of money around for State social provision. Beveridge was to define full employment in terms of 'there are always more vacant jobs than men seeking jobs',[91] and he came close to promising jobs for life when adding that 'if demand is directed wisely ... there is no reason why most people should not continue normally in their chosen occupations and their settled homes so long as they desire'.[92] Beveridge hoped that full employment would change trade union attitudes and provide 'an occasion for reviewing rules and customs as to the use of manpower'.[93] but the change in the balance of power in the labour market made the end of restrictive labour practices even less likely, especially since full employment was bound to be effectively defined as everybody having a job irrespective of whether they were fully employed doing it.

One consequence of the expansion of State social provision was to diminish the role that many unions had played in providing benefits for their members, and to concentrate their activities still more on to job protection and the pursuit of better wages and conditions, this time in a much more favourable economic climate. In the 1920s, Keynes had written of the trade unions that they were 'once the oppressed, now the tyrants', and their 'selfish and sectional pretensions need to be bravely opposed',[94] but, still in possession of their legal immunities, the unions had become very much an Estate of the Realm in the 1940s. 'I sometimes wonder ... who governs this country – the Government or the Transport and General Workers Union', James Chuter Ede, the Chairman of the then Labour Government's Emergency Committee, said to Arthur Deakin, the General Secretary of the TGWU, at the time of the Dock Strike of 1948. Deakin replied: 'That is a question I would prefer you to answer, Home Secretary.'[95] The 'answer' would not have been an easy one to make because the Dock Strike of 1948, like that of 1949, was unofficial. Far from governing the country, these events showed that the leaders of the TGWU, the largest and potentially most powerful of the unions, could not always control their members, any more than the Trades Union Congress at the centre of the movement could necessarily control the TGWU, or any of its constituent unions. At times, the trade union movement acted as a coherent whole, but at others as a disparate one, and what, on the part of its critics, came to be the common portrayal of the union movement as a massive negative force impeding national economic progress, only needs to be qualified in the sense that the defects of British management in both the private and the public sectors was more than a matter of denial of prerogatives, and that the Keynesian or Managed Economy Welfare State was flawed from its conception as a form of economic and social order that would arrest, let alone reverse, Britain's relative economic decline.

Those who wished to label the new order as Keynesian social democracy had the social elitism that continued to characterize British life to explain away, not least because Keynes himself had practised it along with, more forgivably in his case, intellectual elitism as well. The neutrality of the *Employment Policy* White Paper towards forms of ownership of property caused Aneurin Bevan from the Left to reject the document on the grounds that Keynesianism risked rendering a Labour Party committed to nationalization functionless.[96] If Bevan had known that Keynes had told Friedrich Hayek that his anti-collectivist tract *The Road To Serfdom* was 'a grand book', and that 'morally and philosophically I find myself in agreement with virtually the whole of it; and not only in agreement with it, but deeply moved agreement',[97] he would have been even more alarmed, although possibly not as much as many Keynesians. Keynes had been clear anyway that 'no obvious case' had been 'made out for a system of State socialism',[98] much as Beveridge had written that 'the necessity of socialism ... has yet to be demonstrated'.[99] What Keynes had been looking for were economic arrangements for Britain that worked better than the Marshallian Social Service State had done in the inter-war period, and he lived to see his ideas adopted, though, of course, inevitably mixed with politics. Indeed, like Roosevelt's New Deal before it, the British Keynesian or Managed Economy Welfare State proved to be more impressive as a political phenomenon than in terms of economic performance. When *The General Theory* appeared, one of the old guard, Jacob Viner had got it right when he had written that 'in a world ordered in accordance with Keynes's specifications there would be a constant race between the printing press and the business agents of the trade unions, with the problem of unemployment largely solved if the printing press could maintain a constant lead and if only volume of employment, irrespective of quality, is considered important'.[100] Though Keynes did not share his socialism, James Meade described Keynes as 'My God'.[101] If so, Keynes was to be another Earthly God That Failed.

4
Ghost in the Machine: The Electoral Revolution of 1945 and the Veto

'When I reached the Dorchester for my luncheon with [J. Arthur] Rank, there was a huge board (with results) in the hall. Many people were watching it, mostly with glum faces. Already Labour had gained over a hundred seats.' So wrote the former spy, Sir Robert Bruce Lockhart of the Foreign Office in his diary for 26 July 1945 about the outcome of the General Election. 'When I came down from Rank's room, the faces round the board were even glummer', Bruce Lockhart recorded. 'Labour had now over 300 seats with over 150 more results to come. A complete majority over *all* other parties was therefore certain ... . Labour had won a complete and, to the extent of its magnitude, a startling victory.'[1]

'You've had a revolution', President Truman said to King George VI on meeting him at Portsmouth seven days after the Labour Party's resounding victory. 'Oh no! We don't have those here', replied the monarch,[2] and, indeed, nothing comparable with, say, the constitutional upheavals of the seventeenth century had occurred or was at all likely. What had taken place was an electoral revolution. The 1945 Election witnessed the defeat of the Conservative and Unionist Party, which, together with its allies, had dominated British politics since the Representation of the People Act of 1918 had created a modern mass electorate. At every inter-war General Election, the Conservatives and their allies had secured more votes than their Labour or Liberal rivals, and one consequence of that electoral record was that, with the brief exceptions of the minority Labour Governments of 1924 and of 1929–31, Conservative or Conservative controlled Coalition or National Governments had been in office throughout the period. The Conservatives and their allies had won the General Election of 1935 handsomely, obtaining 53.5 per cent of the votes cast and a majority of 247 seats over all other parties in the House of Commons, a feat that was unmatched in any later Election in the twentieth century. When the electoral truce that had operated during the Second World War was abrogated following the defeat of Nazi Germany, the Conservatives were widely expected to win the 1945 Election too, not least because they were led by Churchill, previously the Prime Minister of the victorious wartime Coalition Government. That Labour triumphed and went on to form its first majority Government was, then, a remarkable event. For, by obtaining more votes than the Conservatives, and, in part, as a result, securing a substantial Parliamentary majority, the Labour Party had confirmed the political position that the prominence of its Ministers in the work of the wartime Coalition Government from 1940 onwards had won for it. The pattern of British electoral politics had changed from one of Conservative dominance to that of a two major party system, and the General Election of 1945 had emphasized this in dramatic fashion.

As many political myths came to surround the General Election of 1945, it seems best to set out the actual facts. The numbers on the electoral register who recorded their vote is sometimes shown as 73.3 per cent of those eligible,[3] or, when allowance is made for two-member constituencies, 72.8 per cent.[4] The Labour Party secured 11,967,746 votes, representing 48 per cent of those cast, which resulted in it winning 393 seats. The Conservatives and their allies obtained 9,972,010 votes, representing 39.6 per cent of those cast, which meant that they won 210 seats. The Liberals attracted 2,252,430 votes, representing 9 per cent of those cast, which led to them securing 12 seats. Of the other parties, the Independent Labour Party retained its 3 seats – all in Glasgow; the Communist Party won 2 seats, retaining Western Fife and winning Mile End; the Irish Nationalists retained the two member seat of Fermanagh and Tyrone; and the Common Wealth Party retained the Chelmsford seat that it had won earlier in the year at a by-election. In addition, 17 Independents were elected.[5] The net swing against the Conservatives and their allies compared with the outcome in 1935 was 23 per cent in Birmingham, 18 per cent in Portsmouth, Southampton and Plymouth, 17.5 per cent in London and Leeds, 14.5 per cent in Edinburgh, 14 per cent in Sheffield and Manchester with Salford, and 11.5 per cent in Bristol. The net adverse swing was 6.5 per cent in Liverpool, and 2.5 per cent in Glasgow [6] where of their seats the Conservatives lost only Kelvingrove, and then by a mere 88 votes.[7] In Scotland as a whole the net swing to Labour was 7 per cent, in contrast with Wales where the figure was 12 per cent. The comparable swing in the counties around London was a remarkable 18 per cent, and no less than 20 per cent in the counties of the West Midlands. The net swing to the Labour Party in England and in the country as a whole was 12 per cent,[8] and, as one consequence, in a House of Commons that now had a membership of 640 instead of 615, Labour obtained a net gain of 209 seats compared with its position when Parliament was dissolved, 79 in constituencies which had never returned a Labour MP before.[9] Among the less predictable Tory victories were winning Lloyd George's former constituency of Caernarvon Boroughs;[10] the unseating of the Liberal leader, Sir Archibald Sinclair, in a very tight contest at Caithness and Sutherland;[11] and the defeat of another Liberal, Sir William Beveridge, at Berwick on Tweed,[12] though it was probably too much to hope that this result was a punishment inflicted by the voters concerned for gross opportunism on Beveridge's part. At Hammersmith North, D.N. Pritt, elected as a Labour MP there in 1935, and subsequently expelled from the Party for left-wing excesses, won the seat easily in 1945, driving the official Labour candidate into third place.[13] Such setbacks for Labour were few. In London, Labour increased its share of the 62 seats available from 27 to 48. In Birmingham, the city of the Chamberlain political dynasty, Labour had taken none of the 12 seats available in 1935, but in 1945 it took 10 out of the 13. Liverpool returned 8 Labour MPs and 3 Conservatives in 1945, exactly the reverse of the 1935 results. In Manchester, where the Tories had previously held 6 seats to Labour's 4, in 1945 the Conservatives secured 1 solitary seat to Labour's 9. Labour took all the seats in Bradford, Nottingham, Hull, Leicester, Plymouth, Stoke-on-Trent, Wolverhampton, and Cardiff. This time, Salford went Labour, as did the two member seats at Blackburn, Bolton, and Preston. So did Sunderland and Southampton. Labour even won two of the Portsmouth seats. Labour took Taunton, Kidderminster, St Albans, Winchester, Wimbledon, Barnet, and, by 44 votes, Cambridgeshire. Five members of Churchill's Caretaker Cabinet were defeated, including Harold Macmillan at Stockton-on-Tees.[14] What mattered above all was that the Labour Party had a majority of 146 over all other parties and groups in the House of Commons.[15] It was a famous victory.

'No socialist who ever saw it will forget the blissful dawn of July 1945', Michael Foot was to write later in Wordsworth-mode about Labour's General Election victory in 1945.[16] Another believer was to observe that 'for British socialism it was, of course, its one great historic moment'. Recapturing the atmosphere on 26 July 1945, he wrote: 'Mr and Mrs Attlee driving up to the Palace in their Standard 10 fifteen minutes after Churchill had left in his chauffeur driven Rolls, the crowds of Labour supporters surging up the Mall and chanting not

"We want the King" but astonishingly "We want Attlee," even Mr Herbert Morrison and Professor [Harold] Laski overreaching themselves in fulsome tribute to the new Prime Minister at the packed victory celebration that night in the Central Hall.' [17] When the new Parliament met, in the Debate on the Address, the first ever Labour MP for Watford, John Freeman, was later described by a future Labour Cabinet Minister, Denis Healey, as speaking for a whole generation[18] when he declared that 'on every side is a spirit of high adventure, of determination, a readiness to experiment, to take reasonable risks, to stake high in this magnificent venture of rebuilding our civilization, as we have staked high in the winning of the war ... . We have before us a battle for the peace, no less arduous and no less momentous than the battle we have lived through in the last six years. Today the strategy begins to unfold itself. Today may rightly be regarded as D-Day in the Battle of the New Britain.'[19] It later became a form of conventional political wisdom to believe that the election of the first majority Labour Government led not only to 'a massive transfusion of new blood' into the British political elite but also 'ushered in a new social, political, and economic settlement. A radical programme was carried through by a Government of giant figures who built a Welfare State, and an economy run for full employment and high and sustainable economic growth on Keynesian lines with its commanding heights in public ownership. That settlement endured until Margaret Thatcher's counter revolution.'[20]

With 1945 in mind, Lewis Namier wrote afterwards that 'General Elections are the locks on the stream of British democracy, controlling the flow of the river and its traffic',[21] which well-known observation invited the response that many of the most important changes in the direction and content of British politics had little to do with General Elections. British Governments had twice declared war on Germany in the twentieth century without recourse to General Elections. It may remain a matter of debate whether the First World War or the Second had the most radical effects on British society, but no other events or ideas changed both Britain's role in the world as dramatically or the content of its political discourse as importantly as the waging of two total wars. The outcome of the 1945 Election represented 'the Waterloo of the Conservative Party', according to the supposedly dispassionate authors of the first ever Nuffield Election Study,[22] who, in effect, gave an affirmative answer to the familiar political question of the day, namely: 'has Labour come to stay?'[23] On this view, Labour's victory in 1945 was 'the manifestation not simply of a transitory mood at one

General Election, but of a genuine and cumulative increase over many years of popular support for socialist policies that had been advanced with increasing precision in every phase of the Labour Party's history. This support did not derive simply from successful advocacy ... . It came from the logic of events and the maturing development of circumstance. These had shaped the minds of men and women increasingly and inevitably to an understanding of the validity and inevitability of socialist principles.'[24] Of the 1945 Election, D.N. Pritt, a covert Communist, wrote that 'we all ... had the same sort of experience. We found the electors in an unusually quiet and thoughtful mood, not really excited or stirred. They were quiet because they knew what they wanted; they wanted a Socialist Government, that is a Government which would lead them some way along the road to a society planned to give opportunities for a full life to all its citizens – towards a Socialist Britain.'[25] The notion that voters were more 'intelligent and thoughtful' than usual, as Emmanuel Shinwell was also to suggest[26] because they came up with a particular result, need not be taken seriously as an explanation of Labour's victory in 1945. *The Economist*, for one, felt the need to complain that 'it is becoming almost a rule now, especially in urban areas, that Labour meetings are orderly, but that Labour [and Communist] hecklers do their best to prevent free speech at Conservative and often at Liberal meetings'. The same journal also observed that 'on the national stage, in the newspapers and on the wireless, the roles have been reversed. Here the Labour Party has conducted its campaign with great dignity and good feeling, while the Conservatives have resorted to stunts, red herrings and unfair practices to an extent that has disgusted many of their friends and followers.' Churchill got much of the blame for this, with *The Economist* pompously suggesting that his behaviour 'confirm[ed] all the often expressed doubts about his qualities as a peacetime leader', while, at the same time, regretting that Churchill's recent conduct together with his action in becoming the Leader of the Conservative Party in 1940 ruled out him serving as 'the rallying point for a truly national policy of social and economic regeneration', presumably as Prime Minister in some form of peacetime Coalition Government.[27] Quite why the Labour Party would see its interests as being served by such an arrangement was not explained.

'There is one superlatively good thing about the result of the [1945] General Election – it leaves no doubt about the will of the people', *The Economist* declared. 'The Labour landslide is complete and surpasses the wildest dreams of Transport House ... . Beyond any possibility of mistake, the country wants a Labour Government and a socialist programme.'[28] Certainly, it had been stated in *Let Us Face The Future* that 'the Labour Party is a socialist party and proud of it', with 'its ultimate purpose at home [being] the establishment of the Socialist Commonwealth of Great Britain'. If this conjured up the nightmare world of Sidney and Beatrice Webb, the manifesto reassured those electors who took the opportunity of reading it that 'socialism cannot come overnight, as the product of a weekend revolution. The members of the Labour Party, like the British people, are practical minded men and women.'[29] This was hardly a call to the barricades, and one notes that earlier in the campaign *The Economist* had observed that 'this is not one of those elections when there is a Great Issue ... there is almost total absence of positive proposals put before the country in a form specific enough for them to be grasped'. *The Economist* believed that, like the Conservatives, the Labour Party had 'the task of distinguishing themselves from the common mass of the Coalition [Government]' policies. It argued that 'nobody can tell from the Labour speeches and manifestoes what they would propose to do in the next four years. On coal, to take only one instance, their advocacy of nationalization has considerably less specific content than the [Conservative Caretaker] Government's proposals.' Hence, *The Economist* talked of 'The Blindfold Elector' of 1945,[30] with the implication that the Conservative, Labour and Liberal manifestoes were much the same in content. In fact, there were sufficient proposals for the public ownership of the Bank of England, the fuel and power industries, inland transport and the iron and steel industry in *Let Us Face The Future*[31] to mark that document off from *Mr Churchill's Declaration to the Electors*, though not from the *20 Point Manifesto of the Liberal Party*. This stated that 'Liberals believe that the controversy for and against nationalization is out of date', before asserting that 'where public ownership is more economic, Liberals will demand it without hesitation', with the coal industry being made into ' 'a public service' in some way maintained 'without subsidies'.[32]

When it came to social policy, the electors were assured that the Liberals supported increased provision for education,[33] and that they would not be satisfied 'until there is a separate dwelling for each family at a reasonable rent'.[34] The Liberals said that they had 'detailed proposals for improved health services',[35] and, not surprisingly, they stressed their association with 'the Beveridge schemes for social security and full employment'.[36] The Conservative document had a similar commitment to full employment, and Churchill reminded the electors that his previously promised Four Years' Plan for expanding State social provision had already begun to be implemented in the form of 'the Education Act [of 1944] for which the new Minister of Labour [R.A. Butler] is greatly respected'. The Tories promised 'an all out housing policy',[37] while also stating that 'one of our most important tasks will be to pass into law and bring into action as soon as we can a nationwide and compulsory scheme of national insurance based on the plan announced by the Government of all parties in 1944'.[38] The Conservative manifesto also said that 'we propose to create a comprehensive Health Service covering the whole range of medical treatment from the general practitioner to the specialist, and from the hospital to convalescence and reha-bilitation; and to introduce legislation for this purpose in the new Parliament'.[39]

Let Us Face The Future promised that a Labour Government would proceed with 'a housing programme with the maximum practical speed until every family in this island has a good standard of accom-modation', and one feature of increased provision for education would be 'the raising of the school leaving age to 16'. There was also to be a 'new National Health Service',[40] and 'legislation extending social insur-ance ... to all'.[41] How was this all to be paid for? The Liberals combined pledges to expand public expenditure with 'a progressive reduction in the burden of taxation'.[42] *Let Us Face The Future* promised 'social provi-sion against rainy days, coupled with economic policies calculated to reduce rainy days to a minimum',[43] and 'taxation which bears less heavily on the lower income groups'.[44] Churchill combined promises of greater public spending with a commitment to 'an early reduction in taxation', but he did remind electors that 'the State has no resources of its own. It can only spend what it takes from the people in taxes and borrowing. Britain is now a nation of taxpayers ... . The willingness of this generation to bear their fair share of sacrifices must, though we hope for relief, be continued ... the plans for social progress which we are determined to carry out, cause and require a much higher expendi-ture than before the war. The burden must be borne by all citizens as taxpayers. There is no easy way of one section getting great benefits from the State at the expense of another. The nation can have the services it is prepared to pay for. Where all benefit, all will have to contribute. The revenue is not created by waving a magic wand.'[45]

Those economic liberal sentiments aside, the manifestoes of the leading political parties had much in common, certainly as regards domestic policy, and the same observation could also be made about defence and foreign policy, the Empire-Commonwealth and the United Nations and hopes for world peace. This was what would be expected after a period of Coalition Government drawn from members of those parties. The stage was set for a boring General Election, and, except for the politically committed, this may well have been how many voters saw the campaign. Three-quarters of those responding to an opinion survey in April 1945 had not even bothered to check to see if their names were on the electoral register.[46] The turnout for the July 1945 Election was much the same as in the elections of the inter-war years,[47] and, even making allowance for the dislocation present in a country still at war, this electoral fact does not square with subsequent tales of an enthused electorate. It may be that, whatever their own voting intentions, when they had any, many electors were either uninterested or, as some 84 per cent of intending voters told one survey before the Election, they had already made up their minds. In February 1945, when asked by an opinion survey about the outcome of the next election, a plurality of respondents predicted a Labour victory.[48] This proved to be a better forecast that those made by political commentators and by many Labour politicians. Ernest Bevin expected a Labour victory, but he had no idea of the size the majority would be.[49] Herbert Morrison felt unable to predict the outcome of the election with any confidence. Earlier he had thought that it might prove to be very close between the Labour Party and the Tories and that the Liberals might hold the balance. As the campaign progressed, Morrison was impressed by the optimism of local Labour Party workers, but he wrote that off as amateur enthusiasm.[50] Hugh Dalton wrote in his diary that 'my hunch is that we have won about 80 seats, giving us about 240, with 30 for the odds and ends, including the Liberals, and 370 for the Government, giving them a majority of about 100'.[51] Three weeks after Labour's victory, Attlee confessed that 'in his most optimistic dreams he had reckoned that there might, with luck, be a Conservative majority of only some 40 seats'.[52] Barbara Castle recorded that 'nobody in the Labour Party expected the landslide that happened, except Aneurin Bevan, who had some sort of political antennae which told him there was a ground swell of discontent'.[53] Shinwell recalled that both Bevan and himself expected a Labour victory.[54] Anthony Wedgwood Benn was at Transport House on the day of the declaration of the Election results, and recorded that 'we never thought we would win. Who thought we would beat Churchill? He'd won the war single handed.'[55]

With their record of electoral success, it would be unsurprising if most Tories believed that a Conservative victory was a foregone conclusion, or, for that matter, some electors thought the same, possibly being one partial explanation for the unimpressive turnout. Once the campaign opened, Churchill chose to stir things up, either believing that he could afford to indulge himself, or it may have been that Bruce Lockhart was right after the Election when he said of Churchill that 'his trouble is that he likes and always has liked dogfights',[56] or, as the Tory, Quintin Hogg maintained, Churchill was one of the worse electioneers of the century because 'he had absolutely no idea of how other people felt or thought'.[57] For whatever reasons, in his radio broadcast that opened the campaign, Churchill chose to launch an attack on the Labour Party by declaring that 'no socialist system can be established without a political police', meaning 'a sort of Gestapo'.[58] No doubt anything resembling the Soviet system of government would have that character, or, indeed, any other remotely practicable socialist regime, and the Labour Party had a socialist commitment in Clause 4 of its Constitution, and a current Chairman in Harold Laski whom a court of law in a libel case was soon to decide had preached socialist revolution. A Socialist Britain would be a police state, and the time would come in the 1970s and 1980s when elements in the Labour Movement would try to impose such a regime. In 1945, though, the Labour leadership comprised people who had been Churchill's colleagues in his wartime Coalition Government, who had obtained a measure of political stature and prominence from the experience, and an image of being men of responsibility and moderation, even if none of them seems to have been particularly popular as individuals.[59] The close relationship of the trade unions with the Coalition Government had also enhanced the status of the wider Labour Movement. 'I remember listening to Churchill's first election broadcast in 1945 in the Carlton Club, when he referred to the possibility of a Gestapo in Britain with rather more perspicuity about fundamental political attitudes than practical advocacy or wisdom', Hogg wrote. 'The Club was entranced. "You might be interested to know", I said offensively, "that that speech will cost us at least 250,000 votes." I was not popular. "It must be wonderful to be as certain of yourself as that", said a critic.'[60] The critic was right about the precision of an electoral forecast of that kind, and it was also impossible to know if the speech only really offended the educated classes, as one who actually watched it being delivered maintained,[61] or 'the vast majority of the public, especially the class of new young voters' whom Bruce Lockhart asserted alienated by 'the faulty election tactics of the Tories' which he considered explained 'the magnitude of Labour's victory'.[62] Hogg believed that 'it would be the greatest of mistakes to put down our defeat to bad propaganda', though he himself criticized the behaviour of 'a large section of the Press supporting the Conservative Party [who] took the opportunity to denounce the whole system of controls (which no one proposed to remove) and to organize a chase of that mischievous and irresponsible figure, Professor Laski'. Of the Tories themselves, Hogg maintained that 'our [radio] broadcasts were dull and ill planned; our broadcasters knew nothing of the technique. Our literature was confused, negative and unconvincing. Our organization was improvised and ineffective, and nobody bothered to read and expound our election manifesto. In short, we were beaten and perhaps we deserved it.'[63]

'I personally think that Churchill had an overpowering effect on the 1945 campaign', R.A. Butler was later to say, adding: 'I thought the Gestapo speech a great mistake and it did cloud the whole Election'.[64] Butler also observed, though, that 'surveying the wreckage in the summer of 1945, which I had been almost alone in predicting, I resolved ... to ensure that we did not go into another election with the propaganda victory already lost'.[65] Far from deserting political ideas, though, in preparing his Gestapo speech, Churchill had been influenced by reading Hayek's *Road to Serfdom*, at least according to Harold Macmillan. He believed that the Prime Minister's broadcast 'shocked and angered ordinary folk', but it was not decisive, since 'the Election was lost before it started'.[66] Churchill did not appreciate this, but, if he did dominate the Election campaign, then at least this ensured that it was conducted on his chosen ground. Noting opinion poll data, one authority on British elections stated that the comfortable Labour lead over the Conservatives that had been recorded in the Gallup Poll since 1943 declined during the 1945 campaign,[67] and the 18 per cent lead in January 1945 and that of 16 per cent in April and of 12 per cent in May was down to 6 per cent once the campaign was under way in June.[68] Sceptics will note that the most accurate Gallup Poll came after the event, when respondents were asked how they voted, and, in contrast with some later exercises of this kind when more electors than should have done recalled voting for the winning side, this survey reflected the actual outcome of the votes cast, and, thus, a margin of victory for the Labour Party of approximately 9 per cent.[69] Churchill's concentration of fire on the Labour Party's socialist commitment did not seem to do the Tories any electoral harm in 1945, but what was more interesting was that it did not do them as much good as past experience might suggest, or, indeed, that of later times. Even British politics has phases when radical opinions have more popular appeal than usual, and the first half of the 1940s seems to have been one of them. The performance of the Conservatives in wartime

parliamentary by-elections was very poor,[70] and opinion survey material showed in March 1945, for instance, that if a Popular Front,
including the Communists, opposed the Tories, no less than 55 per
cent said that they would vote for it as against 24 per cent for the
Conservatives.[71] The declaration in *Let Us Face The Future* that 'Labour
believes in land nationalization and will work towards it'[72] normally
would be considered a bold one, but not in a political context in
which, in April 1945, 51 per cent of those surveyed favoured such a
measure as opposed to 30 per cent who disapproved.[73] In May 1945,
when asked in an opinion survey if the Communists actively supported another party's candidate at a General Election whether or not
this would make them more or less inclined to vote for that candidate,
as many as 18 per cent said more inclined and only 30 per cent said
less inclined,[74] which figures suggested a tolerance of Communists that
was remarkable both by British standards and compared with any
other period. The popular radicalism of the time was 'at least a half-
formed socialist ideology', according to D.N. Pritt, who noted that 'a
substantial number of the new Labour Members acknowledged – many
to me personally and some publicly – that they owed their victories
partly to the support given to them in their election campaigns by the
Communist Party'.[75] Of the General Election victory itself, Palme Dutt
wrote that 'this glorious political leap forward in Britain' was 'the
counterpart of the sweep to the Left throughout Europe',[76] though
only Willie Gallacher and Phil Piratin were elected to the 1945 House
of Commons as overt Communists. Dutt himself finished third and last
in the contest for the Birmingham Sparkbrook constituency, with the
defeated Conservative candidate, Leopold Amery, obtaining over four
times as many votes as he did. Amery recorded that 'the wretched Dutt
... forfeits his deposit in addition to the very large sums that he and
Communist headquarters must have spent'.[77]

The outcome of the 1945 Election was explained in different terms
by Lord Beaverbrook, the owner of Express Newspapers and a former
Conservative Cabinet Minister, whose leading role in the Tory campaign in 1945 few Conservatives found helpful. That Beaverbrook's
planned 'victory feast' at Claridge's had turned into 'a last supper' drew
from him several reflections, some of them shrewd. One explanation
that he gave for the Tory defeat was of the boredom, 'the swing of the
pendulum,' and 'time for a change' type. In other words, the National
Governments of the 1930s, or the 'Old Gang' as their political enemies
described their leaders in *Guilty Men*, had accumulated too many
grievances against the Conservatives for them to continue to prosper

electorally. 'It was a mistake to believe that the public were thinking of the war and Mr Churchill's record as our national leader', Beaverbrook wrote. 'They were thinking of before the war and the Tory Party's association with mass unemployment ... . The unpopularity of the Party proved too strong for the greatness of Churchill and the affection in which he is held by the people.' Beaverbrook thought that 'it was unfortunate that the blows intended for the heads of Mr [Neville] Chamberlain and his colleagues should fall upon Mr Churchill'.[78] During the 1945 Election there seems to have been a belief on the part of some voters that it would be possible to vote against the Conservatives, but that Churchill would in some way continue to be the Prime Minister, and in his last radio broadcast Churchill went to the trouble of emphasizing that 'there is no truth in stories being put about that you can vote for my political opponents at this Election whether they be Labour or Liberal without at the same time voting for my dismissal from power'.[79] Churchill's departure from the post of Prime Minister may have concerned the electors less than he must have thought. Churchill's conduct of the war attracted very high levels of support, at least as measured by contemporary opinion surveys, but, once Germany had been defeated and there had been at least a partial restoration of partisan politics, when asked in another survey in the summer of 1945 who they would like to see leading the new Government after the war, only 20 per cent of the respondents said Churchill. This was only impressive in comparison with, say, Attlee, who was named by only 4 per cent. The most favoured peacetime Prime Minister was reported to be Sir Anthony Eden with 31 per cent, [80] which was one more piece of evidence of Eden's relative popularity, and this figure meant that over half of the respondents preferred to have a Conservative incumbent in 10 Downing Street, a finding that was in some contrast with both voting intentions and the actual outcome of the Election, and possibly indicative of widespread ignorance of the political system, or at least of one not involving government by coalition, actual or contrived, which, after all, had been the experience since 1931.

Those given to scepticism about political opinion polls had years of pleasure to come at the expense of believers, if they lived long enough, but one confirmatory piece of evidence that the scale of Churchill's personal popularity at the time of the 1945 Election was exaggerated by the likes of Beaverbrook was his own performance in the Woodford constituency. Churchill's only opponent was an Independent candidate who advocated a one day working week and who was described by one of Churchill's biographers as 'crazy'.[81] Maybe so, but the man obtained 10,488 votes or 27.5 per cent of those cast,[82] which outcome acted as a reminder that admiration for Churchill was by no means universal in 1945. While paying tribute to the 'matchless moral services' that Churchill 'rendered to the nation and to the world in 1940 and 1941,' *The Economist* was of the opinion that 'Lord Baldwin would have done far better' for the Conservatives in 1945 than they did under Churchill's leadership.[83] In the literal sense this was nonsense, but one could see that the Churchill of the 1945 Election did not fit in with the Baldwin model of the man of moderation thought to be essential for Tory electoral success, despite its failure to work in 1923 and 1929.[84] As a veteran of thirteen contested elections, Lord Winterton advanced the view that a 'supreme genius of world renown' like Churchill would rarely prosper in democratic politics compared with politicians like Baldwin, Attlee, and Truman who could affect to be 'just ordinary men',[85] and this was one reason why the Tories lost in 1945.[86] It may be that Eden, for example, would have done better than Churchill in 1945, if only marginally, with his variant of the Baldwin model, which was one of socially stylish 'reasonableness'.

After exonerating Churchill from blame for the Tory defeat in 1945, Beaverbrook attempted what an adoring biographer believed to be 'a deeper analysis': 'Once the middle class had been made up of small self-employing businessmen, whose national political interest lay with the Conservative industrialists or the Liberal exporters and merchants. But now, to an increasing degree, the middle class is composed of salary earners, whose relationship to the capital structure is precisely parallel to that of the wage-earning proletariat, although on a higher financial plane, and whose future is concerned with pensions, like the worker, rather than investment like the capitalist.'[87] In casting around for an explanation of the Conservative defeat that he had conspicuously failed to predict, Beaverbrook's musings took in some of the conventional wisdom of the time that was to be repeated later. In fact, there had been no sign in the late 1930s of any serious erosion in support for the then National Government, and, indeed, its by-election record suggested that if a General Election had been held then, the Conservatives and their allies would have won again.[88] It may well be that the Conservatives would have won again in 1945 if the franchise had been confined to the 1935 electorate, or what actively remained of it, and that there was no large scale transfer of allegiance, merely some Tory abstentions, some people being prepared to vote Labour this time because the odds against them were less daunting, and disproportionately Labour voting

from those who had been too young to vote before, who were numerous, given that there was a gap between the two General Elections of
nine years and eight months.

One later estimate was that Labour attracted 61 per cent of the new
electors in 1945,[89] and, in part, this would reflect the predominance of
Labour voting in the Armed Forces. 'When the constituency boxes
were opened, I was well down', Leah Manning wrote of her experience
as a Labour candidate at the count in Epping in 1945. 'But when the
soldiers' vote came to be counted, my pile crept up and up. I was well
in, by a majority of over a thousand.'[90] The Armed Forces' vote was an
important feature of the 1945 Election and in close contests, like that
at Epping, a decisive factor, but, overall, the number of Service personnel registered to vote was about three million out of an electorate of
around thirty three million.[91] As there were about four and a half
million men and women of voting age in the Armed Forces, it seems
that many were disfranchised.[92] Only 59.4 per cent of those Service
personnel registered to vote did so.[93] As for the middle class being
won over by the Labour Party, one estimate was that in 1945 only
22 per cent voted that way, though that those who did were primarily
drawn from the lower middle class,[94] which lent some credence to
Beaverbrook's guesswork. The development of State bureaucracies
made the middle class even less reliable for the Conservatives. In an
employee culture, the Labour Party was the most obvious defender of
many forms of employment, especially in what came to be called the
public sector of the economy. Much more important, certainly numer-
ically, was what happened in the working-class part of the electorate.
What, of necessity, have to be estimates suggest that the percentage of
working-class electors voting Conservative was about 37 per cent in
1922, 47 per cent in 1924, 31 per cent in 1929, 56 per cent in 1931, 50
per cent in 1935, and 31 per cent in 1945. In other words, there had
not been much sign of a downward trend in working-class Tory
support before 1945,[95] and among the factors keeping it alive was arrogance of the kind that Emmanuel Shinwell, the Minister of Fuel and
Power in the Labour Government, displayed in 1947 when he told the
Conference of the Electrical Trades Union that 'we know that you, the
organized workers of this country, are our friends and, indeed, it could
not be otherwise; as for the rest they do not matter a tinker's cuss'.[96]
Those working-class anti-heroes outside the ranks of organized labour,
not least women, were unlikely to be impressed by such dismissive attitudes, and, even after 1945, despite the interposition of the trade
union leaderships and the 'liberal' intelligentsia, the Conservatives still

had good reason to believe that the broad mass of the electorate shared many of their values, and perhaps to such an extent that for many such people to vote Labour as they regularly did, at least from 1945 onwards, was 'deviant' and a display of 'false consciousness'.[97]

Working-class Conservative voting attracted earnest studies, replete with the apparatus of the social sciences,[98] but, in much the same way as the contemporary tendency for women to disproportionately vote Conservative was merely noted, it was never clear why middle-class socialists and 'liberals' escaped the attentions of such investigators, since they were 'deviant' too, and their views on, say, 'moral' issues were the ones that tended to be aberrant. There were enough of such people to be found in the Labour Party for those in the mass of the population with a taste for social deference to have no need to look elsewhere. Since, probably because of the middle-class nature of its authorship, the Marxist model was of little use in the analysis of British politics, a more convincing model for this period, though one still bound to understate the complexity of the social structure, would be one which certainly involved widespread deference on the part of the mass of the population in relation to the constitutional monarchy, and which took account of attitudes towards the people in between that would range from admiration for particular skills and, to a lesser extent, educational attainments, where recognized, and envy of possessions, all the way through a form of tolerance, as if of aliens, to contempt, and, for some, hatred. Of course, Aneurin Bevan expressed a form of class hatred when, in 1948, he described the Tories as 'vermin',[99] but the virulence of this class war language could not obscure the presence of the socially privileged on Bevan's own side. The flavour of the distance between the socialist intellectuals and the masses was encapsulated by a joking remark made by Hugh Dalton: 'I once told Douglas Cole that we could only win power by the votes of the football crowds. He shuddered and turned away.'[100] If the Labour Party, though, did not represent the views of 'the football crowds' whom did it represent, and what was socialism supposed to be if it was unrelated to them?

That the Labour Party at last could claim the voting allegiance of the majority of the working classes in whose interests it had originally been formed did not make the House of Commons of 1945 into a People's Parliament. 'Overnight ... Parliament had become unmistakably the great national forum', Michael Foot, elected for the first time, believed.[101] When speaking on the Third Reading of the Trade Disputes and Trade Unions Bill, Sir Hartley Shawcross, the Attorney General, boasted that Labour were 'the masters of the moment and not only of the moment but for a very long time to come'.[102] If the socially privileged such as Shawcross and Foot were in Labour's ranks, who exactly were 'the masters'? A contemporary survey showed that half of the Labour MPs came from the professions and were doctors, teachers, lawyers, civil servants, and technicians, and there were no less than 33 Labour journalists. There were far fewer trade unionists than before. [103] It was of a later Commons intake that an MP from a mining constituency was to remark that to progress in the Labour Party 'you now need callouses on your behind instead of your hands', as, for instance, the number of teachers grew at the expense of the manual workers,[104] but it was of the Labour intake in 1945 that one socialist celebrated the changed social composition of the Party in Parliament on the basis that this meant that it had 'ceased to look like a faction or a sect – representing, as it were, just one estate of the nation – and had come instead to look like a truly national party commanding the support of the whole people'. On this basis, Winchester men like Hugh Gaitskell and Richard Crossman were especially welcome,[105] and Woodrow Wyatt was nothing less than 'the symbol of the new type of Labour MP', being 'the son of a pre-school headmaster in Esher, the product of a minor south-coast public school'.[106]

One satirist maintained that the politics of the 1945 Parliament, even the 1940s, had been dominated by 'the radical middle classes ... the Herbivores, or gentle ruminants, who look out from the lush pastures which are their natural station in life with eyes full of sorrow for less fortunate creatures, guiltily conscious of their advantages, though not usually ceasing to eat the grass'. To such people, the working classes were cast into the role of 'the lovably human but essentially inert objects of benevolent administration'. The Carnivores among the middle classes took a more robust view of why they were socially privileged, though the satirist's use of Evelyn Waugh as typifying this set of attitudes was misleading, since Waugh was talented as well as distasteful. The satirist went on to suggest that this domestic split in the privileged classes rather than any struggle between classes was the basis of democratic politics,[107] and as a description of the nature of the British political class or nation or elite it was better than most, though it took no account of the intrusion of trade union power. That said, Herbivores versus Carnivores could join Roundheads versus Cavaliers and Normans versus Saxons along with, one supposes, Left versus Right, Us and Them, and Pareto's classification of Lions and Foxes[108] as a means of categorizing political behaviour and attitudes. To even consider most Conservatives as Lions or Carnivores or Cavaliers would grant them an image of vigour and courage and assertiveness in their divine right to govern that bore little relation to their often pusillanimous political behaviour, which was hidden for some behind a shield of snobbery.

As for the Labour Government and the contemporary House of Commons in which it had a substantial majority, one historian of impeccable 'liberal' credentials suggested that the British Nationality Act of 1948 might well not have been drafted to grant the status of British subject to all Commonwealth citizens in the spirit of the 'open door' if the arrival of the *Empire Windrush* carrying West Indian immigrants had taken place earlier in the year than it did.[109] Nobody could have been under any illusions about what popular opinion would be on such an issue of public policy, which would have been to imitate the White Australia policy that still survived the legislation.[110] House of Commons opinion was another matter, and restrictive legislation might well have run into difficulties in an elected Chamber that, for example, was prepared to vote in favour of a five-year suspension of the death penalty as part of the Criminal Justice Bill of 1948. An opinion survey suggested that only 26 per cent of those asked approved of this initiative.[111] Moving that the relevant clause should be read a second time, the Labour lawyer, Sidney Silverman asked:

> Where can we find a better cross-section of the community than this elected House of Commons? We are not delegates; we are not bound to ascertain exactly what a numerical majority of our constituents would wish and then act accordingly without using our own judgment. Edmund Burke long ago destroyed any such theory. We are not delegates. We are representatives. Our business is to act according to our consciences, honestly looking at the facts and coming to as right a judgment as we may.[112]

What Silverman failed to add was that Burke made his famous declaration about the role of the MP after he had been elected for Bristol in 1774, and that, such was the unpopularity that his independent behaviour caused, Burke felt it impolitic to face the electors there again in 1780.[113] Meanwhile, in 1948, James Chuter Ede, the Home Secretary, had detected 'an increasing volume of uneasiness' on the part of the public about capital punishment, but this had been about an 'unusual run of successive reprieves' that he had granted.[114] Ede added: 'I share the view of Burke that we are not delegates, but, on the other hand, one of our duties is to ensure in matters like this that we keep respect for the law alive in the hearts of the people who have to submit to its administration ... . I do not think that public opinion in this country shares the view ... that there is something intrinsically wrong in taking the life of a person who has deliberately and of malice aforethought taken the life of another person'.[115] The hereditary House of Lords voted against the relevant clause,[116] thus showing itself more in tune with popular opinion on the death penalty than the elected House of Commons. A majority of the Labour Cabinet also proved to be in favour of capital punishment, though in its deliberations the Cabinet seemed to be more concerned with the difficulties with the House of Lords than with the conflict between House of Commons opinion and that of the public, and with finding some means of limiting the number of executions.[117] Eventually, a Royal Commission was set up to examine the subject, which, conveniently, did not report until 1953. One former Home Office Minister, Lord Winterton, observed in the relevant debate that 'I never thought that I would live to see the day in the House of Commons when there would be shown ... more sympathy for murderers than for their victims.'[118] An 'enlightened' outlook towards criminals was one that was to gain ground among lawmakers, though the Saxons or common people tended to continue to be less than 'understanding'.

It may well be that, as one contender for the accolade of latter-day Edward Gibbon wrote, 'by the time they took the bunting down from the street after VE Day and turned from the war to the future, the British in their dreams and their flinching from reality had already written the broad scenario for Britain's post-war descent'.[119] On this view, 'Britain came out of the Second World War as an obsolescent industrial economy with grievous weaknesses. Instead of first devoting all possible resources and effort to remedying this, she chose to load this economy with the vast and potentially limitless cost of the Welfare State, placed current expenditure before capital investment, and thus set the pattern of the next thirty years.'[120] In a liberal democracy, though, the electorate had to be persuaded of the necessity of some form of programme of 'national efficiency' involving, as it seemed very likely to do, high social costs with widespread unemployment in what it would have hoped would be the interim period, while awaiting problematical long term benefits for the economy. Even dressed up, this would have been an unlikely message to win sufficient support in 1945 in competition with the more comfortable attractions of the Keynesian Welfare State. That the State should be widely seen as the Universal Provider in terms of guaranteeing particular jobs for life, and, as a result of the Distribution of Industry Act of 1945, even, in principle, guaranteeing the location of choice, as well as a range of social services, was only to be expected. The British State had just won another total war. It was not surprising that the British Constitution that comprised the constitutional monarchy, Cabinet Government, 'the Mother of Parliaments,' even the party system, and the career Civil Service was described with seriousness and in Namierite prose as if it was one of the wonders of the world.[121] With a machinery of government deemed to be second to none, it was natural to assume that the State could undertake more roles than it had been previously common to assume were within its capacity to perform, and that there was the money available for the State to act.

The situation had been different in 1918, when, as Churchill wrote, once the Armistice had been declared, 'a new set of conditions began to rule ... . The money-cost, which had never been considered to be a factor capable of limiting the supply of the armies, asserted the claim to priority the moment the fighting stopped.'[122] The Coalition versus the Rest electoral contest of 1918 was not replicated in 1945, which, if only in the ease of retrospect, made the anticipated historical parallel between the two General Elections of a victory for the Great Man seem strange. It may be that the folk memory of the record of the Lloyd George Coalition Government of 1918–22 did not do Churchill much good, even if probably few would remember that he was a member of it. Lloyd George's pledge 'to make Britain a fit country for heroes to live in'[123] and, more specifically, to build 'homes fit for heroes',[124] had not been honoured, not least because it could be protested that the money was not available once the peacetime economy faltered. By 1945, that the money had been found for a second total war may well have suggested to enough of the electorate to make a difference to the result that Reconstruction could be financed in peacetime, and this may have been what the plurality wanted, even a majority, given that 63 per cent of respondents to an opinion survey in July 1945 felt that provision for housing was the main problem facing the incoming Government.[125] So it may be that Bevin displayed a shrewd awareness of popular concerns, if little honesty, when he promised in the election campaign, in the absence of actual plans and a time scale, that a Labour Government planned to build five million houses.[126]

Bevin's record as Minister of Labour added credibility to remarks he made about demobilization and the return to employment,[127] and, according to survey evidence, demobilization was as important an issue as pensions and social security.[128] One familiar popular belief about the 1945 General Election in later years was that Servicemen and their families disproportionately voted Labour because they were the safest bet when it came to swift demobilization on the basis that Churchill would go looking for another war and then the men would never get home. A social survey led by G.D.H. Cole in advance of the Beveridge Report found 'more of the same' to be the prevailing attitude towards State social provision, and, to the irritation of the questioners, much in the way of apathy and no evidence of any desire for a social revolution.[129] This is not to say that there was not more socialist or radical sentiment in the population in 1945 than usual, though probably less than in 1919 when the Triple Alliance was humiliated, or humiliated itself. By 1945, the Conservatives were as overdue for a defeat in a General Election as the Labour Party was for a victory that would give it the opportunity to form a majority Government, and since the prevailing view in the Labour Party was that another defeat was likely there was less call for it to act in a 'responsible' manner before the Election, which may have given it an advantage. For a country that had avoided defeat and occupation, the 1930s were the most recent Hard Times available, and, in the strange atmosphere of wartime Britain with much in the way of social dislocation and with her Army expelled from the continent of Europe for four years, there seemed to be enough discontent in sufficient of the electorate to make the difference to grant office to the Labour Party with its promise of a cost-free New Jerusalem. What was being sought may well not have been anything resembling a Brave New World in economic and social policy, or bravery by any conceivable definition, but security – a Safe New World or, if one prefers, a Better 1930s. *Let Us Face The Future* was exactly the wrong title for the Labour manifesto. It was about The Past, especially the recent past, and remedying its ills. There was to be no going back. In this way, what could be called a 1945 Veto came to characterize British politics, with the Labour Party and the trade union movement that provided its financial and institutional base as its guarantor. Soviet imperialism ruled out a Safe New World in one obvious sense, and the views of the voters were to come to be defied in Home Office matters, but for nearly thirty years the mass of the British electorate's love affair with the Keynesian Welfare State persisted until the consequences of the relative national economic decline associated with that economic and social order came to be so obvious and humiliating that the Veto of 1945 was lifted and the political economy of the Cruel Real World returned.

5
Wheat and Tares Together Sown: The Attlee Labour Governments 1945–51

Those who 'walked with destiny'

'That first sensation, tingling and triumphant, was of a new society to be built, and we had the power to build it', Hugh Dalton was later to write of the Labour Party in 1945 as it formed a Government that had a commanding majority in the House of Commons. 'There was exhilaration amongst us, joy and hope, determination and confidence. We felt exalted, dedicated, walking on air, walking with destiny.'[1] There was singing too when the new Parliament assembled, as Dalton recorded in his diary for 1 August 1945: 'The Tories sing for Churchill, "For He's A Jolly Good Fellow," and we reply with "The Red Flag".'[2] This singing of the socialist anthem was said to have stunned House of Commons officials, and caused Oliver Lyttelton on the Conservative Front Bench 'to fear for my country'.[3] There may have been no justification for this reaction since several Labour MPs did not even know the words of their anthem, with 'Red Ellen' Wilkinson choosing to sing for Churchill anyway, and then the Conservative, Colonel Clifton-Brown was re-elected to the post of Speaker of the House of Commons,[4] which behaviour signified continuity in the British constitutional arrangements. Certainly, in his relationship with Attlee as the Labour Prime Minister, George VI had continued to act in the conventional manner of a constitutional monarch meaning that, in the Bagehot formulation, he retained 'the right to be consulted, the right to encourage, [and] the right to warn', and his official biographer thought that his interventions in the appointment of the Foreign Secretary in 1945, and the timing of the General Election of 1951 were important,[5] which seems to have been so in the latter instance. The normally unemotional Attlee was said to have wept when George VI died in 1952.[6] As for the House of Lords, the Labour Party had made it clear in its manifesto that 'we will not tolerate obstruction' from that institution,[7] and, when this occurred in the case of legislation to nationalize the iron and steel industry, the delaying powers of the Upper Chamber were reduced from two years to one by the Parliament Act of 1949. Nevertheless, the composition of that Chamber remained one of hereditary peers. As for the Higher Civil Service, believed by Laski, among others, to be naturally antipathetic to a Labour Government, Attlee recorded that 'I always found them to be perfectly loyal ... . That's the Civil Service tradition, a great tradition. They carry out the policy of any given Government ... . They were all anxious to do the best that they could by a Labour Government.'[8] Morrison paid tribute to the Higher Civil Service in his study of the British Constitution called *Government and Parliament,*[9] which treated the machinery of British central government as being very nearly perfect. The behaviour of the Higher Civil Service that Morrison and Attlee lauded reflected a sense of public service on the part of many officials, but it was also the case, of course, that the Labour Government retained much of the extensive apparatus of wartime bureaucracy and, hence, the relevant Civil Service posts, and it then further developed the machinery of public administration. Though, thereby, new institutions were created, the established ones were largely left alone, as they would tend to be by a Labour Government that, unlike later ones, had no need to play at reforming them, because it had a programme, much of it the work of others, but a programme nevertheless.

Since Clement Attlee had led the Labour Party to victory at the General Election, it might be thought that it would be a formality that he would then become the Prime Minister, but Herbert Morrison pressed his own claim with the help of Laski. 'If the King asks you to form a Government you say Yes or No, not "I'll let you know later"', Attlee observed. 'You try to form a Government, and if you can't you go to the King and tell him so, and advise him to ask somebody else.'[10] This interpretation of the British constitutional practice may well have mattered less than Bevin's unwillingness to press his own claims to be the Prime Minister, urging Attlee to 'go to the Palace straightaway',[11] though it remains unclear whether Bevin was motivated more by loyalty to and admiration for Attlee than hatred of Morrison. So, Attlee survived, and praise for his record as Prime Minister became so familiar that one historian suggested that it became a Gold Standard against which the performance of his successors tended to be measured.[12] There was and is no need to go along with the Labour Party view of history that modern British politics did not begin until 1945, and Attlee in his own writing made it evident that he was well aware that Baldwin had already patented the role that he himself was to play. 'Great men must be kept harnessed if they are not to upset the democratic applecart', Attlee wrote, specifically citing Lloyd George and Churchill, but surely not forgetting that Bevin actually was in that league or that several of his Labour colleagues were under the impression that they were too; and his implication was that there was a vital part to be played by political leaders like Baldwin who were 'second or third rate'.[13] Attlee plainly saw himself in this category, though before 1940 he would be best described as a political fool, falling into the familiar trap of those who rejected Christianity of seeing socialism as a secular religion delivering Heaven-on-Earth through such unlikely means as the League of Nations or nationalizing the coal mining industry.

Like the Labour Party he led, it was the Second World War that gave Attlee his opportunity to make an important contribution to British political life. With Churchill running the war, Attlee was effectively the Prime Minister on the domestic front. Being placed at the centre of the machinery of government in this way was an excellent apprenticeship, and, for one, Field Marshal Alan Brooke remarked on a wartime Cabinet run by Attlee in Churchill's absence being 'finished in half the time',[14] and of another such meeting being 'luckily run by Attlee which shortened matters considerably'.[15] In the early days of the Labour Government in 1945, the Field Marshal was 'very impressed with the efficiency with which Attlee ran his Cabinet. There was not the same genius as with Winston, but there were more businesslike methods. We kept to the agenda, and he maintained complete order with a somewhat difficult crowd. Our work was quickly and efficiently completed.'[16] Far from learning how to do the job of Prime Minister from Churchill, Attlee may well have been the better Chairman of the Cabinet, and the terseness of style for which he became noted may have been developed in reaction to Churchill's tendency to be garrulous. There had not been much sign of economy of words in Attlee's often embarrassingly poor public speeches in the 1930s. Of the subsequently best-known put-downs, 'thank you for your letter, contents of which have been noted',[17] and 'a period of silence on your part would be welcome',[18] both were directed against Professor Laski, and not a leading politician, who might have been swift-witted enough to hit back, or too powerful to take on. Like Baldwin, presumably Attlee smoked a pipe because he was addicted to nicotine, but its use by the master as a prop to sustain what was accepted in those days as an image of sagacity could not have been lost on Attlee. If Attlee came to translate a reputation as a man of few words into a pose, with the resort to the pipe used to punctuate discussion on his own terms, it was still the case that it was a form of wisdom to learn to say little because he had little of value to say. Attlee was 'orderly, regular, efficient and methodical to a degree that put him in a different class from any of the Prime Ministers who followed him', according to one official who worked with a number of his successors,[19] and it may well be that 'the country was never so well-governed, in this technical sense, than under Attlee'.[20] Of course, there is more to political leadership than the moving of paper in the manner of a glorified higher civil servant and impressing such people, but the Labour Governments that Attlee led had both taken on and sought a greater range of responsibilities than any other peacetime government before or since, and Attlee had to lead the way in moving the great weight of resulting business at speed, probably fearing that otherwise his colleagues along with himself would sink beneath it, which fate, at times, threatened. As Prime Minister, it could be said that Attlee had the advantage over many other peacetime Prime Ministers in the range of talent that he had at his disposal both in forming the Labour Governments and in sustaining them, but the price to be paid for this was that there were an uncommon number of prima donnas to be found in the leading group within the Labour Party of the time.

The Labour Governments of 1945–51 tended to be often portrayed both then and later as being dominated by the Big Five, namely Attlee, Bevin, Morrison, Sir Stafford Cripps, and last, and certainly least, Dalton. Attlee was of the opinion that a Prime Minister was 'only the first among equals',[21] which was the most that he could have expected to be in this company, except that from the time of his resignation from the post of Chancellor of the Exchequer in November 1947, as the result of an indiscretion, Dalton was to count for a lot less than before. 'Well, I had had it, my personal high tide; and I had gone under', Dalton wrote. 'All the rest, I thought, would now be anticlimax ... and I was not far wrong'.[22] Dalton was to return to the Cabinet as Chancellor of the Duchy of Lancaster in May 1948, and in February 1950 he became Minister of Town and Country Planning, and then Minister of Local Government and Planning in January 1951, but he was no longer in the inner circle of the Cabinet. Dalton had hoped to be Foreign Secretary when the Labour Government was formed, but that appointment had gone to Bevin. As we have noted, some say that George VI persuaded Attlee to deny the Foreign Office to Dalton, whom he disliked, preferring Bevin whom he described as 'a real Englishman'.[23] The monarch acted as if he believed that the socially privileged Dalton, educated at Eton and Cambridge, was a fraud for becoming a socialist, but this was not a view that was likely to appeal to Attlee, educated at Haileybury and Oxford himself, and later the Prime Minister said that his motive in denying Bevin the Treasury, which he wanted, was that 'Ernie and Herbert [Morrison] did not get on together. If you put both on the home front there might have been trouble, therefore it was better that Ernie should operate mainly in foreign affairs.'[24] Morrison himself had wanted to be Foreign Secretary, and he had to be persuaded to become Lord President of the Council and Leader of the House of Commons, successfully asking to be designated 'number two' in the Government with the unofficial title of Deputy Prime Minister,[25] which position he retained when he did eventually move to the Foreign Office in March 1951.

Cripps was appointed as President of the Board of Trade when Attlee first formed the Labour Government, eventually becoming Chancellor of the Exchequer in succession to Dalton. 'For leadership in the Labour Movement, Stafford had a most unfit upbringing', Beatrice Webb had written of Cripps, who had the misfortune to be her nephew, 'Born and bred in a luxurious Tory household, brilliantly successful as a Winchester scholar, winning a New College scholarship which he refused in order to study science ... at University College [London], he married, at a little over 20 years old, a wealthy girl with a millionaire mother. Hence he was able to settle in a charming country home of his own as a well-to-do squire. It is to his credit that he became a successful barrister, the youngest KC at the Bar, earning a big income ... . Then he was suddenly selected as Solicitor General by Macdonald in ... 1930 and thus entered Parliament ... as a Front Bencher. He knew nothing whatsoever about the internal life of the Labour Movement ... . From the first he had a subconscious contempt for his colleagues, old and young alike ... [failing] to consider their views to be of any importance. He organized first the Socialist League, then the Popular Front, practically in direct opposition to the Labour Party [National] Executive. How could he expect that his rivals for leadership, Hugh Dalton more especially, should not succeed in getting rid of him?'[26] Cripps was expelled from the Labour Party in 1939 and not reinstated until 1945. 'He is an enigma', Mrs Webb wrote of Cripps, [27] as well she might of a man whom Jimmy Walker the trade unionist dismissed as 'still in [his] political childhood' in the 1930s,[28] when he contrived to have faith in Christianity and Marxism at the same time.[29]

Bevin thought Cripps was 'more than halfway to Moscow' as late as 1947,[30] but one biographer was probably nearer the mark when he described Cripps by that stage as having replaced Archbishop William Temple as the national apologist for Parliamentary Christian Democracy.[31] Cripps's support for nationalization was subject to the condition that 'the democracy controlling the State's actions must be imbued with the Christian spirit'.[32] Like Attlee, Cripps had been a political fool in the 1930s even if his foolishness had tended to take a different form, and he too was rescued by the opportunities afforded to him by working in and with Churchill's Coalition Government. Even his role as a Communist fellow-traveller had made it seem politic to make him the British Ambassador in Moscow, and he was later to conduct the Cripps Mission to India, and also to be Minister for Aircraft Production for the latter part of the war, in which post his experience in management in the munitions industry during the First World War may well have been an advantage, as, indeed, would be the case with his duties as President of the Board of Trade. A devout Anglican, Cripps's early morning briefings at the Board of Trade were likened to prayer meetings, and Morrison believed that Cripps saw himself as a political Messiah.[33] Cripps was an unusual character, and, though his taste for knitting was not widely known,[34] it was hard not to believe that his nicotine addiction[35] was ignored by commentators because it did not fit in with the Puritan image encouraged by his tee-totalism[36] and vegetarianism.[37] Brendan Bracken was not alone in viewing this 'White Gandhi' with distrust, though he recognized in 1947 that 'Cripps has a great following', believing that this was because 'the British public like either fat men or high-minded skeletons'.[38] When, in that year, Cripps had come to believe that Attlee should be replaced as Prime Minister because the Government lacked direction, it was not himself that he wished to promote but Bevin. Dalton was of the same opinion, but recognized one obvious obstacle to any such change. When matters came to a head in September 1947, Morrison told Dalton, and, thus the world, that 'he wanted to be Prime Minister, not for any reason of vanity, but simply because he could do the job better than anybody else could'. Dalton observed, 'I thought this rather engaging!'[39]

It also proved to be the case that Bevin had no wish to play Lloyd George to Attlee's Asquith, taking the line that 'Attlee was the best Prime Minister any Labour Government could possibly have and anyone who wanted to get rid of him was a fool'.[40] Undeterred, as Dalton recorded, Cripps went to see Attlee 'to try to persuade the little man' to make way for Bevin, to be bought off by the Prime Minister making him Minister for Economic Affairs in charge of economic planning, which meant taking over responsibilities that Morrison had previously exercised. Attlee also proposed the setting up of 'a small committee of senior Ministers – our present Inner Cabinet of Five plus Christopher Addison [the Leader of the House of Lords] – to be publicly announced, and to take much detail out of the full Cabinet'.[41] A Prime Minister of Attlee's temperament was unlikely to have allowed much in the way of detail to have reached the Cabinet, and it seems more likely that the arrangement was designed to meet the needs of the moment with Dalton's resignation making for further change shortly afterwards. The appointment of Cripps as Minister for Economic Affairs made for needless duplication, and it was one more piece of evidence that ideal structures of government organization of the Webbsian variety rarely cohere with the rough trade of politics that Attlee, in this instance, felt required Cripps being given a different role.

When the composition of the Labour Government as a whole was finally announced, *The Economist* had observed that 'Mr Attlee has not, after all, gone in for boldness or for experiment. Both in its personnel and in its structure, his new Government is conservative, and the emotion that list of appointments arouses is much more that of anticlimax than of exhilaration.' While conceding that 'some of the appointments' were 'excellent', the journal wrote of 'Old Wine in Old Bottles', and urged the Prime Minister 'to aim at a lowering of the average age of his Cabinet by the 15 years or so that would bring it on a parity with Parliament itself'.[42] Attlee had abandoned his earlier ideas about a Cabinet of 10, mainly composed of persons with extremely light departmental duties,[43] which, indeed, would have been a bold departure from normal peacetime practice. Later, Attlee ideally would have preferred to have a Cabinet of 16,[44] but that which he first formed in the summer of 1945 had 21 members, and the second Ministry that he formed in February 1950 had 18 members. Only Attlee, Morrison, Lord Jowitt as Lord Chancellor, James Chuter Ede as Home Secretary, Tom Williams as Minister of Agriculture and Fisheries, and Lord Addison in various roles, were members of the Cabinet for the entire six years and three months of Labour rule. As we have seen, that Attlee's original Cabinet had too many old men in its ranks was one criticism made of it, and much the same was said even after the reconstruction of October 1947. Lord Pethick-Lawrence and Lord Stansgate departed at that time, but Lord Addison, by then 78, stayed on. That there was a place in the Cabinet for the supposedly unimpressive

George Isaacs as Minister of Labour and National Service all the way down to January 1951 was remarked upon adversely by one historian, who also criticized the presence in the Cabinet of another trade union veteran, George Hall, who was Colonial Secretary for 14 months, and in the Government as First Lord of the Admiralty for several years after that. A.V. Alexander, as Minister of Defence, was said to have old fashioned views on defence and colonial matters,[45] but then so would many people in the Co-operative Movement, and Alexander was, in part, in the Cabinet to represent them and their place in the coalition that was the Labour Party.

Bevin was said by Dalton to be always urging Attlee to appoint more trade unionists to the Cabinet,[46] and that element in the Labour Movement was well represented at that level. 'You've got to have a certain number of solid people whom no one would think particularly brilliant, but who ... can give you the ordinary man's point of view', Attlee said, having in mind 'little George Tomlinson',[47] when brought into the Cabinet as Minister of Education. Attlee believed that 'you must [also] put in people who are likely to be awkward',[48] and, Tomlinson's predecessor at that Ministry, Ellen Wilkinson was in this category. 'A number of the plotters [against Attlee in 1945] had been given jobs', Shinwell observed. 'It is not bad tactics to make one's enemies one's servants.'[49] Ellen Wilkinson proved to be the only female Cabinet Minister of the Attlee era, lasting only 18 months as Minister of Education before dying in early 1947, some thought of natural causes, others that she committed suicide.[50] Morrison, her lover at one stage,[51] did not have the courage to send flowers to her funeral for fear that it would damage his political standing.[52] Shinwell himself owed his position in the Cabinet to being a trouble-maker whom Attlee may well have thought would be better in than out,[53] as, indeed, would be the case with Aneurin Bevan, the only member of the original Cabinet below 50, being 47. 'I made it clear he was starting with a clean sheet', Attlee said of Bevan,[54] and in terms of actually running anything of importance relating to the machinery of government this was only too true. Bevan was at least experienced in the House of Commons, which was not characteristic of many of the 1945 Labour intake, and, besides the virtues of experience and the needs of party management, this was one reason why so few of that intake were Ministers from the outset. Subsequent experience was to show that Attlee was right to have a low opinion of, for instance, Richard Crossman's abilities, which left just three men who, at least in retrospect, could be said to have been obvious choices for early advancement. One of them, Harold Wilson, was in the Government from the beginning, being made Parliamentary Secretary to the Ministry of Works when Tomlinson was Minister there.[55] By March 1947, Wilson had become Secretary for Overseas Trade, and six months later, at the age of 31, he replaced Cripps as President of the Board of Trade.[56] Hugh Gaitskell was seriously ill at the time of the 1945 Election,[57] but within a year he had become Parliamentary Secretary to the Ministry of Fuel and Power and the Minister there in October 1947. The only other obvious early omission from the Government was Evan Durbin, who then replaced Wilson at the Ministry of Works only to die as the result of a swimming accident as early as September 1948.

'If he doesn't measure up to the job, you should tell him', Attlee was to say of his dealings with Ministers,[58] thus feeding an image of ruthlessness in discarding failures. Yet, Arthur Greenwood was the only major Cabinet Minister whom Attlee dismissed, and in this case, by October 1947, Greenwood's alcoholism was too obvious to ignore.[59] Two months later, Attlee accepted Dalton's offer to resign, choosing not to save a Minister who had plotted against him. When dismissing John Wilmot as Minister of Supply, also in 1947, 'Attlee had looked very uncomfortable',[60] and not, thus, 'the good butcher' of legend. More in character was Shinwell always being in the Government and even back in the Cabinet from February 1950 onwards, and the similarly talismanic John Strachey being given Ministerial office at all. Attlee's main concern had to be to keep the Government together; and until the resignations of Bevan and Wilson from the Cabinet in April 1951, which occurred at a time when he was ill and Morrison was in charge, Attlee was successful in this. Of many Governments, it could be said 'Thank God for the Civil Service', but when the monarch made this observation about that formed by Attlee in 1945,[61] his estimate was wrong. For this was a Government of more stars than most. 'I had not much idea about destiny', Attlee was later to say,[62] but what the team that he led did have was the ability to govern effectively across most of the range of public policy.

Cold warriors and commonwealth men: the defence, imperial and foreign policies of the Attlee Governments

The Defence, Imperial and Foreign policies that the Labour Governments of 1945–51 pursued followed, naturally enough, from the roles that its political leaders perceived Britain as having or wished her to have in the world at that time, and the country's capacity to fulfil those chosen roles. Britain's economic difficulties were an obvious and perennial restraint upon her freedom of action, and so was the need to accommodate to American behaviour and wishes. This latter consideration had not been as prominent a factor when, for instance, in his book, *The Labour Party in Perspective*, published in 1937, Attlee had written about what constituted a socialist foreign policy. 'Social justice should be the basis of a peaceful world', Attlee had said. 'Socialists of all countries are united by a common rejection of the doctrines and ideals of militarism, and are convinced that the political and economic salvation of mankind lies in the broadest and most generous co-operation.'[63] Attlee believed that the already doomed League of Nations was 'a World Commonwealth in embryo',[64] and wanted the British Armed Forces to be assigned to an international police force. [65] Attlee associated imperialism with capitalism, thus calmly ignoring the behaviour of the Russian Communists in constructing the Soviet Union as well as the activities of the Comintern in promoting the further expansion of Soviet imperialism. Indeed, Attlee envisaged a future British Labour Government pursuing a policy of international economic co-operation with the USSR, which was described as being 'largely governed under socialist inspiration'.[66]

As for the contemporary British Empire-Commonwealth, Attlee had recognized that the Dominions, meaning Canada, Australia, New Zealand, and South Africa, already had self-government, and he wished to see this principle extended to India and Burma as well as to the colonial empire accompanied, of course, by socialism, believing that the spirit of the Brotherhood of Man should determine relations between different races, though he noted 'the exceptional position in the Union of South Africa' with white minority rule. This had implications for future arrangements in the colonial empire, and prospectively deleterious ones, but Attlee thought that how South Africa organized its internal affairs was a matter for the Union Government,[67] which attitude the Labour Government that he led was to take even after the introduction of the policy of apartheid in 1948. As Prime Minister, Attlee's ideas about the future of the British Commonwealth and Empire stayed much the same as before, but then so did his faith in a world organization, this time the United Nations. The Attlee Governments came to be both Cold Warriors and Commonwealth men, and if the latter role came to them as second nature, the antagonism that was to be displayed towards the Soviet Union followed from experience and needed a formidable ally to be effective. If the containment of Soviet imperialism was, as George Kennan wrote, 'a test of the overall worth of the United States as a nation among nations', then before 1947, she failed that test. Far from starting the Cold War, the Americans were slow to 'experience a certain gratitude to a Providence which, by providing the American people with this implacable challenge, has made their entire security as a nation dependent on their pulling themselves together and accepting the responsibilities of moral and political leadership that history plainly intended them to bear'.[68]

'You don't keep a dog and bark yourself, and Ernie was a very good dog', Attlee later said of his relationship as Prime Minister with Ernest Bevin, who was the Foreign Secretary until April 1951,[69] and of their behaviour at the Potsdam Conference in the summer of 1945, Sir Alexander Cadogan of the Foreign Office wrote of Bevin that 'he effaces Attlee and at the Big Three meetings he does all the talking while Attlee nods his head convulsively and smokes his pipe.' Cadogan believed that 'Bevin will ... do well. He knows a great deal, is prepared to read any amount, seems to take in what he does read, and is capable of making up his own mind and sticking up for his (or our) point of view against anyone. I think he's the best we could have had.'[70] Harold Nicolson soon learnt that 'the Foreign Office are delighted with Bevin. He reads with amazing rapidity, remembers what he reads, cross-examines the experts, and having once mastered his brief, acts with vigour.'[71] Bevin was well described by Cadogan as 'the heavyweight of the Cabinet',[72] and a man who probably could have become Prime Minister himself in 1945 and again in 1947 if he had so wished. Attlee may well have given Bevin a freer hand than later Prime Ministers were to grant their Foreign Secretaries, barring Churchill in the case of Eden, but, as we have seen, Attlee had what passed for ideas of his own, and plenty was heard about them, especially at first, not all of his behaviour being consistent with the knowing Cold Warrior image that he was to seek for himself. 'There is always a tendency on the part of some people in the Labour Party to over-simplify foreign affairs', Attlee later said. 'It's partly due to a certain woolly idealism ... . They mean well but they don't like looking at unpleasant facts.'[73] This would have been a good description of the Attlee of the 1930s, but the people whom Attlee had in his sights were those Labour MPs who were associated with the *Keep Left* pamphlet published in 1947 and the Group that took its name, who argued that, together with other Western European countries, Britain could and should pursue a socialist foreign policy, and one independent of both the USA and the USSR.[74] 'We and we alone can prevent the Third World War,' declared Richard Crossman,[75] and called upon the Prime Minister to disown 'the Fulton [Speech] policy which regards Russia like Nazi Germany, and is seeking allies to join in and suppress her'.[76] Attlee's recollection was that 'some of them thought we ought to concentrate all our efforts on building up a Third Force in Europe ... . But there wasn't either a material or a spiritual basis for it at that time. What remained of Europe wasn't strong enough to stand up to Russia by itself. You had to have a world force because you were up against a world force ... . Without the stopping power of the Americans, the Russians might easily have tried sweeping right forward. I don't know whether they would, but it wasn't a possibility you could just ignore. It's no good thinking that moral sentiments have any sway with the Russians, there's a good deal of old-fashioned imperialism in their make-up ... . Their foreign policy has been carried on in much the same way from the days of Queen Catherine the Great. Some of our friends wouldn't see that.'[77]

They were not alone, certainly at first. For, as late as January 1947, Attlee, full of belief in the effectiveness of the United Nations as an assurance of world peace, and sceptical about the arguments of the Chiefs of Staff for the maintenance of a British presence in the Middle East that the Soviet Union would see as being of offensive intent towards her, observed in a memorandum that 'unless we are persuaded that the USSR is irrevocably committed to a policy of world domination and that there is no possibility of her alteration, I think that before being committed to this strategy, we should try to come to an agreement with the USSR. ... It does not seem to me to be too difficult to deal with points of friction.' What the Chiefs of Staff had advanced, according to Attlee, was 'a strategy of despair'.[78] To write in this manner also meant that Attlee was taking issue with Bevin, who had stated in April 1946 that 'the Russians have decided upon an aggressive policy based upon militant Communism and Russian chauvinism ... and seem determined to stick at nothing, short of war, to obtain her objectives. At the present time her aggressive policy is clearly directed to challenging this country everywhere, partly because HMG are the leaders of ... social democracy in Europe and partly, no doubt, because we appear the less formidable of Russia's only two rivals as Great Powers.'[79] So, Bevin's response to Attlee was to say that 'it would be Munich all over again ... if we speak to Stalin as you propose', taking the line that in relation to Greece, Turkey, and Iran, 'he is as likely to respect their independence as Hitler was to respect Czechoslovakia's and we shall get as much of Stalin's goodwill as we got of Hitler's after Munich'. Bevin argued that 'the present rulers of Russia ... believe they have a mission to work for a Communist world'.[80] Attlee was still unconvinced that Soviet expansionism was sufficient a threat to justify a military presence in the Middle East of the order that Bevin thought necessary, but he gave up his opposition when the Chiefs of Staff made it evident that they would resign unless he did.[81] If, instead of vapid internationalism and prospective appeasement of Stalin, Attlee had contested this policy on the grounds of its financial cost in the context of Britain's severe economic difficulties he would have had a stronger case than that which he advanced, although it would probably have made no difference to the outcome.

What was interesting was that Attlee put forward none of these arguments when, also in January 1947, the Labour Government, or rather only some members of it, decided that Britain should manufacture her own atomic weapons. As the British Government saw it, the Americans, or, at least, Congressional opinion had reneged on the assurances that seemed to be given in the Quebec Agreement of 1943 that Britain would continue to share in peacetime in the benefits of research and development of atomic energy, and hence the weaponry, that she had the right to anyway because of the scale of her contribution. The McMahon Act of 1946 ruled out further collaboration. 'Our Government, having made an agreement from which it had gained immeasurably, was not keeping its word and performing its obligations', wrote Dean Acheson, which behaviour 'was to disturb me for some years to come'.[82] More immediately, the Labour Government had to decide what to do about it, and Attlee believed that 'the manufacture of a British atom bomb was ... essential to our defence', because 'we couldn't allow ourselves to be wholly in [the Americans'] hands ... there was always the possibility of them withdrawing and becoming isolationist again'.[83] The decision to make an atomic bomb was made on 10 January 1947 by the Gen 163 Committee of the Cabinet comprising Attlee, Morrison, Bevin, Lord Addison, then Secretary of State for the Dominions, Alexander, who was Minister of Defence, and, from outside the Cabinet, Wilmot, the Minister of Supply.[84] Dalton and Cripps were excluded from this committee, having opposed manufacturing atomic weapons on grounds of cost in October 1946. They had been told by Bevin, 'That won't do at all, we've got to have this ... I don't mind for myself, but I don't want any other Foreign Secretary of this country to be talked at or by a Secretary of State in the United States as I have just had in my discussions with Mr [James] Byrnes. We have got to have this thing over here whatever it costs ... . We've got to have the bloody Union Jack flying on top of it.'[85]

'[Bevin's] manner was so aggressive that both the President and I wondered how we would get along with this new Foreign [Secretary]', Byrnes was to write of the Potsdam Conference,[86] and, indeed, Truman's first impression of Bevin was one of toughness.[87] Byrnes came to admire Bevin saying that 'he lived up completely and whole-heartedly to his agreements – he had debated vigorously and some-times harshly before entering into them, but having committed himself he would carry out his contracts to the full'.[88] Bevin had cer-tainly approached the role of Foreign Secretary with his usual self confidence. 'You see, I've had a good deal of experience with foreign-ers: before the last War I had to do a good deal of negotiation with ships' captains of all nationalities', Bevin stated. 'These people, Stalin and Truman, are just the same as all Russians and Americans; and dealing with them over foreign affairs is just the same as trying to negotiate a settlement about unloading a ship. Oh yes, I can handle them.'[89] At first, Bevin persuaded himself that he would be at an advantage in dealing with Stalin because the dictator would remember that in 1920 'his dockers' had refused to load the *Jolly George* with munitions for use against the Bolsheviks, and that the Council of Action of which Bevin was a leader had opposed British military inter-vention against them.[90] Even when, entirely unsurprisingly, Stalin did not display the slightest gratitude for this behaviour, Bevin could still say at a meeting of Commonwealth Prime Ministers in 1946 that 'the Soviet policy of expansion has engendered its own dynamic which may prove too strong for [Stalin] in spite of all his shrewdness and power. I don't think he's planning for war, but he may be unable to control the forces he's started. We've always got to be prepared for that.'[91] Since, in Attlee's words, to put the matter mildly, Stalin was 'a pretty ruthless tyrant', and, thus, 'a man you could do business with because he said yes and no and didn't have to refer back',[92] Bevin's interpretation of Stalin's role in the Soviet system was idiosyncratic to say the least.

As late as the Moscow Conference of March 1947, Bevin had difficulty in reading Stalin, recognizing his ability to portray himself as a man of moderation and reasonableness, though his admiring biogra-pher pointed out that, unlike Roosevelt, Bevin did not allow his nego-tiating position to be affected by this perception.[93] Bevin's view as expressed in early 1946 was that 'you can never ... deal with the Russians if you lie down and let them walk over you',[94] and his declara-tion in 1945 that 'Left understands Left, but the Right does not' was not about prospective relations between a Labour Britain and the

Soviet Union, but about the contemporary political situation in France.[95] This was just as well, since the Left was particularly poorly placed in dealing with the Soviet Union because, if what had been called the Russian experiment failed, then, without the model, socialism failed too. So, excuses had to be found, and such events as The Great Terror had to be disbelieved. One of his advisers later wrote that Bevin resented being labelled as a man of the Right, and, indeed, people of that political inclination might well smile wearily at Bevin saying in 1945 that the work of the League of Nations needed to be carried forward 'in order that the dreams of a Parliament of Men may eventually be realized.'[96] This may well have been for Labour Party consumption, though Bevin was an admirer of the International Labour Organization. Bevin chose to present his preferred policy objectives in relation to the Middle East under the heading of 'Peasants rather than Pashas',[97] though there seems no evidence that practice followed suit. Bevin was to be the author of the Colombo Plan of 1950 for aid to underdeveloped Commonwealth countries,[98] and he was not above sentimentality about the emergence of the multi-racial Commonwealth.[99] Nonetheless, as will be seen, Bevin was to express reservations about Britain giving up her Indian Empire. What worried Bevin was the effect of the example presented by Britain's retreat from India upon her overall position. As he stated at the beginning of 1947: 'Without the Middle East and its other potential resources, he saw no hope of our being able to achieve the standard of life at which we are aiming in Great Britain'.[100]

So, Bevin was a complex man, if one who came to command the respect of the Foreign Office. There were those who maintained that this was the case because Bevin did as they wished. When he first went to that department, Bevin was understandably distrustful of the Foreign Office civil servants because of their social elitism. One of the officials, Gladwyn Jebb, reassured him by comparing him with Thomas Wolsey, a butcher's son from Ipswich, who had been the equivalent of a Foreign Secretary four hundred years before, and who had also become a Cardinal. Bevin grandly informed Jebb that he did not mind the upper class, who were often 'intelligent and amusing', and that he loved his own lower class, which was 'the backbone of this country', but that he could not abide the middle class, who were 'self righteous and narrow minded'. Jebb thought that Bevin's dislike of intellectuals was unfortunate, and mused about the lack of educational opportunities available to 'poor Uncle Ernie'.[101] The notion that Bevin would have necessarily benefited from higher education and that his talents would have been suitably recognized showed a touching faith in the university examiners and ignored the need to parade 'acceptable' views in many subjects in order to score heavily in the honours finals examinations. Bevin seems to have been a bitter enough character as it was without having to endure this, and, though, as he was to find in dealing with the situation in Palestine his experience of life did not always provide him with the insights that were necessary, nobody has a perfect record, and, across most of the range of foreign policy, there was advantage in Bevin remaining a raw talent. 'He's a big bumble bee caught in a web and he thinks he's the spider' was how Bevin at the Foreign Office had been described to Bevan,[102] and Dalton recorded the view of a former adviser that 'after only two months' indoctrination Bevin had become more devoted than any of his predecessors for a generation to the career diplomat and all the Old Boys in the FO'. Thus officials such as Cadogan and Sir Orme Sargent had survived, whereas Dalton implied that he would have known better.[103] The notion that Dalton would have made a more effective Foreign Secretary as a consequence, or on any basis at all, need not detain us beyond noting that Jebb's observation that 'Dalton was not as intellectual as all that'[104] would have been one of the least of the man's problems.

As for Bevin's relationship with his Foreign Office advisers, Sir Roderick Barclay recalled that 'we were treated rather as a benevolent uncle might treat some promising nephew who had talent but still a good deal to learn about the ways of the world ... . The suggestion that Ernie was in the hands of his Foreign Office officials shows a complete misunderstanding of his character. He had a very strong will, normally knew just what he wanted and had very clear ideas about ministerial responsibility. Though he was open to argument it was very difficult to persuade him to do something if his instincts were against it. It was slightly easier to head him off some course which he had in mind to follow, and he never resented it.'[105] In reality, the social composition of the Foreign Office was no guarantee of conservative advice or of Conservative allegiance, given the social origins of so many on the Left, and if traditionalism was wanted in relation to, for example, the Middle East, Bevin needed no prompting, as was evident from a memorandum that he and the then Colonial Secretary, George Hall, submitted to the Cabinet in August 1945 about the fate of the former Italian colonies. 'They flank our main line of Imperial communication by sea and air to India, Australia and New Zealand through the Mediterranean and the Red Sea and provide bases from which Egypt, the Sudan and Kenya could be attacked', Bevin and Hall wrote. 'We must therefore ensure that they do not come under the control of any other State which is potentially hostile or incapable of providing for the maintenance of orderly conditions and for their defence in peace and war.'[106] It was the case that some leading Foreign Office civil servants developed a particular view of ideologically motivated Soviet expansionism, as expressed most importantly in a memorandum in April 1946 written by Christopher Warner,[107] but that such a body of official opinion promoted a policy momentum that Bevin was too poorly placed to resist, and, indeed, was swept along by,[108] does not amount to a convincing argument. A classic working class authoritarian like Bevin, granted the power of decision and armed with a considerable intellect and, thus, not solely reliant on animal cunning, would be unlikely to be overawed by his departmental advisers. Bevin's views on Communism and on dealing with Communists would be most likely to have been formed by his experiences in the TGWU and the Labour Movement more generally rather than by reading memoranda, though he would not be above using the arguments deployed there by Warner and others for his own purposes. One of those advisers, Frank Roberts, wrote that Bevin 'listened to and accepted advice, but he was very much his own man, making up his own mind for himself with many ideas of his own',[109] adding that 'those who suggested that he fell unduly under official influence could not have known him'.[110]

'It is now an accepted thing that when Bevin, the Foreign Secretary, speaks, the Tories applaud and the Socialists remain glumly silent', Lord Beaverbrook observed about the House of Commons as early as November 1945, with his rich socialist biographer adding that Bevin outdid the Americans in his zest for the Cold War.[111] At that stage, if the Americans were waging a Cold War it was against Britain and her Empire-Commonwealth in the interests of promoting a new world economic order, and, far from confronting the Soviet Union, the Americans strove to translate into peacetime the relationship with that tyranny fostered by the supposed Grand Alliance that had defeated Nazi Germany and her allies, once the USSR and the USA had joined the fray, though only after being attacked. In victory, this Unholy Alliance had served its purpose, and that such bodies as the Security Council of the United Nations and its Assembly and the Council of Foreign Ministers proved to be arenas of conflict should have come as no surprise. That the Americans were later to show the zeal of the convert in waging the Cold War could disguise neither their earlier slowness to react, nor their crass behaviour in treating Britain and the Soviet Union in an even-handed-manner, and Bevin was far from being a Cold

Warrior from the outset. Indeed, according to Bevin's biographer, in their early dealings with him, Stalin and Molotov his Foreign Minister, thought Bevin naïve in trying to establish what the Soviet Union wanted to ensure good relations, since they saw Britain as being in decline with her Empire in prospective dissolution,[112] and, of course, they were aware of the economic plight of Western Europe which might well just fall into their lap, and there were large Communist parties in Italy and France to give history a push. According to Bevin's own account, in late 1947, after warning Molotov off trying to 'get Austria behind your Iron Curtain,' and telling him to leave Turkey and the Straits alone and Korea too, he did at last get a reply to the question of 'what do you want?' and this was 'a unified Germany'. Bevin was incredulous: 'Why do you want that? Do you really believe that a unified Germany would go Communist? They might pretend to. They would say all the right things and repeat all the correct formulas. But in their hearts they would be longing for the day when they could revenge their defeat at Stalingrad. You know that as well as I do.' Molotov did, but it made no difference.[113]

Inevitably, the fate and future of Germany was the most immediate European problem. If Bismarckian Germany had been too big and powerful for the political stability of Europe, this had been even more the case with the Germany of 1939. The solution that eventually emerged was for Austria to be returned to a separate status with the Big Two and a Half having zones of occupation, together with one for France, and for Bohemia and Moravia to be returned to form part of a revived Czechoslovakia. The remainder of the Germany of 1939 ended up divided into three. Poland was assigned former German territory, including the former East Prussia, being moved westwards in the process because the Soviet Union had herself annexed previously Polish areas. Within what remained of Germany was divided up into zones of occupation, as, indeed, was Berlin, the Bismarckian capital city. In 1949, the British, American, and French zones were combined to form the Federal Republic of Germany, or West Germany, and in 1950 the Soviet zone became the German Democratic Republic, or East Germany. So, in contrast with what happened after the First World War, when the military bands had marched back to a Germany that not all Germans had to believe had really been beaten and which country was only left wounded by the subsequent peace treaty, the Germany of 1945 had been destroyed and its territory had been carved up and subject to foreign military presences that proved to be long-lasting. In 1919, it would have been better if Germany had been treated in a tough manner or a tender one, but the virtue of the arrangements that emerged after 1945 was that Germans were to experience both, depending on which side of the Iron Curtain they were located. There were Berlin crises to survive, but the problem of what to do with Germany had been solved for the foreseeable future.

What to do about the Soviet Union was a problem that, at first, Britain was left by the Americans to deal with, and, though Bevin could not be said to have simply reacted to events, the strategy that he pursued was, of necessity, well described as rough and ready,[114] since it could not be within his power to bring about a planned progression from the Treaty of Dunkirk of 1947 with France, to the formation of the North Atlantic Treaty Organization in 1949.[115] Naturally enough, Bevin wanted Britain to have as much freedom of manoeuvre as possible in conducting her foreign policy, and, at times, he seemed to think of Britain, the remainder of Western Europe, and their colonies as the future basis of a position more independent of the USA. Thus, as late as October 1948, Bevin told Dalton that he was trying 'to organize the middle of the planet – W[estern] Europe, the Mediterranean, the Middle East, the Commonwealth ... . If we only pushed on and developed Africa, we could have [the] US[A] dependent on us, and eating out of our hand in four or five years. Two great mountains of manganese are in Sierra Leone etc. [The] US[A] is very barren of essential minerals, and in Africa we have them all.'[116] On this evidence, the criticism of the unsuitability of Orme Sargent as a senior adviser to Bevin on the grounds that he represented 'the FO of, say, 1910'[117] missed the point that, in some respects, Bevin's reading of the modern world had its similarities. Nonetheless, whatever Bevin's hopes for an eventual way out of Britain's predicament, and however irksome the role of junior partner in the relationship with the USA could be, as he wrote in February 1947, 'the partnership is worth the price' because ' only if we were to find ourselves alone with our political objectives widely divergent from those of the United States would our financial nakedness be fully apparent to the world'.[118]

In fact, the economic difficulties that overtook Britain at that time forced Bevin to approach the Americans requesting them as a matter of urgency to take on the financing of military activity in Greece against Communist insurgency as well as support for Turkey. The State Department's reaction was to recognize that 'the British Government is really convinced that it is unable any longer to expend funds, supplies, and manpower in the Near East in the future as it has done in the past', and to accept that it was necessary for the USA to intervene financially if Soviet pressure was to be resisted and the continued independence of Greece and Turkey assured.[119] As the Truman Administration had already agreed to share the costs that Britain incurred in maintaining her occupation zone in Germany,[120] it was always probable that the State Department would respond favourably in relation to Greece and Turkey. The main obstacle was likely to be Congress, and at the crucial meeting with that body's leaders, Dean Acheson, then Under Secretary of State, declared that:

> in the past eighteen months, Soviet pressure on the Straits, on Iran, and on Northern Greece had brought the Balkans to the point where a highly possible Soviet breakthrough might open three continents to Soviet penetration. Like apples in a barrel infected by a rotten one, the corruption of Greece would infect Iran and all to the East. It would also carry infection to Africa through Asia Minor and Egypt, and to Europe through Italy and France, already threatened by the strongest domestic Communist parties in Western Europe. The Soviet Union was playing one of the greatest gambles in history at minimal cost. It did not need to win all the possibilities. Even one or two offered immense gains. We and we alone are in a position to break up the play. These were the stakes that British withdrawal from the Eastern Mediterranean offered to an eager and ruthless opponent.

Acheson's words won over the isolationist Republican Senator, Arthur Vandenberg.[121] This form of appraisal advocating a policy of containment of Soviet imperialism had been made before by George Kennan in his famous Long Telegram from Moscow in February 1946,[122] as well as by Clark Clifford, a Special Counsel to the President, in September of that year,[123] but it was now to become American foreign policy in the form of the Truman Doctrine. President Truman told a Joint Session of Congress on 12 March 1947:

> At the present moment in world history nearly every nation must choose between alternative ways of life. The choice is too often not a free one. One way of life is based upon the will of the majority, and is distinguished by free institutions, representative government, free elections, guarantees of individual liberty, freedom of speech and religion, and freedom from political oppression. The second way of life is based upon the will of a minority forcibly imposed upon the majority. It relies upon terror and oppression, a controlled press and radio, fixed elections, and the suppression of personal

freedoms. I believe that it must be the policy of the United States to support free peoples who are resisting attempted subjugation by armed minorities or by outside pressures. I believe that we must assist free peoples to work out their own destinies in their own way. I believe that our help should be primarily through economic and financial aid which is essential to economic stability and orderly political processes ... The free peoples of the world look to us for support in maintaining their freedoms. If we falter in our leadership we may endanger the peace of the world – and we shall surely endanger the welfare of our own nation.[124]

The Truman Doctrine was a dramatic rejection of American isolationism and an assertion of that country's responsibilities of world leadership.

Since in enunciating the Truman Doctrine, the American President had said that totalitarianism spread and grew in 'the evil soil of poverty and strife ... when the hope of a people for a better life has died',[125] it would seem in retrospect that there was a natural progression to the Marshall Plan if Western Europe was to be made economically secure, but the domestic politics of the matter made for complexity, and the speech made by General George C. Marshall, the then Secretary of State, at Harvard on 5 June 1947 was a carefully weighted one:

The truth of the matter is that Europe's requirements for the next three or four years of foreign food and other essential products – principally from America – are so much greater than her present ability to pay that she must have substantial additional help or face economic, social, and political deterioration of a very grave character. Before the United States Government can proceed much further in its efforts to alleviate the situation and help start the European world on its way to recovery, there must be some agreement among the countries of Europe as to the requirements of the situation and the part those countries themselves will take in order to give proper effect to whatever action might be undertaken by this Government. It would be neither fitting nor efficacious for this Government to undertake to draw up unilaterally a programme designed to place Europe on its feet economically. This is the business of the Europeans. The initiative ... must come from Europe. The role of this country should consist of friendly aid in the drafting of a European programme and of later support of such a programme so far as it may be practical for us to do so.[126]

Whether as the result of reading about Marshall's speech in *The Daily Herald*, as one biographer wrote,[127] or, according to another biographer, hearing an account of it on the radio, Bevin reacted at once, explaining later that he saw the prospect of what was to become known as Marshall Aid as being 'like a lifeline to sinking men' and one to be 'grabbed ... with both hands'.[128] There was no Marshall Plan in being at the time, and Marshall's speech had made no distinction between the needs of Western Europe and those European countries effectively under Soviet rule. Since the Soviet Union was bound to appreciate that, as Bevin put it, the implementation of Marshall's proposals would be 'the quickest way to break down the Iron Curtain',[129] their policy was bound to be obstructive, and, indeed, Molotov as Soviet Foreign Minister did his best to wreck the relevant Paris Conference of July 1947, eventually withdrawing. So, Western Europe only was to be the recipient of the European Recovery Programme, and it was made clear to the British Cabinet by Will Clayton as Under Secretary of State that it would be difficult to persuade Congress to approve of the Programme without the countries concerned showing in 'a concrete and substantial way [how] they proposed to help themselves, how long it will take and by what steps – what minimum assistance is required from the US, why it is necessary, and when the load on the US would be reduced', and there would need to be 'some proposals regarding a closer integration of [the Western] European economy'.

Bevin remarked that 'in Europe we can't reach a customs union at once',[130] and, while he welcomed the Marshall programme, he proved to be determined to ensure that Britain's problems were not just 'lumped' in with those of her continental European neighbours.[131] Bevin emphasized that 'Britain with an Empire is on a different basis', and that the nature of her dollar problem was different too.[132] Naturally wishing to retain for Britain that 'little bit of dignity we have left',[133] Bevin emphasized that unless the relationship with the USA was one of a financial partnership it would come to resemble that between the USSR and Yugoslavia.[134] This analogy was not the most obvious one to use given Bevin's contemporary prediction that 'Yugoslavia would gradually come west',[135] which he made presumably on the basis that, unlike all but Albania of the countries in Eastern Europe, Yugoslavia's Communist regime was not a consequence of 'liberation' by the Red Army, which meant that she had some scope for an escape from the Soviet system. Indeed, in June 1948, the independent behaviour of the Tito dictatorship was to lead Stalin to expel

Yugoslavia from the successor organization to the Comintern, the Cominform, an expulsion that Bevin greeted with caution.[136] In the meantime, Bevin had led the West-European response to the Marshall initiative, and played his part in ensuring that the Organization for European Economic Co-operation involved only intergovernmental relationships and no transfer of sovereignty to a supranational body.[137] Even if the speed of the peacetime self-generated recovery of the Western European economies was the cause of the payments crisis of 1947, as one thesis maintained,[138] that dollar crisis had to be addressed, and Marshall Aid was instrumental in providing the additional resources that promoted further economic progress[139] as well as the political stability of the countries most as risk.

'Britain cannot stand outside Europe and regard her problems as quite separate from those of her European neighbours', Bevin stated in January 1948, which anticipated the establishment of 'a Western Union',[140] and led directly to the Treaty of Brussels between Britain, Belgium, the Netherlands and Luxembourg that was signed two months later. Before that happened, the Communist coup in Czechoslovakia in February 1948 changed the political context in which Bevin could hope to involve the Americans in the defence of Western Europe. By early March, there was evidence of State Department thinking along the lines of 'US participation in a North Atlantic-Mediterranean regional defence agreement based on Articles 51 and 52 of the United Nations Charter and including initially Great Britain, France, Benelux and Italy'.[141] When Norway came under Soviet pressure, Bevin advocated the establishment of 'an Atlantic security system' which would 'at once inspire the necessary confidence to consolidate the West against Soviet infiltration and at the same time inspire the Soviet Government with enough respect for the West to remove temptation from them and ensure a long period of peace. The alternative is to repeat our experience with Hitler and to witness helplessly the slow deterioration of our position until we are forced in much less favourable circumstances to resort to war in order to defend our lives and liberty'.[142] The Soviet authorities blockaded Berlin from June 1948 to May 1949 necessitating an airlift by the USAF and the RAF, which was a masterpiece of organization, and which succeeded in sustaining the people of West Berlin as well as demonstrating the willingness of both the British and the Americans to combat not only the immediate threat to their interests in that city, but also their awareness of the example that would be given not just to Western Europe but to the world if weakness was displayed in this confrontation.

There was to be an extensive USAF presence in Britain from the Berlin Crisis of 1948–9 onwards, and a number of bases were established. Bevin 'welcomed the presence of US bombers in the UK at the present time', but 'he was anxious to see [these] peacetime arrangements put on a more definite basis'. Bevin secured an agreement from the American Ambassador in London, Lewis Douglas, that Britain could terminate the arrangements should they no longer be considered to be in the interests of common defence, but while they lasted it did seem that American aircraft flew from British soil on an unconditional basis, which, in principle, included those carrying atomic weapons.[143] Whether these arrangements were worth the risk depended on what interpretation was made of Soviet intentions, especially once it was evident that as early as September 1949 that, at least in part because of the activities of its spies, the USSR was in possession of atomic weapons. Informality had the advantage that the American Congress was not directly involved, given that, as Acheson observed, the Truman Administration's experience in seeking the necessary acceptance of the North Atlantic Treaty bore out Alexis de Tocqueville's maxim that in America every political question is soon transformed into a judicial one.[144] It was not until well into March 1949 that Bevin was able to tell the House of Commons that agreement had been reached between the Governments of the USA, Britain, France, Canada, Belgium, the Netherlands, Luxembourg and Norway in regard to the proposed North Atlantic Pact, and that the Governments of Denmark, Iceland, Italy and Portugal had also been invited 'to be associated with us in this great enterprise'. Bevin said that 'this new Pact brings us under a wider roof of security' than that provided by the Treaty of Brussels, 'a roof which stretches over the Atlantic Ocean and gives us the assurance of great preponderance of power'. Bevin added that 'Article 5 [of the proposed Pact] sets forth the essential principle of collective self defence between us, and Article 6 contains a ... definition of the area within which the signatories will regard an attack upon one of them as constituting an attack upon them all'.[145] Since Italy was to be a member of the North Atlantic Treaty Organization, it was always likely that Greece and Turkey would become members too, and they were invited to join in 1951.[146] The North Atlantic Treaty was signed in Washington on 4 April 1949, and Sir William Strang, who had been Permanent Under Secretary at the Foreign Office at the time, later wrote of Bevin that 'no single act during his term of office as Foreign Secretary gave him a more satisfying sense of achievement than the signature of the North Atlantic Treaty'.[147]

What Bevin saw as Britain's unique position in the world was described by him in November 1949 in terms of her presence in the 'three great sectors of the Free World ... the Commonwealth, North America, and Europe', which were 'all interrelated', and 'the United Kingdom, not only now but always, will have to reconcile its responsibilities to all three; we cannot isolate ourselves from any of them. In addition, of course, we have our overriding obligations to the United Nations'.[148] Since, by the beginning of 1948, Bevin had written off the record of United Nations as 'disappointing',[149] the view of Britain's role in the world that he had was essentially that of Churchill's 'three circles', though he had fewer illusions about American intentions, most certainly after their behaviour over the problem of the Palestine Mandate. 'The fate of the Jewish victims of Hitlerism was a matter of deep personal concern to me', Truman later wrote in relation to his many interventions and those of his Administration into this matter, 'I have always been disturbed by the tragedy of people who had been made victims of intolerance and fanaticism because of their race, colour, or religion. These things should not be possible in a civilized society.'[150] Indeed, and, without success, Truman was to attempt to secure civil rights legislation to remedy the social situation in the Deep South and elsewhere in his country, in part for electoral reasons. Such considerations were also influential in the Truman Administration's approach to the future of Palestine as there was a Jewish Lobby and vote present in American domestic politics and not a comparable Arab one, and the Democratic Party's interests needed to be protected in the contests for Congress and, in particular, New York, and, of course, Truman himself needed to win the Presidential Election of 1948 to retain office.

If there was a time to settle the Palestine problem, it had been in the 1930s, when the British Government had both responsibility and, if not power, then more room for manoeuvre without the intervention of others. By 1945, the situation had changed, and, when in the November of that year, Bevin announced a review of the Palestine problem it was to be an Anglo-American Committee of Inquiry that conducted it. Bevin would have known that he was stating the obvious when he said that the British Government had 'a dual obligation to the Jews on the one side and to the Arabs on the other',[151] though critics such as Crossman, a member of the Committee, and, who like many in the contemporary Labour Party, was a Zionist, chose to act as if this was not so. This did not mean that in this matter Bevin was the soul of realism, certainly at the outset. 'I will stake my political future on solving this problem', Bevin stated, 'but not in the limited sphere presented to me now'.[152] This meant that he did not expect to be judged solely on the question of Palestine, but on how 'the Jewish problem' as a whole was settled. The Jewish people needed 'a proper opportunity for revival'.[153] Even at this stage, Bevin recognized that the United Nations would become involved, and inevitably so, given that it was the successor organization to the League which had granted the Palestine Mandate to Britain in the first instance. Indeed, that involvement and that of the Americans explained why the Palestine problem was a Foreign Office matter, and, thus, of direct concern to Bevin, and not just the responsibility of the Colonial Office. Drawing on his experience in industrial relations, and against overwhelming evidence to the contrary, Bevin seemed to assume that a deal could be done, and, as we have seen, he approached the Palestine problem with his usual confidence. Events such as the bombing of the King David Hotel by Jewish terrorists, and the execution by them of two Army sergeants who had committed no crime, eventually forced the British authorities to withdraw.

In February 1947, Bevin summed up the predicament of the British Government in Palestine by saying that it had 'no power, under the terms of the Mandate, to award the country either to the Arabs or to the Jews, or even to partition it between them'. The Government had been faced with 'an irreconcilable conflict of principles. There are in Palestine about 1,200,000 Arabs and 600,000 Jews. For the Jews, the essential point of principle is the creation of a sovereign Jewish State. For the Arabs, the essential point of principle is to resist to the last the establishment of Jewish sovereignty in any part of Palestine ... there is no prospect of resolving this conflict by any settlement negotiated by the parties.' So, Bevin concluded, 'the only course now open to us is to submit the problem to the judgement of the United Nations'.[154] One historian was to suggest that the British authorities could not be said to have acted harshly in its handling of the Palestine problem because the numbers of deaths among British subjects far exceeded those among other groups, including the Jewish terrorists.[155] The methods of Nazi Germany and of the Soviet Union were not available to those British authorities, and the same historian emphasized the importance of the success of the Jewish terrorists was to be in demonstrating to nationalist leaders in other colonies the advantages of urban guerrilla warfare against an imperial power like Britain that observed civilizing self-restraints in response to it.[156] Britain's abdication of responsibility was followed by what can now be seen to have been the First Arab-Israeli

War, which was won by the Jewish forces, and the independent state of Israel was established. 'You seem to have forgotten that Clement Attlee and Ernest Bevin plotted to destroy the Jews in Palestine and then encouraged the Arabs to murder the lot', Crossman declared to Sir Frank Soskice in 1954, 'I fought them at the time as murderers. I can never trust them again and you can't expect me to forgive them for genocide'. Soskice was shocked by this outburst,[157] and possibly concerned about Crossman's mental balance. That Bevin acted as he did because of anti-Jewish prejudices was to become a familiar charge,[158] and some would say that with his social origins such feelings would not be unusual at that time, though this would be to neglect the anti-Semitism evident among the socially privileged, notably, Keynes,[159] and, of course, Karl Marx,[160] whose followers were forced to strive to emphasize that his distaste was for Judaism and not for Jews without explaining the distinction in practice and avoiding the question of what the fate of the Jews would be if they did not concede to *history*. Nobody would suspect Bevin of having 'liberal' sentiments, but he would seem best described as an anti-Zionist,[161] and, as a British Foreign Secretary he had to take account of his country's interests in the Arab world, not least as regards oil, as well as seeking a means of alleviating the plight of Jewish people. Nobody with much sense now believes, as the likes of Crossman did, that there is, or was in, say, 1945–7, a simple solution to the Palestine problem. Bevin was guilty of arrogance in this matter and of failure, but, as one biographer suspected at the time, Bevin's failure was not to seem so complete to future generations than it did to some of his contemporaries.[162]

'It seems to me that the time to take action to establish Dominion status [for India] is now – to develop or improvise the form of Government to carry on through the war but to remove from all doubt the question of Indian freedom at the end of the war', Bevin had written to the then Secretary of State for India in 1942, but, when the idea was advanced by the Cripps Mission, the Indian Congress Party turned the idea down.[163] 'The India conquered by Great Britain is an impossible unit for a sovereign state', Beatrice Webb wrote at the time, citing 'its powerful eighty million Mohammedan [minority], its princely provinces, its discordant religious sects and castes. Even within Congress itself there is no common living philosophy – Nehru is a Communist, Gandhi is a visionary of a fantastic type, the majority being just ordinary profit-making businessmen, or rent-receiving landlords, with a medley of inexperienced reformers of the democratic brand, and a smattering of orthodox and pious Hindus.'[164] This sour analysis left out observations about the number of lawyers in the Congress ranks, but it did point up the complexity of the future of India, which reality, for example, eluded many American critics of British colonialism. 'We need a man to do in India what [Lord] Durham did in Canada', Attlee told the War Cabinet in 1942, which was to save that country for the British Empire,[165] and, four years later, Bevin was to compare Attlee's statesmanship in relation to Indian independence with that of Durham.[166] Nevertheless, in January 1947, Bevin had written to Attlee over India to say that 'we appear to be trying nothing except to scuttle out of it, without dignity or plan', and that 'we knuckle under at the first blow' had implications in 'Malaysia, Ceylon and the Middle East, with a tremendous repercussion on the African territories'.[167] On the more immediate matter of Indian independence, Attlee denied that British policy lacked dignity, and told Bevin that 'you must offer a practical alternative'.[168] As for the partition of India that followed independence, the view of Vallabhbhai Patel that 'whether we like it or not, there were two nations in India'[169] may well have understated the divisions on the sub-continent, but it had more realism than Nehru's assertion that there would have been no partition at all if Lord Louis Mountbatten had been appointed as Viceroy of India a year earlier than was the case.[170]

It does seem that developments in the Indian sub-continent after 1945 were the opposite of what the Labour Government had hoped to achieve, which had been a united federal India as part of what the Chiefs of Staff planned to be a new Asian system of defence.[171] India, Pakistan, Burma and Ceylon were granted their independence in 1948, which meant that the jewel of the British Imperial Crown was removed from its setting. It was remarkable that even when India became a republic in 1949, she wished to remain a member of the Commonwealth, and much was made of this flexibility in the 'new wine in old bottles' mode by constitutional experts such as Sir Ivor Jennings. Less was heard of Burma refusing to join the Commonwealth, and of the Republic of Ireland electing to leave. For that country, as its Prime Minister, J.A. Costello, said, 'the pirouetting on a point of a pin was over'.[172] Eire had stayed neutral even in the Second World War, which behaviour made her secession both sensible and welcome, and it was unfortunate that Britain did not make the break with her in 1949 more definite. As for Australia and New Zealand, two countries that had fought against Nazi Germany and her allies, Britain was excluded from the ANZUS Pact of 1951, which organized the defence arrangements of those countries around a relationship with the USA.[173] The two countries remained a source of food, and the gold production of South Africa provided reasons to postpone the question that Attlee had anticipated of what place such a country could have in a multi-racial Commonwealth. It could not be said that the Labour Government did not treat that form of Commonwealth seriously, with one example of this being Britain taking India's intentions into account when, in January 1950, and in the face of American disapproval, Bevin chose to recognize the Communist regime in China as that country's *de jure* government. Bevin told Ambassador Douglas that 'Chinese Communists were first and foremost Chinese and that they were not capable of becoming Russians overnight',[174] and the British attitude towards recognition of the Communist tyranny was pragmatic, not approving, unlike that of the Americans who preferred to still recognize the defeated Chinese Nationalists as the government of China even when they were driven out to Formosa and other offshore islands.

When, with encouragement from Stalin, the communist regime in North Korea attacked South Korea in June 1950, the American troops in the latter country were, at first, almost driven into the sea, but, following General Douglas MacArthur's brilliant riposte at Inchon, American forces not only defeated the invaders but set off into North Korea, with some of them reaching the boundary with Manchuria at which point they were attacked by Chinese Communist forces. Britain was herself having to cope with Communist insurgency in Malaya, and sent troops to Korea as part of what was officially a United Nations military presence. When, in reaction to the advance of the Chinese Communists, MacArthur seemed to be beyond political control, and there was talk of an all-out war to restore the Nationalist regime in China with the possible use of nuclear weapons, the British Government was alarmed, and, in December 1950, with Bevin too ill to travel, Attlee flew to see President Truman in Washington. 'The contribution of two men, Truman and Attlee, to saving the peace of the world in 1950 has not been sufficiently recognized,' Morrison was later to write, 'It may well be that if different men and different parties had been in control in the United States and Britain at the time of crisis, the third, and possibly final, world war would have broken out'.[175] Attlee's Washington visit was better described as a needless distraction,[176] and such was the limited value of the talks that Acheson was 'left ... with a deep dislike and distrust of the "summit conference" as a diplomatic instrument'.[177] The transcript of the talks bear out this view,[178] and so does Acheson's less than admiring summary of what Attlee said. 'The line of Mr Attlee's argument was that the position of our forces in Korea was so weak and precarious that we must pay for a cease fire to extricate them', Acheson later wrote, 'He believed that withdrawal from

Korea and Formosa and the Chinese seat in the United Nations for the Communists would not be too high a price. There was nothing more important than retaining the good opinion of Asia ... President Truman and General Marshall [stated] that the preservation of [American] defences in the Western Pacific and the belief of the Asian peoples in [her] fighting power were a path to securing their good opinion'.[179] Truman's line was that 'the only way to meet Communism is to eliminate it. After Korea, it would be Indochina, then Hong Kong, then Malaya',[180] and Acheson pointed out that 'if we surrender in the Far East, especially if this results from the action of our allies, American opinion will be against help in the West to those who had brought about the collapse'.[181] Attlee raised the 'difficult and delicate question of MacArthur',[182] but it was for Truman to decide the fate of the domestically popular General, which he did by dismissing him in April 1951.[183]

The likes of Senator Knowland detected 'a Far Eastern Munich' resulting from the Attlee visit, but the Prime Minister had not got his way over Korea, and, as Acheson wrote, the visit was soon forgotten in Washington,[184] though not, of course, as Morrison's words showed, in Labour Party mythology. Naturally, Attlee made no mention of his proposals for a United Nations withdrawal from Korea in order to appease Communist China when he subsequently reported on his visit to the House of Commons.[185] Supporting the Democratic Administration of Truman was a wiser form of appeasement, given that, though they conveniently forgot this foolishness later, Truman's Republican opponents were uninterested in confronting the Soviet Union in Europe, and all for war with Communist China. Even in January 1951, of recent Cabinet meetings, Gaitskell said to Dalton that 'he was very much troubled by [the] anti-Americanism of many. With Strachey it was pathological ... [Gaitskell] had been so much upset by the Cabinet decision on Thursday, 25th January to tell Gladwyn [Jebb] to vote against the American resolution at [the] UN that he had been to Clem and said that he would have to reconsider his position if this was adhered to. He thought that his stand on this had had some effect on Clem and on the Cabinet['s] revised decision the next day'.[186] Whether Gaitskell was as influential as he thought may be doubted, given that, in the meantime, Washington accepted a British and Canadian amendment to their Resolution, which modified it.[187]

Ill health forced Bevin to miss these particular Cabinet meetings, and in March 1951 he ceased to be Foreign Secretary, then becoming Lord Privy Seal until his death the following month. Bevin was described by *The Times* as being 'like Mr Churchill, a visitor from the eighteenth century; he was of the company of Chatham and Samuel Johnson. His place, one felt, was among the big men, men of strong hearts and strong opinions.' *The Times* said that this 'working class John Bull had his weaknesses; he had, certainly, a full measure of pride and prejudice; he made his mistakes, some serious. But there was no questioning his greatness.'[188] Of course, Bevin was said by some to have started the Cold War. If so, this would have added to his reputation in the same manner as that of Churchill was enhanced by his combative behaviour towards Nazi Germany. The reality was that the Bolshevik Revolution of 1917 had been a declaration of Cold War at the very least on Western civilization. For those on the Left, whether overt Communists or not, the Soviet Union or Empire had to succeed as a political venture, and, certainly, it could not be allowed to fail. This political position had its logic, but, though, of course, what Lenin rightly called 'useful fools' would choose to place the best possible interpretation on Soviet behaviour and intentions, it was not incumbent on others to follow suit. Far from waging Cold War on the Soviet Union from the outset in 1945, Bevin could be criticized for placing so much emphasis on seeking an accommodation with that tyranny, when no terms were at all likely to be available that did not threaten Western interests. Once he had perceived this, Bevin did lead the way in opposing the Soviet dictatorship, not least because the Americans took their time about taking on this task, which slowness tended to be concealed by their later behaviour. Bevin could not declare the Cold War even if he had wanted to because the state of the British economy was such that, as he complained to Attlee in 1947, 'I am expected to make bricks without straw' in conducting his country's foreign policy.[189] Bevin was to be accused especially by those given the opportunity of retrospect of having delusions of grandeur about Britain being a Great Power in 1945, which in some respects was a criticism of substance, but, until the declaration of the Truman Doctrine, the Americans did not face up to their responsibilities, not least in confronting Communism, and there was only Britain to do this. The maintenance of conscription in relation to the Armed Forces, even extending the period to be served to two years in 1950, with Bevin as an advocate of that change,[190] was a demonstration of the seriousness with which the Attlee Governments took the defence of British interests, which were extensive and threatened by Communism.

The care that Bevin took to draw American men and money into Western Europe in the form of NATO and Marshall Aid showed that he was well aware of where power really lay. Then again, when it came to the retreat from her imperial role, given the carnage immediately afterwards, Britain could be accused of undue haste in quitting India, but not of clinging on, and if this latter charge had some substance in the Middle East, there was the matter of the security of oil supplies as well as the nature of the successor regimes. The existing ones were often distasteful enough. Bevin would have retreated from Egypt, and, thus, the Suez Canal Zone, but the Egyptian regime insisted on pressing its claims to the Sudan, thus ruling out a settlement, as the British Ambassador in Cairo made clear in 1946.[191] As for the Far East, Malayan tin and rubber were dollar earners, and it was not just in Britain's interest but also in that of the West as a whole that the Communists should be defeated in the civil war there. The real point about the Commonwealth and Empire was that it was still of some material advantage to Britain in a situation in which she was in economic difficulties, but what should have been clear even at this time was that it was one thing to run a British Empire-Commonwealth and another to simply be one of the members of the Commonwealth, even the most senior one, because it could not serve as a comparable basis of political power. Since men from what were known as the White Dominions and from the colonies had fought with Britain in the Second World War, it was understandable that there were feelings of amity with those countries that had no necessary counterpart in relationships with the countries of Western Europe.

Usually with hindsight, Bevin has been criticized for his cautious attitude towards Britain's role in Europe even by the otherwise admiring Frank Roberts, one of his Foreign Office civil servants, whose argument was that in 1945 and immediately afterwards with Western Europe in ruins and the new Governments essentially having been the exiled wartime ones formerly based in London, Britain had the leadership of Europe in her grasp and she was pressed in vain by such great Europeans as Paul Henri Spaak to seize it. Roberts did not suggest that Bevin was a 'Little Englander', and not surprisingly so, given Bevin's close interest in European issues and good relations with leading politicians there, notably Spaak.[192] Bevin's much cited observation that 'if you open that Pandora's Box you never know what Trojan 'orses will jump out'[193] was said of the Council of Europe not European integration as such. Nevertheless, if Bevin had made the remark about the course of twentieth-century European history down to the 1940s it would have had some justification, though not, of course, to those who knew what came next, or to those rewriting history as Jean Monnet-style ideologues. After the experience of the Weimar Republic, that Western Germany would go on to be a successful liberal democracy was not known at the time, or even that it would be securely established at all, in which venture Bevin played a part. Since Western Europe was in ruins, it remains unclear quite how Bevin was to anticipate the economic progress that then followed, though, of course, through his actions, he did his best to ensure the vital bonus of Marshall Aid. Britain did not have the economic resources to lead Western Europe anywhere, and the Americans who did possess them had an agenda of their own, which, as Bevin said in his last major speech, was 'pressure upon us to integrate',[194] and this was not intended to provide Britain with a surrogate Empire in Western Europe but to subsume her within it, with her actual Empire-Commonwealth consigned to history. That Britain failed to sign up with the Schuman Plan for a European Coal and Steel Community at the outset in 1950 was also supposed to be a missed opportunity, with Morrison's comment that 'we cannot do it, the Durham miners won't wear it'[195] being seen as evidence of needless insularity. Frank Roberts thought that the reason that Bevin did not grasp at membership of the Community in the same way as he had seized on Marshall's Harvard Speech, despite his strong advocacy of Franco-German reconciliation and of West German participation in Western institutions, was because he felt, with much justification, that the Schuman Plan had been designed to exclude Britain much as we had been excluded from its preparation, and that the last minute approach to him was presented in terms that expected and got a negative response.[196] Bevin and the rest of the Labour Government were presented with a supranationalist plan in line with Monnet's grand design for a united Europe in the spirit of take it or leave it, and chose to leave the venture to a group of countries that had been defeated and occupied during the Second World War, which Britain had not fought in order to surrender her status as a nation state.

'Here is the new Foreign Secretary, who shows to all the world that his main thought in life is to be a caucus boss and a bitter party electioneer', Churchill said of Herbert Morrison in July 1951,[197] by which time the Leader of the Opposition was attacking an easy political target. Morrison's tenure of the post of Foreign Secretary only lasted between March and October 1951, but, at least according to one of his officials, it was sufficient time for Morrison to demonstrate his inadequacy for the role, and to obtain the reputation of being the worst Foreign Secretary since Sir John Simon.[198] Even his official biographers suggested that Morrison in his prime would have done better, adding that he would certainly have failed with more style and better grace.[199] The same observers wrote that Morrison had hesitated about taking the post of Foreign Secretary, doing so in the end because he believed that to go to a great department of state would further his leadership ambitions. As they recognized,[200] this interpretation differed from Attlee's recollection about Morrison's behaviour, which was that 'he seemed to want [the Foreign Office] badly and turned down every other suggestion I made to him ... . So, in the end, I appointed him. Rather bad luck for him as it turned out.'[201] It was 'bad luck' that Morrison's period coincided with the uncovering of a spy scandal involving Guy Burgess and Donald Maclean, two Foreign Office civil servants who defected to their paymasters, the Soviet Union. In view of the work involved, it may have been 'bad luck' that, soon after becoming Foreign Secretary, Morrison had to deputize for Attlee, because the Prime Minister was ill, though given his desire for the succession, Morrison may have welcomed the distraction. He continued to take a close interest in the Festival of Britain, even answering Parliamentary questions on the subject in May 1951, leading Sir Anthony Eden to suggest that, as Foreign Secretary, he ought to be concentrating his attention on international affairs. Morrison replied that 'I do not take the superior view of the Foreign Office which the right hon. Gentleman seems to take.'[202] Morrison had ministerial responsibility for the Foreign Office and not for the Festival arrangements, and if Acheson was underrating Morrison's political record when he dismissed him as having 'no feel for situations beyond the sound of Bow bells', there was substance in his observation that Morrison 'knew nothing of foreign affairs'.[203]

The Foreign Office view seemed to be that Bevin had not been able to pronounce the names of various foreign places, but, at least, unlike Morrison, he knew where they were. 'He seemed to lack not only the background knowledge but also the ability to comprehend the essentials of the problems before him', an official later wrote, 'It was not long before this became apparent both to his colleagues in the Cabinet and to Parliament – with disastrous results.'[204] This affected Morrison's political reputation, but whether it made much difference to the conduct of foreign policy in relation to such intractable problems as Egypt and the Abadan crisis could be doubted. The Abadan crisis occurred when a Nationalist regime in Iran led by Mohammed Mossadeq nationalized the Anglo-Iranian Oil Company in which the British Government had a majority shareholding. When Morrison engaged in some unconvincing Palmerstonian sabre rattling, Dalton recorded: 'I said [to Attlee] Morrison mustn't try to compensate himself for having been a conscientious objector in W[orld] W[ar] I and against arms before W[orld] W[ar] II'. Attlee agreed, saying that 'we must certainly keep in close touch with [the] US Government'.[205] As late as 1945, Britain might just have been able to act alone to protect her interests, but by 1951 Attlee in particular thought that 'the use of force was out of the question',[206] and American opposition to such a course of action was made obvious by Acheson.[207] Morrison came to see that the overthrow of the Mossadeq regime could be better achieved in the long run by covert means, as was brought about in 1953,[208] but, of course, he could not say this publicly. That Britain could profitably be bullied may well have been the lesson that Washington drew from the Abadan crisis,[209] but that the Labour Governments' period of office ended on such a low note did not detract from its impressive character of its overall record in external affairs as well as in defence.

The completion of the New Jerusalem project: the economic and social policies of the Attlee governments

'For the time being Ministers would do well to assume that ... we are, with the imminent cessation of Lend Lease, virtually bankrupt and the economic basis for the hopes of the public non-existent', Keynes informed the Labour Government in a memorandum dated 13 August 1945, adding that 'it seems ... that there are three essential conditions without which we have not a hope of escaping what might be described, without exaggeration and without implying that we should not eventually recover from it, a financial Dunkirk. These conditions are (a) an intense concentration on the expansion of exports, (b) drastic and immediate economies in our overseas expenditure, and (c) substantial aid from the United States on terms which we can accept.' Keynes thought that 'it is probable that after five years the difficulties would have been largely overcome' anyway, with 'an age of abundance' to follow,[210] but American aid was essential in the meantime because otherwise he was concerned that 'our people would not accept what was coming to them',[211] because 'at home a greater degree of austerity would be necessary than we have experienced at any time during the war', and 'there would have to be an indefinite postponement of the realization of the best hopes of the new Government'.[212] It was in this 'most grim' political and economic context, as the Chancellor of the Exchequer, Dalton, called it,[213] that Keynes was to conduct the negotiations to obtain the American Loan, without the financial security provided by which the Attlee Government might well not have felt able to make the early start that it did with implementing the

Beveridge Report among many other measures. Dalton was later to gloat: 'By the end of the 1945–6 Session we had passed Acts of Parliament nationalizing the Bank of England, the Coal Industry, Civil Aviation, and Cable and Wireless; two Finance Acts embodying my first and second Budgets, and my Borrowing (Control and Guarantees) Act; a National Insurance Act substantially increasing pensions and other benefits; a National Insurance (Industrial Injuries) Act: an Act establishing, at one blow and in full plenitude, a National Health Service; a New Towns Act and a Trade Disputes and Trade Unions Act … . This was assuredly a record legislative harvest, of which we might feel proud'. Thus, 'for the Labour Government, 1946 was an Annus Mirabilis'.[214] In his second Budget, that of April 1946, Dalton said that as regards constructive plans for the Development Areas, as the former Distressed Areas were called under the Distribution of Industry Act of 1945, 'I will find … with a song in my heart whatever money is necessary to finance useful and practical proposals'.[215] The tune was soon to change.

'We are sitting here today as the representatives of a victorious people, discussing the economic consequences of victory', Oliver Stanley commented from the Conservative Front Bench in the debate on the American Loan in December 1945, 'If a visitor were to come … from Mars … he might well be pardoned for thinking that he was lis-tening to the representatives of a vanquished people discussing the economic penalties of defeat'.[216] If so, the Martian would have been more perceptive than the Attlee Government or its Conservative oppo-nents or the British electorate. The statistical material presented during the Washington negotiations spelt out the reality. 'Before the war the UK was dependent on imports for two-thirds of the food consumed by its people and, apart from coal, for the bulk of the raw materials used by its industries', the relevant White Paper stated, 'But the UK paid for such requirements by the proceeds of its exports and by the earnings of its shipping and other services rendered to overseas countries and of its investments abroad. The effect of the war was to bring about a severe dislocation of the UK position in several respects, which will inevitably take some years to remedy; namely, loss of exports, loss of overseas investments, loss of shipping, increase of overseas debt, and loss of reserves.' Britain's export trade had shrunk to less than one-third of its pre-war volume. More than half of the pre-war tonnage of British mer-chant shipping was lost during the war. The net income from overseas investments was estimated as being less than half that received in 1938. In addition, Britain had incurred huge overseas debts in the form of accumulated sterling balances, together with a burden of current expenditure abroad that was not simply going to cease with the end of hostilities, and which had to be sustained at a time when British exports and other sources of overseas income were insufficient to finance even an import programme on the barest minimum level, and when the UK had insufficient reserves from which to fill the gap.[217]

The American Loan might well ease what Keynes called 'our financial embarrassments' in the short run, but it and later Marshall Aid was never going to be used to remedy what Keynes termed 'the celebrated inefficiency of British manufacturing'. Keynes thought that 'shipbuilding seems to be the only traditional industry where we fully hold our own', in which assessment he was to be proved wrong, and went so far as to suggest to the Cabinet that 'if by some sad geographical slip the American Air Force ... were to destroy every factory on the North East coast and in Lancashire (at an hour when the directors are sitting there and no one else), we should have nothing to fear'. Keynes believed of British industry that 'provided we have never made the product before, we have the rest of the world licked on cost',[218] and, once more, he proved to be too optimistic. Then again, there was the role of the trade unions to be taken into account. The Trade Disputes and Trade Unions Act of 1946 was 'a straight repeal of vindictive and objectionable Tory legislation', according to Dalton,[219] but the ineffectual Act of 1927 had not taken the unions back to the days of the Taff Vale case of 1902 when they could be sued in a corporate capacity for damages said to have been caused by the actions of its officers.[220] The state of the labour market had kept the unions down until full employment came with the war, accompanied, of course, by the retained legal immunities, and by the presence of Bevin at the heart of the machinery of government, as, of course, he continued to be after the Coalition gave way to the Attlee Government. Arthur Deakin, Bevin's successor as the General Secretary of the TGWU, Tom Williamson, the General Secretary of the General and Municipal Workers' Union, and Will Lawther, the President of the National Union of Mineworkers, formed a right wing triumvirate that worked closely with the Labour Government. 'This close co-operation with the Government is a golden opportunity for us, but it deprives us of our independence', one contemporary union official pointed out, adding that: 'It makes us have a double loyalty. The two loyalties clash all the time and no one has told us how to combine them ... . Our Movement is basically a sectional movement for the benefit of small sectional interests, but now we are expected to give them up for the benefit of the nation. But can we do that without being disloyal to our members and giving up the tasks for which we are appointed? We were not meant to be public servants to guard the interests of the nation; we were appointed to protect our members and to guard and further their interests within the framework of the law ... . It is all right having the national interest in mind but we are not the right people to have it.'[221]

'Besides two arms and two legs for oratory, gesticulation and move-ment, socialism has two heads and two hearts which are always at war with one another', Keynes had grandly informed a group of socialists in 1931. 'The one is ardent to do things because they are economically sound. The other is no less ardent to do things which are admitted to be economically unsound. I mean by economically sound, improve-ments in organization and so forth which are desired because they will increase the production of wealth; and by economically unsound things which will, or may, have the opposite effect.' Keynes believed that 'three *motifs* exist, variously compounded, in the breast of every socialist ... . For English purposes one might perhaps sum up the *motifs* as the political, the practical, and the ideal.'[222] One could recognize the political commitment of the Labour Party to socialism as an ideal, but what was commonly missing was the practical *motif*. Ten years before the victory of 1945, Dalton had published a book called *Practical Socialism in Britain*, but this title was cruelly deceptive since this sup-posed magnum opus did not provide the formally programmatic Labour Party with a programme, let alone arrangements for the transi-tion to socialism. If there was to be a planned economy, where were the plans for it? Socialism seemed to have as many definitions as Christianity and similar bitter disputes about what was the true faith, but the rejection of the market system had to be common ground. This had to mean public ownership of the means of production, distribu-tion and exchange, as in Clause 4 of the Labour Party's Constitution. In place of consumer sovereignty, there had to be rationing and price controls. There had to be direction of labour, and the control of its rewards, and, indeed, the regulation of any other forms of income. Fully developed, this was a command economy, begging the question posed by the daunting scale of the responsibilities undertaken and the apparatus required, what would the mechanism be, or who would the men and women be, that could possibly have the abilities to issue viable commands?

Public administration in the context of a total war had given the Higher Civil Service experience of running a command economy without financial constraint, but economic reality returned with a vengeance in the summer of 1945. As for economic planning, Morrison seemed grateful that the Attlee Government was able to inherit the wartime machinery,[223] especially since the Labour Party's own preparations had not advanced much beyond the stage of declaring such planning to be desirable. Exactly how a mixed economy should be run had also proved to be as elusive a subject for socialists as it had been and was to continue to be for others, and, this time, and given the Labour Government's objectives, it was the inherited wartime array of controls that proved to be invaluable. There were various financial controls over capital issues and foreign exchange transactions, over import controls and also allocation schemes for most important materials, as well as food rationing. There were manpower controls involving the direction of labour, and controls over the means of production, which were reinforced at the consumption stage by the rationing of clothes, furniture and fuel. Investment demand was limited by licensing schemes regulating building and machinery.[224] Morrison's recollection of the Labour Government's initial approach was that 'the ad hoc use of economic and financial controls came first, together with a limited amount of economic planning'.[225] One economist pointed out though that a manpower budget continued to be included in the *Economic Survey* until as late as 1950, observing that, since there were few means of ensuring that the targets were met, the targets were somewhere between a forecast and a qualified hope.[226]

There can have been few more daunting economic inheritances for a British Chancellor of the Exchequer than that which Dalton faced in the summer of 1945, and few holders of the post were as inadequate in relation to the task as he was. Dalton was fond of pointing up the iniquities of the British social class system, and he was speaking from experience, given that few owed so much to social privilege as he did in relation to what little he achieved in life. That Dalton had been educated at Cambridge, one of the two great centres of learning in Britain for the study of economics, and that he had held an academic post at the LSE, the other leading institution, might have been seen as qualifications for being Chancellor, but to say that Dalton was well past his best by 1945 should not be taken to say that Dalton's best ever was good enough, though this was hidden for some by a form of social confidence, loudly expressed. On the other hand, the contemporary economic situation was so bleak that it has to be questioned whether any Chancellor of the Exchequer could have done much better in relation to what one gifted economist called the 'management' of the economy,[227] the inverted commas being justified not only by Britain's reliance on overseas trade when the days of being able to dictate the terms on which it was conducted had long gone, but also by the great difficulty in practice of knowing how the domestic economy was faring in fact, as opposed to how it was portrayed in the official statistics. R.H. Tawney, no less, had written an account of why the transition from a wartime to a peacetime economy had gone horribly wrong after 1918, which was not up to much as economic history but effective as a political warning not to do the same after the end of the Second World War, meaning not to decontrol the economy and so usher in a brief inflationary boom followed by a slump and dear money.[228] As it happened, Keynesianism had displaced Marshallian economic orthodoxy, and the Labour Government had no intention of dismantling economic controls, and there was the commitment to full employment.

When Chancellor in 1951, Gaitskell stated that 'it is the firm policy of His Majesty's Government to keep unemployment at the lowest level compatible with the avoidance of inflation. The experience of the last few years has shown a level of about 2 per cent at the seasonal peak', though he defined 'the full employment standard of the United Kingdom as a level of unemployment of 3 per cent at the seasonal peak'.[229] On this basis, the Attlee Governments did rather better than expected in pursuing this objective, though, of course, those Governments, like their successors into the 1970s, interpreted full employment in the spirit that every man should have a job irrespective of whether or not he was fully employed doing it.[230] 'We should aim at balancing the Budget, not necessarily every year, but over a period of years, deliberately planning Budget surpluses when trade is firmly good and deliberately planning Budget deficits when trade is bad or when it is threatening to go bad; but balancing, over a period, surpluses against deficits', Dalton stated in 1945,[231] thus convincing one observer that it was only in a broad sense that his approach was Keynesian, while conceding that this had been the case with the *Employment Policy* White Paper too.[232]

On Budgetary policy, Dalton recognized that 'in recent years thought on this subject has moved very far from its old orthodox bearings',[233] and if he had not entirely cast off his Marshallian intellectual shackles the same had been true of Keynes himself. Dalton acted on the belief that 'the risk of inflation now is less than the risk of deflation later',[234] and shared with others the fear that a serious unemployment problem might still emerge in the immediate post war period.[235] 'We must in the years that lie ahead borrow as cheaply as we can', Dalton had stated in the summer of 1945,[236] and in his first Budget Speech that

October he declared that 'there is no sense, or so it seems to me – I hope no high authority will differ from me – in paying more than we must for the loan of money; and I have endeavoured … to bring [interest] rates down'.[237] Though the space that Dalton devoted to the matter in his memoirs might suggest otherwise, allied to the anxiety to make it clear that Keynes's approval had been sought and given,[238] Dalton's original statement had made it clear that the Labour Government was continuing the policy of its predecessors, namely, 'cheap money and low interest rates'.[239] Of course, Dalton's intention was to reduce 'not only the debt charge in the Budget … but also the cost of borrowing by industry and by public bodies, including local authorities',[240] and, thus, promote economic activity. What was portrayed as the Daltonian experiment with cheap money was confidently pronounced by one economist to have been undoubtedly a failure,[241] while another questioned whether cheap money was seriously harmful since investment demand was high anyway and subject to direct controls, and home demand was not a major cause of the two crises of 1947 that undermined what this particular economist described as the Labour Government's previous air of unquestioning assurance.[242] One crisis involved the convertibility of sterling in July 1947, which had been insisted upon by the Americans. Dalton recalled 'much official optimism' on the part of the Treasury about the consequences of this policy,[243] and on that of the Bank of England too, to judge from the surprised reaction of its Governor, Lord Catto, who stated: 'Suddenly, everybody wanted dollars, and convertibility, even for current transactions, became too great a strain and had to be suspended.'[244] So, 'after six weeks of convertibility we called it off', Dalton recalled, writing that 'it should have been obvious for some time that this retreat would be inevitable', though he found it to be 'a personal humiliation and a bad setback to the Government'.[245]

'If 1946 was Annus Mirabilis, 1947 was Annus Horrendus', Dalton wrote,[246] and the fuel crisis ensured that this was so. 'Prime Minister, you should not let yourself be led up the garden path by the statistics', Emmanuel Shinwell, the Minister of Fuel and Power said to Attlee in June 1946 when advising him to ignore the predictions made by his economic adviser, Douglas Jay, that there would be a fuel crisis in early 1947. 'You must look at the imponderables.' A twenty-minute soliloquy followed.[247] 'Everybody knows there is going to be a serious crisis in the coal industry except the Minister of Fuel and Power', Shinwell declared in October 1946. 'I want to tell you that there is not going to be a crisis in the coal industry, if by crisis you mean that industrial organization is going to be seriously dislocated and that hundreds of factories are going to be closed down.'[248] This was exactly what happened. In his diary entry for 7 February 1947, Dalton recorded: 'Today, at this morning's Cabinet, Shinwell [the Minister of Fuel and Power] suddenly asks permission to tell the House of Commons this afternoon that all electricity must be cut off from industry in London, South East England, the Midlands and the North West, and from all domestic consumers all over the country between nine and twelve, and between two and four each day. This is a complete thunderclap, following the usual rather hopeful tales we have had from him during the past week. Only two days ago he was saying that he supposed we ought to give a priority to keeping all the generating stations well supplied, even if this means cutting off some other people. The weather has been very bad, but the root cause of all this trouble is the insufficient stocks with which we started the winter ... . We thus enter a fuel crisis which continues from day to day. There is snow, frost and burst pipes everywhere.'[249] *The Economist* commented that the Government 'could not have prevented a fuel shortage; but they could have prevented a generalized economic paralysis ... . The responsibility of the Government is collective; but the blame also falls specifically on Mr Shinwell. It is known that the Micawber policy was peculiarly and personally his. It was he who insisted on waiting to see if anything turned up and on hoping against hope that it might turn out to be a little coal ... . But important though fuel is, the real cause of the gloom that is now felt across the country lies in the revelation that has been made of the quality of the Government's economic planning in general ... the planned economy has bitten off more than it can chew ... . There is not enough Ministerial wisdom or administrative wisdom to go round.'[250] That the coal mining industry was about to be nationalized had not proved to be an incentive for either the owners or the miners to improve productivity or output in the meantime,[251] and there was a coal supply crisis before the bad weather took its toll.[252] The cold weather seemed to get most of the blame for the fuel crisis from the electorate, or at least the Labour Government's standing appeared to be only temporarily damaged,[253] but the effects within the Government were a different matter. Of the fuel crisis, Dalton wrote that 'it was certainly the first really heavy blow to confidence in the Government and in our post war plans ... . Never glad, confident morning again!'[254]

Why this was so was illustrated by one of Bevan's boasts made to the Labour Party Conference in 1945. 'This island is almost made of coal and surrounded by fish', Bevan had declared, 'Only an organizing genius could produce a shortage of coal and fish in Great Britain at the same time.' This sally was said to have won Bevan the loudest laugh of the Conference,[255] and the implication was that economic planning was easy and that nationalization was a panacea. Of the Attlee Government in its early days, one of its economic advisers, James Meade, observed that

> in internal policy there is already a conflict between the different main meanings that may be given to the idea of Socialist economic planning. Broadly speaking, there are on the one hand those (led by Cripps at the Board of Trade) who believe in the quantitative plan-ning of the economy commodity by commodity. Such a Gosplan could not, in my opinion, be carried out without socializing all or most industries (which is expressly not the policy of the Labour Party) and, possibly, without losing freedom of choice of consumers and workers as to what they will consume and what they will work at. On the other hand is what I think of as the Liberal-Socialist solu-tion under which certain industries which must in any case be large scale monopolies (e.g. electricity, railways, etc.) are completely socialized and run on 'market' principles of pricing and costing, while the rest of industry is made to compete by anti-restrictive practice legislation. Steps are taken to maintain total aggregate demand – partly (i.e. in the case of the socialized sector of the economy) by quantitative planning and programming and partly by planning certain categories of demand by such means as tax and subsidy policy, the rate of interest, the rate of exchange etc. to see that private investment, consumers' expenditure or exports are of the desired magnitude. I am pretty sure that Morrison, who most fortunately as Lord President is the Economic Section's Minister, is going to be the leader of the second school of thought.[256]

As it happened, Meade's successor as Director of the Cabinet Office's Economic Section, Robert Hall, thought that Morrison was unable to understand the briefs presented to him. The same official welcomed Cripps being made Minister of Economic Affairs in September 1947 because 'Cripps is a realist and able to understand a problem very quickly',[257] but whether this made much difference in terms of economic planning remained unclear.

Cripps may have had a British style Gosplan in his mind, but when Harold Wilson succeeded him as President of the Board of Trade, what he inherited was primarily the system of wartime controls. There were no less than eight government departments with responsibilities for British industry, and a ninth was created in 1951 with the establishment of the Ministry of Materials. The Ministry of Supply was responsible for iron and steel, non-ferrous metals, vehicles, engineering and explosives. The Ministry of Food was responsible for the procurement, distribution and price control of essential foods and feed stuffs. The Ministry of Agriculture and Fisheries was responsible for farming, horticulture, agricultural machinery and fisheries. The Ministry of Fuel and Power was responsible for the coal, gas, electricity and oil industries. The Ministry of Transport was responsible for transport services other than civil aviation, road building and parts of the quarrying industry. The Ministry of Works was responsible for building and building materials, and civil engineering. The Admiralty was responsible for shipbuilding and repairing. The Board of Trade was responsible for all industries not assigned to another department, of which the most important were textiles, chemicals, rubber and paper. The Board of Trade was also responsible for the general administration of insurance and company law, price policy and price controls, the distribution of industry, commercial relations with other countries, bankruptcy, patents, the census of production and distribution, as well as the range of controls affecting production, raw materials, imports and exports.[258] The Board of Trade's guide to raw materials controls comprised 90 pages, and one internal investigation doubted that 'there is any man in the Board of Trade who knows what is controlled'.[259] Since the structure of the Board of Trade in his time involved no less than 19 divisions,[260] keeping track of its activities was bound to be a challenging task for Wilson. Though Gaitskell was to dismiss him as 'weak, ambitious and overworked',[261] Wilson proved to be an effective Minister, even finding time for three trips to Moscow for negotiations with his Soviet counterpart, Anastas Mikoyan, which Wilson later described at length and in unconvincing dramatic style,[262] and which others believed to be of little value.[263] 'If he's ambitious, why doesn't he try to hit a headline against monopolies?' Dalton was to ask about Wilson,[264] plainly unimpressed by the activities of the Monopolies and Restrictive Practices Commission that had been established by legislation in 1948. This Commission had worked so slowly that one economist estimated that it would take it 8,000 years to cover the whole of industry. Trade union behaviour was explicitly excluded, and the Labour Government lost office before it could abolish resale price maintenance,[265] and if getting rid of price fixing was a curious ambition in relation to socialist criteria, so was Wilson's eventual 'bonfire of controls'.[266] There seems no reason to dissent from the gloomy verdict of two socialist writers who later commented that if there had been no Korean War it was probable that Labour Government planning in 1951 would have been almost entirely confined to Budget policy and some balance of payments controls.[267]

The Dalton-inflationary and Cripps-deflationary generalization about the economic policy of the Labour Government could not survive knowledge of the contents of Dalton's Budget Speech of 12 November 1947, which one contemporary economist correctly said largely set the pattern for 1948 and subsequent years in terms of fiscal policy.[268] 'This is the second time in three years that I have had to present to the Committee [of Ways and Means] a Supplementary Budget', Dalton had said, 'My reason today is that we must strengthen still further, and without delay, our budgetary defences against inflation.'[269] This Dalton proceeded to do, which reality tended to be obscured by the manner of his subsequent resignation. If he had survived his indiscretion, Austerity Dalton would not have politically suited a man whose eyes were said by critics to be 'blazing with insincerity'.[270] Austerity Cripps was just right for the times, at least as far as the Roundheads were concerned. 'There, but for the grace of God, goes God' had been Churchill's famous joke about Cripps,[271] and Cripps did tend to clothe his political behaviour with Christian principles. Speaking in 1947, Cripps said that the 'first call' to the country was 'to put into practice in our industrial life those basic principles of honesty and honour which we have so long declared to be the foundation of our spiritual life', and 'to submerge all thought of personal gain and personal ambition in the greater and deeper desire to give our all to secure the future prosperity and happiness of our people'.[272] Cripps's economic strategy was clear: 'You will see, then, that as long as we are in this impoverished state, the result of our tremendous efforts in two World Wars, our own consumption requirements have to be the last in the list of priorities. First are exports ... second is capital investment in industry; and last are the needs, comforts and the amenities of the family.'[273] One later outside assessment was that Cripps was dependent on the advice of officials such as Robert Hall, and that his contribution was to add a resolute public manner allied to drive and moral fervour.[274]

A year after his resignation, Dalton was to concur with the view that his resignation had 'made possible the coordination of the Treasury and the planning machine', but thought that this 'double burden' was only being borne successfully 'because Cripps is so brilliantly on top of his form. I am sure that this set-up cannot last'.[275] Indeed, Cripps's health was to be broken by overwork. Robert Hall himself said of Cripps that 'he did not really understand the basis of economic planning as we developed it'. Hall played down the importance of the inheritance of economic policy from Dalton because 'it was not part of a plan ... . Cripps from the first thought that the problems should be treated as a whole, as is clear from the opening words of his first Budget speech. He brought in Edwin Plowden [as Chief Planning Officer] and it was under him that the main instruments [of economic planning] were developed.' Hall added that 'his weakness was really his emotional belief in socialism, which allowed Nye Bevan to defeat him on several crucial matters ... it was the constant tendency of government expenditure to rise which was the great handicap of the Government ... and Nye was the main force behind this, not only on health but on ... extravagant housing and in his general pressure. Stafford would never stand up to him in the end and that was why Nye said that (in effect) he had out manoeuvred him on several occasions. This was because Stafford's conscience was against him'.[276] On this view, Cripps was not Iron Chancellor enough in relation to the control of public expenditure, though one area in which he had a success that was to elude others was that his period of office was associated with a wages policy that actually worked. This policy lasted from February 1948 to October 1950 in which period wage rates increased by only 5 per cent at a time when retail prices rose by 8 per cent. The right wing leaders of the TUC promoted the policy to explicitly support the Labour Government and to preclude outside interference with its preferred voluntarist tradition of collective wage bargaining.[277] That the period of wage restraint lasted as long as it did was a remarkable example of the coherence of the contemporary Labour Movement. Aside from accumulated grievances, two blows finally undermined the policy, the second of which was the inflation that resulted from the outbreak of the Korean War. The first was the devaluation of the pound sterling on 19 September 1949. Characteristically, Cripps had made the maintenance of the existing exchange rate into a matter of honour, and this factor together with his serious illness delayed a decision that might have been presented as a considered move and not a crisis measure if it had been made in, say, April. When the devaluation took place five months later it was of the order of 30 per cent to a new fixed rate of 2.80 dollars to the pound.[278]

When poor health forced Cripps to relinquish the post of Chancellor of the Exchequer in October 1950, his natural successor was Hugh Gaitskell, who had been called in to support Cripps in his work even when still Minister of Fuel and Power, and more explicitly so when he had been made Minister of State for Economic Affairs in February 1950. Gaitskell's role was well described as 'Vice-Chancellor of the Exchequer',[279] and, though, he had never been in the Cabinet, when accepting the Chancellorship itself he recorded that 'I made sure that I really was to be Number 4 in the Government as Stafford had been'.[280] Aside from the ridiculous Shinwell, those most aggrieved by Gaitskell's promotion the new Chancellor identified as Bevan, who seemed to be humiliated by this promotion over his head, and Wilson, whose jealousy Gaitskell found irrational in view of his age.[281] Unlike Morrison, who thought Gaitskell to be too young to be a threat to his own hopes of eventually succeeding Attlee as Leader of the Labour Party,[282] Wilson may well have appreciated that Gaitskell's promotion made him the most likely nominee of the Right and Centre for the succession. Being nearly ten years younger than Gaitskell did not alter the reality that Wilson had been in the Cabinet for more than three years and that he had been passed over for the Chancellorship, for which post he could see himself as well qualified, at least in the sense that he had an academic training in economics. In years to come, Wilson's political behaviour tended to be either attributed to excessive careerism, or, in the opinion of some members of the intelligence community, to obtaining advancement so as to better serve the interests of his Soviet masters. Whatever the motivation, Wilson had given little public sign of being a man of the Left before the autumn of 1950. Though overshadowed by Bevan, in terms of succeeding him Wilson had the advantage that Bevan was more than 18 years older than he was. 'It was a battle between us for power – he knew it and I knew it', Gaitskell was later to observe about the contest that took place between him and Bevan over the Budget of April 1951,[283] which was to lead to the resignation from the Government of Bevan, Wilson, and a lesser figure, John Freeman.

Whether the absent Attlee, undergoing lengthy hospital treatment at the crucial time, would have found a means of compromise that eluded the deputising Morrison was doubtful. If Bevan had to move on from being Minister of Health, becoming Minister of Labour and National Service in January 1951 was unlikely to have been his preferred destination, and when he was not even considered for the succession to Bevin at the Foreign Office, one interpretation of his behaviour was that he seemed to be seeking a pretext for resigning from the Government.[284] Referring in his personal statement to that of Bevan the previous day, Wilson said on 24 April 1951 that their resignations had not been made on the 'narrow issue' of the introduction of National Health Service charges for teeth and spectacles, but the 'more fundamental one' that 'the Budget ... included a rearmament programme which I do not believe to be physically practicable with the raw materials available to us'.[285] Wilson had been consistent on this point, but it had been unconvincing when Bevan had used it too because on 15 February 1951 he had pledged that the Government would implement the rearmament programme in full,[286] in some contrast to the more cautious earlier commitments made by Attlee[287] and Gaitskell.[288] Wilson challenged the need for charges on teeth and spectacles to be made, arguing that the financial contribution made in the context of the rearmament programme was small, but their importance was that 'the principle of the free Health Service has been breached'.[289] The principle for there being prescription charges, though, had been conceded in the National Health Service (Amendment) Act of 1949, which provision Bevan as Minister of Health had defended in December 1949 as relating to only 'a very small aspect' of that Service's activity and 'not a considerable retreat from the position we have taken up'.[290] Bevan explained his behaviour in this matter of social policy as demonstrating 'the danger of compromise',[291] and, though he was probably well described by a contemporary *Daily Herald* journalist as looking around for an issue on which to break with his colleagues, Bevan's main motive was to combat what he perceived as the Labour Party's 'drift to the Right'.[292] In his opening speech to the Labour Party Conference in 1948, Morrison had argued that 'consolidation' should be the basis of the Labour Government's future programme and appeal to the electorate. He used the word no fewer than three times,[293] though there could be no mistake about what he meant, certainly not on Bevan's part. For Bevan really believed that 'there is only one hope for mankind – and that is democratic socialism',[294] and, as he was later to say that 'it is essential that we should keep clear before us that one of the central principles of socialism is the substitution of public for private ownership. There is no way round this.'[295] In other words, the Keynesian or Managed Economy Welfare State was not enough.

'Public enterprise must "behave in their financial management and accountancy procedures in accordance with the rules normally observed in industrial and commercial firms"'. So ran Article 9 of the Ordinance of 16 January 1945 by which the French Government nationalized the Renault car factories.[296] Similar clarity of objectives was absent from the nationalization legislation passed by the Labour Government elected in Britain six months later. The Labour Party had been committed to universal nationalization since 1918: but debates within the Party concentrated on forms of organization (effectively, public corporations versus some form of workers' control) and not on how to run the various enterprises once they were nationalized. The fact of nationalization was deemed to be sufficient. In the 1930s, notably in his book *Socialization and Transport*, Morrison had played a prominent part in persuading the Labour Party to adopt the public corporation form of organization, and he was to pilot the Attlee Government's nationalization programme through Parliament, thus establishing a base from which the nationalized industries came to dominate the provision of energy, public transport, communications, and iron and steel. These nationalized industries soon ran into difficulties. The official historian of the nationalization programme later contended, unconvincingly, that it did not matter that the Labour Party had no detailed plans of its own on which to establish the nationalized industries on operational terms;[297] and an official historian of the nationalized electricity industry pointed to the various blueprints that others had produced, implying that they made Labour Party preparations unnecessary.[298]

The McGowan Committee in 1936, the Reid Committee in 1945, and the Heyworth Committee also in 1945 had published thorough reviews of the electricity distribution, coal mining and gas industries respectively; but neither their efforts nor those of the higher civil servants at the then Ministry of Fuel and Power could adequately take the place of Labour Party plans for the practical operation of the nationalized industries. The Party, which believed in planning *per se*, needed plans of their own for how to run nationalized industries, not least because the future prospects for socialism in Britain were intimately bound up with the success or failure of nationalization. It was a task that should not have been delegated to others, and the 'confession' of the contemporary Minister of Fuel and Power, Shinwell, about the absence of plans was an honest admission of the Labour Party's and his own irresponsibility.[299] The McGowan, Reid, and Heyworth Reports had not recommended management units on a national scale,[300] nor were there other departmental reports that amounted to blueprints for running nationalized industries.[301] No serious consideration was given to the British Petroleum solution where the Government exercised a measure of control through a majority shareholding. Full scale nationalization using the public corporation form or organization was what occurred. The public corporations that were established included, among others, the National Coal Board, the British Transport Commission, the British Overseas Airways Corporation, British European Airways, the National

Gas Council and the Central Electricity Authority; together with, in some cases, supporting regional organizations. Morrison declared in 1946 that the establishment of public corporations like the National Coal Board would mean that 'we shall get the best of both worlds. We shall get business management, public accountability, but not meticulous political control.'[302]

The nationalization legislation in general granted Ministers greater powers to intervene than their inter-war counterparts had possessed, which some were to use to limit price increases,[303] and gave little specific indication of the commercial and financial aims that the public corporations should pursue. For instance, the National Coal Board was charged with the duties of 'securing the efficient development of the coal mining industry, and ... making supplies of coal available, of such qualities and sizes, in such quantities and at such prices, as may seem to them best calculated to serve the public interest in all respects'. The relevant legislation also established the 'break even rule' that 'the revenues of the Board shall not be less than sufficient for meeting all their outgoings properly chargeable to revenue account ... on an average of good and bad years'.[304] The relevant statutes laid down no rules for determining the 'right' levels of investment, output, prices and costs that would take the place occupied by the criterion of profitability in private enterprise.[305] The public corporation model had proved to be an unhappy double compromise. On the one hand, as regards the extent of political control, public corporations were a compromise between a government department and a private company. On the other hand, as regards the actual operations of the nationalized industries, they were a compromise between a commercial enterprise and a social service.

'Beveridge called for a crusade to slay the five giant evils which afflicted our society – poverty, ignorance, disease, squalor and idleness. Within three years of our electoral victory, the Labour Government had provided the legislative framework and created the organization designed to rid our country of all five.' So later wrote James Griffiths, the Minister of National Insurance at that time, adding: 'To the Family Allowances Act we added four others – Industrial Injuries, National Insurance, National Health and National Assistance. During those same years, Ellen Wilkinson and George Tomlinson, at the Ministry of Education, began to implement the 1944 Education Act. The school leaving age was raised to fifteen.' Griffiths said that 'together these six Acts of Parliament provide the foundation of Britain's Welfare State'.[306] They did indeed, though the Butler Education Act, which related to England and Wales only, was very much a Conservative measure, as reflected the composition of the House of Commons in the time of the wartime Coalition Government, with the private education system of Public Schools preserved alongside a State system characterized by the selection of children at eleven plus with an academic grammar school education for the often small minority who passed, thus providing a form of equality of opportunity and a possible route to a university education. All children were to receive at least four years of secondary education, although few seriously believed that the secondary modern schools to which most of them were assigned had parity of esteem with the academic grammar schools. The failure to develop a system of grammar technical schools proved to be as important a flaw in the Butler dispensation as was the relative neglect of further education. The Labour Party's preference was for comprehensive secondary education, but the Ministers of Education in the Attlee Governments .concentrated on implementing the Butler arrangements.[307]

The Family Allowances Act of 1945 was passed on the initiative of the Churchill Conservative Caretaker Government. Though hostility towards family allowances on the part of some of the leaders of the Labour Movement had diminished by that time, there had been earlier evidence of it.[308] Griffiths himself wrote that it would have been appropriate to call the relevant legislation the Eleanor Rathbone Act,[309] and the Independent MP had campaigned perennially for family allowances. Miss Rathbone was not a socialist, and, indeed, she had wanted Churchill to win in 1945 because she thought that he would be more likely than Labour to stand up to the Soviet dictatorship.[310] The Churchill Caretaker Government also introduced a Bill to carry out the proposals agreed under the Coalition relating to industrial injuries insurance. This had the Prime Minister's explicit support,[311] with the Bill's appearance being attributed by one senior official to Churchill having done this at the request of Bevin as an indication that the Conservatives would implement the Coalition's social insurance plans if re-elected.[312] When Griffiths moved the Second Reading of what became the National Insurance (Industrial Injuries) Act of 1946, Osbert Peake for the Conservatives observed that 'here we have a measure devised by one Government and published in the form of a Bill by that Government being adopted *in toto* by that Government's successor after a General Election'.[313] Griffiths also introduced the National Insurance Act of 1946, the forerunners of which were the Old Age Pensions Act of 1908 and National Insurance Act of 1911 from the Liberals, and, from the Conservatives, Neville Chamberlain's Widows, Orphans and Old Age Contributory Pensions Act of 1925.

The legislation of 1946 adhered to the principle of universality,[314] which meant that it embraced 'everybody from the barrow boy to the Field Marshal', and it was also the first Insurance Act in any country which brought under its cover the self-employed and those defined as not being gainfully employed.[315] This was to enact the relevant proposals in the Beveridge Report, and this was also true of the National Assistance Act of 1948.[316] The aim of this Act was stated to be 'to terminate the Poor Law',[317] which it did formally, though, in practice, the household means test had been effectively abolished by the Determination of Needs Act of 1941 promoted by Bevin.[318] The physical buildings remained, of course, and the local authority old people's homes may not have seemed to those who entered them to be much of an improvement. National assistance was to be centrally funded and intended to be a last resort that would be little needed with a social security system characterized by dignity and entitlement. Of the implementation of national insurance, Griffiths stated that the Labour Government had 'endeavoured to give a broad subsistence basis to the leading rates',[319] and critics pointed out that the cost of living index used made the levels of benefit less than they should have been, especially when the low level of family allowances was taken into account.[320] The brutal and obvious reality of the situation was that recognized, for instance, by one sympathetic historian of the Attlee years, which was that without the American loan the Welfare State measures would not have been possible, and, indeed, there would have had to have been cuts in the existing social services.[321] The third Rowntree social survey of York found that, compared with 1936, by 1950 there had been a marked decrease in primary poverty, and that important factors in this change had been the increased provision of social security allied to full employment.[322]

The Ministry of Health was Bevan's preferred and actual political destination in the Labour Government. He had said that he would only accept a real job,[323] but the difficulty with being Minister of Health was that it was actually two jobs, one of which was involved the main ministerial responsibility for the Government's housing programme. 'I never spent more than an hour a week on housing', Bevan was alleged to have later told Dalton. 'Housing runs itself.'[324] Bevan had many calls on his time, but he must have been well aware that he had inherited a housing crisis and of the political need to solve it. 'We had to establish our housing policy on one fundamental principle, the principle that so long as there was a shortage of housing and of labour and building materials our main aim would be to provide that the vast majority of the houses to be built should be for letting to those in need', Bevan declared in 1947,[325] adding that 'for a few years to come we are going to be judged by the number of houses that we build. In ten years' time we shall be judged by the kind of houses that we build and where we are building them, and I am not going to be panicked into doing a bad job.'[326] In other words, the house building programme was not only concentrated on the construction of council housing for rent, but the quality and size of the houses were to be exemplary. 'I was not happy about housing', Dalton was later to write about taking over responsibility for it as Minister of Local Government and Planning in January 1951, 'I tried to loosen up some of the regulations and leave the local authorities more freedom. I left them free, for instance, to include either one or two WCs in a three-bedroomed council house. On this point, Bevan had been a tremendous Tory. Always, he had said, there must be two.'[327] Middle-class people or those from farther up the social scale like Dalton would expect such facilities, and Bevan's Housing Act of 1949 omitted the phrase 'working classes' that had been present in earlier and similar housing legislation,[328] which was in line with his declaration that 'we don't want a country of East Ends and West Ends, with all the petty snobberies this involves'.[329] Far from wanting the creation of working-class ghettoes that mass council housing estates promoted, Bevan acted as if the middle classes would come to prefer such housing to owner-occupation. In the late 1930s, the number of new houses completed per annum averaged 300,000,[330] and even his indulgent official biographer conceded that this magic total would have been all the more readily attainable if Bevan had agreed to cut standards.[331] In the context of the time, that approximately 200,000 houses a year were built would have seemed more of an achievement, but for Bevan's earlier and characteristic boast that 500,000 a year would be built with proper planning.[332] In his frustration, Bevan once asked the Cabinet, 'Where are all the people I need for my programme?' Attlee replied, 'Looking for houses, Nye.'[333]

Since Assumption B of the Beveridge Report was that 'a comprehensive national health service' would be established,[334] and the Coalition Government had promised as much in 1944, then, provided the country's economic circumstances permitted this, some form of service was going to be created in the immediate post-war period whether or not the Labour Party won the General Election. The form that the National Health Service actually came to take, though, was very much determined by Bevan as Minister of Health, with the important help of a senior official called John Hawton. The wartime

Emergency Hospital Service was well described as marking a secular shift towards a nationally planned and rationalized hospital service,[335] but peacetime arrangements that were meant to be permanent were bound to run into opposition, and not only from the medical profession. In October 1945, when Bevan made it clear to the Cabinet that he wanted to nationalize the hospital system,[336] Morrison opposed this, not least because it would further weaken local government at a time when it was losing other functions.[337] Since this weakening was one consequence of the nationalization programme that Morrison himself was charged with implementing, he seemed to be wanting to draw the line somewhere. Bevan was determined that his own nationalization plan would not be a casualty, arguing that a new and different system was needed, given that anyway the voluntary hospitals were receiving up to 90 per cent of their income from the State, and a local government hospital service would be bound to be unequal in operation over the country, which would be unfair to a public paying equal contributions.

As for the administrative arrangements envisaged, these fitted in with the regional structure of local government that the Labour Party favoured.[338] Bevan was to do nothing about regionalization in the form of elected bodies, but this did not stop him from wearing down the opposition within the Cabinet to his National Health Service proposals, and he proceeded to introduce the relevant legislation for England and Wales, with the Secretary of State for Scotland doing so for that country. The National Health Service was to be 'available to everybody ... and not made conditional upon any insurance qualification',[339] with the financial base coming primarily from central government taxation.[340] The Service was to have a tripartite structure comprising a hospital and specialist service, general practitioner services and local government services. Bevan's approach was to maintain that he would engage in consultation with the various vested interests in the medical profession, arguing that 'there will not be negotiation ... the House of Commons must assert its supremacy, and not allow itself to be dictated to by anybody, no matter how powerful and how strong'.[341] In reality, Bevan had to take advantage of the main division in the medical profession, and buy off the hospital specialists with the important help of the distasteful Lord Moran of the Royal College of Physicians. 'I stuffed their mouths with gold', Bevan was reported to have said of the deal.[342] 'Thus, the top doctors obtained *à la suite* terms in the Health Service: part-time payment for loosely defined sessions, the secret disposal of Treasury funds to those of their number whom Lord Moran [and the other heads of the Royal Colleges] thought more meritorious, the lion's share of the endowments of the teaching hospitals to pay the costs of their researches, and the right to private practice – much as before', wrote one historian of the hospital system, adding that 'the consultants had gained regular remuneration without any loss of freedom and were being trusted to use this freedom responsibly ... . The teaching hospitals had retained their independence, whatever nonsense it made of the regional design.'[343]

Of course, this was an unelected regional structure, since the medical profession would not accept any arrangement that risked them becoming anything resembling salaried government officials. The general practitioners were said to fear for their clinical independence, which they also seemed to think was threatened by the abolition of the purchase and sale of practices. Bevan would not concede on that matter, and the conflict between him and the British Medical Association led by Charles Hill, who had fame of a kind as the BBC's Radio Doctor, persisted most of the way down to the actual inauguration of the Service. Hill later wrote that the BMA secured five of their seven objectives in this battle,[344] and general practitioners were to prove ungrateful for their biggest benefit from the National Health Service, which was greater certainty of income compared with the former arrangements. One commentator was later to suggest that the trial of strength between the elected Government and the medical profession demonstrated the brutal power of vested interests, and that, though for the sake of pride, the National Health Service was represented as a socialist measure, it was the captive of those interests.[345] That an ideal system of socialized medicine had not been established mattered little compared with the greater accessibility to medical services that was made available to the mass of the population. 'After 5 July [1948], the Minister of Health will be the whipping boy for the Health Service in Parliament', Bevan declared. 'Every time a maid kicks over a bucket of slops in a ward an agonized wail will go through Whitehall.'[346] Though much misquoted later, Bevan had pointed up the centralized character of the new Service, and that by May 1950 a Cabinet committee had to be established to try to keep control of Health Service expenditure,[347] since Bevan showed little willingness to do so, emphasized its cost. Where the resources were to come from to sustain the National Health Service was not a question that exercised the mind of Bevan. He had seized the time.

A combative reconstruction government

'This great nation has a message for the world which is distinct from that of America or that of the Soviet Union', Bevan had stated in his resignation speech. 'Ever since 1945 we have been engaged in the most remarkable piece of social reconstruction the world has ever seen. By the end of 1950 ... we had assumed the moral leadership of the world'.[348] Similarly, R.H. Tawney believed that a Social Democratic Britain would provide the world with an envied alternative to Soviet Communism on the one hand and American capitalism on the other.[349] A sympathetic economic historian wrote of the Attlee Government's economic policy record that, in terms of the aims set out in the election programme of 1945, it was obviously highly successful: full employment was maintained, to almost universal surprise; there was no repetition of the great inflationary boom of 1919–20 and the slump that followed; the entire programme of nationalization was carried out; the National Health Service was successfully launched; the Welfare State was put on a solid foundation.[350] 'The Labour Government of 1945–51 was, by any test, one of the most crucial in British history', an admiring political historian has written, adding: 'Its impact upon the development of modern Britain, at home and overseas, was immense in almost every aspect. Like the Governments of Peel, Disraeli, Asquith and Lloyd George, and perhaps Gladstone's first term of office, the Attlee Government wrenched the course of British history into significant new directions. The consequences were profound for Europe, the North Atlantic community, and the developing world, no less than for the political, social, and economic evolution of Britain itself. For perhaps the last time in the experience of the British people, a Government was able to place its imprint upon external circumstances, rather than have to respond, passively or helplessly to them.'[351]

The Attlee Governments were at their most impressive in the spheres of defence and the conduct of imperial and foreign policy. The Labour Party of the 1930s had been opposed to even adequate provision for defence, which had made nonsense of its opposition to the Appeasement of Nazi Germany. As might be expected after a total war, the Labour Governments of the 1940s certainly took a radically different attitude to defence, even conscription, and in the 1951 Budget the reaction to the perceived lessons of history was to come to seem excessive. The Labour Party of the 1930s had favoured the Appeasement of the Soviet Union, but there was none of this from Bevin as Foreign

Secretary, who, to his lasting credit, was to become the quintessential Cold Warrior. There were to be only too many who were to say that the Britain of the Attlee Governments had the delusion of still being a Great Power, and, given the country's dramatically reduced economic circumstances, how ridiculous this posturing was supposed to be. All depended on one's interpretation of Communism, and, thus, of the intentions of the Soviet Union, and there was no shortage of people in intellectual life and journalism who wanted the West to lose. For those who wanted the West to prevail, and who saw the Soviet Union as an adversary much like Nazi Germany had been, the threat had to be confronted, and, at first, only Britain saw the necessity to perform this role. When the USA finally took on her responsibilities for world leadership, Britain became her only effective ally. Grim reality was the prime determinant of the defence and foreign policy of the Attlee Governments; and, when it came to their conduct of imperial policy, the granting of independence to what had been the Indian Empire, behaviour that represented the antithesis of Britain having delusions of grandeur, dominated the record.

The Attlee Governments were the first to run a peacetime Keynesian or Managed Economy Welfare State. The Churchill Coalition Government had shared authorship in the creation of that economic and social order, and as Reconstruction Governments those of Attlee achieved so much more after 1945 than the Lloyd George Government did after 1918, though the radically different world conditions and the overthrow of the previous economic orthodoxy and American aid benefited them. The Attlee Governments got too much political credit for the Welfare State and too little of it for skilled economic management in playing their part in effecting the transition to a peacetime economy. The nationalization of the hospitals proved to be the only measure of public ownership that attracted much lasting admiration outside of the ranks of the producer interests involved. The National Health Service always was a special case, and in the form it was introduced very much Bevan's creation, but the establishment of a substantial public sector of the economy exempted from market disciplines was to disappoint the advocates of nationalization, with excessive hopes breeding excessive disappointment, especially given the unimpressive record of, notably, the coal mining industry and the railways under private ownership. Of course, a New Jerusalem had been promised. When the social security measures came into force on 5 July 1948, which was also the date of the inauguration of the National Health Service, Attlee marked the occasion by stressing with historical accuracy the all-party nature of the creation of the Welfare State,[352] but Bevan did so with his 'Tory vermin' speech. 'The eyes of the world are turning to Great Britain', Bevan declared, adding that 'we shall have people coming here as to a modern Mecca'.[353] There was to be no shared authorship for the New Jerusalem, and 'consolidation' was not enough. It already had to be as regards the redistribution of income, since the bulk of what had occurred had taken place during the war rather than under the Attlee Governments,[354] and what they had done had been to hold the line. Nobody with much sense did come to see Britain as a Mecca because that country needed an economic miracle and she did not bring it off, and not surprisingly so given that the economic and social order that had been the subject of Reconstruction had been primarily designed to put the world of the 1930s right.

The Attlee Governments may well have attempted to do too much, which was why, as one sympathetic observer commented, so many of the leading Ministers and officials were worn out by the scale of responsibilities undertaken.[355] There is now no shortage of severe criticism of the Labour Governments' failure to lay the basis for a modern economy instead of shoring up the old one,[356] and a willingness can be detected, on the part of those who did not live through the period in particular, to be sceptical of the favourite interpretations of it of many of those who did.[357] Historical revisionism has its imperatives, of course, but it should be said that, while the most famous of Labour Governments included Ministers fit to rank with any of any period, and one who had greatness, the Attlee Governments, of course, had their incompetents. Far from being banished to the back benches after the fuel crisis, Shinwell was to be Secretary of State for War and then Minister of Defence, in which roles he seemed to be sustained by those below him in the manner of a table tennis ball on top of a fountain. It was fitting that the intellectual John Strachey was the Minister responsible for the ridiculous groundnuts scheme, as well as, for a time, the introduction of bread rationing, a measure that had been avoided at the height of the Battle of the Atlantic, and for trying to encourage the public to eat a form of fish called snoek, which was said to be good for them, and which those who risked it said it tasted like wet newspaper. The Americans or Lord Woolton would probably have found a more encouraging name for this unappetising fish, but Strachey could expect no help in such matters from his Parliamentary Secretary, the grim Dr Edith Summerskill, who, as a feminist, was the last person in the world who could have been expected to establish any form of rapport with the beleaguered housewives of the 1940s.

Rationing and austerity disfigured a political landscape that the Labour Governments imbued with a form of Roundhead earnestness that ensured that such as the Lynskey Tribunal would find very little in the way of wrongdoing. The Labour Government's overall majority was reduced to 5 as the result of the February 1950 Election, and the Conservatives obtained an overall majority of 17 following the October 1951 Election.[358] In the first instance, the turnout was 84 per cent of those entitled to vote,[359] and in the latter contest, the comparable figure was 82.5 per cent.[360] These were to prove to be the highest turnouts in the history of universal suffrage in Britain in the twentieth century. The Labour vote of 13,948,883 in 1951[361] was not bettered until 1992, when the Conservatives finally achieved this in the context of a much larger electorate. The radical mythology of 1945 might not be entirely convincing, and many interpretations of the 1950 and 1951 Elections were possible, but lack of political interest certainly by British standards could not be one of them. The Safe New World had been built and the brief Golden Age of the Labour Party was over. The Labour Party and Movement had produced a Government fit to rank with any in peacetime, and one man of greatness, Ernest Bevin.

6
Fast Falls the Eventide: The Churchill Conservative Government 1951–5

Elected on probation

'Winston has crawled back into Downing Street', Lord Moran wrote in late October 1951 in the aftermath of the Conservatives having obtained only a majority of 17 in the General Election, though he found that, far from this outcome being 'a great disappointment to him', Churchill was relieved simply to be back as Prime Minister,[1] and if this meant a return to office on any remotely politically acceptable basis at all then, for once, Churchill reflected the dominant mood in the Tory Party. Churchill was well described as 'not ... a Conservative at heart',[2] and, ideally in 1951, he may have wanted to lead a Coalition Government including the Liberals. He had spoken in support of Violet Bonham–Carter at Colne Valley in the Election,[3] and, when composing his Cabinet, he offered the post of Minister of Education to the Liberal leader, Clement Davies, who refused it.[4] For several years afterwards, the conventional wisdom was that between 1945 and 1951 the Conservatives had made themselves into the most effective Opposition of the century, having had their policies revamped by R.A. Butler and his 'backroom boys' as thoroughly as Lord Woolton as Tory Chairman had reconstructed the party machine.[5] There had been a Woolton Revolution in organization, but, however seriously such as the One Nation Group took their activities, the Butler 'Revolution' was primarily presentational. The Conservatives had a Statist tradition anyway, one which had been on display in the National Governments of the 1930s, and, if their behaviour then had come to be seen as not Statist enough, as members of the wartime Coalition Government the Tories had committed themselves to what proved to be the most popular parts of the Keynesian dispensation. The Attlee Governments had passed the relevant Acts of Parliament. So, when it came to running the New Jerusalem, the Conservatives had to prove their credentials, and to encourage a favourable response to the question that Bevan had once mockingly put, *Why Not Trust The Tories*? Hence, the main task for Butler and others engaged in framing Conservative policy was that of the politics of reassurance. To adapt one of Beaverbrook's contemporary criticisms, what Tory reform only too often amounted to was Statism without socialists, and he was right too about most Conservatives who spoke the language of economic liberalism being 'more concerned with freedom than with enterprise'.[6]

Commitments to denationalisation in the 1951 Election manifesto were limited to the iron and steel industry and road haulage, not least because to do more would antagonize the trade unions, who were to retain their legal immunities. As for the private sector, in the context of the rearmament drive, there was to be an Excess Profits Tax.[7] That had been Churchill's idea.[8] The 1950 Election manifesto promised to 'abolish the existing rationing system' and that controls would be 'reduced to the minimum necessary',[9] though 'rent control must continue until there is no housing shortage'.[10] It had been the Party Conference of 1950 that had induced the one radical commitment in the next manifesto in what Butler called 'a famous wave of hysteria' which led to the call that the next Tory Government should promise to build 300,000 houses a year. Butler had serious doubts about this pledge which he believed would make it difficult to restore the economy, but Woolton, once reassured that meeting the target was feasible, stepped forward to endorse the proposal in 'beaming surrender'.[11] It may have been that somewhere in the back of the minds of the delegates there lurked a memory of Eden and then Churchill at the 1946 Conference recycling the Conservative notion from the 1920s of 'a property owning democracy',[12] which chimed in with the sentiment of 'an Englishman's home is his castle', and with individualism as opposed to collectivism. Churchill had made use of the term before,[13] but what, in contemporary political circumstances, it amounted to in specific terms seemed unclear even to Tories.[14]

The Tories had good reason to fear that there was not enough in the 'New' Conservatism to override the reinforced class prejudice that sustained the mountain of votes that they still found ranged against them, and resorted to slogans of the Set The People Free variety. Churchill inveighed against Labour's 'class war,'[15] though, of course, the still socially exclusive Conservatives were waging one too. The Maxwell Fyfe reforms were supposed to undermine this form of elitism

within the Parliamentary Party, and, according to Woolton, to represent 'Tory democracy in action'.[16] Nevertheless, when the social back-
grounds of successful candidates in the 1945, 1950, and 1951 Elections
were compared it was found that there was little change in the type of
Conservative candidate chosen to contest seats which the Tories had
any chance of winning.[17] Few of the electors whom those candidates
faced had probably heard of Butler's Charters, let alone read them,
and, if recognized and believed, the housing pledge that Butler
opposed may well have counted for much more in extra votes for the
Conservatives, at least to judge from the salience of the issue in
samples of public opinion. Bodies such as the Housewives League,
derided at the time as little more than a Conservative front organization, possibly offended as many voters as they won over, but the
Labour Governments' association with austerity and rationing may
well have disproportionately alienated women voters,[18] and, indeed,
anybody who thought as a consumer. Woolton tried to catch this
mood when he declared that 'a little more red meat would not do us
any harm'.[19] Though the Tories were unconvincing as advocates of the
private enterprise system, there was still the American example of a
higher standard of living on display in magazines and in the crowded
cinemas in the Golden Age of Hollywood to bring home a message
that even Conservative believers thought it risky to preach in the face
of the 1945 veto. To some extent, the Tories owed their victory in the
1951 Election to the fact that there were 366 fewer Liberal candidates
than there had been in that of 1950,[20] in which Election the
Conservative recovery owed a great deal to a recasting of the constituency map that favoured the Tories,[21] a factor which also explained
a Conservative majority in the House of Commons in 1951 when the
Tories polled 231,067 fewer votes than Labour.[22] The Safe New World
was not in danger from the Conservatives, as they had striven to stress,
but they were only allowed back into office on probation anyway.

'A most brilliant Cabinet of all the talents'?

Churchill was 'spoiled for choice' in selecting his Cabinet in 1951,
according to Woolton, 'It used to be said that Asquith ... had selected a
most brilliant Cabinet of all the talents, but Churchill's new Cabinet ...
would ... have stood up against any of its predecessors for personal
ability and breadth of experience'.[23] More certainly, Churchill's
approach to Cabinet-making was unusual. He conducted much of it
from his bed, and, according to Macmillan, he thought it a splendid

idea to issue the list of Cabinet appointments by instalments on the grounds that it kept up the public's interest. Macmillan, not on the first list, found this procedure puzzling, as did Woolton, and both of them were alarmed at Churchill initially making himself not only Prime Minister but Minister of Defence too.[24] Churchill, though, always intended to make way for another, and his eventual choice was Field Marshal Alexander,[25] who took over in March 1952, and proved to be no politician and an ineffectual Minister of Defence.[26] Churchill seemed to be trying to recreate the wartime arrangements as far as possible, and the short-lived and extraordinary appointment of 'Pug' Ismay as Secretary of State for Commonwealth Relations[27] was only one instance. The 'Overlords' experiment illustrated Churchill's state of mind. Lords Woolton, Cherwell, and Leathers were assigned a supervisory role in relation to groups of departments. Leathers had the resounding title of Secretary of State for the Coordination of Transport, Fuel and Power.[28] As a businessman, Leathers had no taste for the controversies of peacetime politics. In September 1953, Churchill told Moran: 'The Overlords are going. Leathers has wanted to resign for a long time. I only kept him by calling him a deserter.'[29]

That Eden would become Foreign Secretary was obvious, but Churchill used his discretion to advantage in the appointments he made to the posts of Chancellor of the Exchequer and Minister of Labour. Churchill appointed Butler to the Treasury, ruling out the expected choice, Oliver Lyttelton, who was told the news by Churchill who was 'in bed, in a quilted flowered bedjacket, the garment slightly reminiscent of Don Pasquale'. Churchill, inevitably smoking a cigar, treated Lyttelton to what seemed like a public oration. Lyttelton who was 'deeply disappointed' not to have got the Treasury, accepted the post of Colonial Secretary.[30] Lyttelton was 'an outsize Elizabethan figure', as David Maxwell Fyfe described him, but to the Labour Party he was 'the embodiment of the harsh, insensitive capitalist'.[31] The emollient Butler would not be so easy a target, and the same proved to be true of Sir Walter Monckton as the Minister of Labour. Macmillan was one who was relieved that Maxwell Fyfe had been appointed Home Secretary rather than Minister of Labour on the grounds that the latter's speeches and writings had alarmed the trade unions.[32] 'I have the worst job in the Cabinet for you', Churchill told the reluctant Monckton,[33] and he gave the best job to Macmillan, who, as Minister of Housing and Local Government, was given the task of realizing the pledge of building 300,000 houses. The tearful Churchill informed Macmillan that 'it is a gamble – [it will] make or mar your political career. But every humble home will bless your name, if you succeed.'[34] With 'the real free enterprisers and deflationists' excluded from its ranks, Crossman spotted that 'the general make up of the Churchill Cabinet means that it will only be very slightly to the Right of the most recent Attlee Cabinet. Just as Attlee was running what was virtually a Coalition policy on a Party basis so Churchill may well do the same.'[35]

At the Churchill Government's first Cabinet meeting, 'Winston was in a state of mental and physical activity truly remarkable in a man within a month of 77', Maxwell Fyfe wrote, adding that he looked 'pugnaciously cherubic'.[36] Moran later advanced the thesis that Churchill was too old and too ill to be Prime Minister once more in 1951. Moran was not a member of Churchill's inner circle,[37] but his views on Churchill's physical state have their interest, and so do the gems that he picked up in conversation with his patient whose confidence in him he betrayed. Moran's attempts to explain Churchill's personal and political behaviour in terms of amateur psychology were tedious. The professional variety might have been of some use in explaining Moran's peculiar request to be made Minister of Health in 1951, which the astonished Churchill turned down.[38] Unlike Moran, John Colville, Churchill's Principal Private Secretary, was well placed to assess Churchill's ability to do the job of Prime Minister from 1951 onwards, and recalled that when he returned to that office a sheaf of Action This Day labels of the kind that he had frequently used during the War was placed before his seat at the Cabinet table. They remained there for three and a half years, and they were never used. Colville suggested that 'this was symbolic of the change which had taken place. The sense of urgency had not entirely vanished, but it was no longer Churchill's constant companion. Slower to anger, content to feed his golden carp and to play bezique, more amenable to argument and readier to listen to advice, he was nonetheless the undisputed master of the House of Commons and of the Cabinet. He was distressingly deaf, less resilient than of old, quite often lazy, but, when he chose, he could still rise to the heights of oratory, could charm a discontented colleague, turn aside a question with a reply which made the House of Commons laugh.'[39] Churchill suffered a stroke on 23 June 1953. While the speed of his recovery from that blow was remarkable enough to make him seem superhuman, inevitably Churchill's powers were diminished thereafter. Churchill was later accused of clinging to office to deny Eden, and his behaviour was to have that effect, but the fact remains that if

Churchill had relinquished the Prime Ministership in the summer of 1953 or immediately afterwards the succession would most likely have gone to Butler because Eden was incapacitated through illness at the time.

Reflected glory: the defence and external policies of the Churchill government of 1951–5

The Coronation of Queen Elizabeth II on 2 June 1953 was to be the last great imperial occasion in British history. Amidst the pageantry and the presence of the Commonwealth leaders and the representatives of the many colonies, this reality may well not have seemed obvious to many on a day when the news came through that a Commonwealth team had climbed Mount Everest. Britain still seemed to be running a Commonwealth on which the sun never set. Of Churchill's 'three circles' of British influence in the world, it was the Commonwealth in the form of the Dominions that seemed to attract the most popular domestic affection, being favoured destinations for emigration, and with their contribution to Britain's war effort being another reminder of the closeness of the relationship. American slowness to go to war made for the 'special relationship' with the USA being perceived in a much more instrumental manner. The notion of closer political involvement with the defeated countries of Western Europe was a matter of interest for a minority of the political class. Churchill's continued political presence masked the reality of Britain's diminished place in the world. If the 'three circles' existed anywhere except in his mind, it was Churchill that held them together.

Eden seemed to be both a popular and commanding Foreign Secretary, and, he recalled that Churchill had remarked of their relationship that 'you could put each of us in a separate room, put any questions of foreign policy to us, and nine times out of ten we would come up with the same answer. This was certainly true.'[40] Maxwell Fyfe, for one, believed that 'Winston was determined not to oppose his successor, and none of the other members [of the Cabinet] had the knowledge or experience to question or contradict Eden's policies. I doubt if a Foreign Secretary has enjoyed quite so much independence since Lord Rosebery ... . This entrusting of a vital aspect of government to one man, however competent, was in a sense an abrogation of the role of the Cabinet, and in our relationship with Europe in particular it meant that we were bound by Eden's hostile approach to a matter in which he was nominally opposed by Churchill, Macmillan, and myself at least.'[41] Macmillan wondered if he should have resigned from the Government over Europe.[42] In fact, Eden's relationship with Churchill was not always harmonious, and he did not enjoy more freedom of manoeuvre as Foreign Secretary than Bevin had done.

Eden was opposed to closer political involvement with continental Europe, with his feelings being encapsulated by his observation that 'if you were to open the personal mail arriving from overseas in any post office in England you would find that 90 per cent of it came from beyond Europe, from Australia, Canada, India, Africa, anywhere, indeed, where British soldiers and administrators had served or British families settled. How could we ignore all that?' Eden saw Britain as being an active and enlightened European nation with a world role, and not as a limb of Europe.[43] A united Europe as a romantic concept was bound to appeal to Churchill in Opposition with time on his hands and with phrases to spare, but in practical terms a Europe divided by the Cold War was the brutal reality, and in that context the encouragement of the cohesion of Western Europe was imperative, and Churchill's advocacy was primarily designed to support Bevin in his endeavours, and to please and involve the Americans. When he became Prime Minister, Churchill did not, as some allege, become too old and ill to pursue the matter.

As he had defined the European issue, the main job was done with the establishment of NATO. Again in this context, Churchill had encouraged the formation of a European Army[44] that would involve the West Germans. 'The French approached this from a constitutional rather than a purely military point of view', Churchill later observed of the Pleven Plan for a European Defence Community, whereas he had been thinking in terms of 'no supranational institutions', and 'national armies ... under a unified allied command'.[45] Anything else would be 'a sludgy amalgam', Churchill believed, 'What soldiers want to sing is their own marching songs!'[46] So, 'we are not members of the [EDC], nor do we intend to be merged in a Federal European system', Churchill declared in 1953. 'We feel we have a special relation to both ... we are with them, but not of them. We have our own Commonwealth and Empire.'[47] It was the French National Assembly and not the British Government that undermined the Pleven Plan in 1954. Eden then played an important part in devising arrangements that brought West Germany into a Western European Union, and for her to be rearmed within NATO, together with undertakings by Britain and the Americans to maintain armed forces in continental Europe.[48] With Dulles having threatened an 'agonizing reappraisal' of the American commitment to the defence of Western Europe,[49] meaning, effectively, a retreat to its periphery, Eden had acted to protect the wider interest. In much the same manner, Eden also contributed to achieving a settlement in 1954 to what Churchill had called the 'stubborn problem' of Trieste,[50] which had soured relations between Italy and Yugoslavia.[51] Such practical achievements did not save the Churchill Government from later being said to have missed opportunities to have seized the leadership of Western Europe, oddly by observers who accused it of having delusions of grandeur, and who elected to play down the reality that the critical relationship had to be that between France and West Germany.

That 'the United Kingdom was in a totally different category, as far as United States policy was concerned, to any power in the world' was how John Foster Dulles, the Secretary of State in the Eisenhower Administration described the 'special relationship' between the two countries in 1953,[52] though much depended on what the issues were and the weight of Congressional opinion. Eisenhower believed that he had known 'no greater man' than Churchill,[53] and he stated that 'there's just nobody, in a war, I'd rather have fighting alongside me than the British',[54] and, before being elected, he seemed clear about there being a 'special relationship'.[55] As President, though, Eisenhower did not think of this in terms of Churchill's vision of a common Anglo-American front 'from Korea to Kikuyu and from Kikuyu to Calais'.[56] Churchill and Eden got on no better with Eisenhower and Dulles than they had done with Truman and Acheson. Eden was to describe Dulles as 'a preacher in the world of politics', and to place on record how difficult it was to work with him,[57] and an official wrote that the tempo of Dulles's mind was entirely out of harmony with Eden's, 'like two lute strings whose vibrations never coincide'.[58] Churchill was bound to dislike a Secretary of State who attracted the description of 'Dull, Duller, Dulles',[59] and, despite the warmth of their private correspondence,[60] he was critical of Eisenhower,[61] especially when the President opposed his initiatives. Though Dulles was a useful scapegoat for the British to blame when things went wrong in Anglo-American relations,[62] the Secretary of State was well aware that when his uncle, Robert Lansing, had pursued policies disapproved of by President Wilson he had been dismissed. So, Dulles may have acted as if he ran American foreign policy, and it suited the President for that to be believed, but the fact was that Eisenhower was in control.[63]

Whether Eden recognized this reality may be doubted, but Churchill had good cause to appreciate it in dealings with Eisenhower over relations with the Soviet Union. For, once Stalin had died in March 1953,

Churchill saw an opportunity, as Macmillan later observed, to be 'not only ... the greatest War Minister but ... the greatest peacemaker in the world',[64] though the Ambassador in Moscow made it clear that the new Soviet Government's talk of peaceful co-existence with the West was only that of 'the snake and the rabbit'.[65] Churchill chose to believe otherwise and to press Eisenhower for a summit meeting with the new regime, which behaviour he persisted with even beyond the Bermuda Conference of December 1953, at which the President argued that 'there had been no change since Lenin' in Russian ambitions to undermine the West, describing the Soviet Union as a whore regime. The French leaked these remarks to the newspapers,[66] which would not have harmed Eisenhower's standing, given that contemporary American domestic politics was dominated by the anti-Communist crusade of Senator Joe McCarthy, who served the cause of traitors past and present, and of the Left for the foreseeable future, by the indiscriminate nature of his campaign. Eisenhower's behaviour did not stop Churchill from continuing to believe that 'meeting jaw to jaw is better than war',[67] and at times, such as during the visit to Washington of June 1954, Eisenhower seemed to agree to a summit meeting if a preceding Anglo-Soviet meeting was successful. On the return journey, Churchill contacted Molotov as a first step to meeting with Malenkov, despite Eden's opposition to the initiative, and deliberately without consulting the Cabinet, which body proved hostile to the idea when it found out. Macmillan thought at one stage that the Cabinet was in danger of breaking up on this issue, and after an acrimonious meeting on 23 July 1954 this was a possibility, before another foreign policy initiative from the Soviet leadership rendered the notion of a bilateral meeting redundant.[68] Though Churchill craved to be the peacemaker and to cultivate the Americans not least to that end, he still believed that 'peace through strength is necessary',[69] which meant his Government proceeding with the policy of Britain having its own nuclear weapons, and it was at Washington in 1954 that he told Eisenhower that Britain intended to develop her own hydrogen bomb.[70]

'It was impossible not to be conscious that we were playing second fiddle', Eden's private secretary wrote of Churchill's visit to see Truman in January 1952,[71] later observing that 'the Americans are not backing us anywhere. In fact, having destroyed the Dutch Empire, the United States are now engaged in undermining the French and British Empires as hard as they can'.[72] Eisenhower privately agreed that, for instance, the British had governed India better than the Indians were governing themselves, but 'to Americans liberty was more precious than good government'.[73] The defence of liberty did not, of course, rule out American business interests prospering as a result. The CIA took the lead in finding a solution to the Anglo-Iranian oil crisis in 1953, to be toasted after the coup by the restored Shah with the words, 'I owe my throne to God, my people, my army, and to you'. In place of its former monopoly, the Anglo-Iranian Oil Company only had the same 40 per cent share as the leading American companies. Acheson had earlier remarked to the British that 'you must learn to live in the world as it is',[74] and this was certainly one lesson. In the differences between Britain and Saudi Arabia over the Buraimi Oasis in 1952, Washington, with American oil interests involved, chose to adopt the unconvincing pose of impartial mediator. 'Those who are not with us are against us ' was one British official's conclusion,[75] and Eden commented retrospectively on American failure to support its friends in the hope of being popular with their foes. Eden cited the Baghdad Pact of 1955, which the Americans had encouraged as a Northern Tier against Soviet expansionism, while leaving Britain to be its only Western member, and seeking to take credit for not joining with those hostile to the Pact, notably Egypt.[76]

When the Ambassador in Washington, Sir Roger Makins speculated about 'the Americans [being] out to take our place in the Middle East',[77] the reality was more complex than this because, at this stage, the Americans seemed to want power without responsibility as well as political benefits from displaying their dislike of Old World colonialism, which was supposed to be qualitatively different from New World colonialism as practised by the Americans themselves, for example, in their informal empire in Central and South America. That the Americans had a Panama Canal Zone was supposed not to be the same as Britain having a similar military presence in the Suez Canal Zone in Egypt. By keeping their own distance from the British and the French, and with their own 'special relationship' with Israel in some way not supposed to count, the Americans acted as if Arab nationalists could be won over to the West, with Dulles believing, over Buraimi, for example, that there was something called 'public opinion in Saudi Arabia'.[78] As if Eden's difficulties with the Americans were not enough, he had his own with Churchill's interventions in Middle Eastern matters. Eden overrode Churchill's wishes when promising self-government to the Sudan,[79] and that behaviour and the Foreign Secretary's conciliatory conduct of relations towards Egypt offended what became known as the Suez Group of Tory backbenchers as well as the Prime Minister, who remarked that 'he never knew before that Munich was situated on the Nile'.[80] Egypt had been a part of Britain's informal empire since 1882, and, as recently as the ten years down to 1946, her Ambassador, Sir Miles Lampson, had effectively ruled the country. A group of army officers had overthrown King Farouk in 1952. Power then passed, eventually openly, to one of their number, Colonel Gamal Abdel Nasser. The Anglo-Egyptian Treaty of 1936, negotiated by Eden himself, had made provision for the presence of British troops in the Suez Canal Zone for the next twenty years. As various terrorist attacks emphasized, there was no prospect of this arrangement continuing, Eden negotiated an orderly withdrawal in 1954 subject to what, in terms of practical politics, could be no more than the theoretical right to return in specified circumstances. Churchill had tended to view the policy in much the same way as the Suez Group rebels as one of 'scuttle',[81] but, such were what he believed to be the strategic implications of the development of the hydrogen bomb, that he intervened in the debate to speak of 'the obsolescence of the base'.[82]

Eden was credited by one Foreign Office diarist with 'a large share of responsibility for preventing [Britain from] becoming involved in war in the Far East in the 1950s',[83] which assessment invited the qualification that British troops fought in the Korean War, with Eden being involved in achieving an eventual Armistice,[84] and that Britain was currently also combating Communist insurgency in Malaya. Since, in Africa, Britain was also engaged in dealing with the Mau Mau uprising in Kenya, Eden was bound to be aware, as the same official suggested, that, despite the granting of independence to the Indian Empire, his country was still overstretched in terms of worldwide commitments,[85] even though Eden 'could never quite reconcile himself to its inevitable consequence – growing American dominance and self-assurance in international affairs'.[86] Churchill did see this, and observed in 1954 that 'Eden was sometimes very foolish: he would quarrel with the Americans over some petty Central American issue which did not affect Britain.'[87] Britain still did have interests in the Far East, and, since her Government did not always, even often, interpret the changing situation there in the same manner as the Americans did, even Churchill could not expect Eden to stay silent.

After the overthrow of the Nationalist regime in mainland China and the Korean War, the Americans were determined to oppose the further spread of Communism, and they took this resolve to the point of contemplating using force to maintain French colonialism in Indo-China to prevent the Viet Minh rebels from conquering the area. Britain feared that such a Communist victory would be undermining of her position in Malaya.[88] An international conference convened at Geneva in 1954 considered the future of Indo-China, with Eden and Molotov as co-chairmen. After tortuous negotiations in which Eden in particular displayed considerable skill, a form of settlement was found that divided up Indo-China into North Vietnam, South Vietnam, Laos, and Cambodia, with the last two countries granted neutral status. The Settlement was close to what Dulles had wanted, especially when it came to where the division of Vietnam was made. The Chinese described Eden as 'the King of the Conference',[89] and, as in Ireland, India, and Palestine, the British habit of partitioning as offering something to every party was in evidence. The agreement of Communist China was crucial to the success of the Geneva Settlement. Contemporary Chinese foreign policy was supposed to be based on the Five Principles of Peaceful Coexistence,[90] but what mattered was why China needed a period of peace. One domestic reason was the need to concentrate on ensuring the success of the first Five Year Plan. Further, China had no wish to repeat the experience of the Korean War, having learnt then that the Soviet Union would not come to their aid. The Geneva Settlement served China's strategic interest in that it removed foreign troops from China's borders, and, if only half of Vietnam was to be in Communist hands, the remainder could be undermined by guerrilla warfare as the Chinese knew better than anybody else. With the Americans choosing to stay on the sidelines at the time that the Settlement was made, while eventually being unable to leave South Vietnam to its fate, the 'real gain for peace' that Eden believed to have been achieved[91] proved to be a temporary one. It may well be that the Geneva Settlement represented the last example of an independent British policy exercising significant influence in the resolution of a major international crisis.[92]

If, as Lord Franks suggested, British foreign policy in the first decade after 1945 was based on 'a kind of confidence trick', because Britain acted as a Great Power though she did not have the resources,[93] such were Eden's achievements, especially in his golden year of 1954, it was understandable that there were those who considered him to be 'a great Foreign Secretary'.[94]

One-nation Butskellism: the economic and social policies of the Churchill government of 1951–5

When Butler first met his senior Treasury advisers as Chancellor of the Exchequer in 1951, he recalled that 'their story was of blood draining from the system and a collapse greater than had been foretold in 1931'.[95] In the manner in which he was supposed to have reacted to this grim inheritance, and then conducted economic policy, Butler was to be famously described by *The Economist* three years later to have practised Butskellism, a term that it devised by merging the names of Butler and his Labour predecessor as Chancellor. *The Economist* observed: 'The Mr Butskell who is in office at the moment has been extraordinarily lucky. He took up his duties at a time of grave economic crisis, used the one political weapon that his other half had shunned for political reasons – the weapon of the Bank Rate – and found that it worked even more effectively than he, his civil servants, or ... even the previous Mr Butskell's critics had ever expected. Partly as a result of this, but partly also as a result of a fall in import prices, he was able to introduce a mild first Budget and a very popular second one.'[96] That it was all luck was the interpretation favoured in a popular study of the time that seemed to aspire to be taken as seriously as Keynes's journalism. The economist concerned, Andrew Shonfield, assigned himself a role akin to a *film noir* private detective, seeing obvious solutions, usually Keynesian ones, with those in authority displaying no such wisdom. Thus:

> The Conservatives benefited from a quite extraordinary windfall in British foreign trade, starting at the beginning of 1952 and continuing through until the middle of 1954. What happened was that the prices of the basic materials which this country buys abroad – costing some €1,500 million in all in 1951 – fell by no less than one-quarter over that period. That alone produced nearly €400 million of extra purchasing power a year, without anyone lifting a finger. At the same time the prices that our exports fetched in overseas markets were steadily edging upwards. By 1954 the combined effect of the favourable bargain, which allowed us to sell our manufactured goods more dearly while buying our exports more cheaply, was to increase the foreign exchange earnings of Britain from the same amount of work done and the same amount of goods sold abroad by some 12 per cent.

With a low rate of investment and with additional output being made available for sale in a home market that was being decontrolled, Shonfield concluded that it was 'really no wonder that the British consumer, who was left in sole possession of the field, was able to go on a tremendous buying spree for a couple of years'.[97]

That said, though, Butler believed in 1951 that the economic situation was 'worse than 1949 and in many ways worse even than 1947',[98] and, if the Cabinet had allowed him to have his own way, he would not have become involved in practising Butskellism. By early 1952, the Treasury had become concerned not just about the economic situation, but about the behaviour of the Americans, which 'would be more readily understandable if their purpose was to weaken the UK economy, rather than to strengthen it'.[99] The way out of the predicament was to allow sterling to float, which proposal was called the ROBOT scheme, an acronym composed from the names of the leading Treasury and Bank of England officials involved. Opposition was inevitable from those who thought ROBOT to be 'revolutionary',[100] or those who believed that the economic situation was insufficiently desperate to justify the scheme.[101] Crucially, Churchill distrusted Butler as a former Chamberlainite, requiring him to have for a time unwanted Ministerial support from Sir Arthur Salter, whom Churchill described as 'the best economist since Jesus Christ'. Butler recalled that 'for thirteen months [Salter] wrote me numberless minutes in green ink'.[102] After his experiences as Chancellor in the 1920s, Churchill also distrusted the Bank of England and the Treasury, and for a few uncomfortable months the latter institution's work was subject to a Treasury Ministerial Advisory Committee,[103] including Woolton, who preferred business methods to those of the Civil Service.[104] Though the relevant papers make sufficiently clear the part played by the officials in the ROBOT affair,[105] the same cannot be said of the Cabinet minutes relating to the critical meetings held on 28 February 1952 and the following day. Salter portrayed himself as having led the way in stopping ROBOT,[106] and the credit was also claimed for Cherwell,[107] who had influence over the Prime Minister in the role of licensed eccentric. The majority of the Cabinet proved to be opposed to the ROBOT plan, and Butler believed that 'in the long term ... the decision not to free the pound was a fundamental mistake. The absence of a floating exchange rate robbed successive Chancellors of an external regulator for the balance of payments corresponding to the internal regulator provided principally by the Bank Rate. If such a regulator had existed, and a floating rate been accepted, Conservatives would have been saved some of the uncertainties and indignities of "stop-go" economics and Socialists the traumatic experience of a second formal devaluation [in 1967].'[108]

Lyttelton wrote of the Cabinet majority that opposed ROBOT that 'they prefer a genteel bankruptcy'.[109] 'If the bold stroke had been taken then, with everything risked on a single throw', Shonfield wrote, 'it would have imparted a sharp point and a coherence to Conservative policy instead of the havering and flabbiness that came upon it in subsequent years'.[110] If ROBOT had been implemented in 1952, there might well have been no further Conservative Governments for some time. For what was being argued, in terms of hard political reality, was that a Tory Government with a majority of 16 could effectively devalue the pound, and deflate the economy with one consequence being a considerable increase in unemployment in what it would be hoped would be the short run, and survive in electoral terms in an economic and political context in which supposedly competitive industries were to ensure that their workers had jobs for life performed in much the same way, and the State was to be the guarantor of employment. Even the harshest scholarly critic of the economic policies pursued by the various Governments of the Keynesian era did not believe that Churchill and his Cabinet could have proceeded with ROBOT in 1952, not least because they lacked the war chest funded by the proceeds of North Sea oil that the Thatcher Governments used to ride out the political storm,[111] and, by that time, economic expectations had also changed considerably.

Frustrated over ROBOT, Butler was only able to proceed with his version of Butskellism. In November 1951, the Bank Rate had been raised from 2 to 2.5 per cent,[112] and in the Budget of March 1952 it was raised to 4 per cent 'to fortify the currency'.[113] The *Economic Survey* subsequently observed that the net effect of the Budget measures was 'to leave consumers' real purchasing power virtually unchanged', because 'the reduction in food subsidies and ... increases in indirect taxes ... roughly matched ... the effects on personal incomes ... of the income tax concessions and the increase in national insurance and other transfer payments'.[114] In the 1953 Budget, Butler took sixpence off the standard rate of income tax, reduced purchase tax, abolished the excess profits levy in a bid to make the country 'nimbly competitive', and there were inducements to stimulate capital investment. 'We can lighten our load and liberate our energies', Butler declared, though he was unable to reduce the 'terrible burden of taxation' to even 'moderate' levels.[115] 'In 1952, I introduced an emergency Budget, and last year an incentive Budget, [and] so this year I am proposing a carry-on Budget', Butler declared in 1954,[116] and not surprisingly so, since 1953 seemed to be the most prosperous year in British economic history. *The Economist* had written then that 'if the Chancellor was right last year ... he had a liberal share of good luck. That is no very sound basis for confidence in this year's guess.'[117] A year later, 'Budget Bulls-eye by

Accident' was the same journal's verdict on how things had worked
out down to 1954,[118] at which time Butler believed 'sweeping reductions in taxation' would have been 'unjustified'.[119] It proved to be
unfortunate that Butler did not take the same attitude in his 1955
Budget, but, as *The Economist* said of his task before the event, 'his signposts are pointing in different directions'.[120] It did seem as if by this
stage Butler had come to act as if monetary policy provided a form of
painless discipline for the economy that would work wonders,[121] but,
whether this was so or not, he did risk cutting sixpence off the standard rate of income tax in the pursuit of 'confident expansion'.[122] In
addition, the *Economic Survey* was able to report that by the end of
1954, 'the main body of controls over the direct economy had been
removed, and freedom had been restored both to consumer and producer'.[123] Since some forms of food rationing had lasted until that
summer, and building controls had lasted until that November,[124]
what Butler once called 'the confines of restriction'[125] had been slowly
removed. It was only in February 1955 that the non-convertibility of
sterling was relaxed, and even then it was a halfway measure, with the
process not being completed until 1958.[126]

When Walter Monckton was made Minister of Labour, Lord
Margesson, the former Tory Chief Whip, said to his modern successor,
James Stuart, 'What are you doing with that old oil can in the
Cabinet?'[127] To buy off the trade unions would have been a fitting
answer. Monckton recorded that 'Winston's riding orders to me were
that the Labour Party had foretold grave industrial troubles if the
Conservatives were elected, and he looked to me to do my best to preserve industrial peace'.[128] Monckton was soon to declare that 'I am a
firm believer in government by consultation and consent, and I shall
do everything I can to carry out that principle in the conduct of my
Ministry'.[129] For his part, Churchill made every effort to socialize with
the right wing triumvirate that still essentially ran the TUC, inviting
them to dine with him, and even urging his doctor to treat Arthur
Deakin when that union leader was ill on the grounds that he was 'a
very important person'.[130] Industrial peace was secured by Monckton
'at the risk of entering into compromises that could only have an
inflationary effect', Woolton wrote, adding that this policy of appeas-
ing the unions 'greatly disturbed some of us in the Cabinet',[131] but
there was little that they could or would do about it. In late 1953,
Butler was sent for by Churchill and told: 'Walter and I settled the rail
strike in the early hours of the morning on their terms. We did not
think it necessary to keep you up.'[132] Churchill knew what he was

doing, remarking about Monckton that 'he is worn out giving way'.[133] As was the intention, the union leaders were impressed with Monckton, with Tom O'Brien declaring that 'only a narrow political bigot would deny the excellence of the job done by the present Minister',[134] whom Deakin described as having 'given us a square deal and we have been able to do things that were difficult to do under our own people'.[135] *The Economist* was less impressed with Monckton, remarking about the Minister's settlement with the rail unions in December 1953 that 'he should not forget the truth behind the applause that his skill in negotiation has earned. His triumph is really one more retreat from reality.'[136]

'Very soon severe competition from Germany and Japan must be expected in our export markets', Churchill had declared in 1951,[137] and the evidence drawn up by the Anglo-American Council on Productivity made it brutally clear that Britain would be poorly placed to meet it or, indeed, any other form of serious foreign competition. A successor body called the British Productivity Council was supposed to promote remedies, though Monckton believed that the Government itself needed to act to halt a relative economic decline that opened up the prospect of 'the relegation of the United Kingdom to the second division of the industrial league'. The President of the Board of Trade, Peter Thorneycroft, took the line that private industry should be given the opportunity to put things right first.[138] Since he did not propose the creation of relevant machinery to enable State intervention to promote greater industrial efficiency, what Monckton most likely had in mind was no more than exhortation on the part of the Government, which behaviour would be compatible with the manner in which he dealt with wage settlements. The harsh reality was that private enterprise was a misnomer for a sector of the economy that had come to be all too dependent on the Statism that had been practised from the time of the National Governments onwards, and whose relentlessly exposed inefficiencies were only in part a matter of trade union obstructionism. That there was not a competitive private enterprise culture in Britain was reflected in the attitudes of the contemporary Tory Party, as Beaverbrook had recognized, and it was evident in the behaviour of the Churchill Government towards the nationalized industries. Since the partial denationalization of the iron and steel and road haulage industries was as far as that Government was prepared to go, not least to avoid antagonizing the unions, that still left the problems of what to do about the management of public enterprises in a mixed economy, underlined in 1955 by the Cameron Report which argued that the employees of the British Transport Commission should receive 'a fair and adequate wage' meaning that 'a railwayman should be in no worse case than his colleague in a comparable industry'.[139] The implication was that when the Commission could not fund this from its revenues, the Treasury should make up the difference, which made nonsense of the theory of public corporations having self-contained finances. It might be said that the Government had done this anyway by using the nationalized industries as loss leaders in combating inflation by limiting price increases. Otherwise, the Tories confined themselves to institutional tinkering with regional decentralization being seen as a means of emphasizing commercial principles. The Fleck Committee, however, reported in 1955 that the National Coal Board was one organization that was too decentralized already.[140] It was a fair criticism of the Conservatives of that time that in relation to the nationalized industries they found it easier to talk of geography and lines of command than of pricing policies and rates of return that were implied by the private enterprise principles in which they professed to believe.[141] The Churchill Government's uncertainty about private ownership even extended to land in the case of the Crichel Down Affair of 1954, which reality was not hidden by the sacrificial resignation of the Minister of Agriculture concerned, Sir Thomas Dugdale.[142]

It was essential for the Party to show 'a true Conservative attitude ... rather than a me-tooing to Socialist solutions', Iain Macleod wrote to Butler in 1950[143] about *One Nation,* a publication to which he had contributed. So had Enoch Powell, who said of the pamphlet that 'it argued that because the Labour Government had sought in health, in insurance, in education, in housing to supply through the social services an average standard for all, it had thereby in practice failed to meet the requirements of those in greatest need. The Health Service, by attempting everything at once, had starved some of the most essential branches like dental health and mental treatment; by building council houses only, the nation had obtained fewer houses altogether; by endeavouring to eliminate differences of educational opportunity, the State was threatening the standards of the ablest; the changing age structure of the population had been too little regarded in the planning of national insurance. The machinery of the Welfare State was not helping the weak by its repression of the opportunities and independence of the strong.'[144]

The advocacy of selectivity instead of universality in State social provision surfaced when Macleod and Powell published *Social Services: Needs and Means* in 1952, and *Change is Our Ally* followed two years later. Keeping things the same was the effective motto of the Churchill Government. The Minister of Education, Florence Horsbrugh was not even in the Cabinet at first. Social security and health were not candidates for change. Certainly, Macleod did not rock the policy boat when he became Minister of Health as early as May 1952 not long after impressing Churchill in a debate on the National Health Service Bill.[145] Macleod had chosen Bevan as his target when declaring that 'I want to deal closely and with relish with the vulgar, crude and intemperate speech to which the House of Commons has just listened'.[146] In this style, Macleod observed that 'to have a debate on the NHS without [Bevan] would be like putting on *Hamlet* with no one in the part of the First Gravedigger',[147] and much was made later of Bevan being absent for the second part of Macleod's speech,[148] which ignored how ineffective his earlier interruptions had been when present.[149] However combative he was in debate, Macleod practised 'me-tooism' as Minister of Health, being content to run the existing arrangements,[150] and it was the Treasury who insisted on the Guillebaud inquiry into the cost of the NHS in a search for economies which the Committee failed to find.[151] As the Committee took the advice of Brian Abel-Smith and his ally, Richard Titmuss, who was busy developing the academic subject of social policy and administration based on State social provision being able to be perpetually expanded, its conclusion that the NHS provided value for money was as inevitable as was the avoidance of where in the long run the money would be found. The Conservatives had no intellectual troops of this calibre, and fielding other people's ideas was bound to be their experience until they equipped themselves to move beyond endorsement.

When Macmillan became Minister of Housing and Local Government with the task of ensuring that 300,000 houses a year would be built in the near future, his Labour predecessor, Dalton, declared that 'he won't be able to build any more, if as many as I'.[152] In this instance, one political charlatan misjudged another. 'In the battles which I had with the Treasury and with others of my colleagues on housing matters, I felt that Churchill was always on my side', Macmillan recalled. 'For he knew as well as I that whatever else might emerge which would throw lustre on the Administration ... the one easily measurable and ... ascertainable success would be the progress of the housing campaign.'[153] Macmillan made much of bringing in Percy Mills and Ernest Marples to run the housing programme,[154] and of copying the approach of 'the old Ministry of Supply',[155] but the most important common feature that the later Ministry of Housing had with that organization was the wartime style of financing. That the 300,000 houses target was met by December 1953 was not surprising given the scale of the resources diverted to the venture at the expense of industrial investment. There was more emphasis on building for private ownership than before, but when it came to legislation affecting rent control Churchill insisted that it 'must be so designed to bring no financial benefit to the landlords'.[156]

'Prudence and appeasement'

'By a long stretch the most successful peacetime Ministry that the country has seen since 1918', wrote one Tory historian about this Government,[157] and another considered that 'Churchill's was a quite exceptional Government. Guided by him, and containing a large number of genuinely wise and honest men ... [it] often pursued policies it regarded as being in the national rather than party interest.'[158] The scale of bipartisanship in the spheres of defence and foreign policy was no more remarkable than in the Attlee years, and in domestic policy, where most of the electoral rewards lay, the overriding concern of the Churchill Government would be better described as the unsurprising one of seeking to further the interests of the Conservative Party, and, if this was disguised at times by the legacies of Coalition thinking, the behaviour tended to be that of office at any price. After the Prime Minister's serious illness in 1953, what drive and direction the Government had possessed was diminished, and one example of this was the Government's failure to deal with the question of New Commonwealth immigration, raised initially by Labour MPs. All that was needed was an amendment to the Nationality Act of 1948 to make British practice the same as that of other Commonwealth countries, but, though Churchill sought action, he seemed no longer up to insisting on it, and nothing happened.[159]

Churchill had stated at the outset of his Government that 'what the nation needs is several years of quiet, steady administration, if only to allow socialist legislation to reach its full fruition'.[160] Butler privately observed in 1952 that 'Winston is so brave in war and so cowardly in peace; the Tory Government ought to convey the impression of people who are absolutely certain of themselves; as it is, they convey the impression of a wobble.'[161] A Treasury official wrote of the Government in 1953 that 'whenever anything happens that they do not like, their first instinct is to use the power of the State to stop it', giving as examples attempts to halt price increase in the transport, coal and steel industries 'if necessary by increased subsidies. It is not very surprising that Tories have no principles ... it is historically right and inherent in Conservatism. But it is surprising that they are such cowards.'[162] In the aftermath of the First World War, Churchill had stated that the watchword of the then Government should be 'prudence and appeasement',[163] and as in 1951 he perceived the nation to be 'split in half' by 'class and ideological strife',[164] understandably this was his approach once more. Churchill had then described his Government's programme as being 'houses and meat and not being scuppered – though perhaps not going broke is going to be the principal preoccupation'.[165] Gaitskell took a different view about the economic climate, and looked ahead to the next Election when 'the intelligent Tories will... want to say "no war: no unemployment: no cuts in social services. Just good government." If I am right about this they will want to stay in power for three or four years, and I do not really see why they should not.'[166] That this was a shrewd assessment was evident as early as the Sunderland South by election in May 1953 when the Tories won that seat from Labour.[167]

'By 1954 ... nearly all State trade had been given back to private enterprise', Butler recalled. 'Competition had been restored in the steel and road haulage industries. Most price controls were abolished. Thousands of controls on the allocation of materials and the manufacture and sale of goods were removed. Import controls had been greatly relaxed. The great commodity markets had been reopened. Above all, food rationing and other restrictions on consumption had been brought to an end.'[168] In 1954, one economist wrote, 'the food ration books were finally burned in an orgy of bonfires and barbecues organized by local Conservative constituency associations. Building licensing was abolished. In October the way that Britain rode over the London dock strike ... showed that stocks appeared to have reached a state of real strength ... . Butler told the Conservative Party Conference: "I give you a slogan: invest in success," and he propounded the vision of doubling Britain's real standard of living within twenty five years. A mood of expansion was in the air. There was every sign that Mr Butler had managed to establish for his country and party that strange, mystical but immensely valuable thing *la puissance d'une idée en marche*.'[169] The implication was that in 1954 Britain had been close to achieving an economic miracle of the kind that West Germany was currently experiencing, and that Butler would have brought this off if he had not played his cards badly in his 1955 Budget. The reality that Britain did not have an economic and social order capable of delivering such a miracle was not recognized at the time, and even if it had been, the electorate exercising the 1945 veto would not have permitted an alternative. Building more houses and getting rid of rationing and legislating to introduce commercial television and, thus, break the BBC monopoly hardly added up to 'the march to freedom' that Butler enthused about,[170] but neither did it constitute cowardice in the domestic political context of the time.

The Conservative Government of 1951–5 conducted itself as if its guiding principle was 'Who Dares Loses'. By the time of his retirement in April 1955, Churchill, the supposed arch anti-appeaser, had achieved his desired objective of domestic peace at any price, if with a Cavalier flourish.[171] As the Tories reaped their subsequent electoral reward, Shinwell summed up what was to be the character of British politics until the Thatcher era when he declared that 'at the last General Election we had to fight Churchill ... this time we are fighting Snow White and the Seven Dwarfs'.[172]

7
The Reckoning: The Eden Conservative Government 1955–7

The smack of infirm government

Within a week of becoming Prime Minister in April 1955, Sir Anthony Eden announced that a General Election would be held in the following month. As the Conservative Government had maintained full employment and the Welfare State, and as the economy seemed to be characterized by boom conditions, a Tory Election victory was always the most likely outcome. Just to make certain, many later thought, or as an act of economic policy mismanagement, which seems more likely, Butler's Budget in April 1955 included a sixpence reduction in the standard rate of income tax. At the Election in May 1955, the Conservatives' overall majority in the House of Commons increased from 17 to 58,[1] only just short of the 60-seat margin anticipated by Woolton as Party Chairman.[2] Eden pronounced the outcome 'better than I had dared hope'.[3] The Conservatives obtained 49.7 per cent of the poll,[4] which was the highest percentage obtained by any political party or alliance of them since 1935, and it was to be neither equalled nor bettered during the rest of the twentieth century. During the Election campaign, the Austrian Treaty was signed by the USA, the Soviet Union, France, and Britain leading to the withdrawal of foreign troops from Austria, and that country's unification, independence, and neutralization, for which Eden had been negotiating for years.[5] The Geneva Summit Conference in July 1955 gave Eden an opportunity to star on the world stage, even if, as might be expected on the Acheson principle, little was achieved. All told, Eden's Prime Ministership could hardly have got off to a better start than it did in its early weeks. Yet, a mere 20 months later, in January 1957, in the wake of the Suez adventure, Eden felt compelled to resign.

The decline in the authority of both Eden and the Government he led was swift even before the Suez crisis. Attlee's explanation was that Eden had an unenviable task in following Churchill as Prime Minister, and that Eden lacked experience of running a team.[6] Further, as Churchill had earlier observed, Eden had 'no experience at all of home affairs. He has always done the Foreign Office, and done it well. But I don't know how he will get on with all the home stuff.'[7] Strictly speaking, Eden had Ministerial experience at the Dominions Office and the War Office, but both had been for a matter of months, which meant that Eden's political career had been overwhelmingly concerned with foreign affairs. Eden continued to intervene, much to the irritation of Macmillan, the actual Foreign Secretary down to December 1955. 'He kept on sending me little notes, sometimes twenty a day, ringing up all the time', Macmillan recalled. 'He really should have been both PM and Foreign Secretary.'[8] Eden preferred to appoint the compliant Selwyn Lloyd as Macmillan's successor. Though it was foreign affairs, the area of his expertise that brought Eden down, there was no doubting his unsurenesss of touch outside that sphere, especially when it came to economic policy. 'Get rid of Butler', Woolton had advised Eden on the latter's first day as Prime Minister,[9] and Butler should have gone for his own sake in May 1955 instead of, as it turned out, making way for Macmillan as Chancellor of the Exchequer in December 1955, to become Lord Privy Seal and Leader of the House of Commons. Staying on as Chancellor meant that Butler had to introduce restrictive economic measures made necessary by the nature of the boom that, as it turned out, the April 1955 Budget had fuelled, and by a run on sterling consequent on rumours that ROBOT was to be revived, speculation added to by Butler's continued presence at the Treasury. The raising of indirect taxes in the 'pots and pans' Budget of December 1955 proved to be a damaging way to leave.[10] That Eden himself had no ideas of any value about economic policy was evident both from his Bradford Speech of January 1956, and from the minutes he wrote to Macmillan as Chancellor.[11] As for Macmillan himself, one economist of the private detective genre was being indulgent in suggesting that Macmillan had come to the Treasury 20 years too late.[12] Macmillan's solitary Budget in April 1956 was memorable only for the introduction of Premium Bonds,[13] and for eventual improvements in economic statistics, the existing ones being often 'too late to be useful' making them like 'looking up a train in last year's Bradshaw'.[14] Meanwhile, with the Butler boom brought to a halt, the economy stagnated. Macmillan was to give the Prime Minister and his colleagues such poor advice on the consequences for sterling of embarking on the Suez expedition that some suspected him of having done so deliberately to bring Eden down. This was too generous.

'It is difficult to advocate a property-owning democracy to the tune of "Your kettles will cost you more"', Eden wrote of the political environment after Butler's second Budget of 1955.[15] That, within months, the economic situation soon became difficult for the first time since 1952 inevitably caused political problems for the Eden Government, as did, ironically and partly through Eden's initial popularity, the Conservatives coming to have a more comfortable majority in the House of Commons. After playing themselves in under Churchill, some in the Party now wanted an inning of real Toryism. In terms of domestic politics, this seemed to mean some sort of reassertion of the values of the private enterprise system.[16] The Conservatives, though, had been returned to office on the basis of the successful practice of Butskellism, and, when, by the standards of the time, its by-election performances deteriorated, the likeliest explanation was that the Government was unsuccessfully practising 'me-tooism' rather than any wish on the part of the electorate for a greater resort to market solutions to economic problems. The 1945 veto had not gone away. The Labour Party was divided by Bevanism, and, with its nightmare scenario of what a return to Tory rule in 1951 would mean disproved by events, it was reduced during the 1955 Election to slogans of the 'what price tea?' variety.[17] Nonetheless, Labour had obtained 46.4 per cent of the poll.[18] Eden was used to popularity and the relatively sheltered and recently bipartisan world of foreign affairs, but that he was more exposed as Prime Minister should not have been unexpected. Critics such as Malcolm Muggeridge in *Punch* and Randolph Churchill in *The Evening Standard* could and should have been written off by Eden as being of unsound mind, but Eden had good cause to treat the unrelated hostility of the Berry family who owned *The Daily Telegraph* as constituting a deliberate vendetta against him.[19] 'There is a favourite gesture of the Prime Minister ... . To emphasize a point he will clench one fist to smack the open palm of the open palm of the other – but this smack is seldom heard', that newspaper wrote on 3 January 1956. 'Most Conservatives ... are waiting to hear the smack of firm government'.[20] Rumours that Eden was going to resign and make way for Butler then circulated, and, instead of disregarding them, Eden, who had been Prime Minister for a matter of months, reluctantly agreed with his inept Press Secretary, William Clark, that a denial should be published.[21] Unhelpfully,

Butler also issued a statement that was characteristically elliptical: 'My determination is to support the Prime Minister in all his difficulties.'[22] One of those difficulties, according to Eden, was that Attlee had ceased to be the leader of the Labour Party in December 1955. He had held on to the post long enough to ensure that Gaitskell and not Morrison would succeed him. Eden later wrote of Morrison being passed over as being nothing less than 'a national misfortune', and of Gaitskell that 'in all my years of political life I had not met anyone with his cast of mind and approach to problems'.[23] This was a curious observation, since upper-middle-class intellectuals who advocated one of the many forms of socialism, as Gaitskell did, had come to be numerous in British politics, and Gaitskell was not unusual in preaching egalitarianism while practising a Frognal Set life style. Bevan was commonly quoted as having described Gaitskell as a 'desiccated calculating machine', though he privately recognized that Gaitskell was 'highly emotional'.[24] Gaitskell only too often used his intellect to justify what his emotions desired. Moral certainty in an arrogant form characterized the irreligious Gaitskell, and if, in public life, Eden had not met such people, he should have counted his blessings. If Eden came to dislike and distrust Gaitskell, it was over his behaviour in the Suez crisis. Before that, Gaitskell recorded about Eden that 'he treats me as though I were a member of his Government',[25] which was Coalition thinking on Eden's part, or, at least, that of bipartisanship, familiar to him when Foreign Secretary, but not to be counted on when Prime Minister.

If his health had permitted, and if the Suez crisis had not taken place, Eden might well have held on as Prime Minister until the economy turned up sufficiently for the Tories to both enjoy a full term of office and another Election victory, as was to happen under Eden's successor. As things actually turned out, there was more to Eden's performance as Prime Minister than the thesis that he had been kept in the role of heir-apparent for too long. When Churchill had said that 'I don't believe Anthony can do it',[26] an implication was that Eden was at most one of life's number twos anyway, and not the man to lead a Government, or, for that matter, to successfully shape one. Too many passengers were tolerated, with Monckton being retained to eventually become Minister of Defence, though the worst example was the Home Secretary whom Eden had inherited, Gwilym Lloyd George. The over-promoted Lloyd George, who wished capital punishment to be retained, showed little political sense in declining to recommend mercy in the case of Ruth Ellis, which was being played up by the newspapers at the time. The Home Secretary may have thought that Mrs Ellis would soon be forgotten like Mrs Merrifield hanged in 1953 for poisoning her employer. The reformers certainly forgot about that old lady, but Mrs Ellis proved to be better material, being much younger, blonde, and her act of murder was the more dramatic one of putting four shots into her faithless lover. Mrs Ellis was hanged in July 1955, and, if a contemporary opinion survey was to be trusted, only 24 per cent of those sampled thought that a woman who had been convicted of murder should not be executed, as opposed to 60 per cent who believed that she should.[27]

Unwisely, given that the likely outcome was bound to irritate Tory activists, the Conservative Government allowed a Private Member's Bill proposing that the death penalty should be suspended for a period of five years to have the time for a Second Reading in early 1956. The reformers were led by Silverman once more[28] with two former Home Secretaries, Chuter Ede[29] and Morrison[30] joining their ranks. It seemed that the responsibility for the death penalty had proved too much for them. The inevitable Commons majority effectively for abolition was overturned in the House of Lords. The Cabinet certainly gave the matter of capital punishment plenty of attention,[31] and eventually came up with what Butler was to call 'the rather curious Homicide Act of 1957',[32] which seemed to please few, but which proved the form of compromise that would pass the Commons. Silverman's contemporary Tory counterpart on the backbenches was the equally distasteful Sir Cyril Osborne, who, with similar zest, pursued his particular obsession – the advocacy of restrictions on Commonwealth immigration. This policy had its adherents within Eden's Cabinet, which discussed the matter at length. By the autumn of 1955, draft restrictive legislation had been prepared, but Eden chose not to proceed with it.[33] The biographer who wrote that Eden could not know how important the issue would become[34] made a feeble defence of his behaviour. Eden knew that it was important: otherwise, why did he and his Cabinet grant the matter so much attention? Eden's diary and papers offer no explanation about his failure to act. Eden's belief in the multi-racial Commonwealth might have been a factor, as might his wish to be well regarded by the holders of 'liberal' opinion, the very people who were to delight in his political eclipse.

In relation to his political career, Eden would have passed the Napoleonic test of 'has he luck?' with flying colours well into 1955, but then luck ran out for him as it did temporarily for the Tories. The Eden

Government's sole achievement in domestic policy was said by one historian to be the White Paper on Technical Education of 1956.[35] Even the most severe critic of British policy in this area praised the document and its political author, Sir David Eccles, the Minister of Education. A decade earlier, a committee chaired by another Conservative, Sir Eustace Percy, had proposed the creation of Royal Colleges of Technology, so called to counteract the academic snobbery of the universities, but the 1956 initiative preferred to call them Colleges of Advanced Technology, and there was also to be investment in technical colleges.[36] At this stage, the funding was not made available to render the initiative as important as Eccles hoped, and, without doubting that much of higher education needed to be made less determinedly irrelevant to the needs of the private sector, the overriding need was for technical training to be made more widely available rather than technical education. The Conservatives had few allies among the educationalists or in intellectual life generally, which meant that they tended to have to respond to the ideas of others. So, for instance, when a Royal Commission reported on the Civil Service in 1955, its findings on pay were dominated by the thinking of the socialist Barbara Wootton, recommending that salaries should be based on 'fair comparisons' with outside groups.[37] The Eden Government made changes at the Treasury that suggested that it was unhappy about the style of leadership that Sir Edward Bridges had provided as Head of the Civil Service, but it conceded the principle of comparable pay to that Service, with one motive presumably being the numbers of white collar Conservative voters involved, despite the implications for public expenditure and expectations. No doubt, as its representatives insisted, the Civil Service could be said to be a special case, but there was no shortage of other groups who made claims for 'fair' rewards before other contemporary committees of inquiry.[38]

The Wootton notion of a rational wages policy[39] was absurd except in the context of a static and autarkic economy, but since 1951 in order to sustain full employment and to combat inflation, the Conservatives had been fortunate not to have to resort to a national incomes policy. For the present, when the Government pronounced on *The Economic Implications of Full Employment* all that emerged was exhortation plus reassurance that nothing much needed to change. Nothing came of a general review of industrial relations that Eden initiated. Eden came to favour a 'period of reflection' before official strikes took place, though not legislation to impose this nor for anything else relating to the trade unions, several of whose leaders shared the

Government's concern about the number of unofficial strikes.[40] These did not include Frank Cousins, whose arrival as leader of the TGWU in early 1956 marked the beginning of the end of the period of co-opera-tion between organized labour and the Tory Government that dated back to 1951. 'We accept that in a period of freedom for all we are part of that all', Cousins famously declared,[41] as if 'Conservative freedom works' was more than a slogan. What eventually became the Rent Act of 1957 easing rent restriction was to be later announced, but other-wise this was a Tory Government that tended to prefer keeping eco-nomic liberalism confined to the sidelines. Thus, when the Herbert Committee on the Electricity Supply Industry came up with proposals on pricing policy that even suggested the disinterment of Economic Man, the Government concentrated on the proposed organizational reforms.[42] A contemporary economist shrewdly identified the climac-teric of 1955 in relation to the conduct of macroeconomic policy,[43] but, in the familiar manner of the true believer, concluded that Keynesianism was not at fault because it had not been properly tried.

With its Foreign Secretary becoming the next Prime Minister, it was only to be expected that the view of the world that informed the exter-nal policies of the Churchill Government was translated to its succes-sor, at least down to the Suez crisis. Eisenhower had welcomed the succession by granting Eden the summit conference that Churchill had been denied, and one consequence of the Geneva Conference was that the then Soviet leaders, Marshal Bulganin and Nikita Khrushchev, were invited to make an official visit to Britain. When they came in April 1956, they were given a 'polite but restrained' welcome, according to Eden.[44] Bulganin and Khrushchev met the Queen and Churchill, and had a sight-seeing tour of London, and a dinner at the House of Commons with Labour Party leaders that proved so disastrous that Khrushchev informed the gathering that if he lived in Britain he would be a Conservative. Whatever Eden thought about that, he was to be embarrassed by a British Secret Service exploit concerned with the Russian cruiser, moored in Portsmouth Harbour, that had brought the Soviet leaders. As a result, a Commander Crabb was missing, presumed dead. Eden had not authorized this exploit, and, indeed, knew nothing about it, as a subsequent statement in the House of Commons made clear. Khrushchev had some fun at Eden's expense at the time, but there was sufficient amity for an agreed final communiqué to be issued. Churchill's son wrote of that document that it was 'of so flatulent a character and so studded with clichés that many people at the time supposed that Sir Anthony himself must have taken a large part in its preparation'.[45] The Soviet visit seemed to support the thesis that Britain was still an important player in international affairs, and Eden treated the Churchillian 'circles' definition of Britain's role as still valid. Preparations for colonial independence continued as did the problems associated with running some of the countries concerned in the meantime. Thus, for instance, the Eden Government faced a difficult situation in Cyprus in resisting terrorism conducted by those who wanted to impose union with Greece by force. Archbishop Makarios associated himself with this movement, and in March 1956 he was deported, with the Colonial Secretary, Alan Lennox-Boyd observing presciently that His Beatitude would return to eventually become Head of State in Cyprus.[46].

Much more important in the long run for Eden's reputation was his refusal to take seriously the Messina Conference of 1955 that was to lead to the Treaty of Rome of 1957 and the subsequent formation of the European Economic Community or Common Market. Butler summed up the prevailing attitude of the British Government at the time when he referred to 'archaeological excavations at Messina', meaning that those present were digging up a past that he thought had been buried once and for all with the collapse of the EDC. Butler said that Eden was 'even more bored' than he was with this attempt to relaunch 'Europe'.[47] When Foreign Secretary in June 1955, Macmillan had publicly praised 'the European idea' as a means 'by which [the] long feuds of centuries between France and Germany may be ended',[48] and privately written that 'our purpose should definitely be ... the strengthening of everything that leads to the unity of Europe on a basis which is acceptable to the British Government, that is what we used to call a confederation as opposed to the federal concept'.[49] When at the Treasury in November 1956, Macmillan declared that 'I do not believe that this House would ever agree to our entering into arrangements which, as a matter of principle, would prevent our treating the great range of imports from the Commonwealth at least as favourably as those from the European countries.'[50] Macmillan's statement expressed the contemporary reality on 'Europe' in British politics that the 'missed opportunities' school of writing on the subject was later to gloss over. Serendipity seems the most convincing explanation of why Messina came to matter. Lloyd told the Americans that 'the pursuit of the Common Market by the Community of Six would lead to the repetition of the EDC experience', meaning that 'after exhaustive negotiation and agreement on a treaty, France in the long run would refuse to ratify'.[51]

That this did not happen was explained by the exceptional circumstances brought about in the politics of the Fourth French Republic by the Algerian conflict which gave Guy Mollet as Prime Minister a position of temporary dominance from which his contribution to promoting integration was of an order that led one observer to write that Mollet was more important to the 'relaunching' of Europe than Messina.[52] The matter was more complex than that, not least in relation to Konrad Adenauer's particular vision of West Germany's political interests and determined pursuit of its realization, but two things were straightforward enough for the British Government to recognize and act upon. As Macmillan's son stated in the relevant debate, one was that 'though ... the Commonwealth is still our biggest market, it is not the market which is expanding the fastest', which was what he called 'the six Messina countries'.[53] The other was American enthusiasm for Messina and European economic integration, which, Eden recorded, matched what they had displayed towards the EDC.[54] It did not matter whether or not, say, the Monnet vision of a United States of Europe was 'boring', because a crucial fact of Cold War life was that the Americans did not think so, which was one reason that greater Western European unity would continue to be sought, and so there was cause to ensure that developments, if any, took the free trade area and inter-governmental form that would suit British interests best. Since Monnet himself did not anticipate how important Messina would be for 'Europe', the most telling criticism of Eden for sending a higher civil servant to Messina instead of a senior Minister or a Ministerial team was the pragmatic one that matters relating to an important and growing market were under high level discussion, and British interests needed to be vigorously protected. Eden was never comfortable with economic matters, and, as for pleasing the Americans, Eden thought that Britain could often get them to do what they wanted, and that she could sometimes act with a measure of independence, but the matters had to be finely judged. In the Suez crisis, Eden's judgment was wrong.

The Suez crisis

On 26 July 1956, the Egyptian dictator, Colonel Nasser nationalized the British-and-French-owned and Egyptian-registered Universal Suez Maritime Company, and, thus, effectively, the Suez Canal itself. Previously, the USA, followed by Britain, had declined to make available loans needed by the Egyptian Government to enable it to build the Aswan High Dam, a massive irrigation and hydroelectric project. Nasser's policy of engaging in arms deals with the Soviet bloc had enraged Dulles, and Eden had been alienated by, among other behaviour, Nasser's interventions in Jordan, then another part of Britain's informal empire, much as Egypt had been until a few years before. On 1 March 1956, King Hussein of Jordan dismissed the Englishman, Sir John Glubb, from command of that country's army, the Arab Legion. If we believe Anthony Nutting, the Minister of State at the Foreign Office, later to resign over the Suez adventure, Eden blamed Nasser for the dismissal of Glubb Pasha, and concluded that the dictator had to be eliminated, or else he would destroy Britain's position in the Middle East and that of himself as Prime Minister.[55] Eden was later to write that 'some say that Nasser is no Hitler or Mussolini. Allowing for a difference in scale, I am not so sure'.[56]

In the immediate aftermath of the seizure of the Canal, Gaitskell was not one of the doubters. 'The fact is that this episode must be recognized as part of the struggle for the mastery of the Middle East', Gaitskell declared in the House of Commons on 2 August 1956, adding that 'if Colonel Nasser's prestige is put up sufficiently and our's is put down sufficiently, the effects ... in that part of the world will be that our friends desert us because they think we are lost, and go over to Egypt'. Gaitskell stated that 'we cannot forget that Colonel Nasser has repeatedly boasted of his intention to create an Arab empire from the Atlantic to the Persian Gulf', and he emphasized the threat that the dictator's ambitions represented to Israel, Jordan, Iraq and Saudi Arabia. Of Nasser's behaviour, Gaitskell said: 'It is all very familiar. It is exactly the same that we encountered from Mussolini and Hitler in those years before the war.'[57] Eden's initial reaction to the news of Nasser's act of nationalization was to take the matter to the Security Council, and Gaitskell recorded: 'I said "Supposing Nasser doesn't take any notice?" Whereupon [Lloyd] said, "Well, I suppose in that case the old-fashioned ultimatum will be necessary." I said that I thought that they ought to act quickly, whatever they did, and that as far as Great Britain was concerned, public opinion would almost certainly be behind them. But I also added that they must get America in line. This should not be difficult.'[58] In his Commons speech, Gaitskell had concluded that 'while force cannot be excluded, we must be sure that the circumstances justify it and that it is, if used, consistent with our belief in, and our pledges to, the Charter of the United Nations and not in conflict with them'.[59] Gaitskell wrote at the time that 'had we attacked the Government at this moment we could very easily have been framed as unpatriotic and behaving in an irresponsible manner', and that 'I tried in my speech to preserve a balance', describing what he had to say on the United Nations as 'terribly important'.[60] Gaitskell wrote to Eden the following day giving a 'friendly warning' that the Labour Party would not support the use of force unless 'Nasser were to do something [else] which led to his condemnation by the United Nations as an aggressor'.[61] Those unwilling to join in the campaign to grant Gaitskell the status of sainthood could conclude that he was trying to have it both ways by talking tough and effectively precluding approval of anything resembling action. Inevitably, the bellicose rhetoric was only too memorable, and, as the Suez crisis progressed, Gaitskell was easily portrayed as leading the Opposition from behind, which interpretation was flattering. When fighting took place, Gaitskell used a broadcast to urge the Tories to overthrow Eden.[62] To call this 'irresponsible' would be kind, since this particular form of 'Eden must go' appeal was bound to be counter-productive.

The conventional wisdom became that the Suez crisis was comparable only with that of Munich in the political divisions that it caused. This may have been true of the political nation, but the reality was that the Munich Agreement secured a level of popular approval that was denied to the Suez adventure. It took courage for Churchill and his few allies on the Right to oppose Munich. The Labour Opposition in 1956 had the easier task. The difference was that when the 'peace at any price' policy of Munich failed, the National Government could be portrayed as having neglected the national interest, and the Churchillians had the patriotic card in their hand. Over Suez, the Eden Government behaved foolishly, but going to war to assert British interests was difficult to present as national betrayal. Gaitskell had no problem in showing that what Eden betrayed were the ideals of liberal internationalism to which he had subscribed, but, once British troops went into action, the Labour Party inevitably faced the 'unpatriotic' charge that Gaitskell had feared along the lines of the message of contempt that its intellectuals in particular attracted of 'any country but your own'. So, at the gutter level of politics, in 1940, *Guilty Men* worked as a form of fake history, but when Michael Foot tried to repeat the formula over Suez there was no market. When *The Daily Mirror* ran a campaign against The War of Eden's Face on the analogy of The War of Captain Jenkins's Ear, it soon had to drop this because of falling sales. When Bevan famously addressed a rally against Suez in Trafalgar Square on 4 November 1956, this may well have marked the revival of the street politics of demonstration and of the gutter, which was ironic given

Bevan's love of Parliament. Ironically, too, given the standards that Gaitskell tried to set himself in public life about rationality in discussion, the behaviour of the Labour Opposition in the House of Commons led that Chamber to resemble a bear garden,[63] to which state the Commons was to revert only too often thereafter. 'The booing and the screaming started whenever Eden entered the Chamber, and it went on from there', an official present recalled, 'And it was a significant moment when Eden ... announced the surrender of Port Said. The Labour uproar vanished into a ghastly, sickly silence.'[64]

'Nobody I talked to had a word to say for the Government's policy, which they all felt was reckless because it separated us from the Americans, without whom we could not survive', Crossman recorded,[65] and if his assessment of opinion in The Establishment was accurate then, for once, those who could be described as its members had got it exactly right. As Crossman himself recognized, the Labour Opposition's 'United Nations right or wrong' line[66] was beside the point. This was that without the explicit support of the USA, there was no sense in attacking Egypt. Eden acted as if he could present the Americans with a fait accompli, but, effectively, because of the American domestic political timetable, this meant taking immediate military action. Eden wrote that 'a criticism was subsequently made that we and the French, as the powers principally concerned, should have reacted at once and forcibly reoccupied the Canal. There are two answers to this. The first answer is political. As signatories of the Charter of the United Nations, we were bound first to seek redress by peaceful means ... we knew that we must at some time take the issue to the Security Council. We might even be able to prod them into action. To accept this did not mean abandoning the use of force as a last resort.'[67] Eden's second answer was military: 'Unless the action could have been carried through exclusively by airborne troops, there was no alternative to an expedition from Malta. Unless we could fly all the forces needed, they had to swim. The nearest place from which to swim was Malta, a thousand miles away. Cyprus has no sufficient harbour for landing craft or transports. There is no escape from these logistics.'[68]

Nasser himself later recalled that before nationalizing the Suez Canal Company, the Egyptians had assessed Britain's military capabilities and concluded that 'Britain would not be ready to have any military movement before three or four months. We thought at that time that it would be possible to reach a sort of settlement during those three months'.[69] Nasser's assessment of British military potential was correct. Britain was organized to wage the Cold War and to deal with colonial insurgency and not much in between. Anthony Head, the then Secretary of State for War, was later to maintain that critics who complained about the lack of an immediate British military response had to have had in mind an airborne operation to seize the Canal. 'All the responsible military advice, both British and French ... unanimously rejected' that course, Head recalled, adding that proceeding would probably have meant 'the resignation of those military advisers who had been overruled'. It would have taken six days for reinforcements to be shipped from Malta,[70] and, since Arnhem, it had become military doctrine that paratroops were only to be used if they could be supported within 24 hours. 'British planners ... overlooked an important distinction that at Arnhem we were confronted by Germans, whereas at Suez our enemy was of a somewhat less martial character', Churchill's son observed.[71] Of the Chiefs of Staff, Mountbatten's opposition to military intervention was of an order that Field Marshal Templer called him 'yellow',[72] though Templer's own advice was that an effective invasion force could not be mounted for six to seven weeks.[73]

This meant that negotiations had to be engaged in and that they would involve the Americans. When the British Ambassador in Washington informed Eden that 'Nasser could hardly have chosen a better time for his action in terms of American domestic politics',[74] he was only stating the obvious, as he would have been if he had added that there was never much likelihood that President Eisenhower, running for re-election as an architect of world peace, was going to be seen publicly supporting Britain and France, two colonial powers, in any military adventure against Egypt. The USA believed herself to be in competition with the Soviet Union for the allegiance of the Third World, recently invented at the Bandung Conference of 1955, at which, Eisenhower had noted, more than half of the world's population were represented,[75] or, at least their rulers were. Wooing the supposedly uncommitted nations was a waste of resources because their self-interest was bound up with their status. However unrealistic the Americans were in some of their perceptions, Eisenhower was not going to change them to suit the convenience of the British and the French. At the outset, Eisenhower had despatched Robert Murphy to London, who was told by Macmillan that if she did not accept Egypt's challenge, 'Britain would become another Netherlands'.[76] Murphy wrote of Eden that he had 'not adjusted his thoughts to the altered world status of Great Britain, and he never did' and that he 'expected to play the diplomatic starring role which he had performed for so long between the wars and during World War II'.[77] Murphy recorded that there were those in Washington who regarded Eden as 'slippery, ' and that 'it was obvious that Eden and Dulles were uncomfortable with one another',[78] bearing out an earlier diary note of Eden's that Dulles was 'no doubt glad to be rid of me'.[79] When Dulles arrived in London, he was soon to say that 'a way had to be found to make Nasser disgorge what he was attempting to swallow'. As Eden wrote, 'these were forthright words' which 'rang in my ears for months'.[80] They did not disguise the reality that Dulles was on a delaying mission. As Murphy wrote, 'If ... Dulles ever was actually convinced of the possibility of organizing a Canal Users Association to operate the Suez Canal, I was not aware of it ... it seemed to me that he was skilfully working for time in the hope that public opinion in western Europe would harden against military adventure.'[81] On 13 September 1956, when asked if the USA would join Britain and France in forcing a SCUA convoy through the Canal, Dulles replied that 'I know nothing about a plan to shoot a way through ... . We certainly have no intention of doing so'.[82] Eden was in the midst of 'two difficult days in the House' when he learnt of Dulles's ad lib comments,[83] and he knew as well as everybody else that Nasser was being told that he had nothing to worry about from the Americans if he did defy SCUA. *The Devil and John Foster Dulles* was an excellent title for a study of the Secretary of State, since the two had at least a nodding acquaintance, but the *Dulles Over Suez* view of the crisis ignored the reality that 'leave it to Foster' was not how Eisenhower treated foreign policy, only its detail. The President was in charge.

The initial reaction of the American Joint Chiefs of Staff on 31 July 1956 was that Nasser must be broken. They thought this should be accomplished by economic and political means. If, however, these were tried and proved insufficient, Britain should then use armed force, and the USA should declare herself in support of this action. Eisenhower thought that 'it was wrong to give undue stress to Nasser himself', though he described him as embodying 'the emotional demands of the people of the area for independence' and for 'slapping the white man down'. Eisenhower said 'we must consider what the end could be. It might well be to array the world from Dakar to the Philippine Islands against us'.[84] If it suited its holders, 'world opinion' would be condemnatory of US behaviour anyway, ignoring American efforts not to be counted as 'the white man'. Eisenhower was to learn that most neutralist countries tended to criticize the Anglo-French armed intervention at Suez, while almost ignoring the contemporaneous Soviet suppression of a revolt in Hungary,[85] noting in relation to 'the Moscow line' that 'Nehru seemed to be ... buying their entire bill of goods'.[86] That Eisenhower seemed surprised by this behaviour was remarkable, but, whatever the failings that he displayed in his handling of the Suez crisis, inconsistency was not one of them. 'In my telephonic and other communications with Prime Minister Eden I frequently expressed the opinion that the case as it stood did not warrant resort to military force', Eisenhower later recorded,[87] and he spelt out as early as 31 July 1956 what the American response would be to the use of force. 'There would have to be a showing that every peaceful means of resolving the difficulty had previously been exhausted', Eisenhower wrote to Eden. 'Without such a showing ... I personally feel sure that the American reaction would be severe.'[88]

With the Suez Canal functioning smoothly, as Eisenhower had predicted,[89] a form of settlement seemed the obvious solution. Christian Pineau, the French Foreign Minister, was obstructive during the most promising of the negotiations, or so Lloyd informed Eden,[90] but sufficient was achieved in discussions that involved the UN Secretary General, Dag Hammarskjöld, and Mahmoud Fawzi, the Egyptian Foreign Minister, for Lloyd to say on 19 December 1956 of a letter that Hammarskjöld sent to the Egyptian Government on 24 October that 'there is set out the broad lines of a scheme which, if properly worked out in detail, could be regarded as complying with the six principles'[91] that Britain had been treating as the basis of a peaceful settlement. In the most comprehensive study of the Suez crisis, Lloyd was said to have told the Israeli Prime Minister, David Ben-Gurion that it was possible that there might be agreement with Nasser in a week about the running of the Canal.[92] Lloyd himself wrote that he told the Cabinet that he was 'very doubtful' about 'the prospects for a negotiated settlement'.[93] Lloyd also recalled that he had tried to point out to Ben-Gurion 'the dangers in a military operation of the kind he was proposing. There would be an immediate appeal to the Security Council. If the British and French vetoes were used, the Uniting for Peace procedure would possibly be invoked. The matter would be referred to the General Assembly, the majority of whose members would be hostile ... . The United States' attitude would be uncertain. Canada would probably be against. Under this kind of pressure the military operation after a few days might have to be halted.'[94] Lloyd's observations to Ben-Gurion were made at the Sèvres Conference on 21 October 1956 and the following day, to which he travelled incognito. Pineau had recognized that 'the English are incapable of acting without a pretext', and the French and Israeli Governments had come up with a plan. In essence, Israel was to pre-emptively attack Egypt and the British and French were to intervene to safeguard the Canal. Part of the plan involved the RAF bombing the Egyptian air force at its bases.[95] Broadly, events followed the plan. Lloyd later stated that 'there was no prior agreement' about the Israeli attack that began on 29 October 1956.[96] Eden was 'to say it quite bluntly to the House that there was not foreknowledge that Israel would attack Egypt'.[97]

When the Anglo-French forces finally invaded Egypt on 6 November 1956, Nasser, pretending that he had a choice, later said that he had no intention of fighting them. He intended to sit back and let world opinion save him.[98] In the event, American political and economic pressure did save Nasser as the Anglo-French forces were forced to withdraw, being replaced by a United Nations force. Far from *Cutting the Lion's Tale*, Nasser himself could do little. The Egyptian Army had been defeated by the Israelis once again. The Anglo-French forces had some difficulty in taking Port Said, but the ceasefire came with them probably only 24 hours from taking the entire Canal. Meanwhile, the Egyptians had taken the precaution of blocking the waterway. Britain was now dependent on the Americans for oil and also for aid in stemming a run on sterling. The Chancellor of the Exchequer, the initially bellicose Macmillan, was now all for pulling out. The Americans remorselessly enforced a withdrawal, and Eden complied on 22 December 1956. Troops belonging to the United Nations and a salvage team took over. Returning from an extraordinary rest cure in Jamaica on 14 December 1956, Eden made the strange statement: 'Does anyone suppose that there would have been a United Nations Force but for the British and French action? Of course not.'[99]

The Suez adventure was a fiasco. As Nutting wrote: 'we had achieved none of the objectives, whether pretended or real, with which we had set out ... . We had not separated the combatants; they had separated themselves. We had not protected the Canal; it was blocked. We had not safeguarded British lives and property, but had subjected them to the gravest hazards. Nor had we achieved our real aim of seizing control of the Canal. Least of all had we toppled Nasser from his throne.'[100] Legally, Britain had been on weak ground regarding her claims to the Canal Company. Militarily, the expedition took so long to mount that the eventual and predictable victory over Egypt looked like an anti-climax, although that description was even more fitting for the painful withdrawal. As for halting with the conquest of the Suez Canal in sight, nobody but Churchill could have put the humiliation more succinctly: 'I would never have dared; and if I had dared, I would certainly never have dared stop.'[101] The British Ambassador, Sir Harold Caccia, was present in Washington shortly after Suez 'when Dulles asked Lloyd why on earth we did not go through with the operation'.[102] Lloyd was surprised, given that 'Dulles was the man who had led the pack against us', and replied that 'if you had as much as winked at us we might have gone on'. Dulles replied that he could not have done that.[103] Dulles was a useful scapegoat, and, when replying to Britain's request for economic help, George Humphrey, the Secretary of the Treasury, provided a memorable quote when he said, 'You will not get a dime from the US Government ... until you've gotten out of Suez.'[104]

Neither man mattered compared with Eisenhower. Macmillan's assessment that 'Ike ... will lie doggo'[105] proved to be hopelessly wide of the mark. That the USA lined up on the same side as the Soviet Union and against Britain and France at the United Nations was an indictment of Eisenhower's conduct of American foreign policy. The West should have drawn the line in relation to Arab nationalism in 1956, for it was not only in Iraq that the failure of what became the Eisenhower Doctrine was to be demonstrated. More immediately, the Suez crisis and the supposed need to act in accord with the United Nations Charter provided Eisenhower with political cover for inaction over the Hungarian Revolution, feeling able to maintain that 'Hungary was ... as inaccessible to us as Tibet'.[106] It was far safer to be seen to act firmly in 'a family spat' with Britain and France.[107] Gaitskell seemed to think that Suez prevented 'the whole world' from being 'united in denouncing' Soviet aggression in Hungary,[108] as if that would have made any difference. Bevan had some difficulty in dealing with Soviet behaviour since he had hailed Khrushchev's denunciation of Stalin in February 1956 as the precursor of liberalization.[109] Such a development would destroy the system that Khrushchev aspired to run, and the prime purpose of his denunciation had been to assure the CPSU membership that under his leadership they were safe from being purged. Nehru considered that 'Soviet action in Hungary spelled the eventual death knell of international Communism.'[110] The Soviet Empire was doomed only when her leaders failed to crush revolts in colonies such as East Germany, Poland and Hungary with exemplary ruthlessness.

'Much of the subsequent controversy over the Suez decision has been about the trees and not about the wood', Eden was to write. 'The main question is whether inertia would have brought better results for the peace of the world than action. I think not. I thought and think that failure to act would have brought the worst of consequences, just as I think the world would have suffered less if Hitler had been resisted on the Rhine, in Austria or in Czechoslovakia, rather than Poland.'[111] Thus, for Eden, the Suez crisis was *Full Circle*, to cite the title of the relevant volume of his memoirs. It was really *The Reckoning*, to take the title of the wartime volume, though a needless one. When in relation to the Suez adventure, Churchill declared that 'I would not have dared to do it without squaring the Americans',[112] he was only stating what ought to have been obvious to Eden. 'Anthony, have you gone out of your mind?' was Eisenhower's reaction to the Suez invasion,[113] and one official who had been close to him wondered if Eden had gone mad.[114] Then there were those who believed that Eden's poor health or at least the treatment of it affected his judgment. More convincing was the argument of the best of the many biographers, and a friendly one, who thought that Eden still saw Eisenhower in wartime terms when he had been below him in the political hierarchy and as a social inferior rather than as the leader of the Western Alliance.

On this view, Eden had not adjusted to Britain having a secondary role in relation to the USA.[115] The decision to fight on in 1940–1 against Nazi Germany and to prosecute the Cold War against the Soviet Union had both been predicated on the USA taking on the responsibilities of world leadership. In the context of the Pax Americana, for much of the time Britain's position in her relationship with the USA resembled that of the constitutional monarch within her own political system, which, as we have noted before, meant the right to be consulted, to encourage and to warn. The real power lay elsewhere. Bevin and then Eden had displayed considerable skill in particular circumstances in exercising more influence than this analogy suggests, so much so that Eden then overreached himself. As her 'finest hour' further faded into history and relative economic decline persisted, Britain's authority would have been diminished eventually anyway, but there was no need for Eden to gamble it away. If the USA had not been prepared to intervene in Indo-China without British support in 1954, why did Eden think that Britain could intervene in Egypt without American backing in 1956? Military action had to be immediate or not taken at all, and, given Britain's experience in running the Canal Zone after 1952 how was the area, once won back, to be held down, and if Nasser was deposed, which was by no means certain, who exactly was to rule Egypt in his place? As Mossadeq had learnt, there were other ways to undermine Nasser. There was no guarantee, of course, that the Americans would cooperate in this, and some would say that Eden's domestic political position was no longer strong enough to permit him from abstaining from seeking a confrontation with Nasser. Since the French were convinced that Nasser was the author of their troubles in Algeria, they were going to go ahead anyway, and, if in a stronger position, Eden could have let the French and the Israelis get on with it, making clear British moral support for their behaviour, though the requirements of the United Nations Charter prevented participation. Eden never seems to have considered playing Perfidious Albion, or to have taken American warnings seriously. When the Suez adventure failed, Eden's days as Prime Minister were numbered, and, on grounds of ill health, he resigned in early 1957.

8
The Failure of the Middle Way: The Macmillan and Home Conservative Governments 1957–64

'Supermac' and the Whig supremacy 1957–60

'Macmillan was a Whig, not a Tory ... he had no use for the Conservative loyalties and affections; they interfered too much with the Whig's true vocation of detecting trends in events and riding them skilfully so as to preserve the privileges, property and interests of his class.' So wrote Enoch Powell,[1] appalled at the ruthlessness with which Macmillan pushed aside Butler in order to replace Eden as Prime Minister. Much of Macmillan's subsequent behaviour and that of the Governments he led could be interpreted as justifying Powell's analysis all the way down to his ridiculous choice of successor. However unimpressive he had been at the Foreign Office and at the Treasury, from the beginning of 1957 to mid-1961, Macmillan commanded British political life. A foolish socialist cartoonist dubbed him 'Supermac', and, successfully for a time, Macmillan cultivated an image of 'unflappability', a form of Edwardian effortless superiority. Macmillan was said to see Butler as his social inferior,[2] though even he must have wondered if marrying into the Devonshires was worth the personal humiliation it brought, and nobody could take seriously any suggestion of intellectual superiority. Bevan was not alone in disliking merit being spurned when Butler was passed over,[3] and, for Macmillan, to judge from the defensive nature of his over-extensive memoirs, social confidence was not enough. 'Only six', Butler was supposed to have remarked of the number of volumes. Of course, Churchill had written six volumes about being the wartime Prime Minister, and, while many noted that the titles of the volumes of Eden's memoirs had a Churchillian ring to them, so had those of Macmillan: namely, *Winds of Change*, *The Blast of War*, *Tides of Fortune*, *Riding The Storm*, *Pointing The Way*, and, last

155

and certainly least, *At The End of The Day*. On the Churchill scale, like everybody else, Macmillan was bound to be found wanting. Staying ahead of Butler proved to be challenging enough for Macmillan, and their rivalry was a continuing feature of this period of government.

What Powell failed to appreciate about Macmillan was the importance of his intellectual deference towards socialism. This proved to be more than advocating further doses of Conservative Statism than even the National Governments of the 1930s were able to practise, given the constraints of traditional public finance. Macmillan's pilgrimage to the Soviet Union in 1932 had been a strange venture, especially as he knew that he would only see what he was shown,[4] and one notes his fear expressed to the future President Kennedy in 1960 that 'Communism will triumph, not by war, or even subversion, but by seeming to be a better way of bringing people material comforts'.[5] The West had cause to fear Soviet military might and KGB espionage, but not the competition of economies that 'peaceful coexistence' was supposed to promote. If Macmillan was not converted to socialism in the 1930s, he acted as if he was convinced that it would prevail. Among the proposals in his book, *The Middle Way*, published in 1938, were that economic activity should be coordinated by a National Economic Council, on which would be represented the relevant Ministers and government departments and the employers and the TUC, whose task would be to draw up 'a comprehensive plan'. A nationalized Bank of England, a National Investment Board, and a Foreign Trade Authority would be involved in its implementation. There was to be a minimum wage. There was to be a National Nutrition Board. Not surprisingly, as Macmillan's company had published *The General Theory*, there were references to Keynes's thinking, though whether Macmillan really understood his thesis could be doubted, given his observation, which echoes a familiar socialist lament, that 'all these things that are denounced as impossible in the cause of peaceful progress immediately become possible for the purposes of war'.[6] When Macmillan eventually came to the Treasury and then as Prime Minister, one economist-turned-detective recorded that officials used to count how many times he would refer to his inter-war constituency of Stockton and the level of unemployment it had suffered, and that there must be no repetition.[7] This was later to be portrayed as compassionate Conservatism, but since Macmillan's social snobbery was said to be marked even by the standards of the Tory elite of his generation,[8] his view of what he called 'ordinary people'[9] would not be much different from that he would have towards domesticated animals. Macmillan was not alone among British politicians in fearing the mass electorate and feeling the need to humour the beasts, though the fatalism that he displayed in the face of a supposed socialist future always was unjustified, and not only because of the deterrent value of the forbidding example of the Soviet Union. What, in criticism, J.K. Galbraith called *The Affluent Society* was bound to prove a more attractive destination than socialism. Once expectations were raised, the contemporary reality was that Britain did not have an economy capable of delivering the desired goods and services at the required pace. Macmillan knew this and privately likened contemporary British industrialists to a collection of grandfather clocks, and the most that could be done with them was wind some up and gently tap others as a form of encouragement. Nothing much would be achieved until the next generation came along.[10] With this outlook, the most that Macmillan could do was to gamble with the economy. This approach worked for a time.

On 10 January 1957, when Macmillan first met the monarch as Prime Minister he warned her 'half in joke, half in earnest, that I could not answer for the new Government lasting more than six weeks. She smilingly reminded me of this at an audience six years later'.[11] Kilmuir's memoirs testify to the low state of Tory morale in early 1957,[12] but there was no hard evidence that the Suez adventure had undermined the Conservatives in electoral terms. Those who thought otherwise would point to the Tory defeat at the Lewisham North by-election on 14 February 1957, which was the first instance of a Government losing a by-election since the Attlee Government's sole reverse of that kind at Glasgow Camlachie on 28 January 1948. The Conservative vote at Lewisham North, though, had been divided by the intervention of an Empire Loyalist, and, if there was a specific issue to explain the outcome, legislation to decontrol rents would seem the best bet. In any case, the net swing against the Tories was less than it had been at Tonbridge just before the Suez crisis broke.[13] Macmillan still retained Eden's comfortable majority in the House of Commons, and, with no need to hold another General Election until 1960, the Government could wait for the economy to turn up. Macmillan was shrewd in his Cabinet appointments. Butler was made Home Secretary, in which role he was unlikely to endear himself to Conservatives. Lloyd was retained as Foreign Secretary. Few writers can resist quoting *The Economist*, which pictured Lloyd returning to the Foreign Office 'down a long, cold arch of raised eyebrows'. Fewer went on to read that journal's concession that Lloyd's retention had 'the real advantage that the Cairo newspapers will not be set crowing'.[14] Macmillan felt that he could dispense with Head as Minister of Defence, bringing in the abrasive Duncan Sandys. Peter Thorneycroft was made Chancellor of the Exchequer. Kilmuir was retained as Lord Chancellor, and he noted that, of the 1950 Parliamentary intake, Iain Macleod, Reginald Maudling, Harold Watkinson, and Ernest Marples were all given prominent posts within the Government. Only five of Macmillan's Cabinet had been in the wartime Coalition Government, and only a similar number had been in Churchill's 1951 Cabinet.[15]

By keeping Lloyd as Foreign Secretary, Macmillan was making it clear that the Government would not be apologizing for the Suez adventure, which approach was correctly judged to be the one that most Tories favoured. Since he was not 'a very orthodox Tory', that it was Macmillan's intention 'to run the Government ... as a *centre* party' should have been obvious. In March 1957, Lord Salisbury resigned from his post as Lord President of the Council when Macmillan, seeking a solution to the problem of the future of Cyprus, brought Archbishop Makarios back from exile. As Salisbury had been widely portrayed as the 'kingmaker' when Macmillan had succeeded Eden, his departure suited the Prime Minister's interest.[16] In May 1957, Macmillan felt politically secure enough to announce that British ships would in future use the nationalized Suez Canal.[17] The Labour MP, Emrys Hughes, accused Macmillan of 'trying to gloss over the fact that this is the greatest and most spectacular retreat from Egypt since the time of Moses',[18] but it made no political difference. With Britain's first hydrogen bomb having been tested in the Pacific, Macmillan was able to move on, insisting that 'we are a great world power and we intend to remain so .... I am determined that this country should be and remain a nuclear power.'[19] The previous month had witnessed the Sandys White Paper on Defence, which had emphasized reliance on nuclear weapons and Armed Forces comprising only volunteers, meaning the prospective demise of conscription. The statement that 'the new defence plan set out in this [White] Paper involves the biggest change in military policy ever made in normal times'[20] ignored that represented by the introduction of peacetime conscription in the first place. Eden had 'long wished to bring National Service to an end,' and in 1955 his Government announced a reduction in the size of the Armed Forces from 800,000 to 700,000, later envisaging a further cut in numbers to 445,000 preferably by April 1960.[21] Two years after the end of the call-up at the end of 1960, the Sandys White Paper anticipated there being 375,000 in the Armed Forces on an all-regular basis.[22] Reducing the demands that defence spending and the diversion of resources presently made on the economy was an important motive for making these changes,[23] and an implication was that greater reliance on nuclear weapons would save money. Eden had been insistent that Britain 'should not become entirely dependent on the United States for supplies of atomic weapons, warheads or fissile material',[24] and in relation to the nuclear deterrent a further White Paper in 1958 anticipated that costs would not increase significantly in the next few years.[25] This confidence was misplaced, as the costs of research and development proved onerous, and by 1960 the crucial Blue Streak project had to be abandoned. So, Britain's independent nuclear deterrent came to depend on American provision. As for conventional defence, the suspicion that the decision to have an Army of 165,000 was related to the numbers likely to be recruited rather than the commitments to be met was borne out by the Berlin Crisis of 1961, when the Government had to retain existing conscripts beyond their term of service and envisage recalling those recently released.[26] The Sandys White Paper had contained the reservation that if voluntary recruiting failed to produce the numbers required, some limited form of compulsory service would be needed,[27] but, politically, once it was abolished, National Service was not going to return. Much of the later regret about the end of conscription tended to neglect the military necessity for its introduction in the first instance, and to concentrate on its virtues in relation to the inculcation of social discipline. It could not be in the interest of Conservatives to diminish that, but, in the eagerness to free-up money for the purposes of electoral bribery, not even some form of community service was introduced.

'I shall never be happy until our old time closeness has been restored', Eisenhower had written to Churchill in November 1956 about the relationship with Britain,[28] and when Macmillan became Prime Minister he was swiftly in contact, with Macmillan believing it 'better to be the pursued than the pursuing'.[29] It was on Eisenhower's initiative that the Bermuda Conference took place in March 1957,[30] and the President deemed the meeting the most valuable of its kind since the Second World War, though the record suggests that little in terms of specific policy was agreed.[31] The Washington Talks of October 1957 were of a similar character, though a Declaration of Common Purpose was made.[32] Amicable relations had been restored, and in March 1960, with Britain needing to replace Blue Streak, an agreement was made that Britain would receive the Skybolt weapons system from the Americans, subject to it being developed successfully, and there was also the prospect of the Polaris system, though not necessarily as part of a bilateral arrangement. In exchange, the Americans were promised Scottish port facilities for their submarines.[33] Earlier, in response to a further crisis over Berlin, Macmillan took the opportunity to play the honest broker between East and West, and, in February 1959, made the first ever visit to Moscow of a British Prime Minister in peacetime. When there, Macmillan's personal appearance was well described as being one of calculated eccentricity, including the wearing of a foot high white fur hat left over from 1940,[34] which behaviour encouraged suspicion that the visit was primarily designed to impress the British electorate. The Prime Minister's 'voyage of discovery' was more ambitious than that. For, on the principle that 'it's the first step that counts',[35] Macmillan hoped to establish sufficient trust between the Soviet leaders and those of the West for there eventually to be agreement on a ban on the atmospheric testing of nuclear weapons. Progress was slow, but Macmillan persisted with his 'honest broker' role all the way down to the Paris Summit of May 1960, which was wrecked by the Soviet reaction to the U2 incident. Prematurely on the test ban issue, the dismayed Macmillan privately concluded that Britain 'counted for nothing',[36] though he was to intervene to good effect in a meeting of the UN General Assembly the following September attended by many heads of government.[37]

Whether or not Lester Pearson of Canada had been correct in his belief that at one stage of the Suez crisis the Commonwealth had been 'on the verge of dissolution',[38] Macmillan deemed it politically expedient to be seen to rebuild relationships, and in early 1958 he became the first Prime Minister to undertake a tour of the Commonwealth, visiting India, Pakistan, Ceylon, New Zealand, and Australia. Even an accompanying hostile journalist and biographer was impressed by Macmillan and the manner in which he identified himself with the multi-racial Commonwealth, noting his remark that 'at home you always have to be a politician: when you're abroad you almost feel yourself a statesman'.[39] Macmillan certainly staked a claim to statesmanship when, at the end of a tour of Africa, he addressed the South African Parliament in February 1960 and declared that 'the most striking of all the impressions I have formed since I left London a month age is of the strength of ... African national consciousness .... The wind of change is blowing through this continent.'[40] Nobody took any notice when Macmillan had said in Accra that 'the wind of change is blowing right through Africa',[41] but to say much the same in the citadel of apartheid took political courage. On his tour, Macmillan had tended to receive advice from colonial administrators that the African colonies would not be properly ready for independence for 15 or 20 years, but that it would be best to give it to them now because the time that should ideally be given over to learning to run the countries concerned would in reality be taken up by rebellion and repression.[42] As for the risk of establishing what would soon be dictatorships, English history had witnessed Tudor tyranny in one century and military government and tyranny in the next before attaining constitutional rule.[43] Inevitably, Macmillan was accused, not least by Lord Hailsham, of promoting change in Africa with bloody consequences,[44] but independence had already been granted to Ghana in 1957, and it was to be given to Nigeria in 1960. Macmillan had once asked his Colonial Secretary for a profit and loss account of what each colony cost and what benefits Britain got out of it.[45] This was very much that attitude of why are we spending money in and on Accra that would be better spent in and on Accrington. Macmillan also thought that 'Africans are not the problem in Africa, it is the Europeans'.[46] When at the Colonial Office in 1942, Macmillan had suggested that the big white-owned farms in Kenya should be taken over by the Crown and run as state enterprises on the grounds that this would be less expensive than a civil war.[47] Nearly 20 years later, Macmillan reflected that 'if we have to give independence to Kenya, it may well prove another Congo. If we hold on, it will mean a long and cruel campaign – Mau Mau and all that.'[48] In the event, granting independence to Kenya in 1963 did not prove to be as troublesome as Macmillan feared, coming to be overshadowed, like the rest of colonial policy, by the problem of what to do about the Federation of Rhodesia and Nyasaland. This had been established in 1953 on what was perceived as a multi-racial basis, and the leaders of the black majority had come to want representation in relation to their numbers or the break-up of the Federation or both. The leading white politician there, Roy Welensky, believed that 'Macmillan's mind was the most complicated I have encountered in my political life',[49] and Macleod, when Colonial Secretary, was described by Lord Salisbury as 'too clever by half',[50] but the wily Whig pair could not devise a political settlement. That Monckton was at one stage placed at the head of a commission to find a solution was a sign of desperation, as was Sandys eventually being given ministerial responsibility with the same remit. With his usual brutality, Sandys told Welensky that 'we British have lost the will to govern',[51] and, although one present refined this remark as meaning 'by force',[52] it was obvious that the Conservative Government just wanted to be rid of the Empire in Africa, and, for that matter, elsewhere too.

Though Macmillan had 'European' credentials of a kind, by the time that he had become Prime Minister any hope that Britain had of shaping Western European economic arrangements to her liking had gone. The 'miraculous' Venice Conference of May 1956 had settled matters. The British Government had declined to attend, but the Foreign Ministers of what was to be the Six did so, and Pineau for France must have surprised the others present by stating at once that the French Government was in favour of the Spaak Report for a Common Market, provided that arrangements were made to include his country's colonies and overseas territories. Pierre Uri, who worked closely with Monnet, thought that had the British attended 'they would have got the same deal'.[53] The Treaty of Rome was signed on 25 March 1957 and the European Economic Community came into being on 1 January 1958. Meanwhile, the British Government had come up with Plan G, which was a compromise solution comprising a Free Trade Area in industrial goods only involving the Common Market countries and also Britain and the remainder of Western Europe.[54] Quite why the architects of the Treaty of Rome would want to accommodate Britain in this way at this stage was unclear, but Macmillan assigned Maudling to engage in lengthy negotiations,[55] which were brought to an end in November 1958 by the French Government, which simply stated that 'it is not possible to create a Free Trade Area as wished by the British – that is, with free trade between the Common Market and the rest of the OEEC but without the single external tariff barrier around the seventeen countries, and without harmonization in the economic and social spheres'.[56] The French Fourth Republic had only survived as long as it had through the political skills of such as Mollet and Schuman, but the Algerian crisis brought it down to be replaced by the Fifth Republic, with Charles de Gaulle returning to eventually become President under a Constitution said to be modelled on that of Britain in the hope of securing similar political stability. De Gaulle had previously opposed the Common Market because of the losses of national sovereignty involved, but with it being established he was prepared to live with it and exploit its arrangements in the interests of France. Macmillan was only recognizing the obvious when he wrote that 'de Gaulle is bidding for the hegemony of Europe,'[57] with Britain deliberately left on the outside as part of the Outer Seven, the European Free Trade Area, which also included Austria, Denmark, Norway, Portugal, Sweden, and Switzerland.

'It is really too bad that [Roy] Harrod should be so completely incompetent and irresponsible and put all these ideas in his head', Sir Robert

Hall wrote in March 1959 of Macmillan's economic policy preferences, though it did occur to this Treasury official that all Macmillan was doing was to 'manoeuvre us to where on our own arguments we need a lavish Budget'.[58] Macmillan eventually got fed up with Harrod[59] but that he lasted as long as he did was most likely explained by his economic advice commonly being that of ' a stalwart expansionist',[60] much like Percy Mills, who had been ennobled and served in the Cabinet in various roles. 'The PM ... is naturally expansionist and is egged on by Roy Harrod on theoretical grounds and Lord Mills out of ignorance', a Treasury insider complained.[61] When Mills argued that 'another 1929/32 is upon us', Macmillan was 'alarmed',[62] and not surprisingly so, since a Tory political imperative in the 1950s was to avoid a rerun of the 1930s literally at all costs. In this spirit, the most that the Government could hope to do was to issue warnings about worrying economic trends and hope that the trade unions especially would take notice. Thus, when a Council on Prices, Productivity and Incomes was established in the summer of 1957, a Treasury insider wrote that it could 'only be a piece of machinery and not a substitute for resolute action',[63] and, indeed, Macmillan described the role of The Three Wise Men arrangement as an exercise in 'restraint without tears'.[64] A sterling crisis had led to a Bank Rate being raised to 7 per cent in September 1957, its highest level since 1920, and Peter Thorneycroft as Chancellor of the Exchequer declared that 'the Government are determined to maintain the internal and external value of the pound .... There can be no remedy for inflation and the steadily rising prices which go with it which does not include, and indeed is not founded upon, a control of the money supply. So long as it is generally believed that the Government are prepared to see the necessary finance produced to match the upward spiral of costs, inflation will continue and prices will go up.'[65] A leading Treasury official observed that 'the words chosen ... were dangerous as far as economists were concerned',[66] meaning, as Harrod informed Macmillan, that they represented 'an antiquated doctrine' that was 'pre-Keynesian'.[67] The official blamed the economist Lionel Robbins for Thorneycroft getting it into his head that 'the supply of money was the cause of all the trouble',[68] and, when the Chancellor proved determined to limit future increases in public expenditure, the Permanent Secretary of the Treasury, Sir Roger Makins, thought that 'he was being egged on by [Nigel] Birch and [Enoch] Powell, [his junior Ministers] who ... are both rather mad'.[69] Whether this was the case or not, the bargaining within the Cabinet got the difference down to less than one per cent of current expenditure, and Thorneycroft's point was that if this sum of money was trivial, why could it not have been found somewhere else to 'keep us straight'.[70]

Thorneycroft's belief was that 'so long as it is generally believed that the Government are prepared to see the necessary finance produced to match the upward spiral of cost inflation will continue',[71] and he was reported to have privately questioned in Washington whether sound money should necessarily be subordinate to the maintenance of full employment as the prime objective of economic policy.[72] When the entire Treasury Ministerial team resigned in January 1958 rather than concede, Macmillan replied that he rejected 'the implication ... that the Cabinet could not accept the reductions in expenditure proposed because of their fear of ... the electorate'.[73] If Macmillan and the majority of the Cabinet were afraid of the voters in relation to the proposed cuts in Welfare State expenditure, they had good cause. The Ministers concerned ought to have been aware that family allowances were paid direct to mothers, and that disproportionate Conservative voting among females was an important electoral reality. Macmillan felt in a strong enough position to dismiss the resignations of the Treasury Ministers as 'these little local difficulties',[74] and with the compliant Derick Heathcoat Amory installed as Chancellor, he was prepared to gamble with inflation rather than against the 1945 veto. In the short term Macmillan was lucky, with a fall in import prices making for price stability in 1958, as Amory later stated, and with the cost of living benefiting from lower wage increases than had been common.[75] The Government scored an important victory in the London bus strike of 1958. The then Minister of Labour, Macleod, faced down Cousins and the TGWU, and of the meeting that marked the union's surrender, Macleod boasted that he had drawn the blinds of his office so that Cousins would not be seen on his knees.[76] The time was soon to come when it would be Governments that would be on their knees.

'Our policy can be simply stated: Prosperity and Peace'. So stated the Conservative manifesto for the 1959 Election.[77] Macmillan provided reminders of his interventions in foreign policy in a televised broadcast shared with President Eisenhower before the campaign started,[78] and in its final broadcast he reminded the electors of his trip to Moscow in the company of both a map and a globe.[79] The Prosperity theme was the more important, as Macmillan had been aware when he had declared at Bedford in July 1958 that 'most of our people have never had it so good'.[80] When a cartoonist portrayed Macmillan surrounded by consumer durables and saying 'Well, gentlemen, I think we all fought a good fight',[81] he was depicting the Conservatives' electoral strategy fairly. With the Bank Rate down to 4 per cent by November 1958, and credit restrictions removed, the Budget of 1959 was well described as very expansive, indeed the most invigorating since 1945.[82] With what proved to be the boom of 1958–60 well under way, the economy did not need stimulating. Nonetheless, urged on by Macmillan, Amory took 9d off the standard rate of income tax, and 2d off the cost of a pint of beer.[83] The Conservatives obtained 49.4 per cent of the votes cast in the 1959 Election, which gave them an overall majority of 100 seats. The Labour Party secured 43.8 per cent of the votes cast.[84] The 'official' chroniclers of the Election declared that 'the Labour Party has to decide whether it stands for a more efficient and humane administration of the existing Mixed Economy Welfare State, whether it stands for fundamental change, or whether it will continue on its ambiguous course.' The implication was that if the Labour Party did not discard its 'schizophrenic image', then it could not be seen as an alternative government,[85] and, soon, a book called *Must Labour Lose?* spelt out a similar message.

Immediately after the Election, the Gaitskellite MP, Douglas Jay, wrote that if the Labour Party did not change its ways the Tories could be in office for 40 years. Jay wanted changes made in the Labour Party's Constitution, including the commitment to nationalization, and he proposed amending its name to Labour and Radical or Labour and Reform.[86] Gaitskell had no wish to change the Party's name, but, possibly with the earlier behaviour of the West German SPD in mind, he had decided that at the 1959 Conference he would redefine what was meant by democratic socialism, which involved trying to get rid of Clause 4 of the Constitution, which committed the Party to universal nationalization. Gaitskell duly tried and failed,[87] as, indeed, he was bound to do having proceeded without the support of the trade union leaders. The Left scented blood, and, at the 1960 Conference, official Labour Party policy on defence became that of the Campaign for Nuclear Disarmament. Gaitskell vowed to 'fight, and fight and fight again to save the Party we love',[88] and the policy of unilateral nuclear disarmament was overthrown at the 1961 Conference.[89] The intensity of the Labour Party's anguish over losing the 1959 Election followed from the unfounded belief that it was winnable in the first place. The Party retained a substantial base: as Jay pointed out, it won 'over twelve million votes, nearly forty-four per cent of those cast'. Quite why Jay feared 'a long dogfight between Liberals and the Labour Party which could keep the Tories in power for forty years'[90] was unclear, because past Liberal revivals in the 1923 and 1929 Elections had damaged the Conservatives disproportionately, and this was true of the recent Rochdale and Torrington by-elections and the sole Liberal gain in 1959 was of previously Tory North Devon.

Jo Grimond, who had replaced Clement Davies as Liberal leader in 1956, favoured 'the creation of 'a new progressive movement' involving 'the radical side of politics – the Liberals and most of the Labour Party', without which he envisaged what he chose to call the Left being 'in Opposition for years'.[91] Grimond was supposed to have said of his own constituency that its main industry was subsidies,[92] and with him abandoning the discipline of economic liberalism, and, thus, any serious link between the Liberal Party and the world of ideas, the way was open for instrumentalism and the 'politics of protest' and proposing subsidies all round to meet local grievances, real and imagined. The longer the Conservatives were in office, the greater the accumulation of discontents, though whether they would be numerous enough to cause them to be defeated was unclear at the time. What was evident in 1959, except to the pundits, was that the 'Prosperity and Peace' winning formula owed much to special circumstances. As regards Peace, Macmillan was already concerned that the Anglo-American relationship depended too much on personal factors, meaning his friendship with Eisenhower.[93] The next President would be from another generation, and, although, in fact, there was to be personal friendship with Kennedy, it was of a different order, and seen to be such. Prosperity mattered more in electoral terms. The contemporary conventional wisdom was that Keynesianism gave the Government an overwhelming advantage in the timing of Elections, which view reflected the unquestioning faith many had in this form of national economic management. World economic conditions might well not be as favourable again, and, even if they were, it might well be harder to disguise the uncompetitiveness of the domestic economy, especially in relation to the consumerist expectations raised. That much could be worked out in 1959 and 1960, but what could not have been foreseen was the speed of the Government's decline in authority and that of Macmillan himself.

The decline and fall of the Macmillan government 1961–3

Since, as Ambassador to London, Joseph Kennedy had delighted in what he had seen as the prospect of Britain being defeated by Nazi Germany, it was not surprising that Macmillan was apprehensive about his son becoming the American President in 1961.[94] John Kennedy proved not to be amoral, but, inevitably, he was not the knight in shining armour that he was portrayed as being in what passed for contemporary political analysis and even scholarly works. Kennedy would not have been elected in the first place without the help of gangsters, or if his personal behaviour had been known, or if he had not lied about his health. Kennedy had a distinguished war record. So, he had displayed courage, but he still felt the need to pretend that he had written *Profiles in Courage*, and that he was a man of intellect, which fooled many people, especially intellectuals who needed to feel wanted. Kennedy's politics were those of appearance, and, thus, well suited to television. Indeed, as both Kennedy and his wife looked like film stars, as personalities they were almost too big for the small screen. In 1959, Macmillan had led the Conservatives to victory in the first British Election dominated by television, and his cultivated Edwardian image had not counted against him, but, once Kennedy had emerged on the scene, this cultivated persona soon lost its appeal. Macmillan wrote that he felt like 'an old horse, ready to be put out to grass'.[95] Butler thought that the feeling that 'the torch should pass to a new generation ... might not have made headway [in Britain] but for a persistent slump in the Government's popularity which began with the economic crisis of 1961',[96] though the Government came to be harmed too by scandals relating to national security, and by the failure of Britain's application to join the EEC. Familiarity bred excessive contempt for Macmillan's efforts at statesmanship. He had two triumphs to come.

When the Vienna Summit Meeting took place in June 1961, Kennedy and Khrushchev were present. There was no place for Britain and France. The President had been 'impressed and shocked' by Khrushchev,[97] though the record of the conversations gives no clue as to why this should be so.[98] Subsequent behaviour on the part of Khrushchev suggested that he concluded that Kennedy was weak. Thus, came the confrontations over Berlin,[99] and what came to be called the Cuban Missiles Crisis of October 1962. Britain's public exclusion from the resolution of this Crisis finally brought home to the electorate at large what most of the political class had come to see over Suez, which was that Britain's days as a Great Power were either numbered or over. Ironically, not only was Macmillan the first foreign leader to learn of the Crisis, but Kennedy consulted the British Ambassador in Washington, David Ormsby Gore, more closely than any other outsider during it. The decision to intercept the Soviet ships closer to Cuba than had been planned earlier, which, according to the conventional accounts, gave Khrushchev more time to climb down, was a Kennedy decision taken on the advice of Ormsby Gore. Kennedy said that he had come to 'trust David as I would my own Cabinet'. One of his associates described Macmillan as being 'a pretty tough guy' on issues like Cuba.[100] Macmillan observed early on that Kennedy 'may *never* get rid of Cuban rockets except for trading them for Turkish, Italian or other bases. Thus Khrushchev will have won his point'.[101] Kennedy could trade those bases anyway because the era of intercontinental missiles was at hand. The Soviet Union did not need Cuban missile bases. What it wanted was for Cuba to remain Communist, and, for all the talk of Khrushchev being faced down, what he got from Kennedy was a promise of no further invasion of Cuba. If the confrontation had been called the Cuban Crisis, it would be more easily seen that Khrushchev won the point that mattered most to him.

Shortly afterwards, Dean Acheson surfaced once more, declaring that 'Great Britain has lost an Empire and not yet found a role'. Being Head of a Commonwealth with no political structure, or unity, or economic strength was no substitute. Playing the military weak broker between East and West was no long-term substitute either. Acheson felt that Britain's future lay in Europe.[102] Macmillan felt required to reply publicly that 'in so far as he appeared to denigrate the resolution and will of Britain and the British people, Mr Acheson has fallen into an error which has been made by quite a lot of people in the last four hundred years, including Philip of Spain, Louis XIV, Napoleon, the Kaiser, and Hitler'. Macmillan privately thought that the anger that in Britain had greeted Acheson's remarks was not a good sign,[103] and it could also be said that the prevailing tone of political comment that greeted the Polaris deal in December 1962 was foolish. Macmillan persuaded Kennedy to cast aside the American preference for multilateralism, and to let Britain have Polaris missiles with the right to use them in a purely British emergency.[104] It was a masterly piece of negotiation, enabling Britain to have access to this level of advanced technology on the cheap, though, of course, Macmillan could not very well boast of his achievement at the time. Macmillan was to have another and final triumph with his long pursuit of a test ban treaty, though characteristically he told the bemused Americans that he chose Lord Hailsham to lead the British delegation because he might amuse Khrushchev. Robert Kennedy stressed that the President deliberately took the British view, which meant that of Macmillan, rather than that of his own advisers. On 5 August 1963, the Test Ban Treaty was signed by the Soviet Union, the USA, and Britain, and, as Hailsham observed, this was 'the last time that Britain appeared in international negotiations as a Great Power'.[105]

Acheson had misunderstood the extent of the influence Macmillan had with Kennedy, but not, as Macmillan at least publicly maintained, the value of 'the role of the Commonwealth in world affairs'.[106] Though unable to shed Southern Rhodesia in a politically acceptable way, the Macmillan Government continued to scale down the colonial empire, and, under Macmillan's leadership, it was remarkable how swiftly the balance of opinion in the Conservative Party changed in favour of the EEC as opposed to the modern Commonwealth. The Tory minority had no spokesman to match Gaitskell, of whom his widow said, 'Hugh was almost romantic about the cohesive potential of the Commonwealth'.[107] This was evident in his behaviour in relation to what became the Commonwealth Immigration Act of 1962, which Butler, as Home Secretary, described as 'one of the most bitterly fought Bills that I've ever known'.[108] One opinion survey showed 76 per cent support for the measure.[109] Such people had 'wrong and dangerous views', Gaitskell stated, being well aware that the Government was yielding to a clamour to 'keep them out'. Gaitskell declared that 'the test of a civilised country is how it behaves to all its citizens of different race, religion and colour. By that test this Bill fails, and that is fundamentally why we deplore it'.[110] This idealism was in marked contrast with the opposition to restrictions advanced by *The Economist*, which was, like slavery in the past, argued for on the basis of the need for cheap labour.[111] There was no need for an undifferentiated influx of labour because there was only an artificially induced shortage of that factor of production in what was now widely recognized to be a notoriously inefficient economy. Gaitskell was right when he described the legislation as having been pre-pared with 'indecent haste',[112] but only in the sense that what needed to be repealed was the Nationality Act itself, with rights to permanent residence and then citizenship having to be earned, including, of course, access to State social provision. Many immigrants would have little difficulty in showing that they represented value added to the British economy and society, which very much needed newcomers of ability and enterprise, as, for example, Jewish people had demonstrated in the past, and as West Indian nurses were doing at the time. Since even his official biographer recognized that a simple Open Door policy was impractical by this time,[113] Gaitskell's contribution to this debate was self-indulgent and irrelevant.

When Kennedy first met Macmillan, he was rumoured to have banged the table to emphasize the American commitment to Britain becoming a member of the EEC. If so, Kennedy was preaching to the converted, and, having few ideas of his own, the President was most likely only recycling State Department views, and, especially, those of George Ball, who took the Monnet line. Macmillan announced Britain's application to join the EEC on 31 July 1961,[114] later emphasizing as regards the political implications that 'the only practical concept would be a confederation, a commonwealth ... what General de Gaulle ... has called *Europe des patries'*.[115] Gaitskell gave the announcement a cool reception, noting the political ambitions of the EEC project without approval, and that, as Macmillan himself had once said, such integration did not command majority support in Britain.[116] So, it should have come as no surprise when, in October 1962, and with his usual emotionalism, Gaitskell denounced EEC membership: 'It does mean the end of Britain as an independent European state .... It means the end of a thousand years of history .... And it does mean the end of the Commonwealth.' This was because Britain could not 'continue to exist as the mother country' if it was 'a province of Europe' which was 'what federation means'.[117] Those Gaitskellites who wished to believe that their lost leader would have come to see reason on Europe chose to forget his tendency to act as if he had a monopoly of reason. Conservative opponents of entry could not match Gaitskell's conservatism, though their numbers made up for this. Privately, and ignoring the interests of the EFTA countries, Macmillan wrote that 'whether or not ... we shall reach agreement on the vital points of (a) the Commonwealth, (b) British agriculture, I cannot tell. I should judge that the chances are *against* an agreement, unless – on political grounds – de Gaulle changes his mind. For I feel that he is still hostile and jealous'.[118] It might be that Macmillan was using a diary entry to guard his back against future historians, because if this was what Macmillan actually thought, there seemed little point in proceeding with the application, not least because, as Gaitskell observed early on, what the Treaty of Rome allowed for was not negotiations of the kind that Macmillan and his Cabinet envisaged but adaptations.[119]

So, Edward Heath and his negotiating team had an unenviable task. Ball complained to Kennedy that Macmillan was trying to 'slide sideways into the Common Market', and seemed to think that 'a de Gaulle, Churchill, or Roosevelt might have revelled in the flamboyant gesture, the dramatic announcement that Britain had decided to join the Community without reservation, confident that it could work out the necessary adjustments once it was inside and leading the pack; that was the course of action that I urged on my British friends'.[120]

Since it was obvious that France was 'leading the pack', it was not surprising that Macmillan found Ball's interventions unhelpful.[121] 'Kipling's England is dead', Macmillan told de Gaulle,[122] but Macmillan was not under the illusion that a political case for British membership of the EEC would win over the House of Commons and the electorate whom he had to face, unlike Ball. 'Arguments couched solely in tradesman's terms do not lift men's hearts', Ball wrote,[123] but the Monnet ideal never did have sufficient British adherents to suggest that an appeal to economic self-interest amidst widespread apathy was anything other than the best strategy, always assuming that de Gaulle would not block British membership if the opportunity presented itself. That in some way the other members of the EEC would prevent this happening was one unfounded belief that those handling the British application adhered to,[124] and, indeed, the Governments concerned may have suspected that Macmillan was spinning out the negotiations to wear down his Tory opponents and to fit in with British electoral cycle. By the time that the issue came to be formally decided, de Gaulle had rid France of the Algerian problem, and his domestic political position had been greatly strengthened by the Gaullist victory in the November 1982 Election[125] and by the outcome of the referendum the previous month on the direct election of the President that effectively ensured de Gaulle of a second term of office. There proved to be no shortage of explanations about why the French President behaved as he did, even a collection of them,[126] but the balance of evidence would seem to suggest that the Nassau Agreement and the Trojan horse argument that went with it only provided the pretext for de Gaulle vetoing British membership in January 1963. De Gaulle was described by Macmillan to Kennedy as being 'absolutely crazy ... he wants to be the cock on a small dunghill instead of having two cocks on a larger one'.[127] De Gaulle only subscribed to the European ideal to the extent that it served French interests, not least economic ones. 'There will be no Common Market without a C[ommon] A[gricultural] P[olicy]', de Gaulle informed his Cabinet. 'France is only as European as she is agricultural.'[128] Since British membership might threaten France's political dominance of the 'dunghill' that was the EEC in its existing form, it was always difficult to see what advantage there was in it for de Gaulle, whose priorities were elsewhere, as was evident from the treaty with West Germany that soon followed Britain's rejection. Macmillan wrote that what this rejection meant for the Government was that 'all our policies at home and abroad are in ruins'.[129]

The British Government's application to join the EEC had come to be a crucial part of the programme of modernization that the Macmillan Government openly promoted from 1961 onwards. One act of 'modernization' with European overtones with which Macmillan was closely associated was to drive through, despite the opposition of the Treasury and obvious commercial objections, the treaty of 1962 with France that committed Britain to the development of the Concorde supersonic airliner as if the eventual cost did not matter.[130] Previously, in 1961, the Plowden Report on the Control of Public Expenditure had made proposals that, when implemented, pushed the traditional Treasury arrangements to one side in favour of such spending being planned on what was believed to be a systematic basis over a period of years in relation to prospective resources.[131] In principle, what could be presented as rational decision making in what was technically and primarily a task of allocation seemed superior to the amateurism of the Edward Bridges Treasury. In practice, especially in a Keynesian era, the overriding problem relating to public expenditure was to contain it, and projecting spending programmes into the future on the basis of predictions of economic growth rates that were almost bound to be optimistic was to build into the system a formula for inflation. That Macmillan employed Lord Plowden, a socialist, to do this work hardly helped, but it had been Macleod who had intervened in the drafting to insist on a positive line on public spending being taken. The Conservatives developed various plans for elaborating State social provision,[132] none more spectacular than the ten-year Hospital Plan devised by Enoch Powell,[133] whose appointment as Minister of Health in what was bound to be a heavy-spending department may well have amused Macmillan. The Hospital Plan was supposed to save money by rationalization of existing facilities, and Powell's support for policies of community care for previously detained mentally ill people had the same motivation.

That Lionel Robbins was an economic liberal in principle too did not prevent him from chairing a Committee of Higher Education whose Report in 1963 proposed the doubling of the numbers attending universities with the students concerned being given grants. Since it was argued that the system should expand to meet demand as defined by the numbers who obtained at least minimum entrance qualifications,[134] what was being made was an open-ended commitment as regards public spending. Only philistines would object to academic scholarship being advanced as well as safeguarded by an intellectual elite, but expansion of the order engaged in had to have another motivation and one more ambitious than knowledge that the professions were turning towards reliance on graduate recruitment. The prime motivation had to be the unsubstantiated belief that producing many more formally highly qualified young people than before would greatly benefit the economy, though no effort was made to favour vocational studies or numerate ones. The record of British private industry and commerce in international competition was so unimpressive that few doubted that management standards needed to be markedly improved, though quite what the connection was with an increase in the numbers of arts and social science graduates remained unclear. Since the predominant outlook in the universities was antipathetic to private business, it was unsurprising that the preferred destination for graduates remained the public sector. There was also much talk about giving more opportunities for the socially disadvantaged with talent, but the demographic reality was that there were more middle-class young people around than had been recently the case, and it should have been obvious that they would be the main beneficiaries of expansion.

Elsewhere, and in the public sector itself, the Macmillan Government engaged in essays in administrative change, including the reorganization of the Treasury in 1963[135] and the establishment of a unified Ministry of Defence completed the following year. Macmillan had found the brief period during which he had been Minister of Defence in the Churchill Government to be 'frustrating',[136] and he pushed the amalgamation of the Service Ministries through with the aid of Mountbatten.[137] The Macmillan Government also initiated a review of the staffing of the official external services that eventually resulted in a report in 1964 that was sensible in most respects for its time.[138] Further, this Government tried to bring order to the finances of the nationalized industries, adopting a crude rate of return formula as the guide. The need to separate out the economic activities of the public corporations from their social service commitments along the lines of the Herbert Report was recognized,[139] but the Macmillan Government must have known that the nationalized industries were essentially engines of employment with many employees effectively beneficiaries of the Welfare State. 'Fair wage' arguments had been wheeled out once more during the Guillebaud inquiry into railwaymen's pay in 1960, and what to do about the railways became part of the Government's attempts at modernization of the economy. The difficulty of the task was emphasized by the Tory defeat at the Orpington by-election in 1962 by the Liberals, who, of course, went along with the views of the railway travellers that they should be subsidized even more than they were already. The Beeching Report called *The Reshaping of British Railways* was published in 1963. Though derivative in important respects from earlier initiatives, and amateurish in its economic analysis, the Beeching Report contained a plan for rationalizing the railway system by getting rid of 40 per cent of its route mileage, and concentrating the system's operations on its more profitable activities, that could be presented as being radical, and, unrealistically, as holding out the prospect of the restoration of financial order.[140]

Whatever Heathcoat Amory's limitations as a Chancellor of the Exchequer, he knew when to leave, and Selwyn Lloyd's two years at the Treasury between the summers of 1960 and 1962 were to witness the Macmillan Government running into economic difficulties. Though the EEC was supposed to provide economic salvation in the long run, the more immediate problem was how to run the British domestic economy in a manner that made it grow as fast or faster than its main rivals, and without the current curse of relatively high inflation. Since in the financial year 1960–1 wages and salaries had increased by 8 per cent while productivity had gone up by only 3 per cent, it was not surprising that, by July 1961, the Government was looking for a 'pause' in the growth of personal incomes.[141] This Pay Pause was an informal incomes policy by which the Government hoped to use the public sector as an example that private employers would follow, which they did not. In the same speech, Lloyd had referred to the need for greater economic growth, and professed himself to be unafraid of the word planning, and, indeed, announced that he intended to discuss with both sides of industry the means of better coordinating such economic planning activity as existed.[142] The Cabinet proved to be divided over this initiative, with Macmillan recording 'a rather interesting and quite deep divergence of view between Ministers, really corresponding to whether they had old Whig, Liberal, *laissez-faire* traditions, or Tory opinions, Paternalists and not afraid of a little *dirigisme*'.[143] The Macmillan of *The Middle Way* was bound to win, and the National Economic Development Council or Neddy was established in March 1962. The trade unions participated in Neddy, but not in the accompanying National Incomes Commission or Nicky. The union leaders professed belief in a planned economy, but planning was not to extend to their activities. Neddy produced a document called *Conditions Favourable to Faster Growth*, few of which were likely to be met, and a National Plan of a kind called *Growth of the UK Economy down to 1966* published after the five year period concerned had already begun. The economic liberals had a field day: 'the choice of the figure 4 for the annual percentage increase in national product was ... surprising. It represented a rate of growth half as fast again as that which had occurred in the UK in the 1950s, and twice as fast as the average for the first half of this century. The injection of some new impulse, powerful enough to modify long-established trends, was clearly being presupposed. And the only conceivable new factor in the situation was the inauguration of the Plan itself.'[144] Of course, the economists of the detective novel genre saw things differently. The primacy given to defending the pound at its 1949 level was an easy target, though, of course, in order to hold back the demands made upon them, few Governments resist seeking a golden rule that can be appealed to as a form of discipline in much the same manner as the Gold Standard could once be referred to. The prevailing tone of the critique of Tory economic policy was summed up by the title of the book *Sunshades in October.* All would be well with a 'wider understanding of Keynesianism'.[145]

The Macmillan Government's popularity followed the economy down, and the Prime Minister dismissed seven members of the Cabinet in the Night of the Long Knives of 13 July 1962. 'The Government is breaking up', Macmillan told the startled Lord Chancellor, Kilmuir. 'You don't mind going?'[146] Of his own treatment, Charles Hill asked 'was it really necessary to give a departing Minister but four hours notice of his going?'[147] The Chancellor of the Exchequer, Selwyn Lloyd was the most prominent casualty. Lloyd had proved to be either unable or unwilling to deliver policies that met Macmillan's expansionist criteria.[148] 'For the second time the Prime Minister has got rid of a Chancellor of the Exchequer who tried to get expenditure under control', Nigel Birch wrote to *The Times*. 'Once is more than enough.'[149] Reginald Maudling was Lloyd's replacement. Edward Boyle went to what Macmillan still thought was called the Board of Education, and 'another clever young man – Sir Keith Joseph – [became Minister of] Housing and Local Government'.[150] When the reconstructed Cabinet met for the first time, Macmillan believed that 'there *was* a sense of freshness and interest'.[151] Macmillan's behaviour was not a demonstration of Prime Ministerial power as some chose to portray his behaviour.[152] Far from being 'unflappable', Macmillan had panicked in the face of adverse by-election results and opinion poll ratings. Butler considered that Macmillan had created 'one of the strongest young Cabinets of the century',[153] but it was one that left the Prime Minister 17 years older than the average age.[154] The conventional wisdom that, had his health permitted, Macmillan would have

led the Tories to inevitable defeat at the next Election need not be con-
curred with. Those who subscribed to this wisdom tended to argue that
the tide of opinion had been moving against the Conservatives ever
since the days of *Look Back in Anger*, and this led into a revival of political satire, inevitably directed against the Government of the day, some
of it in print in the magazine *Private Eye*, and some of it in the theatre,
and also on television, with the BBC pretending that its presentation
accorded with its commitment to public service broadcasting.
Ironically, the Tory promotion of policies of community care, though
well meant, explained the lack of difficulty in recruiting so many television 'personalities' then and later, together, of course, with the
financial rewards. How much influence the satirists had was unclear,
though it could be observed that in the past those people who visited
Bedlam to laugh at the inmates were unlikely to be seeking political
guidance from them. In addition, it was safe to assume that most electors would have never heard of the Angry Young Men or what passed
for their ideas, though they would have been aware that 'sexual inter-
course began in 1963', and, unlike the poet, many would have hoped
to benefit. The Tories as the supposed 'Party of the family' and of
'respectability' were always going to be in difficulties in the social
climate that was emerging, but the numbers of the excluded and the
disapproving were always going to be substantial.

  The Government rode out the Portland Spy Case and the Vassall Spy
Case, but the next 'scandal' proved more difficult. John Profumo, the
Secretary of State for War, lied to the House of Commons about his
involvement with a prostitute,[155] and, on being found out, he was
forced to resign. Harold Wilson, by this time Leader of the Opposition,
managed to keep a straight face when trying to maintain that his
concern in the matter was the threat to national security involved in
the fact that another of the prostitute's clients was a Soviet official.
'Gaitskell suits us pretty well' had been a shrewd assessment by
Macmillan of his now dead adversary,[156] and it was doubtful if
Gaitskell would have pressed the matter, not least because his own
relationship with Ian Fleming's wife was too well known in politics.
Wilson chose to make the most of the situation, as did what was commonly described as the Tory Press, until eventually Lord Denning's
Report[157] was accepted as showing that the more exotic rumours had
no substance. In this way, the Profumo Affair came to an end in
September 1963, having borne out Macaulay's maxim that there was
'no spectacle so ridiculous as the British public in one of its periodical
fits of morality'.

What, by then, the Conservatives had lost was political London, which largely determined the tone of political discourse. Since relatively few electors followed political matters closely, this did not mean that the next Election was necessarily lost, or that Macmillan, if his health had permitted him to continue, would necessarily have lost it, given that the size of the Government's majority meant that it would not have to face the electorate until the best moment to appeal to their economic self-interest. What there was a consensus about in British politics for thirty years after 1945 was the formula for winning Elections, and, having himself lost then at Stockton, Macmillan knew what it was. When Macmillan wrote of his 'never had it so good' speech that 'my chief purpose was to warn the people of the dangers of inflation',[158] it was only too clear what was meant to be remembered about what he had said. When Amory as Chancellor sought to act in the traditional Treasury manner, Macmillan told him that he was talking rot and thinking like Neville Chamberlain.[159] Gaitskell accused Macmillan of cheating at politics,[160] and much of Macmillan's political posturing almost invited the charge that he was a charlatan. Yet, there was no doubt that Macmillan believed in the Keynesian order and that his Governments aimed to run and develop it capably, and the Prime Minister's successes in defence and international relations meant that he had been a very successful Greek in the American Roman Empire. One observer chose to describe Macmillan as an English de Gaulle,[161] but Macmillan did not have similar importance for the political system to which he belonged and the comparison neglected the level of absurdity that was evident in so much of de Gaulle's personal as well as political behaviour. Even so, such was the political style that Macmillan had perfected that nobody could be sure whether or not he was serious at the time of his resignation in defining inverted snobbery in terms of the relative status of an Earl and a Viscount.[162] That, in October 1963, from his supposed death bed, Macmillan ensured that his successor as Prime Minister would be Lord Home proved to be one political joke too many.

Interlude: the Home government of 1963–4

Macleod and Powell refused to serve in the Government led by the man who soon had himself translated into Sir Alec Douglas Home, though Butler, said to be the focus of their loyalty, accepted the post of Foreign Secretary, which Home had previously filled without distinction since 1960. Lord Hailsham had become Quintin Hogg once more.

Though Macmillan had noticed before what he gently called the man's 'periodic lack of balance',[163] he had made Hailsham his first choice for the succession, only desisting when the candidate demonstrated that he was seriously unbalanced. Such became the need for Hogg to have a prominent Ministry that in April 1964 he was made Secretary of State for Education and Science with Boyle, the previous holder of the post, staying on in the department as the only Minister of State to serve in the Cabinet. Edward Heath was not only the President of the Board of Trade but also Secretary of State for Industry, Trade and Regional Development. To make his mark, Heath drove through the policy of abolishing resale price maintenance, making it evident that he would resign rather than give way to opponents in the Cabinet and in the Commons.[164] Legislation of this kind, Heath believed, would show the Government to be 'a dynamic, modernizing force',[165] but more obvious was his own anxiety to appear radical in a manner suggestive of economic liberal beliefs. In so doing, Heath acted as if *The Economist* had more votes than the small shopkeepers, showing scant regard for the electoral interests of the Conservative Party. The Chief Secretary to the Treasury, John Boyd-Carpenter, made the obvious point that the legislation was put through before the Election, but its provisions would not come into effect until afterwards, which meant that 'the harm done to the Party's electoral chances by the injury done to the retailers would not in any degree be offset by the gratitude of consumers and housewives for lower prices'.[166] This controversial legislation may well have been an important reason why the Tories failed to prosper politically as much as they could have expected from the Maudling economic boom, as Home himself later wondered,[167] probably with good cause.[168]

In terms of the politics of appearance, that Home looked on black and white television like living proof of Darwin's theory of evolution also may have been a serious disadvantage. Then again, even 20 years after the Butler Act of 1944, that Home was drawn from the social elite would not have mattered more than it had done in the case of Macmillan, if it had not been for what seemed to be a widespread perception that Home's abilities were of such a low order that he had become Prime Minister solely because of his membership of what Macleod called 'the magic circle'. Home came to blame Macleod's pointing this out as the main reason why he led the Tories to defeat in the October 1964 Election,[169] by which time it had became obvious even to Macmillan that Home had been over-promoted.[170] The Conservatives polled 1,748, 434 less votes in 1964 than they had done

in 1959, in part because the Liberals secured 1,454,307 more votes
than five years earlier. That the Labour Party polled 9,724 less votes
than in 1959[171] was not suggestive of an electoral upsurge in its favour.
Kilmuir wrote that 'You never had it so good' had been 'both true and
appropriate' in 1959, but the revival of idealism in politics in
subsequent years required the Conservatives to find 'a popular
non-materialistic policy', which it failed to do.[172] There were bound to
be a multiplicity of reasons why the Tories eventually lost office in
1964, but they politically prospered as long as the economy did like-
wise. The rejection of materialism by the broad mass of the electorate
in the name of idealism seems an unlikely explanation of the Tory
decline. The Conservatives had made a materialistic appeal and literally failed to come up with sufficient goods and services, with Labour
then outbidding them. Macmillan believed that his enforced
retirement had been 'a catastrophe for the Party', though the dramatic
use of language would have been better addressed to the long-run consequences of his choice of successor for his wing of the Party.
Macmillan came to see that Butler, as his successor, might well have
led the Tories to victory in 1964,[173] but only when it was too late.

9
The Wrong Revolution: The Wilson Labour Governments 1964–70

Paying the price of 'thirteen wasted years' of opposition

The slogan that the Labour Party eventually devised to describe the period of Conservative rule between 1951 and 1964 was that of 'thirteen wasted years'. The popular history of that era cuttingly observed that the slogan would have been a more accurate description of the Labour Party's record in Opposition during those years,[1] which was certainly the case in terms of serious policy preparation for office, and, on both sides of the 1948 divide, attempts to set out the relevant positions in terms of practical philosophy all failed dismally. That, in 1952, Bevan called his credo *In Place of Fear* raised expectations that he would tell how a democratic socialist system would be organized in obvious contrast with the brutal authoritarian regimes of the existing socialist countries. It turned out that Bevan had no coherent programme that would deliver Parliamentary socialism, and all that he succeeded in doing was to demonstrate that Bevanism had no distinctive intellectual content, which was why it was soon forgotten. When, in 1956, Strachey attempted to establish the principles of democratic socialism in his book *Contemporary Capitalism* his efforts were well described as a halfway house for those tired of the journey.[2] This did not stop Strachey from being dismissive of revisionists such as Anthony Crosland, who neglected 'the central importance of the ownership of the means of production' and the need for a socialist political economy that would mean that they would be bound to become little more than well-intentioned social reformers.[3] For those who thought like Strachey, *The Future of Socialism* was a strange title for Crosland to choose for a revisionist tract that argued that the creed had no prospects except as a form of social democracy, but, like Gaitskell, who had always defined socialism in terms of equality,[4] Crosland continued to think of himself as a socialist. Crosland proclaimed Marxism to be dead. Keynes was believed to have solved the economic problem. So, you could have both consumerism and redistributive taxation at one and the same time, and, hence, by means of public expenditure create what Crosland deemed to be a socially just society. The Fabian tradition represented by the Webbs was dismissed by Crosland with a flourish: 'total abstinence and a good filing system are not now the right signposts to the socialist Utopia'.[5] As Crosland seemed to believe that such a society would be better characterized by 'sex, gin and Bogart',[6] predictably he soon tired of earnest souls like Richard Titmuss,[7] whose rediscovery of substantial levels of poverty in British society was only to be expected since it was defined in terms of relative deprivation, which ensured that any likely level of social expenditure would be declared inadequate by what became the poverty lobby. Evan Durbin had never completed *The Economics of Democratic Socialism*, and Crosland acted as if he had done the job, but the end of the Butler boom in 1955 had undermined Crosland's thesis well before its publication in 1956. The maligned Webbs had always done the work, which was one reason for their past domination. Keynes's *General Theory* had been preceded by years of reworking of its ideas. Crosland had no taste for such activity, which meant that his revisionist bible remained unrevised either by him or anybody else, meaning that the politicians of the Right and Centre who were likely to fill the majority of the posts in a Labour Government had not engaged in the necessary rethinking of their position, a situation not improved by the belief being widely held that they had done this.

Gaitskell had sometimes wished that he led a political party and not a religious movement,[8] and presumably never more so than when he failed to persuade the Labour Party to abandon Clause 4 of its Constitution favouring blanket nationalization. Well before the next Conference in 1960, at which he felt the need to praise the achievements of Communist Yugoslavia,[9] Gaitskell had been forced to accept a statement of Labour's aims that included the conviction that the Party's social and economic objectives could only be achieved through 'an expansion of common ownership substantial enough to give the community power over the commanding heights of the economy'.[10] By 1960, even the loyalist Patrick Gordon Walker feared that Gaitskell had the 'seeds of self destruction in him',[11] but what Gaitskell was trying to do was to rationalize what the Labour Party stood for, with a view to improving its electoral appeal. His failure meant that the

Labour Party remained at least two parties, with the Left having successfully defended its ideological citadel.[12] Indeed, when Gaitskell died
in early 1963, a supposed man of the Left, Harold Wilson secured the
succession. The choice was described by Crosland as being between 'a
crook' – Wilson, and 'a drunk' – George Brown,[13] and the former won
because the candidacy of James Callaghan split the vote of the MPs of
the Centre and Right. In victory, Wilson toasted Bevan's memory,[14]
presumably much in the same spirit in which he assured the gullible
Cousins that he would pursue left wing policies in office.[15] 'Though
enormously intelligent, he is certainly not an intellectual', Crossman
wrote at the time of Wilson, in whom he detected the qualities of
Lloyd George, believing that what Wilson was aiming at was 'the
British equivalent of Kennedy's New Frontier, with a professional
politician at the centre, hard boiled, ruthless but with a basic inner
drive and integrity, and round him a galaxy of talented, able brilliant
men'.[16] The comparison with Kennedy was unconvincing, not least
because, as Crossman himself observed, Wilson was 'not young or
natural or liberated but is a tight, little, careful, calculating man'. It
never seemed to occur to Crossman that when 'I look into those grey
eyes and see nothing',[17] this was because there was nothing there in
terms of what he would consider to be a political philosophy. The only
sense in which Wilson could be considered to be in the same league as
Lloyd George was in his inability to conceal the scale of his personal
ambition, which led to a similar reputation for duplicity, indeed one
that matched that of 'Double Crossman'. If Wilson had a model for
political leadership it was that of Macmillan, whom he admired for
initially deceiving the Conservatives about his real opinions.[18]

Born into that unloved social category, the lower-middle class, the
Labour Party was all that was on offer to Wilson if he wanted a political
career. Wilson had learnt the ways of the Labour Party in much the same
manner that he had deliberately developed a form of political humour
some thought devastating.[19] There was cause to wonder especially in retrospect if Wilson was less of a socialist than Macmillan, and none at all
to consider that his name should be associated with technocratic Centre
Left thinking or that this informed his political behaviour.[20] Those who
later felt fooled by Wilson had only themselves to blame, since it was
always easy to see through Wilson's pose as the ordinary Huddersfield
Town football supporter who had just happened to have picked up an
Oxford First on the way that was supposed to enable him to run anything and everything. To go farther and say that Wilson was without
principles would be to forget his Christian beliefs, which would be one

explanation of the depth of his antipathy towards racialism.[21] Whether or not, by this stage, the Labour Party owed more to Nonconformity than to Marx, Wilson certainly did. Wilson acted as if the Methodist virtues had permeated the broad mass of public servants. Thus, he could advocate bureaucratic solutions to matters of public policy based upon the example of the wartime arrangements in which, as a temporary civil servant, he had taken part. Since finance was not going to be so readily available in peacetime conditions, the analogy was a poor one, but Wilson never lost his faith in administrative machinery or in the ability for it to be refashioned to perform the chosen tasks. So, Wilson may really have believed that the malfunctioning of the Keynesian Welfare State was the fault of Tory misrule.

By the time that Wilson came to deliver his once famous Scarborough Conference speech of 1963, after twelve years of Opposition the Labour Party was only too ready to acclaim him. The treating of socialism and progress in science and technology as being inextricably linked provided Wilson with a useful 'modernizing' theme; though, of course, the difficulties of a Labour Government as the agent of change was evident in the much misquoted phrase about 'the Britain that is going to be forged in the white heat of this revolution [which] will be no place for restrictive practices or for outdated methods on either side of industry'.[22] Since, according to Wilson, there was to be 'no room for Luddites in the Socialist Party',[23] quite how the one that he led was going to persist without the financial support of the trade unions was left unclear. The political commentators led the way in heaping praise on Wilson as a Leader of the Opposition, giving less weight than they should have done to the reality that in this role, unlike Gaitskell, he only faced Macmillan when he was past his prime, while Home was the opponent that Labour would have chosen themselves. Wilson once jokingly likened the Labour Party to an old stagecoach in that if you rattled along at great speed, everybody inside was either too exhilarated or too seasick to cause any trouble, but, if you stopped, everybody got out and argued about where to go next.[24] So, of course, Wilson's strategy in Opposition was to concentrate on keeping the stagecoach moving, with the only destination that mattered being office. At the October 1964 Election, the Labour Party produced a plethora of promises in its manifesto called *Let's Go with Labour for the New Britain*, to be rewarded with a House of Commons majority of 4. On the fair play principle, the Labour Government was always likely to secure an increased majority at the next Election held in March 1966. Following a net swing to the Government of 3.5 per cent,[25] Labour obtained 363 seats and 47.9 per cent of the votes cast, with the

Conservatives securing 253 seats from 41.9 per cent of the poll, and the Liberals winning 12 seats from 8.5 per cent of the votes.[26] On the face of it, a Labour majority of 97[27] should have ensured that the 1966 Election ranked as one of the great Conservative defeats in twentieth century British politics alongside those of 1906 and 1945, but it was to be commonly forgotten. This was because the Labour Government was doomed to failure already. *Time For Decision* had been the title of the Labour manifesto in 1966,[28] but the time for preparation had been the thirteen years of Opposition, and though the 1964 manifesto promised to cure the ills of the economy by socialist planning, and promised no fewer than six plans including a National Plan,[29] none of these existed. So, if, as in 1945, Shinwell had been sent to find such plans, he would once more have found the cupboard bare. Wilson had seemed to see the future development of the Labour Party in terms of the American Democratic Party as a form of 'natural party of government'. The analogy was a poor one because any political party remotely resembling the Labour Party of the 1960s had no place in American politics, which overwhelmingly tended to be conducted on what would be the Right of the British political spectrum. To Wilson, the debate about Clause 4 was a needless theological dispute. This was not so. As he was to find out, without explicit rejection, socialism remained *the* criterion, its attainment was still *the* test.

No better than using matchsticks: the breach of too many promises

'How much better it would have been if we had won in 1959', Douglas Jay wrote mournfully in retrospect about the Labour Government first formed in October 1964.[30] In 1959, the leading Labour figures had been Gaitskell, Bevan and Wilson in that order. By 1964, only Wilson was still alive. His main lieutenants were of lesser stature: George Brown and James Callaghan, who had competed with him for the leadership in 1963. As incoming Prime Minister, Wilson appointed Callaghan as Chancellor of the Exchequer, and thus placed in charge of the Treasury, and Brown was made First Secretary of State at the head of a newly established Department of Economic Affairs. Only Wilson had even been a senior Minister before, but, as Barbara Castle testified, this 'inner triumvirate' ran what passed for the Government's strategy in its early days. With Gordon Walker being initially appointed as Foreign Secretary, despite losing his seat, and with Michael Stewart at Education, Frank Soskice at the Home Office, and Lord Longford as Lord Privy Seal, there was, as Mrs Castle wrote, 'a clear right wing majority in the Cabinet'. Earlier, with Cousins, Crossman, Anthony Greenwood, and herself brought into the Cabinet, Mrs Castle had felt that 'the Left was on its way',[31] but her hopes were dashed, and she noted that Left was not represented in 'the key economic or overseas posts'. Castle recorded that Cousins 'put up a show of being pleased' with being placed in charge of the new Ministry of Technology. Cousins told her that 'he had turned down the Ministry of Labour: too patent a trick if he went there'.[32] Greenwood thought that being made Colonial Secretary was 'small beer'.[33] The appointment would be better described as a reward for not standing in the 1963 leadership contest, and so splitting the vote of the Left. Fred Lee was made Minister of Power. This was to reward him for being the only member of the then Shadow Cabinet besides himself to vote for Wilson in 1963. Even the supportive Mrs Castle thought that the 'flood of appointments' and the 'excess of junior posts' was 'embarrassing' and had 'the appearance of the spreading of rewards'.[34] Wilson was especially generous to the Gaitskellites. Roy Jenkins became Minister of Aviation with the promise soon realized of more to come. Crosland became Minister of State, and, thus, no. 2, to Brown at the DEA. Jenkins was relieved to escape working with Brown at such close range, describing him as having a 'brilliant but uncontrolled personality'.[35] Denis Healey was the only one of Jenkins's contemporaries to go straight into the Cabinet, in his case as Secretary of State for Defence.

Those who took seriously Wilson's slogan of 'modernization' starting with the machinery of government itself must have wondered why Wilson began with a Cabinet of 23 Ministers, despite having criticized Home for such behaviour,[36] and also why, after the 1966 victory, he then needed a Cabinet of 24, taking it down to 21 only in 1969.[37] The imperatives of party management would be a reply, if one that raised the obvious question of how 'modernization', whatever that meant in specific terms, could be brought about by a Government formed from a Labour Party whose incoherence as a coalition required that much attention. Since disarmament was a policy objective and one that was bound to involve the Foreign Office, appointing a Minister of Disarmament attracted Fabian scorn even before the event, though the observer concerned fell for the idea of having a Ministry of Production or Economic Planning, displacing the Board of Trade, which overrated Wilson's taste for rationalization, and of establishing too a Ministry of Research and Technology.[38] The DEA and the Ministry of Technology duly made their appearance. So did the Ministry of Overseas Development, where Mrs Castle was initially placed, although this was merely the previous Department of Technical Co-operation under another name. The new Ministry of Land and Natural Resources only survived and then in emasculated form until 1966. 'The very powerful Civil Service structure in the Ministry of Housing and Local Government was not going to let the responsibility for local authority planning decisions pass out of its control', Wilson recalled, and 'within days' it had won this particular battle, leaving him to reflect that 'I should have acted more firmly'.[39] As Minister of Housing, Crossman had watched with bemusement as the Permanent Secretary there, Dame Evelyn Sharp had fought to retain her administrative empire. Wilson should have reminded her that she was over the normal retirement age anyway, and, if she persisted, dismissed her. This was never likely. One interpretation of why Crossman had been made Minister of Housing was that the Shadow Minister, Michael Stewart had quarrelled with Dame Evelyn over policy, and that this ruled him out.[40] Wilson's preferred explanation was that 'I've made Dick Minister of Housing because he knows nothing about it, and so has no preconceived ideas'.[41] At the time, this manoeuvring tended to be portrayed as little less than political genius, with nobody asking what relationship appointing two unprepared Ministers had to Wilson's supposed belief in technocracy. Crossman had to be given a job because he was a troublemaker. Crossman had imagined himself being 'the head of [Wilson's] brains trust',[42] but Marcia Williams, his Personal and Private Secretary, and Thomas Balogh, the Oxford economist and character, very much in that order proved to be the Prime Minister's closest political intimates. Unlike Bevin, whom he believed had 'a chip on his shoulder when dealing with intellectuals',[43] Crossman wrote that Wilson was 'not afraid of my brutal brain power',[44] as if, having written about Plato, Crossman had delusions that he was in the same league. Bevin would have been likely to have regarded Crossman's reported tendency in Cabinet to engage in self indulgent intellectual pyrotechnics[45] as a sign of madness, and certainly of unsuitability for office at that level. Wilson had seemed determined to sweep aside those who claimed to have been 'born to rule', but the Cabinets that he led increasingly came to resemble an Oxford Senior Common Room in exile, and the parading of academic attainments was suggestive of needing to be seen as 'qualified to rule'. Though the absence of higher education, supposedly more than compensated for by a monopoly of 'common sense', did not ensure the ability to govern, the Prime Minister led the way in demonstrating that past success in the examination halls was not a guarantee.

'Cheeky chappie he may have been', Mrs Castle observed of Wilson, 'but he never seriously challenged the Establishment'.[46] According to Marcia Williams, 'The struggle with The System – or to be more precise, the [Higher] Civil Service – was lost from the start',[47] but then she wrongly believed that 'when Labour took office in 1964 its leaders had already formulated policies on every major question that they thought required action'.[48] It was the incoming Labour Government's own fault if, as a result of being under-prepared for office, it placed itself in a position of extreme dependence on the Higher Civil Service. A career Civil Service was always an unlikely adversary for a Labour Government that, at the outset, added the DEA, Mintech, the Ministry of Land and Natural Resources, plus a Land Commission, as well as the Welsh Office to the machinery of central administration, all of which had to be staffed with senior posts to be filled. Similarly, all the various commissions and committees of inquiry had to be staffed. Far from the Report of the Royal Commission on the Constitution providing an overview of these various investigations, that body was appointed late on in 1968 to head off Scottish nationalism. Far from representing a radical overhaul of British institutions, these investigations were piecemeal and they were too numerous for the talent available to do such work, leading to reports that were undistinguished, especially by Victorian standards. What to do about local government was a serious political question in principle, but in practice Wilson characteristically acted as if it was really a matter of getting the structure right, which meant that the Redcliffe-Maud Royal Commission that dealt only with England anyway had to take functions and financial arrangements as given.

For all Wilson's praise of the career Civil Service in Opposition, when he entered Downing Street he had brought with him Balogh, a bitter critic of the Treasury and of the Bridges administrative culture. Nicholas Kaldor was installed as Special Adviser to the Chancellor of the Exchequer, and Robert Neild also became an economic adviser in the Treasury, and Mrs Castle brought Dudley Seers into the ODM. Bringing in even a small number of outsiders in this way represented a vote of no confidence in the conventional peacetime arrangements, and if Wilson wanted to change the Civil Service some more he would have been aware that a revised version of the traditional Fabian reform programme had been recently published. All Wilson had to do was act, but the necessary level of confidence in dealing with an established institution was missing, and he chose to appoint the Fulton Committee instead to essentially repeat the list of preferred reforms, together with some contemporary management thinking. The subsequent establishment of the Civil Service Department in 1968 was presented as a radical reform, but what it did was to grant the Home Civil Service the status of being an interest in its own right.[49] Those who manufactured and sold nameplates may well have been the main beneficiaries of Wilson's taste for institutional change. Like his frequent Ministerial reshuffles, Wilson's behaviour in relation to administrative organization invited the criticism that it was designed to give the impression of activity to distract from failures elsewhere. Such a view underrated Wilson's Webbsian belief that the ideal machinery of government would cure all, and ignored the reality that, though the performance of the Labour Governments in the spheres of economic and social policy disappointed not only their supporters, their record on Home Office matters was as radical in important respects as that in defence and external affairs similarly tended to be conservative.

Churchill's view that Britain should not allow herself to be 'relegated to a tame and minor role in the world' had been cited by the Plowden Committee on Representational Services Overseas when it reported in early 1964,[50] and, consequently, the unified Diplomatic Service established the following year was not conceived on a modest scale. That the Duncan Committee was asked to go over the same ground only four years later 'in the light of the current need for the strictest economy'[51] was a measure not only of Wilson's taste for committees of inquiry but of perceptions of the pace of Britain's decline. The shedding of imperial responsibilities had meant that the Colonial Office could be merged with the Commonwealth Relations Office in 1966. The Plowden Committee had been unable to agree to the merger of that department with the Foreign Office, but sentiment about the importance of the Commonwealth had changed sufficiently by 1968 for a unified Foreign and Commonwealth Office to be established.[52] 'I do not regard joining the EEC as a problem', Gordon Walker wrote before briefly becoming Foreign Secretary. 'We cannot do so. In certain circumstances the EEC might break up ... we should not adapt our policies in order to save the EEC. We need not continue to insist that we should be in a political evolution of the EEC. It is better to go for the evolution of the Atlantic Alliance.' Gordon Walker's 'I do not like the Channel Tunnel' attitude spilled over into the belief that the need for British 'influence in and around the Indian Ocean' was 'more important than forces in Germany or ... for home defence'.[53] Michael Stewart, who was to be Foreign Secretary twice in Wilson's Governments, favoured EEC membership for economic reasons, and, in some way, to sustain Britain's global influence.[54] Another Foreign Secretary, George Brown, thought that what he continued to call the Common Market 'would give us an economic base big enough to stand up to anything that the Americans or the Russians can do industrially', and he questioned whether 'we could afford to stay outside it'.[55]

Since there was not the slightest possibility that de Gaulle would permit British membership of the EEC, the renewed application in 1967 following a tour of the relevant capitals by Wilson and Brown was doomed to failure from the outset. The Luxembourg Compromise extracted by de Gaulle had stopped the political development of the Community in its tracks, but the notion that, most importantly, West Germany at this stage would risk its relationship with France to serve Britain's purposes always was fanciful. Those who insisted on treating Wilson as some sort of lower-middle-class Machiavelli thought up various reasons why the Prime Minister risked yet another failure, with Heath, for instance, seeing Wilson's behaviour as being motivated by reasons of party management.[56] Probably more important was that Wilson knew that an application, even a failed one, would please the Americans. The inevitable George Ball had advised President Johnson that he should urge Wilson to 'sign the Treaty of Rome with no ifs and buts', and the President had made it clear to the Prime Minister that he favoured this.[57] An important motive too, given Wilson's obsession with what newspapers thought of him and his Governments, might well have been to appease Cecil King of *The Daily Mirror*, who had 'walking with destiny' views in favour of EEC entry.[58] When the initiative was made, though, King was easily persuaded that 'Wilson is in trouble in Rhodesia and in a mess at home and this is, in part, a gigantic red herring to distract attention.'[59]

The antagonism that the British Government's handling of the Rhodesian crisis caused within the Commonwealth served to emphasize that entity's limitations as a source of British influence in the world. In November 1965, the ruling white minority Government in Southern Rhodesia led by Ian Smith had unilaterally declared independence from British rule, and the Wilson Government then tried to bring this regime down. Economic sanctions rather than military action were the means sought to bring the rebels to heel. Wilson told a Commonwealth Prime Ministers' Conference in early 1966 that these sanctions would work 'within a matter of weeks rather than months'.[60] Since only Britain was likely to observe them, effectively the sanctions were on her own economy. The rebel Rhodesian regime had the invaluable support of the white supremacist South African Government to sustain it, and also that of Portugal's nearby colonies. Of the Six Principles that the Wilson Government was supposed to be observing the most important was 'No independence without black majority rule', though the talks with Smith held on HMS *Tiger* in December 1966 could only have proceeded on the assumption that this would be postponed well into the future. This did not stop Smith from turning the proposed settlement down.[61] Nothing was achieved following the talks between Wilson and Smith held on HMS *Fearless* in October 1968. 'There is a touch of Superman about him', Mrs Castle agreed with Callaghan about Wilson as the Prime Minister explained away the failure of the *Tiger* talks.[62] Marcia Williams, who was present, thought that Wilson and Smith had 'more in common with each other than they would probably have liked to admit',[63] but one obvious difference important at the time was that Smith had served with the RAF in the Second World War[64] whereas, as a biographer gently put it, Wilson's efforts to get into uniform in 1939 had been less than strenuous.[65] Wilson seemed to think that his academic record turned everyone else into an inferior,[66] but Smith seemed unimpressed by him, and the politics of appearance worked against Wilson to ensure that, as Mrs Williams remarked, Smith enjoyed 'very great popularity' in Britain.[67] Wilson was much criticized not least by New Commonwealth leaders for his unwillingness to use force to settle the Rhodesian crisis at the outset. Since the nearest British base was in distant Aden this would have been logistically difficult anyway, and as Healey later wrote, 'Southern Rhodesia had powerful Armed Forces and we had no reason to believe that they would not fight us if we attempted to intervene'. Healey thought that Wilson was right to doubt that he would retain political support at home if he waged a war against 'our kith and kin', and even the policy that was adopted aroused such dissent in British Armed Forces that the Defence Secretary had to issue a severe warning to the Chief of the General Staff about this.[68] In these circumstances, it was not surprising that the distasteful Smith got the better of his adversary. Wilson seemed to find compensation in the invasion of Anguilla in the West Indies in March 1969, supposedly to frustrate the island being taken over by American gangsters. 'This is our kind of invasion', wrote Crossman. 'We couldn't invade Rhodesia but we indulge in this sort of posturing'.[69] Another Minister, Richard Marsh recalled that 'Wilson in Cabinet spoke in terms suitable for the D-Day landing ... speaking of the "First Wave" which was only a few London bobbies.'[70]

One of George Brown's first acts when he became Foreign Secretary in 1966 was to replace 'a ridiculous portrait of ... George III ... with a picture of Palmerston'.[71] There was a case for keeping George III in place as a reminder of the limits of American friendship, though George Ball's hostile presence at meetings was possibly sufficient. 'Like so many other Prime Ministers, as his domestic worries increased, Wilson found that dabbling in foreign affairs was a distraction no less enjoyable for being futile', Healey wrote. 'His attempt to mediate in the Vietnam War infuriated [President] Johnson without achieving anything constructive.'[72] As Britain and the Soviet Union had been co-Chairmen at the Geneva Conference on Indo-China of 1954 they had a prospective role in bringing peace to Vietnam. Wilson visited Alexei Kosygin in Moscow in February 1966, and recorded that 'on Vietnam we got nowhere'.[73] A peace initiative resulted from Kosygin's visit to London in February 1967. Whether this represented 'the biggest diplomatic coup of this century', as Wilson thought, could be doubted, though Wilson believed that the Americans had undermined his efforts, thus ensuring that 'a historic opportunity had been missed'.[74] Johnson was dismissive: 'During the many years we spent looking for a peace formula, I learned that everyone who engaged in such efforts came to think that his own particular approach was the one that would, or should, succeed ... . If only we would follow their plan – and as time passed that usually meant giving Hanoi more and more – peace could be achieved ... they did not realize that the proposals they advocated so strongly had already been tried and had been rejected by Hanoi.'[75] On a visit to Washington in December 1965, Wilson expressed 'continued understanding and support for the US position in South-East Asia', though he had made it clear that 'any bombing of Hanoi or Haiphong would create most serious problems for him and his Government'.[76] Of course, the problems would be with the Left of the Labour Party. 'Harold's answer to our restlessness was to launch a succession of "peace initiatives" in Moscow, Hanoi, the Commonwealth and anywhere else where they might seem plausible', Mrs Castle wrote, and she thought that the idea of despatching Harold Davies, a minor Labour figure, to Hanoi on a secret mission in July 1965 was typical of these efforts.[77] When the mission failed to take place, Wilson seemed untroubled, being 'well satisfied with the gesture'.[78]

When the Wilson Government first came to office, it acted towards the Americans as if nothing had changed since 1951, but even the Kennedy-Macmillan form of relationship was not on offer from Johnson. The most that he could muster for Britain was general sentiment: 'it may be an itty bitty place, but that is where mother came from'.[79] Since, unlike Australia and New Zealand, Wilson refused to agree to even a nominal British military presence in support of the Americans in Vietnam, it was not surprising that Washington tended to be dismissive of his diplomatic activities. Of course, Wilson knew that any form of British intervention in Vietnam beyond seeking peace at any price would have outraged the Left, and the facts of the matter were that Britain no longer had a conscript Army and she was heavily committed elsewhere, notably in a confrontation with Indonesia which represented an important contribution to protecting Western interests in South-East Asia. Unimpressed by Wilson's behaviour, Secretary of State, Dean Rusk, raged: 'All we needed was one regiment. The Black Watch would have done ... but you wouldn't. Well don't expect us to save you again. They can invade Sussex, and we wouldn't do a damned thing about it.'[80] Since Britain was the only reliable ally the Americans had in the European theatre, this was bluster. Wilson was to be upset by BBC accusations about his 'overt importuning' of the White House when Richard Nixon became the incumbent.[81] Wilson thought that he had established a good relationship with Nixon,[82] but Henry Kissinger's assessment was that Nixon disliked him, while recognizing that he was a reliable supporter of the Alliance.[83]

Since Wilson's Ministerial reshuffles were sufficiently frequent to seem random in character, it was to be expected that few Cabinet Ministers retained the same role throughout the period of government, and only Wilson himself, Lord Gardiner, the Lord Chancellor, and Healey as Secretary of State for Defence did so. 'I was fortunate in taking office at a time when overdue changes in the planning and organization of defence were already under way', Healey wrote. ' However, my predecessors had failed to make use of these new tools to bring our commitments into line with what we could afford to spend. Their continuing failure to take necessary decisions had left our forces overstretched, underequipped, and underpaid. Every important decision I took to remedy this situation was bitterly opposed by the Conservatives in Opposition. None of them was reversed when they finally took office themselves. It would have been quite possible in 1970 for them to order a new aircraft carrier, to increase the number of Polaris submarines to five, as planned by Macmillan, to build up our forces in the Gulf and Singapore, and to restore the Territorial Army in its original form. Despite their statements in Opposition, they chose to do none of these things. On the contrary, Lord Carrington paid a generous tribute to my work when he succeeded me.'[84] Healey's own side tended to be less admiring. 'Denis is not a very successful speaker either in Cabinet or in

the House', Crossman wrote on 12 January 1968. 'He plays the role of
the young McNamara – the man who is briefed on all the top level
secrets and who can mock and deride any ideas put forward by his
amateur colleagues. The supercilious sneering expert is always in danger
in a British Cabinet but Denis has a further difficulty. After all, he had
already presented us with no less than four successive defence reviews
and he had defended each as it came out with new facts, new figures,
new statistical demonstrations. Moreover I remembered that he had
sold the F-111 to us as an aeroplane essential for defence East of Suez
which would in fact be based East of Suez and not used in Europe. Now
he was defending it as essential to European defence. I got the impression that he could defend it just as brilliantly as essential to Southern
Irish defence.' Healey got the better of Wilson in subsequent exchanges,
but, according to Crossman, he was 'no match' for the then Chancellor
of the Exchequer, Jenkins.[85] The Lord Privy Seal, Lord Longford, stated
that Healey had told him that Britain would be virtually naked without
the F-111.[86] Though Healey presumably believed this, he did not resign
as Longford did over cuts in education expenditure.

Healey was as reluctant as his Prime Minister to give up the idea of
Britain's world role. As a contemporary British General with NATO
observed, 'Healey's basic misunderstanding of defence policy from the
mid 1960s to mid 1970s stemmed directly from his excessive interest
in the Indo-Pacific area.'[87] Healey had to take seriously the threat
to Malaysia, and more specifically, North Borneo, represented by
Indonesian intervention from April 1963 onwards initiated by
President Ahmed Soekarno, a dictator posing as the champion of the
underdog in South-East Asia. With the aid of the UN, Soekarno had
forced the Dutch to withdraw from West Irian, but the British had
been successful in the recent Malayan Emergency, and, though the
Americans refused to take any notice of this example in Vietnam, the
British had learnt the lessons. Confronting Indonesia pleased Australia,
New Zealand, and even the Americans, who had previously foolishly
aided Soekarno, and by August 1966 the insurgents had been defeated
by a military campaign waged by the British with admirable profes-
sionalism.[88] Healey had inherited the political responsibility for the
Confrontation, and got some of the credit for seeing it through. He
received and deserved no credit at all for his handling of another
inherited conflict in Southern Arabia. Healey well described Aden itself
as a 'concrete furnace',[89] and remarked on 'the noise and stench of
Aden's crowded slums'.[90] That Aden was a replica of Hell was well
known to the British Forces stationed there, who might well have been

intrigued to see it later described as a valuable piece of real estate on the basis of it possessing the world's second busiest oil bunkering port. As for the military threat, by mid-1965 Nasser was displaying his usual ineptitude in the campaign that was being conducted in the Yemen.

In early 1966, the Labour Government announced that Britain would be leaving Aden in 1968, which behaviour increased British casualties. As one observer commented, a Marxist regime took over, the prosperity of Aden declined rapidly, and Soviet warships replaced British ones off Steamer Point.[91] The British Government acted as if it had come to the conclusion that it could no longer afford to behave honourably in Aden, which in the contemporary economic circumstances was the case. The last Governor of Aden, Sir Humphrey Trevelyan, chose to pretend that Britain 'left without glory but without disaster', a view that Healey lamely chose to endorse.[92] In the last Defence White Paper for which Healey had responsibility in 1970, it was stated that 'Britain's military role has been transformed over the last five years by the historic decision to withdraw our forces from their bases East of Suez and to concentrate them in Europe. While our military commitments are being reduced in this way, the nation is getting better value for the money it spends on defence; thus, despite the reduction in expenditure imposed by our economic needs, we have been able to increase our contribution to the defence of Europe ... and simultaneously reduce the overstretch from which our forces have suffered in the past.'[93] The theme of bringing commitments into line with resources and to reduce the burden of defence on public expenditure had been continuous, if obvious, features of the four earlier White Papers, thus giving an appearance of consistency. The cancellation of the TSR2 aircraft project had been a dramatic early action on the part of the Government, though this had been the responsibility of Jenkins as Minister of Aviation rather than Healey, and such were the continuing economic difficulties that the Government faced that, as we have noted, the F-111, its replacement, had later to be cancelled too. Moreover, and similarly, the concentration of the British defence effort on Western Europe had been forced on the Labour Government by economic circumstances rather than by choice.

Barely credibly, Wilson had spoken of Britain's frontiers being on the Himalayas,[94] and the Defence Review in 1966 set out the need for a continuing British presence East of Suez.[95] That Review also announced that a new aircraft carrier would not be built.[96] This led the Minister of the Navy, Christopher Mayhew, to resign. Mayhew was opposed to Britain remaining East of Suez, but argued that, if she did, then the new carrier was essential. Mayhew also argued that the figure of £2,000 million at 1964 prices to cover defence expenditure was 'purely artificial', being 'too small if we wish to stay east of Suez and much too big if we do not'.[97] The further decline of the British economy compelled the Wilson government to withdraw from East of Suez. Unlike Crossman, Healey had not conducted himself as if a First in Greats meant that he could simply pick up any subject, however complex. Healey had military experience himself and he prepared himself for office in the sphere of defence in a professional manner. Though in the climate of economic policy failure of the time, Healey's record at the Ministry of Defence was inevitably mixed, he was possibly the only one of Wilson's Cabinet Ministers, aside from Jenkins, who was able enough to rank with some of the best of 1945–51. Arrogance was one reason why Healey's ability did not work more to the benefit of his career, as well as the suspicion on his own side that this former Communist was little different in important respects from a competent Conservative; hence, Carrington's praise for him.

In the politically crucial area of economic policy, in which sphere Wilson had claimed such expertise, the conventional wisdom came to be that his Government was doomed from its first weekend. Wilson made much at the time and later about the balance of payments deficit that his Government inherited from the Tories. This deficit was not a secret and neither was Wilson's recognition that a Labour Government engendered substantially less confidence with international bankers than the Conservatives did or would have done.[98] So, where were the contingency plans? Even the obvious question of what to do about devaluing the pound did not seem to have been addressed beforehand, and Jay recorded that Brown and Callaghan made light of the illegality of the temporary import surcharge that was imposed.[99] Of the Wilson Governments, some sympathetic economists were later to write that 'there seems little doubt that the initial decision not to devalue when they took office in October 1964 was almost entirely political and was dictated by the narrowness of the majority. In such conditions the possibility of being forced into an early Election was considerable and the judgment of the party leaders was that if the Labour Party were to go the electorate after having devalued almost immediately it had taken office ... it would certainly be defeated ... . Having made this decision, it was necessary to minimize the threat to the pound by increasingly categorical assertions that the pound would never be devalued, and even on the charitable assumption that these assertions were intended primarily for overseas consumption they had the effect of making the leaders of the Party feel publicly committed never to devalue the pound ... the real mystery is why the pound was not devalued after Labour won the ... 1966 Election with an overwhelming majority.'[100] When devaluation was forced upon the Government in November 1967, Callaghan as Chancellor of the Exchequer, recalled that 'when I had been in office for one month I was approached by a very senior monetary authority in Europe ... . He said that he believed that we ought to devalue by between 10 and 15 per cent.'[101] With those in international financial circles having such views, devaluation was a certainty, the only question remaining being when it would take place. The sterling crisis brought on by the Seamen's Strike in July 1966 presented an opportunity to devalue. Wilson and a majority of the Cabinet preferred deflation, involving a prices and incomes policy. The other Cabinet Ministers put the case for floating the pound, but they were overruled.[102]

To suggest that the division of authority between the Treasury and the Department of Economic Affairs was an important reason for the Labour Governments' abject economic policy record would be to slide into Wilson's obsession with administrative machinery, as if a new Ministry or three would work an economic miracle. 'The story of the DEA is the record of a social revolution that failed', Brown later wrote, 'It envisaged a wholly novel form of national social accountancy to replace the orthodox financial accountancy by which the Treasury has always dominated British life.'[103] This was a characteristic exaggeration. The DEA was charged with responsibility for long term economic policy, primarily meaning the National Plan, which made its appearance in September 1965 and its disappearance with the July Measures of 1966. In the latter instance, Brown stated that 'he was for growth; we had fallen back into the old Treasury position of past years'.[104] The Labour Government never left this position in the first place. That was what 'sterling first' was bound to mean. As it was in charge of short term economic policy, the Treasury was always likely to score over the DEA not least because politics was commonly played out in the short term,[105] especially by Wilson. As the Treasury had been recently reshaped anyway, an obvious course of action would have been to give these arrangements a chance to work rather than introducing new ones that Wilson later conceded were flawed anyway. 'The Treasury is too fine a machine; I want to put some sand in it', Wilson had said. 'If you put sand in an oyster it produces a pearl.' This earned the reply: 'But you know what usually happens if you put sand into a fine machine.'[106] It was a legend that the DEA experiment had been dreamt up by Wilson and Brown during a brief taxi ride.[107] Balogh had been given that task by Wilson earlier,[108] with the duplication that had resulted from arrangements in the early years of the Attlee Government involving Morrison and Cripps representing a warning. Jay thought that Wilson knew well enough the arguments against creating an institution like the DEA, but he had promised it to Brown, describing this behaviour as 'a prime example of creating bad organization in order to appease personalities – a classic recipe for trouble'.[109] Brown was going to make 'trouble' for Wilson anyway, and Wilson may well have thought that establishing and running a new organization in competition with the most powerful department in Whitehall would keep him busy, as, indeed, would work on the National Plan. For a time, the conventional wisdom among commentators was that the conduct of economic policy benefited from 'creative tension' between the Treasury and the DEA, with the Prime Minister really running things, arbitrating effortlessly between Callaghan and Brown as only he could, given that he was the only one of them with the slightest knowledge of economics. This knowledge on Wilson's part had been much paraded, but it eventually occurred even to the commentators that the results were no better than when the Tory Government had been led by a man in Home who only understood economics through the use of matchsticks.[110] 'I have begun in disgrace' was Callaghan's fear at the outset of his time as Chancellor of the Exchequer. Even a sympathetic biographer chose the chapter headings of 'Baptism of Fire' and 'Blown Off Course' and 'Devaluation and Departure' when telling the story of Callaghan's record at the Treasury.[111] Callaghan saw himself as having been a tax reformer, though the Selective Employment Tax was unsuccessful.[112] Callaghan had introduced that measure in his May 1966 Budget on the advice of Kaldor,[113] who, according to Mrs Castle, had 'a propensity for getting Governments overthrown'.[114] What SET represented was the Labour belief that only manufacturing activity represented good, honest toil. It was a tax on employment that was intended to squeeze labour out of service industries into manufacturing with a rebate going to employers in the latter sector.[115] Whatever was wrong with British manufacturing, it was not that it suffered from a general labour shortage. Indeed, by comparison with its international competitors, it tended to utilize what labour it had poorly, partly because of union restrictive practices. As for the DEA, despite Wilson himself taking direct responsibility for it for a time, it was abolished in 1969.[116]

'When I joined the Ministry [of Technology] it seemed to me that very little detailed thought had gone into this extraordinary venture',

Richard Marsh later wrote. The Ministry had a remit 'to guide and stimulate a major national effort to bring advanced technology and new processes into British industry ... . Frank Cousins used to tell the story of how when he first met the new Permanent Secretary, with his equally new Private Secretary and Parliamentary Secretary, he opened by asking, "Well, what are we supposed to be doing?" only to realize that they had come to hear him tell them just that.'[117] Much like Bevin before him, Cousins found coming into the House of Commons in later life to be a handicap, and in his case he had neither the wartime moderation of party hostilities nor the support of an established department to help him, and the Opposition gave him a hard time.[118] The quest for another Bevin was doomed to failure, and Cousins was all that the contemporary Labour Movement could come up with. Crossman described Cousins in Cabinet as 'usually saying the obvious thing, but he does say it in a working class way' which was 'important' because 'nobody else' did 'in this Cabinet ... . What kind of a new Ministry he is building I have no idea. All I know is that he occupying more and more floors and getting tremendous backing from Wilson, who believes passionately that his new Ministry of Technology has got to succeed if he is going to keep his promise to modernize British industry.'[119] It may well be that Wilson really believed that the performance of British private industry could be transformed in the couple of Parliaments likely to be made available to his Government by the means of a Ministry modelled on the National Development Corporation of the 1940s.[120] Otherwise, Cousins had been knowingly given an impossible job, discrediting himself in the process, and sharing the responsibility for Cabinet policies that, if outside, he would have denounced until the time came that he could tolerate no more of this. Cousins finally resigned on 3 July 1966 over prices and incomes policy,[121] but his authority in the Labour Movement was never the same again.

The successor to Cousins was a politician then known as Anthony Wedgwood Benn. Previously he had been Postmaster General, in which role he believed he had 'opened up ... enormous change in the organization of the Post Office, which is fifty years overdue'.[122] Whereas Cousins could 'talk to leaders of industry in their language', as one of them remarked,[123] Benn had no such experience and, to judge from his own account of his activities, he had little idea of how to run what eventually was supposed to be a super Ministry.[124] 'The Ministry of Technology started off on too small a scale', Patrick Blackett, Cousins's leading adviser there, later wrote. 'We should have started by being bigger and with more of the older departments drawn in. It ought to have been a Ministry of Industry from the start.'[125] A senior official at Mintech described the merger with the Ministry of Aviation in February 1967 as converting the Ministry of Technology, or first Mintech, into a Ministry of Engineering, or second Mintech. In October 1969, Mintech absorbed the whole of the Ministry of Power and many of the responsibilities of the Board of Trade and of the DEA, including the Industrial Reorganization Corporation, and, thus, at last, it became a Ministry of Industry, or third Mintech.[126] Since, presumably because of its administrative culture, Wilson seemed determined not to attempt to translate the Board of Trade into a Ministry of Industry, he and advocates of a Ministry of this kind, such as Blackett, could have worked out before coming into office that an organization much like the 1969 structure would be necessary, and that if an institution such as the Industrial Reorganization Corporation was needed then Mintech was its obvious location from the outset. Mintech proved best at reorganizing itself, no less than three times, and both it and the IRC seemed to show no particular ability to 'pick out the winners' from private industry to support, and, as would be expected in a political climate geared up to job preservation, much of their activity was directed at 'picking up the losers' and creating future losers like British Leyland and Upper Clyde Shipbuilders. It was the Treasury that provided the thinking behind the attempt made in 1967 to bring the finances of the nationalized industries under control with a regime that included rules like marginal cost pricing that looked good in economic text books but which were commonly going to be overridden by political considerations.[127]

When the Donovan Report on Trade Unions and Employers' Organizations was published in June 1968, *The Economist* described it as 'A Report to Forget'.[128] The Donovan Report might well have been shelved if Wilson had not decided to outflank the Tories on the reform of industrial relations,[129] and to assign the task to Mrs Castle. At the Ministry of Transport, Mrs Castle had attracted such publicity in return for minimal achievement that, in a context in which the Government was widely perceived as struggling, what had to be desperation had led to some talk in the political class of her becoming the first female Prime Minister. 'You are to put the life into the Wilson Cabinet Mark 2', the Prime Minister had told Mrs Castle,[130] before persuading her to move to becoming First Secretary of State in charge of the Department of Employment and Productivity. Both Wilson[131] and Mrs Castle claimed credit for thinking up this new name for the

Ministry of Labour. Even then, Mrs Castle feared that Ray Gunter's old job plus responsibility for prices and incomes policy 'didn't seem to add up to enough'.[132] It added up to more than enough conflict with the trade unions and their leaders than an actual or supposed rival to the Prime Minister could normally handle without being politically damaged. 'I don't intend to be Maggie Bondfield Mark II', Mrs Castle needlessly told Wilson,[133] who, surprisingly, did not see the risks to himself and his Government of letting loose a political obsessive with self-destructive tendencies in an area of public policy crucial to the Labour Movement. Mrs Castle wrongly believed that the Donovan Report's thinking had been heavily influenced by the then General Secretary of the TUC, writing that it had 'George Woodcock's finger-prints all over it'.[134] Whereas George Brown retained sufficient origi-nality for some to believe that he possessed 'the finest untrained mind' in politics, the effects of Oxford on his fellow prole Woodcock had been to leave him a master of negativity. Mrs Castle described Woodcock's line as being that 'it was no good trying to have sanctions against unofficial strikers because they wouldn't work', though 'admit-tedly the voluntary policy wouldn't work either, but that was life!' Mrs Castle concluded: 'I couldn't see any revolutionary changes being carried through unless the Government is prepared to impose them on an unwilling TUC.'[135] Jack Jones, the General Secretary of the TGWU, believed that Mrs Castle was 'anxious to do things *for* the workers but not *with* them',[136] and asked her, 'Why don't you stick with Donovan?' She replied that she did not agree with all the Report's propositions, and asked Jones: 'Do you really want the pro-tection of Section 3 of the 1906 Act withdrawing from unregistered trade unions?' Jones said 'of course not', and Mrs Castle concluded that 'if the rebel can amend the Bible, why can't the Government?'[137] That, of course, depended on relative political power.

Mrs Castle produced a White Paper called *In Place of Strife* in January 1969 with an Industrial Relations Bill to follow. Mrs Castle recognized that she was 'taking a terrific gamble and there is absolutely no cer-tainty that it will pay off'.[138] She had rejected Woodcock's fatalism, but his attitude was realistic in contemporary circumstances. About 95 per cent of strikes were unofficial, meaning that they were not sanctioned nor ratified by the union or unions concerned, or unconstitutional, meaning that they took place in breach of the appropriate procedure for dealing with disputes.[139] That there was a Labour Government had not changed the disruptive behaviour of the ordinary union members, and, in contrast to the days of Deakin and Bevin, the union leaders were often to be found on the Left. This was certainly true of Hugh Scanlon, who now led the Amalgamated Union of Engineering and Foundry Workers, and of Jack Jones, who had made his reputation in the TGWU with a style of leadership based on what he called industrial democracy, which meant doing what the union activists in the rank and file membership wanted.[140] Mrs Castle wondered about Scanlon's relationship with the Communist Party.[141] Nevertheless, Mrs Castle acted as if the union leaders shared her belief in Parliamentary socialism, whereas the poor performance of the Wilson Governments encouraged many on the Left to think in terms of the future use of industrial power to obtain socialism. Whatever the views of the various union leaders, the approach to industrial relations that they had in common was the pursuit of the self-interest of organized labour. They believed that this was best secured by free collective bargaining with labour law biased against the employers. So, consistently enough, the union leaders opposed the wage controls that were part of the Government's prices and incomes policy, and opposed industrial relations reforms that interfered with their privileges. Mrs Castle thought that she had 'foxed them all' with her White Paper,[142] but the political reality was different. There was no need for the union leaders to accept the *In Place of Strife* reforms at all. So, when, in May 1969, Mrs Castle told Jones and Scanlon that 'you've had your chance boys!'[143] she showed that she had completely misinterpreted the political situation. The reality of this was that there was considerable support for the unions' opposition to the legislation not only in the PLP, which included many union sponsored MPs, but also within the Cabinet itself led by Callaghan, by this time Home Secretary, satirised by one commentator as The Keeper of the Cloth Cap.[144] 'The crisis is upon us', Crossman wrote,[145] as the union leaders forced the Prime Minister and Mrs Castle to drop her industrial relations reforms in exchange for no more than a 'solemn and binding undertaking' that the TUC would do its best to intervene in and settle unconstitutional strikes.[146] When confronted by Scanlon at the crucial meeting, Wilson treated his behaviour as being the same as when the Soviet Union had brutally suppressed Czechoslovak attempts to gain political freedom in 1968, saying, 'Get your tanks off my lawn, Hughie!'[147] Wilson had no means of forcing Scanlon or any of the other union leaders to back down.

With a worthless reform of the House of Lords having failed as well as its *In Place of Strife* legislation, the Wilson Government were left to hope that something would turn up, especially an economic recovery, in time for the next Election, and that enough of the electorate would be grateful for the many changes that it had introduced, some of which were radical. That little had been done in relation to the social services was blamed on Douglas Houghton, the Cabinet Minister charged with conducting a 'great review' of them. Crossman complained about the wasted years: 'Endless detailed papers have been written ... but under Houghton there'd been no overall review of how the services are working – whether the priorities are right, what reorganization was required, what rethinking of basic principles.'[148] Crossman was made Secretary of State for Social Services in November 1968 at the head of a massive Department of Health and Social Security, and so given the opportunity to do the task that Houghton had neglected to do. Crossman had been warned by Titmuss about the differences between the Ministries of Health and of Social Security that were being merged,[149] and the scale of the numbers and expenditure involved invited the suspicion that the motive behind this administrative reorganization had been to give Crossman a big job that would keep him busy. Crossman had done previous work in the field of pensions, and he pushed ahead with an incomes related superannuation scheme, but ran out of time.

There were those who would have said that when Crosland was appointed as Secretary of State for Education and Science in early 1965 he was well qualified for the post. 'The ideal of social equality requires the first priority to be given to educational reform', Crosland had written, 'The next Labour Government must have a clear, definite, and far reaching policy for democratising entry into the public schools; and this it should implement without further dithering. At the same time it should both accept and propagate the principle of the comprehensive school ... . If socialism is taken to mean a "classless society", this is the front on which the major attack should be mounted.'[150] Like so many egalitarians, Crosland had benefited greatly from social privilege himself, and, to judge from his earnest attempts to make himself knowledgeable about football, he was curious about what passed for the culture of the working classes. Though the 'respectable' working class tended to have a different outlook from the rest, it was not difficult to find hostility to education among the English working classes or to believe that this was the majority view. So, when Crosland issued Circular 10/65 with the ambition to 'destroy every ... grammar school in England',[151] he was closing down the best escape route from the working classes available to its most gifted children, and sentencing them to run the gauntlet of the determinedly ignorant in a setting in which anything resembling serious discipline was soon to be abolished. Far from being an example of the law of unintended consequences, this outcome was predictable. As for the public schools being subjected to some form of mass Fleming scheme, all that happened was that a Commission looked at them. The removal of the State grammar schools was bound to mean in the long run that private education would prosper, which was the opposite of Crosland's egalitarianism, since what had been available without charge to working-class children who passed the relevant test became available mainly for the moneyed. Crosland was to denounce the 'melancholy waiters' who had urged him to wait for this report or research, instead of pressing ahead with comprehensive schooling,[152] but he was to regret that he rushed into the Woolwich Speech of April 1965 that introduced the binary system of higher education.[153]

'Let us move away from our snobbish caste-ridden hierarchical obsession with university status', Crosland declared in launching the polytechnics. The official who thought up the scheme believed it to be 'revolutionary', since the intention was for the polytechnics to stand alongside the universities with distinctive functions related to the needs of industry and technology.[154] Done properly, this would have been an invaluable role, but it was never going to be one that the polytechnics as they were most likely to develop were equipped to do, and they proceeded to spread themselves across the range of subjects in imitation of the universities. Giving them a similar name to that of a severely elitist French institution only served to emphasize the poverty of achievement. 'I'm not frightfully interested in the universities', Crosland had declared,[155] and he took no part in trying to establish the Open University, the political foundations of which were laid by Jennie Lee, one of his junior Ministers, who had the crucial support of the Prime Minister, who believed that 'it was one of the greatest achievements of our ... Government'.[156] Such was the record of the Wilson Governments that one socialist critic looked longingly back to the Conservative Governments of 1959–64 who had maintained a higher rate of increase annually in social service expenditure in real terms than previous post-war governments and a higher rate, if housing was included, than that achieved subsequently under Labour.[157]

'Devaluation from $2.80 to $2.40 announced', Benn wrote in his diary for 18 November 1967 about the fate of the pound, adding: 'The following day [Wilson] did his absurd broadcast on television saying,

"The pound in your pocket won't be devalued."'[158] Mrs Castle thought that Wilson's 'breakthrough' line on devaluation was unconvincing,[159] and, indeed, this failure in economic policy, as Benn observed, was 'a great defeat for Harold',[160] as it had to be given the earlier opportunities to devalue that had been passed up. Wilson seemed to calculate that if an economic recovery could be promoted, enough of the electorate would either forgive or forget to ensure that the Labour Government would win the next Election, and Wilson decided to move Callaghan to the Home Office and appoint Jenkins as Chancellor of the Exchequer to bring this recovery about. Mrs Castle's reading of this appointment was that 'Harold has now finally nobbled his one serious rival: they stand or fall together.'[161] As Jenkins noted, however, Wilson was being 'cartooned at the time as being very much my poodle'.[162] This was because, as Macleod observed, 'Mr Jenkins is the vogue. If he had stood up on Budget Day [1968] and recited a list of trains arriving at Victoria the trendier commentators would have been breathless with admiration.' Jenkins reflected that 'in the long run [the] Budget of 1968, with a couple of reinforcing turns of the screw, worked completely, although the long run was a long time coming'.[163] *The Economist* believed that 'for the first time in Labour's three and a half years of office the smack of firm government resounded through the Commons'.[164] The same journal's verdict on the 1969 Budget was 'It Won't Do' mainly on the basis that too many of the tax increases were on companies and not on consumers. Jenkins was accused of opting 'to get close to the same disastrous stage of internal economic mismanagement as where he himself came in'.[165] Over the *In Place of Strife* legislation, Jenkins had eventually withdrawn his support because 'he no longer thought that the fight was worth the cost',[166] though, not surprisingly, the price of the Government's surrender was the collapse of its incomes policy and rampant wage inflation.

The 1966 Election had been won by 'more than the usual fraud', according to *The Economist*, and by the spring of 1970 it believed that there were those in the Cabinet who thought that a repeat performance would be 'jolly clever', though others were 'sick at heart at ... again living a lie'.[167] Which side Jenkins was on was unclear from 'The Empty Budget' that *The Economist* described him delivering in April 1970.[168] Jenkins found the 'general feeling' on the Labour side was 'one of disappointment',[169] presumably because of the lack of explicit electoral bribes. Mrs Castle would have liked the Chancellor to 'do more', but she thought that 'psychologically he is striking the right note',[170] which meant seeming more responsible than he was in relation to inflation. Of course, the winning trick was supposed to be to time the Election before prices caught up with wages, and thus bring to a politically successful end what *The Economist* called 'a period of Labour economic rule which has been ... unsuccessful in every respect except one ... . The sole real achievement of Labour's rule is that it inherited a balance of payments deficit which amounted to over 2.5 per cent of GNP in 1964 ... and has turned this into a ... surplus [of] around 1.5 per cent of GNP.'[171] Ironically, in the latter stages of the June 1970 Election, adverse trade figures for May were published, which pundits seemed to believe undermined the image of economic competence that the Labour Government was trying to project, thus, in part, explaining the Conservative victory they had failed to anticipate.[172] As the contemporary economy was well described as being characterized by 'stagflation', meaning a combination of stagnation and inflation,[173] Jenkins and his colleagues had done well to suggest competence of any kind. What could not be doubted was that the demise of the *In Place of Strife* strategy had been followed by a period of rising prices and increased unemployment at the same time that was not supposed to occur under the Keynesian order. *The Economist* wrote of 'the more modern Keynesianism-cum-Friedmanism that is now the accepted norm in America'.[174] What recent events had demonstrated was that macroeconomic management had been overridden by microeconomic forces, and whichever party won the Election would be confronted by a trade union movement with the power to humble the elected Government.

Roy Jenkins and the fashioning of the undisciplined society

'Only a very prejudiced man would claim that everything was wrong with the Britain of 1959', Roy Jenkins was to write in *The Labour Case*,[175] before going on to condemn the 'dreary, ugly pattern of life' of the 1950s, with the defining characteristic of that disciplined society supposedly being hypocrisy.[176] When protesting, though too much, that socialism need not be boring, Crosland had condemned 'socially imposed restrictions on the individual's private life and liberty ... the divorce laws ... prehistoric (and flagrantly unfair) abortion laws, obsolete penalties for sexual abnormality, the illiterate censorship of books and plays, and remaining restrictions on the equal rights of women. Most of these are intolerable, and should be highly offensive to socialists, in whose blood there should always run a trace of the anarchist and the libertarian, and not too much of the prig and the prude.'[177]

Jenkins had come to be unconcerned about socialism, let alone facing the task of trying to make it seem interesting. 'Is Britain Civilized?' was the title of Jenkins's gratuitous final chapter in *The Labour Case*. According to him, it could not be when 'the ghastly apparatus of the gallows still exists', when 'the law relating to homosexuality remains in [a] brutal and unfair state', and 'harsh and archaic abortion laws' remained in force as did 'divorce laws which involve both a great deal of unnecessary suffering and a great number of attempts (many of them successful) to deceive the courts'. Though he had himself piloted what became the Obscene Publications Act of 1959 through a Tory-dominated House of Commons, Jenkins thought that 'a strong Home Secretary' would have 'a far better chance of effective Parliamentary support for liberal causes the more the balance in the ... Commons is tilted towards the Labour Party'.[178] So, it proved. By means of Private Members' Bills, for which the Wilson Governments provided the Parliamentary time, the legislation that Jenkins favoured was passed to create an undisciplined society, which many preferred to call the Permissive Society. A novelist observed that the many changes in popular culture that came to characterize the 1960s could not have occurred if National Service had not been discontinued.[179] Perpetual adolescence on the part of males was, indeed, one condition of the immaturity that came to be on mass display and then to persist, but the biggest change was greater freedom for women, eventually, of course, at a price. Anyway, the Swinging London interpretation of the 1960s did not represent life for more than a small minority in the capital itself, and, as for elsewhere, nobody pretended that there was, say, Swinging Oldham. In addition, before the decade closed, the settlement of the Irish Problem that Lloyd George had devised nearly 50 years before had begun to unravel, at first in the name of civil rights for the minority, with, of course, violence to follow.

'Poor old Home Office', Sir Frank Soskice wrote, 'We are not always wrong, but we always get the blame.'[180] Jenkins actually got the blame when the Permissive Society later turned sour, though he was formally Home Secretary for less than two years after December 1965. His immediate predecessor, Soskice, had direct, if reluctant, responsibility for the Race Relations Act of 1965 and indirectly for the Murder (Abolition of Death Penalty) Act of that year, with the Bill in the latter case being once more the work of Silverman. As for the procedure of allowing MPs to vote according to conscience on this issue, as one Tory wryly observed, it was an 'extraordinary coincidence that every [MP] opposite, save one, firmly believes that no man should hang'.[181]

So, the procedure was a fraud, and there was no doubt once more about popular opinion on the matter. In early 1965, an opinion survey found that no less than 70 per cent were opposed to the abolition of the death penalty.[182] The only setback for the abolitionists was that an amendment ensured that the legislation only ran for five years.[183] In 1969, the Government rushed through the decision to make abolition permanent,[184] though a subsequent opinion survey showed that only 27 per cent favoured this policy.[185] There was also no encouragement at all for 'liberals' from popular attitudes towards race relations. In 1965, 87 per cent approved of the strict limitation on the number of immigrants, and 52 per cent thought that immigration that had taken place had harmed the country.[186] 'If we do not have strict immigration rules, our people will soon all be coffee-coloured', Soskice said privately,[187] and what became the Race Relations Act of 1965 was political compensation for the imposition of such rules. In principle, it outlawed racial discrimination, though it took further legislation in 1968 to try to formally prevent this in housing and education. The two Front Benches had effectively agreed that immigration and race relations were not to be matters for party combat, so giving the opportunity, as on hanging, for ignoring popular opinion.

Frustrated in Opposition, and with Edward Heath as the inept Leader of it, Enoch Powell temporarily derailed this arrangement with a speech at Birmingham on 20 April 1968 in which he predicted civil unrest if immigration was not dealt with. 'Rivers of blood' were going to flow.[188] Overnight, Powell was translated from a largely unknown politician to a popular hero at least on this issue. No less than 74 per cent of those questioned in an opinion survey agreed with Powell, and 69 per cent disagreed with his dismissal by Heath from the Shadow Cabinet.[189] Mrs Castle thought that Powell had 'taken the lid off Pandora's box and that race relations in Britain will never be the same again'.[190] Benn believed that 'from the Government's point of view the situation could be very dangerous and difficult'.[191] Crossman feared 'the revolt of the masses which Enoch had let loose' and the appeal made to 'the real Labour core, the illiterate industrial proletariat who have ... revolted against the literate'. Crossman guessed that Powell 'miscalculated the extent of the popular appeal and has been slightly appalled by it. He isn't a fascist but a fanatic.'[192] What these Ministers could not see were three obvious things. Firstly, though nobody could pretend any longer that the evolution towards a multi-racial society in various parts of Britain that Jenkins had lauded 18 months before[193] had any kind of popular endorsement, Powell had not invented a means of bringing mass opinion to bear to prevent it coming to pass. Secondly, while Powell may have inflicted some damage on the Labour voting base, though probably less than that caused by the then Government's economic policy record, his behaviour had been sustaining of the political system more generally in the sense that, while himself little different from the classic mad Professor, here was somebody who actually seemed to listen to and articulate mass opinion on this issue. Thirdly, Powell had, indeed, 'miscalculated'. His objective had not been to act as some sort of safety valve for the political system, but to advance his political career, and this he had ruined. For, 'the enemy within' that Powell raged on about,[194] did not just control the BBC of Hugh Carleton Greene, the Home Office and so on: they continued to run the two major parties. Powell was eventually driven to go to Ulster to find a political home. The 'liberals' must have seemed to be everywhere to him, though, of course, they remained in short supply among the mass of the electorate. One 'liberal' had the courage to go on record and suggest that the manner in which the political class dealt with immigration did much to diminish public faith in British political institutions,[195] though it could be doubted whether this was more damaging than the arrogance displayed in relation to the public's continuing support for the death penalty.

When in Opposition, Wilson had suggested that a promise on the part of the Labour Party to implement in office the recommendation of the Wolfenden Report of 1957 that homosexual behaviour between consenting adults in private should no longer be a criminal offence 'would cost us, at a rough estimate, six million votes'.[196] There was no need to make such an overt commitment, given the resort to Private Member's legislation in supposed matters of conscience, and when appointing Jenkins as Home Secretary, Wilson must have known that Jenkins would promote such a measure. Though an opinion survey suggested that more were opposed to the change in the law than favoured it,[197] the opposition did not constitute a majority view, and, Leo Abse eventually steered through what became the Sexual Offences Act of 1967. Jenkins played an important role in promoting this measure,[198] and in the case of what became the Medical Termination of Pregnancy Act of 1967 it was he who encouraged David Steel to take the legislation forward.[199] In this instance, there was massive public support for abortion law reform where the mother's health was in danger or where the child was likely to be born deformed, but not on the basis that there was not enough money to support another child.[200]

There was also a Divorce Reform Act of 1969. There seemed to be more public support for easier divorce than opposition though not a majority.[201] That there was a lack of outside enthusiasm for changing the law relating to theatre censorship[202] did not obstruct the passage of the Theatres Act of 1968, which, indeed, was unchallenged. One observer attributed this to the forces of social conservatism having suffered too many defeats to make a contest of it.[203]

The particular character of the 1966 Parliament certainly made life difficult for such conservatives, though, on many issues, and over time, their arguments held up better than those of the reformers, who were well named 'the trendies.' Even then, the reforming Abse could be found campaigning for keeping the age of sexual consent at 16, effectively arguing that the line had to be drawn somewhere,[204] as, indeed, in many other respects, social conservatives had been laughed to scorn for suggesting. On the "forbidden fruits" view of sexual activity, the good clean fun 1960s lifestyle was never going to last long, and it did not take genius to guess in broad terms what was to succeed it. Pessimism was always in order about the Divorce Reform Act, for instance, some advocates of which seemed to think that its provisions would make possible a once-and-for-all opportunity for wives in particular to escape from unhappy marriages, and then things would carry on much as before. What was always more likely was that the institution of marriage would be damaged irreparably, and that, for many, it would degenerate into arrangements not much different from those between boyfriends and girlfriends with similar instability, and with the interests of children sacrificed. The reformers' contempt for the wife-and-mother type of woman ignored the reality that the Welfare State assumed the maintenance of the traditional family structure, and that undermining it was to invite open-ended commitments to compensatory public expenditure. Since the traditional family was a conservative institution, in attacking it, the Jenkins of the 1960s was a radical. He was best compared with Tom, and especially Daisy, in *The Great Gatsby*: 'they were careless people ... they smashed up things and creatures and then retreated ... and let other people clean up the mess they had made'.

The New Morality was bound to be much the same as The Old Immorality, and nobody could possibly know how many people were won over to the Labour side by the Permissive Society legislation or how many were alienated. The measures cumulatively may have added up to a social revolution, but it was not the revolution that Wilson had promised, which had been in the performance of the economy. 'The

Government is on the edge of complete disintegration of a kind from which Labour would not recover for twenty years', Mrs Castle declared in July 1966,[205] and, though this assessment underrated the power and the resilience of the wider Labour Movement, the Wilson Government may well have been doomed from that July Crisis onwards. Others would point to the 1967 devaluation. Wilson and his Government cast around for ways to win the next Election. The age at which people became eligible to vote was lowered to 18, presumably on the assumption that young people were radical, as if the minority of usually socially privileged university students who noisily took up opposition to the Vietnam War were in any way representative. Then, to avoid the mistake of the Attlee Government in behaving more than honourably in bringing constituency boundaries up to date, the boundaries were left unchanged. Then, the Election itself was held in June 1970, at least partly in the belief that more Tories would be away on holiday then than Labour's own supporters, and, thus, unable to vote. Playing the Safety First card much as Baldwin had done in 1929, Wilson lost the 1970 Election in a similar fashion, leaving behind a Government whose record in office invited the *Breach of Promise* form of indictment, and a reputation that only the most desperate of revisionist historians would even consider attempting to rescue.

10
The Heath Experiment: The Conservative Government 1970–4

An unnatural disaster

'We're a working-class family and no two ways about it', Edward Heath's father once declared to a biographer.[1] This was strictly true when Heath's father had been a carpenter and his wife originally had been a domestic servant, but not, of course, when the father later became a master builder. In few other countries in the world would such distinctions matter, but Heath always bore the scars of his journey through the British social structure of his time. It was a long haul from a grammar school in Broadstairs to Balliol College, Oxford, to be then commissioned in the Army during the Second World War in which he saw active service, and, after it, briefly, to be a higher civil servant and also a journalist, and then, from 1950, a Conservative MP. As late as 1963, the social elite that had run the Tory Party had been powerful enough to ensure that Lord Home had become its Leader and for a time Prime Minister. Heath supported Home's candidature, and even the admiring James Prior believed that Heath did so because he believed that this was the best way to ensure his own eventual succession.[2] Soon after the Tories had been consigned to Opposition following electoral defeat in 1964, Home was prevailed upon to introduce a system of election for the leadership of the Conservative Party, and, when he stepped down in 1965, Heath defeated Maudling and Powell for the succession. It was easy to believe that Heath had been over-promoted. The supporting roles of Adjutant in wartime and Tory Chief Whip in the 1950s had suited Heath best. Heath's achievement in reaching the Tory leadership and eventually becoming Prime Minister by meritocratic means did not alter the reality that his personality, crippled by his long social climb, ensured that he was to be a mediocre

Leader of the Opposition between 1965 and 1970 and an unsuccessful Prime Minister between 1970 and 1974. The cruelties of the class system meant that, despite his association with yachting and the Albany, Heath was still seen by many as a dull, cold, proud, unconvincing upstart.[3] Heath's manufactured, indeed false, political persona did not hide his lack of social skills, and, allied to a form of blinkered self-satisfaction and obsessiveness, rendered Heath into a political leader best described as an unnatural disaster.

'Modernization' was in political fashion in the 1960s, and, with what proved to be a characteristic lack of concern for his party's electoral interests, Heath had already demonstrated that he was all for it in abolishing RPM when at the Board of Trade. What, though, especially in the contemporary social climate was 'modern' about an apparently sexless bachelor? Of course, Heath had his 'European' credentials, having been thought by some to have failed nobly in what were still called the Common Market negotiations of 1961–3, and 'Europe' did tie in with the 'modernization' image, though as an issue it divided the Tories. Indeed, the Conservatives were divided on several issues, and among many Tories there was a 'murder wish' about the Conservative period of office between 1951 and 1964, from which only the Butler boom years and, less obviously, the apogee of Macmillanite prosperity were exempted. Instrumentalism had been practised. The 1964 Election had still been lost. Real Conservatism was supposed to be the way back to electoral revival.[4] As in 1955, when there had been some heart searching even after a notable victory, the question remained about what exactly this form of Conservatism amounted to. The only distinctive intellectual system available to the Conservatives was economic liberalism, propagated with enthusiasm by the Institute for Economic Affairs since 1957, and Powell and many others took up this creed. Banishing RPM had given Heath economic liberal credentials of a kind, but he was actually a Macmillanite Paternalist with the crucial disadvantage of lacking its social style. So, vocal elements in the Party pressed for market solutions to economic problems, and Heath the unbeliever was placed in an uneasy position, and he often seemed to be leading the Conservatives from the back.

Heath's position was not helped by the Tory defeat in the 1966 Election, though the July Measures shortly afterwards seemed to have paved the way for a Conservative victory next time. In the long wait in between, there was a great deal of earnest activity on the part of Conservative policy groups, initially chaired by the Paternalist figure of Boyle, though Heath eventually thought it wise to dispense with his services. The work of the policy groups popularly surfaced in the form of Selsdon Man, though this was a Wilsonian confection. As Heath himself had long since subsided into 'liberalism' on social issues, it was some harsh sentiments on law and order uttered by Sir Peter Rawlinson that gave the Selsdon meeting in 1970 its profile,[5] and quite why Wilson believed such beliefs to be unpopular defied credulity. Two years earlier, Heath had shared the anger of his leading colleagues about Powell departing from the Shadow Cabinet's agreed line on the issue of Commonwealth immigration, despite having shared in the drafting of a reasoned amendment to the current race relations legislation, and dismissed him.[6] As an outcast, Powell concentrated on establishing a distinctive political position, which combined market philosophy with a form of patriotism, involving not just the racial issue but antipathy to European involvement, which Powell had come to appreciate did not just involve membership of a Common Market. To further his career, Powell needed Heath to lose the 1970 Election, though, ironically, what some called Powellism may have marginally helped the Conservatives to victory. Heath tended to be portrayed as having won a considerable personal victory in the face of overwhelming odds, and he seemed to believe this himself with deleterious effects on his later behaviour. Heath had little in the way of a personal following, and what the Conservatives whom he led faced was a Labour majority in the House of Commons that had been eroded by many by-election defeats, but which was still substantial. During the last few months of the 1966 Parliament, the opinion polls moved in favour of the Labour Government, and, on that basis, which had to be unreliable given the margins involved, the political class concluded that the Tories would lose once more. In the event, the Conservatives won 330 seats compared with Labour's 287, and their overall majority in the House of Commons was 30.[7] The turnout was 72 per cent,[8] which was the lowest since 1935,[9] leading to some talk of the Tory victory being the result of apathy, though the difference in turnout compared with 1945, when the electorate was supposed to have been passionately involved, was slender. The net swing to the Tories from Labour was 4.7 per cent, the largest change in either direction since 1945.[10]

'Mr Heath has won on a programme of change', *The Economist* declared. 'He fought the campaign on his policies, he made commitments, and there has never been any doubt about him sticking to a commitment once he has made it. The electorate has taken him on, knowing what kind of a man he is.'[11] Since what was beyond doubt was that few people cared which party won the Election, and that

Heath was poorly regarded as a political leader,[12] this form of conventional wisdom was poorly judged. Heath had led the Conservatives to a famous victory over the opinion polls and he had also narrowly defeated a discredited Labour Government. Sufficient of the electorate to ensure the Tories office may well have wanted *A Better Tomorrow*, as the Tory manifesto was unimaginatively called, but, in relation to domestic policy, which tended to be the issues that interested electors most, radical departures from the arrangements of the Keynesian Welfare State were always likely to be less in demand than the more efficient management of the current arrangements, especially as lower taxes were promised along with, for example, 'Prosperity for All Areas', 'Homes for All', 'Social Service Advance', 'Better Education', and 'Care for Those in Need'.[13]

The Tories had been well aware that the Labour Party had been unprepared for office in 1964 and of the price paid for this, and there were those who thought that the Conservatives were over-prepared for office in 1970. Of the output of the 36 policy groups, the central theme was said to be 'efficiency, about creating a more American or German style economy',[14] and the quality and range of some of the work done, notably at the Sunridge Park meeting in September 1969 was impressive.[15] The Tories came to office armed with a blueprint for tax reform prepared for them by Sir Arthur Cockfield, an industrialist and former senior official in the Inland Revenue, which included, among other things, a deliberate switch from direct to indirect taxation in the form of the introduction of Value Added Tax.[16] Against that, the Tories never really worked out their position on incomes policy. Maudling favoured such a policy, and Macleod, the Shadow Chancellor did not, and, almost by default, the Conservatives came down against a statutory prices and incomes policy.[17] More fundamentally, the revival of economic liberalism in the Tory Party provided a test of supposed orthodoxy by which the Heath Government was bound to fail. 'The Conservative in principle denies, in practice minimizes, government intervention in the economic field', Powell declared.[18] That was a strange reading of the history of the Conservative Party, not least, to take just one example, in relation to Protection, but by the end of the 1960s economic liberalism was in the intellectual ascendant, unless, that is, the future lay with socialism. Heath had talked the language of economic liberalism at times, not least to mark the Conservatives off from their Labour opponents, and, importantly, to seem different himself, given that he had only too much in common with those opponents in many areas of public policy. Hence, the fuss he made about the style of government and improving its machinery. Heath's preferred economic and social order seemed to be one of efficient collectivism, if, indeed, he believed in any solution to Britain's problems beyond that supposed miracle cure, membership of the European Community, which goal he pursued with messianic zeal.

Heath leads Britain into Europe – at a price

'If we can negotiate the right terms, we believe that it will be in the long term interest of the British people for Britain to join the European Economic Community, and that it would make a major contribution to both the prosperity and the security of our country', the Conservative manifesto declared. The assurance that 'our sole commitment is to negotiate; no more, no less'[19] was, surely, believed by few. That there might well not be a French veto this time if Britain applied had been made more likely by de Gaulle's replacement by Georges Pompidou as President. The prevailing opinion within the British political class had become that membership of the EEC was a panacea that would provide the answer to 'the English disease', as it had become conventional to describe the country's persistent and, some feared, accelerating national decline. 'The arguments over the terms, whether the price of sugar is going to be high enough for the West Indies, and all the rest of the minutiae, are really beside the point', a former editor of *The Economist* declared, catching the mood of desperation. 'It has always been clear, ever since we committed our biggest political mistake for 200 years by refusing to be one of the founder members of the Common Market, that we should have to pay a price to get in ... you do not have to haggle over the subscription when you are invited to climb into a lifeboat. You scramble aboard while there is still a seat for you.'[20] Of course, the political reality was that Heath and his main emissary Sir Geoffrey Rippon had to get the best deal that he could for West Indian sugar producers, and, for that matter, New Zealand farmers, and to be seen to be doing so. Nonetheless, with Australia and Canada defining their economic interests as being less bound up with Britain than at the time of the Macmillan Government's negotiations,[21] the Commonwealth had less prominence as an issue for the Heath Government than for its predecessor, except indirectly in the sense that higher food prices seemed to be the main reason for public opposition as opinion surveys detected. Only 23 per cent of those sampled approved of an application for membership being made at all, and, even when the negotiations were completed, only 18 per cent approved of there being a Festival of Europe to celebrate Britain's entry. At no time during the negotiations was there any evidence of popular enthusiasm in favour of British entry to what the Gallup organization persistently called the Common Market, and, at times, antagonism to this policy seemed to be marked. What was seen as the Common Market did not, though, appear to rank as being of more than minor importance to voters, only 13 per cent of whom were reported as being able to name the Six correctly. One observer thought that this political context made this issue open to leadership,[22] and public apathy and ignorance may well have been a help to the Government, not least in relation to the constitutional implications of entry.

Of the approach that Heath took in the negotiations, his Political Secretary, Douglas Hurd, wrote that 'it would be a great mistake to suppose that he was ready to give the French whatever they wanted. On the contrary, he saw them as tough negotiators with whom we would need again to bargain toughly. But he understood what the [FCO] appeared to ignore, namely the real structure of the European Community. The French had the veto, and on the question of British entry had already used it once. There was no question of them accepting British membership just because the Five wanted us in.'[23] That was surely obvious, as, indeed, was the reality that the French Government would only tolerate British entry if she paid a high and continuing financial price for this, notably in sustaining the Common Agricultural Policy from the operations of which Britain would derive little benefit. As if to emphasize Britain's supplicant role, though the Treaty of Rome did not have a Common Fisheries Policy, one was added at this time, and even the most fanatical of 'Europeans', Sir Con O'Neill of the FCO, later wrote that Britain was mistaken in not making more effort to stop the adoption of this Policy.[24] Ideally, as 10 years before, Heath would have preferred to take the 'Monnet line' and 'just say, outright, Yes, we will become a member of the Community … . Then we could have adjusted ourselves *inside* the Community, and got the Community to adjust at the same time.' Of course, 'the problem about that was … . Parliamentary and public opinion'.[25] House of Commons opinion was one reason why the negotiations were not necessarily doomed to succeed, and it may be that, because of his 'European' credentials, Heath got a marginally less onerous deal than anybody else could have done,[26] though the French still largely dictated the outcome and drove a hard bargain.[27] In an internal history, O'Neill got into difficulties in arguing that Britain had got 'a good bargain' in the negotiations, while trying to have it both ways by observing that 'our success in the

Community will depend less on the nature of the Community and the character of the terms on which we enter it than on our own domestic success, and in particular our own economic performance ... nothing could be more misleading or more dangerous than to suppose that [the Community] offers us a certain remedy for our deficiencies or a panacea to cure the ills from which we have suffered'.[28] Of course, the political attractions of the Community were what excited O'Neill, and, sure enough, the 1971 White Paper argued that 'a Europe united would have the means of recovering the position in the world which Europe divided had lost', leading to a 'more evenly balanced' relationship with the USA and the USSR. It was asserted that 'as a full member of the Community we would have more opportunity and strength to influence events than we could possibly have on our own.'[29] Europe would remain divided anyway because of the existence of the Soviet Empire, and the Community could summon up a united foreign policy in relation to that threat if it wished, but, militarily, the Community did not matter and only NATO did, which meant, primarily, the Americans, and France had already proved to be an unreliable member of that alliance. Not surprisingly, the 1971 White Paper concentrated on the economic advantages that were said to follow from joining the Community. These 'will more than outweigh the costs, provided we seize the opportunities of the far wider home market now open to us. If we do, we shall obtain, as the Six have done since the Communities were founded, a substantial increase in our trade, a stimulus to growth and investment, and a greater rise in real wages and standards of living than we have known in recent years or would be possible if we remained outside.'[30] Britain was believed by the majority of her political class to be unable to put her own house in order, which meant that others had to do the job. That being so, O'Neill's attempt to argue that if membership did not work wonders then Britain herself would be to blame did not convince. The fact of membership was supposed to bring about an economic miracle cure.

Before coming to office, Heath had stated that the Community could not be enlarged without the 'full-hearted consent of the peoples and Parliaments' of the countries involved. Article 237 of the Treaty of Rome stated that adjustments to it needed to be ratified by the contracting States in accordance with their respective constitutional requirements. Since 'the referendum was a device unknown to our Constitution', Heath had meant that 'the voice of the people would speak *through* their elected Parliament', and, not surprisingly, Burke was once again the authority used to justify what Heath called representative democracy.[31]

Being one for 'sound and honest British traditions'[32] when it suited him, Heath took ruthless advantage of them in driving what became the European Communities Act of 1972 through the Commons, playing his part in the further demeaning of that institution. 'It is fashionable and true to deplore the decline in public respect in which Parliament is now held', *The Economist* had observed[33] in the midst of the six days of debate in October 1971 that ended in a Commons majority of 112 on a free vote approving in principle the position that Heath had negotiated with the Six.[34] When it came to the legislation, though, the Labour Opposition was determined to bring the Government down, and, indeed, with the Whips on, Heath made it clear that the Government would resign if the Second Reading of the European Communities Bill was defeated. The outcome was a Commons majority of 8, which was obtained with Liberal support because, as the Leader of the Opposition pointed out, Heath could not get one on the basis of Tory votes as he had wanted, and Wilson had denied him the support of the Labour 'Europeans'. Wilson added that such a majority could not represent 'the full-hearted support of the British people' or even of Parliament.[35] With his place in history at stake – 'the vision of a Britain in a united Europe'[36] – Heath seemed as unconcerned about this as he also appeared to be about minimal public interest. It may well be that by the early 1970s, even a Churchill would have had difficulty enthusing a country about what only the zealots could see as more than a residual commitment: if 'Little England' was not supposed to be good enough, then it had to be 'Europe', though only because there was nowhere else to go. Moreover, as often tended to happen when Heath was personally involved in a venture, almost immediately things went wrong. 'After the Oil Crisis of 1973–4, the Community lost its momentum', Heath was to recall, 'and, worse, lost sight of the philosophy of Jean Monnet'. Heath's overall performance as Prime Minister did not lend credence to his opinion that all would have been well 'if President Pompidou, Chancellor Brandt and myself, the three men who had created the enlarged ... Community, had remained in power'.[37]

A failed style of government

'We are leaving behind the years of retreat', Heath boasted to the Tory Party Conference in October 1970,[38] which, naturally, took the form of a victory celebration. He declared: 'We were returned to office to change the course of history of this nation – nothing less'.[39] What Heath envisaged was 'a change so radical, a revolution so quiet and yet so total, that it will go far beyond ... this decade and way into the 1980s'.[40] Hurd believed that he was not alone in thinking that 'there was a real chance after 1970 that Mr Heath and his colleagues would break out of inherited attitudes and make possible a sharply higher level of achievement by the British people. In short, there was a chance that they could do for Britain what Adenauer and Erhard had done for Germany and de Gaulle for France.'[41] Heath was hardly in the same league as Adenauer or de Gaulle, let alone Erhard. Prospectively, British involvement with 'Europe' did represent a constitutional revolution about which it was wise to keep relatively 'quiet' compared with the promise of economic salvation. In the electorally crucial area of domestic policy what else did the Conservatives' programme amount to? They made much of promises of lower taxation and rationalizing the machinery of government and disengaging from private industry and reforming the trade unions and of combating inflation. There was little reason, though, to believe that the Conservatives had been returned to office on any basis other than a competence vote: namely, to run the Keynesian Welfare State better than the Wilson Governments. There was no evidence that there was much enthusiasm in the electorate for 'revolutions' whether they were 'quiet' or not.

Though Heath maintained that 'our strategy is clear'[42] in fact it was inherently flawed from the outset. For, the supposed 'strategy' embraced both sides of Conservatism at one and the same time, meaning Statism on the one hand, to which Heath subscribed by political preference, as well as economic liberalism. To domestic political problems, there could be public administration solutions and there could be market solutions, and, ideally, the facts of the situation should decide which ought to apply. What could not work was to apply these differing solutions together. This was illustrated by the writings of the contemporary Cabinet Minister, James Prior: 'During Ted's Premiership we were strongly committed to the post-war economic and social consensus in which the basic goal of economic policy was full employment. We recognized the need for an improved Welfare State. We believed in a society in which the social services should be expanded and more done about housing. We were equally committed to working through the institutions which had been developed to implement this consensus approach. Ted himself was a former Minister of Labour, and therefore knew the union leaders well. He wanted to keep the unions closely involved through ... the [NEDC], set up by Macmillan's Government'.[43] There were all sorts of arguments of the social cohesive kind that could be used to justify such policies, but it was fanciful to suggest that an economy better fitted to prosper in international competition was ever likely to result. If it was to be the mixture as before, what substance could there be to the aim of national renewal? As for working with the trade unions, their restrictive practices and legal immunities were formidable barriers to the development of a flourishing economy.

This was why Heath's Government promoted the Industrial Relations Act of 1971. 'There was a fundamental difference between what we set out to achieve and the reforms of the 1980s', Heath later wrote. 'In the Industrial Relations Act, Robert Carr [the Secretary of State for Employment] set out in the spirit of One Nation [Conservatism] to reform the entire field of industrial relations. Our intention was not merely to bring trade unions into line. We had nothing against trade unions as such and, in the early 1970s, neither did the people of this country. What we wanted to change was the balance of power in industry and the climate of confrontation which had begun to develop during the late 1960s. It was the disruptive acts of individual trade unionists which had to be dealt with, requiring us to give new rights as well as responsibilities to the trade unions, as institutions.'[44] Indeed, Part II of the Act listed the Rights of Workers, which included protection against unfair dismissal.[45] Carr stated that the 1971 Act was based on eight pillars, the first of which was the statutory right to belong to or not to belong to a trade union. The second pillar was the right of a union to be recognized, subject to it having the support of a substantial proportion of the relevant group of employees, and to it becoming registered. The third pillar was that of registration, with registered unions being required to organize themselves in line with rules laid down by a Registrar, and among the inducements to register was that unregistered unions had no immunity against tort liability for inducing breaches of any contract. The fourth pillar was the legal enforceability of collective agreements. The fifth pillar limited the legal immunities of unions in relation to, for example, some kinds of secondary industrial action. The sixth pillar involved cooling-off periods for threatened strikes of national importance with provision for strike ballots. The seventh pillar was concerned with the selective enforcement of procedural agreements. The eighth pillar involved the regulation of the bargaining structure.

To implement the legislation, a Registrar of Trade Unions and Employers' Associations was appointed, and a National Industrial Relations Court with the status of a High Court was established.[46] Heath later thought that 'we were mistaken to try to achieve the changes we sought to make through the Industrial Relations Act at one go, rather than by a more gradual series of measures over time, as proved successful in the 1980s'.[47] Prior believed that the approach to that legislation taken by Geoffrey Howe, the Solicitor General and its main author, was 'legalistic in the extreme', and 'we would have been better advised to put our own proposals in abeyance and take up the reforms which the Labour Government had proposed'.[48] Since the trade union movement had refused to accept the *In Place of Strife* legislation when proposed by a Labour Government, it was not very likely that it would accept a Tory version. It was not a matter of House of Commons tactics anyway, because what the trade union movement had demonstrated in 1969 had been the power to overrule the preferred policy of the elected Government, and it was obvious that this power would be used again either to protect union privileges, or, in the case of some elements within the union movement, to damage the economy and with it the British political system. Heath's One-Nation Tory approach was never going to work in a political climate of this kind, and those that would reply that it did for Baldwin in the General Strike, forgot that the economy was less closely integrated then as well as two other factors that were absent this time: namely, the will to win that Baldwin hid behind his Paternalist mask; and the preparations made to ensure victory. It never seemed to occur to those connected with the Industrial Relations Act that unions would refuse to register, thus undermining the legislation from the beginning. Linking together union rights and responsibilities in an even-handed manner in the 1971 Act may have seemed only fair to contemporary One-Nation Tories, but, understandably, the union movement preferred to retain its traditional rights without more controls and duties, and it had the power to insist on this.

'This Administration has pledged itself to introduce a new style of government', Heath and his Cabinet initially declared, which meant 'resolving the issue of the proper sphere of government in a free society'. The State had been 'attempting to do too much'. So, there needed to be 'less government, better government, carried out by fewer people. Less government, because its activities will be related to a long-term strategy aimed at liberating private initiative and placing more responsibility on the individual and less on the State. It will be better government, because the tasks to be done will be better-defined and fewer in number, requiring fewer Ministers and fewer civil servants to carry them out.'[49] Thus far, economic liberals could have no objections, though the creation of the Department of Trade and Industry as well as the Department of the Environment and a renaming that led to there being a Department of Employment suggested that the Heath Government shared Wilson's obsession of playing around with the machinery of central government. Oddest of all was the establishment of 'a small multi-disciplinary Central Review Staff in the Cabinet Office'.[50] That a non-political body of this kind was to pronounce on government policy was peculiar enough, but its head was to be Lord Rothschild, who had been at one time an associate of the Cambridge spies, even thought by some to have been the Fifth Man, always assuming that there were only five. Whatever Rothschild was he was not remotely a Conservative, and, as for the CPRS being portrayed not least by itself as bravely 'thinking the unthinkable', even mild doses of economic liberalism were soon defined by the Cabinet as qualifying for that description. Heath did try to have a smaller Cabinet than his predecessor. There were to be no resignations from the Cabinet, and no leaks of information. Nonetheless, as Prior wrote, 'the tragic death of Iain Macleod in July 1970, a month after he had been appointed Chancellor, was a body blow at the very outset of Ted's Government', even though Prior recognized that he was 'no longer the Macleod whom many of us had ... worshipped'.[51]

Heath's Cabinet did not lack competent Ministers, notably Peter Walker, as well as Sir Keith Joseph at the DHSS and Margaret Thatcher at the DES, but Anthony Barber becoming Macleod's successor at the Treasury was a promotion too far. Elsewhere, Heath ignored Rosebery's maxim that to have a former Prime Minister in the Cabinet was a 'dangerous luxury', and appointed Douglas Home as Foreign Secretary, where he notably defied 'liberal' opinion by insisting in 1971 that the number of KGB spies operating in Britain should be reduced.[52] Reginald Maudling was to prove to be an unfortunate choice as Home Secretary. Brilliant at Oxford without exerting himself unduly, Maudling seemed to expect the rest of his life to be like that. So, when Home had resigned the Tory leadership, Maudling did not feel the need to campaign properly. The succession was supposed to fall into his lap.[53] When this did not happen, Maudling took up a business career. Again, this was supposed to be easy, and Maudling became involved in the Poulson Affair, and eventually its ramifications required him to resign from the Home Office in 1972. Maudling protested his innocence,[54] and he was certainly innocent of business. Even in politics, his chosen career, Maudling's outlook could be peculiar, such as when he took seriously an official's observation that restoring capital punishment would be impractical: 'shall we advertise for a new hangman in *The Times* or *The Daily Telegraph*?'[55]

Being a hangman tended to be a family business anyway, and, if wider recruitment was needed, such was the popular approval of the death penalty, advertising in *The Daily Mirror* might well have been rewarding. Nevertheless, Prior thought Maudling's departure too was a loss: 'Without Iain and Reggie, and with Alec [Douglas-Home] fully occupied as Foreign Secretary, much of the political weight, or "bottom" as Reggie himself would call it, was lost ... . They were political equals of Ted's, and could talk to him in a way that even William Whitelaw and Peter Carrington ... found difficult ... as time went on [Heath] relied more and more on a trio of senior civil servants, led by William Armstrong, Head of the Civil Service, with Douglas Allen, Permanent Secretary at the Treasury, and Conrad Heron, Permanent Secretary at Employment, in support. They were able and loyal advisers, but they were not politicians. This added to the resentment already felt by a number of backbenchers that Ted was not paying sufficient attention to the Party, and fuelled the charges of corporatism which was increasingly being levelled at his Government.'[56] Given Heath's taste for Neddy style consultations with organized interests, this charge was understandable. Quite what benefits Heath expected from consulting trade union leaders, while, at the same time, legislating to diminish their powers, remained unclear.

'We believe that the essential need of the country is to gear its policies to the great majority of people, who are not lame ducks, who do not need a hand, who are quite capable of looking after their own interests and only demand to be allowed to do so', John Davies, the Secretary of State for Trade and Industry, declared in a debate on public expenditure on 4 November 1970, adding that 'national decadence is the consequence of treating us all, the whole country, as though we were lame ducks ... the vast majority lives and thrives in a bracing climate and not in a soft, sodden morass of subsidized incompetence'.[57] What the 'quiet revolution' meant then was that the Government could not be expected to use public expenditure to bale out the 'lame ducks' of private industry. So, the Industrial Reorganization Corporation was abolished, and the Prices and Incomes Board too, although, of course, the Government had to have an incomes policy of a kind for the public sector. The 'N minus 1' formula that it devised led to strikes on the part of the electricity workers and in the Post Office, both resulting in victory for the Government. When, though, Rolls Royce collapsed in early 1971, the Heath Government nationalized the company. It did this primarily 'to ensure continuity of those activities ... which are important to our national defence',[58] but this did not change the political reality that a gaping hole had been torn in the Government's policy of disengagement.[59] Others were to follow. In February 1972, only nine months after announcing the liquidation of Upper Clyde Shipbuilders, Davies was to be found shoring up the company with still more public expenditure. A Communist-led 'work in' and a warning from the Chief Constable of Glasgow about the public order consequences of closing the yards had forced a Government already concerned about the effects on the unemployment figures to back down.[60] These figures mattered because, as Prior wrote of Heath: 'He utterly despised and detested the pre-war Conservative Governments who had tolerated between two and three million unemployed. It was therefore no surprise in which direction Ted decided our economic policy should go when he now had to choose between tolerating a continued high level of unemployment, in the hope that this would keep some control over wage claims and inflation – or trying to run the economy with a higher level of output and growth, and seeking some other means of control over wages and price increases.'[61] In the meantime, the Government had been humiliatingly defeated during the first weeks of 1972 by a strike conducted by the National Union of Mineworkers for which it was totally unprepared. Hurd's diary entry for 11 February 1972 read: ' The Government wandering vainly over battlefield looking for someone to surrender to – and being massacred all the time.' A week later, Hurd wrote: 'From frying pan to fire. Wilberforce gives an immense amount to miners, which they show signs of rejecting.' The reference was to the Wilberforce Court of Inquiry findings that gave the NUM huge wage increases. Heath had to persuade the miners' leaders to accept the offer.[62]

The Heath Government's authority never recovered from this defeat at the hands of the NUM, though the loss of the will to govern along the lines that the Conservatives had proclaimed from Opposition could be detected earlier, with one landmark being their defeat in the Bromsgrove by-election of May 1971.[63] For the Tories to be defeated by the seriously divided Labour Party in a relatively safe seat so soon into the 1970 Parliament was a stunning blow that cast doubt upon the Government's political strategy. Dissension within the ranks of the Parliamentary Party was to become marked,[64] and the manner in which the European Communities legislation was pushed through was not the only reason that these divisions became deeper than in recent times. The English view of Northern Ireland may well have been encapsulated by the complaint in *The Economist* that 'there are very few people left in Ulster ... who are ready to hear reason',[65] and the Heath Government's abolition of the Stormont Parliament and assertion of direct rule in the province was an attempt to try to assert 'reason' that was always unlikely to succeed. Inevitably, the alienation of the Ulster Unionists resulted. Further, in its economic policy, the Heath Government followed up its many retreats by executing an explicit 'U turn' in its economic policy that was well described by one dismissed Minister as representing 'a complete reversal of the policy which we had been elected upon.'[66] In a statement on public expenditure and taxation in October 1970, Barber as Chancellor had declared the Government's aim to be 'to break out of the depressing cycle of high taxation and low growth which has bedevilled this country in recent years',[67] but, not surprisingly, 6d off the standard rate of income tax offset at once by an increase in national insurance contributions, allied to reductions in public expenditure that were only cuts in its rate of growth, and a policy of reining in on State intervention in the economy that was half-heartedly pursued, did not lead to an improved performance on the part of the British economy. Though Barber ended his Budget Speech in March 1971 with the warning that 'all our hopes for the future will be but dust in our mouths if we do not repel the assault upon the value of our money',[68] there was some cause to believe that the electorate soon became less concerned about inflation than the rising unemployment figures.[69]

'The high unemployment route was counter to everything Ted believed in and hoped for Britain', Prior wrote. So, it followed that 'an expansionary strategy' had to be embarked upon, and the 'Barber boom' was launched 'designed to achieve an annual economic growth rate of 5 per cent.'[70] As Barber himself said, that was 'a rate of growth twice as fast as in the past decade',[71] and the means of achieving this was to be massive public spending. Barber privately thought that the level of public expenditure was excessive already, and contemplated resignation rather than associating himself with a policy in which he did not believe. Barber only stayed on out of loyalty to the Party and to the Prime Minister, whose policy it really was.[72] Since the private sector would not invest at the levels and in the places that Heath thought that they should, a new Industrial Development Executive was established in the DTI to do it for them with an array of powers that was well described by a Liberal as 'intervention in private industry on the grand scale', and, indeed, opened up the prospect of 'socialism in our time'.[73] Benn thought so too, describing the machinery and the powers granted under what became the Industry Act of 1972 as representing the 'spade-work for socialism',[74] which observation encouraged others to wonder why the Labour Party had not done the essential preparatory work itself over the previous 70 years, and why Heath was stepping in to help them out. Heath denied not only that the Industry Act of 1972 was 'socialist', but also that 'an abandonment of principle' had taken place at all.[75] The heading in *The Economist* summed up the approach that the Heath Government had now taken to solving the problems of British private industry. This was: 'Blank Cheque'.[76]

Since the Heath Government had restored the Industrial Reorganization Corporation in all but name, it was no surprise when, effectively, the Prices and Incomes Board was restored too. This time, two bodies were deemed necessary: the Pay Board and the Price Commission. Prior thought that the Government was mistaken to opt for a statutory incomes policy in the autumn of 1972,[77] but expansion of the economy on the scale envisaged meant that some means had to be found to contain inflation, and, for all Heath's efforts at conciliating them, the TUC declined to be associated with a voluntary policy.[78] Following the initial Stage I pay and prices freeze from November 1972 to March 1973, Prior wrote, Stages II and III represented 'the most sophisticated pay policy ever introduced'.[79] The sophistication did not matter, of course, if the NUM chose to dissent, which, despite Stage III being largely designed to win its favour, that union proceeded to do. The NUM's hand had been made strong enough anyway after the victory of 1972, but its position was made even more formidable by the effects of the contemporary Oil Crisis in inflating petroleum prices. An overtime ban imposed by the NUM in November 1973 led the Heath Government to impose a three-day working week the following month in order to conserve fuel supplies at electricity stations. The Conservative Government also came to think in terms of a 'who governs?' appeal to the electorate. Lord Carrington, the Party Chairman, was one who thought that this appeal was delayed too long.[80] Whether this was so or not, the Conservatives failed to win the February 1974 Election, obtaining more votes but 4 fewer seats than the Labour Party.[81] The Tories would have still been the largest grouping in the new Parliament if Heath had not spurned the Ulster Unionists,[82] and Heath was left to spend his last weekend as Prime Minister trying to do a deal with Jeremy Thorpe, even though the Liberals whom he led did not hold the balance of power, before ungraciously resigning.

'Heath was an unlucky Prime Minister', one biographer observed, '[Heath] came to office with high hopes of tackling the deep-seated inefficiency and negative class attitudes that bedevilled British industry, but ran into a trade union movement at the height of its obstructive power ... . To his credit, he was not prepared to cow the unions by means of unemployment; instead he tried to buy their support for a form of social partnership ... . But for the miners and the Oil Crisis, it might have worked. As it was, it ended ignominiously in confrontation, blackouts, and defeat.'[83] The assessment that Heath was 'a great man, who achieved a great deal of what he set out to achieve and was, at a crucial time, unlucky' not surprisingly came from a higher civil servant.[84] Leading Britain into 'Europe' had to be Heath's only claim to 'greatness', and, even then, that was dependent on what happened to the Community in the future, and Britain's membership did not bring about the beneficial transformation of her economy that advocates like Heath had predicated. The impressive economic recovery of the countries that constituted the Six had been made before the Treaty of Rome, and, though the Common Market may well have kept this going in a context in which the West enjoyed a remarkable boom led by the USA, the act of joining was not of itself going to improve Britain's economic performance. As it happened, the world economic boom came to a halt, the Bretton Woods arrangements involving fixed exchange rates broke down, the pound was floated, and the sterling area was abolished. Heath could hardly have chosen a worse time to join the Community than 1973. This may have been 'unlucky', and any British Government elected in 1970 would have been in difficulties in a context of substantial rises in world commodity prices, and that led by Heath was unfortunate in that regard. Yet, even the most devoted of 'Europeans' in O'Neill had conceded that Britain had to 'put her own house in order', and in domestic policy the troubles that eventually engulfed this Government were importantly of Heath's own making.

'Conservatism at its best is always empirical, not dogmatic', Heath wrote,[85] and he maintained that his remark in relation to the Lonrho Affair about 'the unpleasant and unacceptable face of capitalism' did not mean that he was hostile to the private enterprise system.[86] Many in the Conservative Party had tired of the Keynesian Welfare State, but this was neither the case with most of the electorate nor with Heath. If, aside from 'Europe', and the need for 'modernization', Heath had any political convictions they seemed to be those of the 1940s in reaction to the 1930s, the world of war socialism and the Attlee dispensation and co-operation with the trade unions. This outlook might help to explain why, for example, the Tories came to office in 1970 with a denationalization agenda that was even more modest than in 1951. A small start was made with selling off council houses. Some State-owned public houses in Carlisle and the South of Scotland were returned to the private sector. So was Thomas Cook the travel agents. A 'second force' airline was permitted alongside what became British Airways, but this was following up the recommendations of the Edwards Committee that had been set up by the Wilson Government.[87] The Heath Government's policy towards the larger nationalized industries was to use them as loss leaders in combating inflation, until the NUM effectively vetoed this.[88] That those industries were so often treated as being outside the remit of 'modernization' was in contrast with the Heath Government's many essays in administrative change that meant central government being reorganized and local government too following what came to be called the Heath-Walker reforms, as well as a worthless recasting of the structure of the NHS. This form of functionalism might well have suited the Webbs, who would surely have approved too of the nationalizations effected by the Gas Act of 1972 and the Water Act of 1973, but it cohered uneasily with Conservatism. So did Heath. Though Heath saw himself as acting in 'the spirit of One Nation',[89] the facts were that of the first twelve occasions on which a State of Emergency was declared under the relevant legislation of 1920, no less than five of them were authorized under the Heath Government.[90]

Heath sought a different style of government to the traditional Tory one, and he got the worst of both worlds by behaving like an inverted Theodore Roosevelt, tending to speak harshly but being unwilling or unable to wield a big stick. Heath's self defeating political style helped to ensure that his Government got no political credit for, say, introducing a Christmas bonus for pensioners that was literally Santa Claus economics, and a part of the biggest rise in social expenditure since the War.[91] In economic policy, Heath did more than steal the clothes of his Party's Labour opponents, and, given what he had said in economic liberal tones before, he looked ridiculous wearing what he did, and so did his colleagues. 'One socialist measure followed another', a backbencher complained, 'with even a 30 per cent levy on land having planning permission where development was not taking place as quickly as the Government wished'.[92] With nothing to lose, Powell asked: 'In introducing a compulsory control of wages and prices, in contravention of the deepest commitments of this Party, has my Right Hon. Friend taken leave of his senses?'[93] Far from going mad, what Heath did was to take the conventional wisdom or, if one prefers, the supposed sanity of the day in domestic politics and economics to its outer limits. Thus, the reform of the machinery of government had to be done properly this time, and if there was to be deficit-financing then it had to be done on the grandest scale, and if there had to be a prices and incomes policy, as all 'serious', 'sensible' and 'responsible' people said there had to be, then it had to be the most comprehensive ever. When all this failed, naturally enough, Heath resented criticism because he had only done what those who mattered had wanted and, indeed, on a scale that nobody else had dared to do. So, to Heath, it was only 'fair' that he should carry on. The electoral arithmetic prised Heath out of Downing Street, but he continued to expect the Conservative Party to support him even after he led them to another defeat in the October 1974 Election, campaigning on an unconvincing Government of National Unity platform. The Tories only claimed 35.8 per cent of the total vote, their then worst electoral performance of modern times.[94] Heath had now led the Conservatives to three defeats in four Elections, but he saw no need to stand down. By staying on as Leader, he effectively ruined the chances of his loyalists, more or less giving the prize to his main adversary, Mrs Thatcher. The Heath experiment was over.

11
The Last Act: The Labour Governments 1974–6

'In 1974 the Cabinet was richer in previous experience than perhaps any incoming Government this century', Harold Wilson was later to write, adding: 'Fourteen members had sat in the outgoing 1970 Cabinet.'[1] In this way, to have experienced Ministers, especially those associated with failure, was deemed to be an advantage. That was not to say that Wilson did not have men well suited to high office to appoint. Healey went to the Treasury, and Jenkins became the first Home Secretary to go back for a second term since Sir John Simon, who 'did not provide an inspiring precedent'.[2] Jenkins was eventually to introduce 'anti-discrimination legislation, both sexual and racial', though he saw his 'primary task as the maintenance of the proper authority of the State, first against the threat of [IRA] terrorism ... but also against a view which I saw as dangerously prevalent within the Cabinet. What the TUC wanted was becoming more important than upholding the rule of law.' Jenkins found it amazing that there was no provision for the independent review of complaints about the police, and he proposed the filling of that gap.[3] Jenkins might well have wished to go to the FCO, but Callaghan was preferred for that role. After that, once Crosland was despatched to the DOE, Wilson was down to the also-rans, notably Mrs Castle, about whom he came to wonder if he had not over-promoted her in the first place.[4] She was to remain as Secretary of State in the DHSS until Wilson's retirement, with one adviser believing that this was because the Prime Minister was frightened of her.[5] Wilson's establishment of the Prime Minister's Policy Unit represented a recognition of some of the weaknesses in the central direction of his previous Governments, but such machinery could only achieve so much in a Downing Street environment in which Marcia Williams continued to be granted more authority than her status merited.[6] With Michael Foot in its ranks as well as Jenkins, the Government that Wilson first formed in March 1974 reflected a Labour Party that, according to one of those Ministers, Edmund Dell, was 'so divided it was difficult even to regard it as a coalition'. Indeed, Dell believed that there was 'no comparable example of such intellectual and political incoherence in a Party coming into office in the twentieth-century history of the United Kingdom'.[7]

The Right and Centre had largely run the Wilson Governments of 1964–70. They may well have been undistinguished Governments by any criteria, but they had been notably vulnerable to condemnation by the use of socialist criteria, and judgments of that kind remained relevant because the Labour Party retained socialist objectives. Wilson had seen no need to do anything about the 1948 divide, acting as if a long period of office and its compromises would ease away the differences, but defeat in the 1970 Election inevitably opened up once more the question of how far a future Labour Government should intervene in a mixed economy. The issue of Britain's membership of the European Community also threatened to tear the Party apart. 'Throughout the period [of Opposition between 1970 and 1974] Labour politicians were to live through a paradox which never properly surfaced', one contemporary observer shrewdly observed. 'The unspoken paradox was this: the proposed planning agreements system between Government and individual firms and a State intervention agency, which [the Left] was to force through as part of the industrial policy, was based upon continental models, but neither they nor their rivals, the Centre Right pro-Marketeers, could acknowledge this. For either side, the public admission of the inherent contradiction could serve to weaken the cause they served.'[8] Those like Jenkins on the Right and Centre of the Party were as fanatically 'European' as Heath. Indeed, Jenkins resigned the Deputy Leadership in April 1972 because the Shadow Cabinet committed itself to a future referendum on British membership of the Community. Jenkins's most revealing objection to referenda was their 'extensive use [would be] the likely enemy of many progressive causes from the abolition of capital punishment to race relations legislation'.[9] A more dispassionate, and certainly more democratic, view would be that, from the perspective of those opposed to being part of the Community, the most advantageous time to hold a referendum on membership would be before joining. Otherwise, it would become a conservative decision, with approval likely.

The translation of Anthony Wedgwood Benn the social democrat into Tony Benn the socialist, was a source of much mirth among his many critics, and some fear. Not content with pressing the referendum idea, Benn wanted to take farther the example that the Heath Government had obligingly given following its U-turn, writing in 1973 that 'these Bills and Acts, together with the prices and Pay Code, constitute the most comprehensive armoury of governmental control that has ever been assembled for use over private industry, far exceeding all the powers thought to be necessary by the last Labour Government'.[10] Benn and the Left then devised *Labour's Programme 1973*, which proposed that a National Enterprise Board should take a controlling interest in the 25 largest British manufacturing companies to promote directed investment on the basis of planning agreements. On the Right, people like Harold Lever dismissed all this as 'a naïve dream' and as savouring of 'the Russian Gosplan'.[11] The examples were nearer home, as Lever knew but could not say. The Right and Centre, and Wilson himself, discredited by the failed Government of the 1960s had to concede ground to the constituency activists, among whom the Left was strengthened by Wilson's curious ending of the proscribed list. They also had to give ground to the unions, among whom the leaderships were dominated by the Left and their activists. This was especially true of the whose strikes had first wounded and then forced the Heath Government to seek a further electoral mandate. As a result of the February 1974 Election, the Labour Party, flourishing a Social Contract with the unions, was able to form a Minority Government, obtaining just 37.1 per cent of the votes cast.[12] In the further October 1974 Election, the Labour Party obtained only 39.2 per cent of the votes cast, and an overall majority of three seats.[13] The Labour Movement had played a major part in bringing the British economy to its knees, and the Labour Government was now doomed to inherit the consequences, and without the consolation of a secure Parliamentary majority to sustain it.

'Labour came to office ... more closely tied to the trade unions' apron strings than in 1964 or 1966', Dell wrote, repeating the then familiar belief that 'the country was becoming ungovernable except with the agreement of the trade union movement'.[14] Mrs Castle believed that the Labour Government's 'new concordat with the trade unions is far more hopeful than the arms-length relationship we had last time'.[15] Healey, as Chancellor of the Exchequer, recalled that 'when I introduced my third Budget in April 1975, I pointed out that the Government had carried out its side of the Social Contract by repealing Heath's anti-union legislation, by starting on the redistribution of wealth and income through its tax changes, and by increasing

old age pensions and other benefits. In fact the value of services provided by the Government, which we tried to get people to see as their
"social wage," amounted to about £1,000 a year for every member of
the working population. But the unions defaulted on their part of
the Contract'.[16] Earlier, Healey had sharply objected when Dell, as
Paymaster General, had described the Social Contract as 'codswallop'.[17]
Politically, in the situation as perceived by many in the electorate, the
Labour Party's special relationship with the trade union leaderships
had superficial short term advantages. Whether the rank and file of the
trade union movement would be obliging was always in doubt. The
leaders only too often led from the back. In the mid-1970s, Jack Jones
of the TGWU seemed to be seen as the most powerful political figure in
the country. The Labour Government might well feel the need to act at
the behest of Jones, or, for that matter, Scanlon of the Engineers, or,
more certainly, the NUM. There was no need, though, for international
bankers to bow the knee, and, sooner rather than later, those countries
who live beyond their means have to satisfy such financial opinion.

'I am the most political Chancellor you ever had', Healey boasted to
Mrs Castle in September 1974, who agreed with him.[18] Healey later
denied that 'my main aim was to make the rich howl with anguish'.[19]
It seems, then, that, in one sense, Healey was not 'political' enough,
and that his economic policy was widely misread. In the case of those
members of the Labour Party committed to – in Benn's phrase – 'a fundamental and irreversible shift in the balance of power and wealth in
favour of working people and their families'[20] they may well have been
misled deliberately. Certainly, neither Prime Minister Wilson nor
Healey had any intention of establishing a National Enterprise Board
with anything resembling wide powers. In May 1974, Healey told the
annual dinner of the CBI: 'I can assure you that the Government has
no intention of destroying the private sector or encouraging its
decay.'[21] Healey later remarked that 'the big mistake [in] the first year
was attempting an expansion of the British economy when all our
trading partners were restricting theirs. So we were bound to run into a
balance of payments crisis'.[22] As Labour had at least partly obtained
office in 1974 on the basis that they could appease the trade unions
more effectively than Heath's Government, whom they accused of
insufficiently expanding the economy when the opposite was the case,
Wilson's Government was poorly placed to pursue anything other
than a Keynesianism-in-one-country approach to economic management, not least because it was in a minority position in Parliament.
Understandably, the electoral reward of a Commons majority of 3 did

not encourage a sterner approach. The outcome of the EEC referendum in June 1975 paved the way for such an approach. The Left's claim to have some special rapport with the mass of the electorate was discredited by their defeat. Wilson had used the electorate to discipline his Party, not being able to do it himself.

There still remained to be settled the question of the distribution of power in the Labour Party, and neither Wilson nor his successor as Prime Minister could bring this about. Wilson took the opportunity to move Benn from being Secretary of State at the Department of Industry to the Department of Energy. At last, too, the Labour Government addressed the problem of runaway inflation. It had little choice about doing this. According to Mrs Castle, Healey was almost desperate at the Cabinet meeting of 12 June 1975, telling Ministers: 'This morning we have had the most severe attack on sterling that we have ever had ... . We have got to stop the slide. I have been talking to the central bankers in Paris and the real reason for this run is the widespread feeling that we lack the will to deal with inflation.'[23] This 'feeling' was well founded. The remedy was supposed to be an incomes policy. 'The threat of statutory powers had obviously concentrated the unions' minds wonderfully', Mrs Castle noted on 7 July 1975.[24] Under Jones's leadership, the unions agreed to a voluntary incomes policy, initially on the basis of a flat rate increase. Dell believed that a statutory incomes policy would have been more effective,[25] but whether the Labour Government could have survived its introduction was doubtful. Early in 1976, cash limits on public expenditure were imposed, pushing aside the Plowden arrangements once deemed the height of sophistication. Wilson resigned as Prime Minister in March 1976 to be eventually succeeded on the third ballot by James Callaghan, whose closest rival proved to be Foot. Callaghan satisfied himself with one act of revenge. He dismissed Mrs Castle. 'I did not believe Jim would sack me', she wrote, 'I didn't deserve that.'[26] Callaghan was unmoved. Jenkins was denied the FCO, staying as Home Secretary until departing for Brussels later in 1976.[27]

Though Callaghan believed that 'I'm Prime Minister of the greatest country in the world',[28] such was the grim nature of the economic analysis that he was initially greeted with in April 1976 that he was to write that 'had I taken it all at face value the only thing to do would have been to throw myself out of an upper-floor window on to the Downing Street pavement'.[29] On the day that he became Prime Minister, Callaghan was told by his Policy Unit that 'a further devaluation of between 5 and 10 per cent in the value of sterling was inevitable'.[30] When first meeting Healey as his Chancellor, Callaghan professed himself to be 'shocked [by] how much had been spent by the Bank of England to support the sterling exchange rate since 1 January 1976. Denis added that we might need to make an approach to the IMF during the summer to replace the reserves we had spent.'[31] Famously turning back at the airport and, thus, away from the annual meeting of the IMF, Healey was to dash to the Labour Party Conference on 30 September 1976. Though he was Chancellor of the Exchequer, Healey was only a delegate and he was limited to a five-minute speech. In it, Healey made it clear that 'I am going to negotiate with the IMF on the basis of our existing policies'.[32] The Cabinet was divided between unreconstructed Keynesians, such as Crosland, devotees of a siege economy, meaning the Left, and the remainder who recognized the need at the time to accept the restrictive conditions that an IMF loan involved. Benn circulated the minutes of the meetings of the Labour Cabinet in 1931, believing them to be 'a complete repeat of what is happening now'. Callaghan was well aware of this historical analogy, and he steered the Cabinet to reluctant agreement with considerable skill, and, some thought, contrived to ease the IMF conditions as well.[33] Healey was later to write that 'Crosland argued persuasively that the situation was already under control. So, in fact, it was, but the markets would not believe it.'[34] Healey insisted that 'we could have done without the IMF loan only if we – and the world – had known the real facts at the time. But in 1976 our forecasts were too pessimistic, and we were still describing our public expenditure in a way which was immensely damaging to our standing in financial markets.'[35] Neither the IMF nor the markets would necessarily have been convinced by more hopeful forecasts,[36] not least because 'official estimates of public expenditure' were 'widely regarded as works of fiction, as [was] the Social Contract'.[37] The brutal reality was that 'the markets wanted blood',[38] and that whatever the Government did it had to have 'an IMF loan because we needed the stamp of approval'.[39]

'Goodbye, Great Britain' had been the reaction of *The Wall Street Journal* to Healey's Budget in April 1975, condemning 'the Welfare State … manic Keynesian syndrome' for the country's plight.[40] Eighteen months later, Callaghan was to tell the Labour Party Conference that 'the cosy world we were told would go on for ever, where full employment would be guaranteed by the stroke of the Chancellor's pen, cutting taxes, deficit spending, that cosy world is gone'.[41] Twenty years after the failure of the Suez adventure had undermined Britain's international prestige, the workings of the economic and social order that she had built in the 1940s, and that she, though nobody else, had prized, had led to the humiliation of the IMF crisis. 'Crosland was saying ... we don't understand economics at all – you can run a much bigger deficit than this without damage', Healey said of the relevant Cabinet debate, before effectively writing off Keynesianism by observing: 'The trouble with theoretical economists is that they don't understand that when you have a deficit you can only finance it by borrowing, and you've got to persuade people that it's worth lending to you, and that they'll get their money back.'[42] Benn thought that 'the death of the social democratic wing of the [Labour] Party occurred in that Cabinet when Tony Crosland said at one stage: it is mad but we have no alternative'.[43] If, to paraphrase Yeats, 'the Centre cannot hold', and those who deemed themselves 'the best lack all conviction', then the way was clear for those 'full of passionate intensity'. Benn had earlier caught a mood when applauding those who treated Foot as 'fake Left' because he was 'Parliamentary orientated'.[44] For a time after the fall of Heath, one adviser recalled that 'there was a real smell of fear in the air, with Labour people in Whitehall and Westminster asking each other which side of the barricades they would join – the miners' or the Army's'.[45] There was no doubt that many on the Left sensed their opportunity. With the Americans defeated in Vietnam, the world seemed not only to believers to be going the Left's way, and, if Britain with no revolutionary tradition seemed an unlikely setting for socialist advance by force, there was sufficient evidence of intent to justify considering the question of who could or would oppose this successfully. After an informal coalition involving the leaderships of the main parties had won the 1975 Referendum for the 'Europeans', the notion of a National Government of 'men of goodwill' being formed to run the country surfaced for a time. The most that eventually happened was a short lived Lib-Lab Pact. The Callaghan Government was left to soldier on alone, only to have what remained of its authority destroyed in spectacular style by a revolt of the wider Labour Movement during the Winter of Discontent of 1978–9. Callaghan had stated in 1976 that 'for too long, perhaps ever since the War, we postponed facing up to fundamental choices and fundamental changes in our society and in our economy',[46] and the overthrow of his Government left the way clear for another with no need to treat the 1945 dispensation with respect. If those trying to break the British political system were not to be satisfied until they faced opponents equally ruthless and, thus, worthy of the challenge, they were to find such an adversary in the next Conservative Government.

Notes and References

1 'A Period of National Humilation and Decline'

1 I[C] Churchill, I, 1948, p. 601
2 I[C] Moran 1966, p. 287
3 I[C] Moran, 1966, p. 254
4 III[A] Hancock and Gowing, 1949, p. 452
5 I[C] Hailsham, 1975, pp. 301–2
6 I[D] Annan, 1990, p. 449
7 I[C] Moran, 1966, p. 353

2 Britain as a Great Power

1 I[D] Rhodes James, VII, 1974, p. 7316
2 I[D] Rhodes James, VII, 1974, p. 7811
3 I[D] Rhodes James, VII, 1974, pp. 7290–1
4 I[D] Rhodes James, VII, 1974, p. 7381
5 I[D] Rhodes James, VII, 1974, p. 7382
6 I[D] Rhodes James, VII, 1974, p. 7900
7 I[D] Rhodes James, VII, 1974, p. 7289
8 II[B] Churchill, I, 1956, p. viii
9 II[B] Churchill, IV, 1958, p. vii
10 II[B] Matthew, 1973, p. 162
11 I[D] Roberts, 1999, p. 617
12 I[D] Rhodes James, VII, 1974, p. 7291
13 III[A] Sayers, 1956, p. 18
14 II[B] Dawson, 1959, p. 249
15 I[D] Rhodes James, VI, 1974, p. 6350
16 I[D] Taylor, 1965, p. 532
17 I[D] Rhodes James, VII, 1974, p. 7346
18 I[D] Rhodes James, VII, 1974, p. 7293
19 III[B] Engerman and Gallman, 2000, p. 489
20 II[B] Blum, 1973, p. 638
21 II[B] Blum, 1973, p. 636
22 II[B] Blum, 1973, p. 363
23 II[B] Anderson, 1981, p. 9
24 II[B] Anderson, 1981, p. 8
25 II[B] Anderson, 1981, pp. 9–10
26 II[B] Anderson, 1981, pp. 19–24
27 II[B] Anderson, 1981, p. 47
28 II[B] Ferrell, 1982, p. 131
29 II[B] Ferrell, 1982, p. 80
30 III[B] Harrod, 1951, p. 576
31 III[B] Gardner, 1980, p. xiii
32 I[D] Roberts, 1991, p. 287

33   **II[B]** Acheson, 1970, p. 29
34   *Punch*, 14.1.1920
35   **III[B]** Skidelsky, 2000, p. 475
36   **III[B]** Kindelberger, 1984, pp. 239–50; **II[B]** Liberman, 1996, p. 89; **II[B]**
      Ferguson, 1998, pp. 412–19
37   **III[B]** Keynes, II, 1971, p. 31
38   **III[B]** Keynes, II, 1971, p. 29
39   **III[B]** Keynes, II, 1971, p. 27
40   *Punch*, 14.1.1920
41   **III[B]** Skidelsky, 1983, p. 234
42   **III{B]** Keynes, XXIII, 1979, pp. 15–17
43   **III[B]** Keynes, XXIII, 1979, pp. 25–6
44   **II[B}**Thorne, 1988, p. 82
45   **III[B]** Skidelsky, 2000, p. 118
46   **III[B]** Skidelsky, 2000, p. 91
47   **III[B]** Skidelsky, 2000, p. 110
48   **III[B]** Moggridge, 1992, p. 657
49   **II[B]** Haynes and Kliehr, 1999, pp. 47–8, 125–6, 138–50; **II[B]** Weinstein
      and Vassilev, 1999, pp. 48, 90, 106, 157, 158, 159, 161–2, 163–4, 165, 168,
      169, 243, 274; **II[B]** Andrew and Mitrokhin, 2000, pp. 139–41, 144, 172,
      186, 187
50   **III[B]** Skidelsky, 2000, p. 242
51   **III[B]** Skidelsky, 2000, p. 241
52   **III[B]** Keynes, XXV, 1980, p. 356
53   **III[B]** Skidelsky, 2000, p. 99
54   **II[B]** Hull, II, 1948, pp. 1472–81
55   **I[B]** HL Deb., 23.5.1944, col. 848
56   **I[B]** HL Deb., 23.5.1944, col. 838
57   **I[B]** HL Deb., 23.5.1944, col. 838
58   **III[C]** Gardner, 1980, p. 384
59   **III[B]** Gardner, 1980, pp. 382–3
60   **III[B]** Harrod, 1951, pp. 631–2
61   **III[B]** Moggridge, 1992, p. 831
62   **III[B]** Harrod, 1951, p. 628
63   **II[B]** Truman, 1955, p. 145
64   **II[B]** Ferrell, 1994, p. 199
65   **II[B]** Acheson, 1969, p. 122
66   **I[B]** HC Deb., 24.12.1945, col. 954
67   **I[B]** HC Deb., 24.12.1945, col. 955
68   **I[C]** Dalton, 1962, pp. 74–75
69   **I[B]** HL Deb., 18.12.1945, col. 782
70   *The Economist*, 8.12.1945, p. 821
71   **I[C]** Dalton, 1962, p. 75
72   **III[B]** Gardner, 1980, p. 201
73   **III[B]** Harrod, 1951, p. 337–8
74   **III[B]** Gardner, 1980, p. 195
75   **I[B]** HL Deb., 23.5.1944, col. 839
76   **I[A]** PRO: T160/1375/F17942/01015
77   **I[B]** HL Deb., 23.5.1944, col. 849

78 **II[B]** Wilson, 1919, p. 456; c.f. **II[B]** Lowell, I, 1896, p. 252
79 **II[B]** Carr, 1991, pp. 119–20
80 **II[B]** Carr, 1982, pp. 349, 364
81 **II[B]** Reiss, 1991, pp. 93–130
82 **II[B]** Bannister, 1992, p. 297
83 **II[B]** LaFeber, 1989, p. 602
84 **II[B]** LaFeber, 1989, p. 284
85 **II[B]** Ambrose, 1984, p. 508

3 The Keynesian Full Employment Welfare State

1 **III[B]** Briggs, 1961, p. 228
2 **III[B]** Beveridge, 1953, p. 319–20
3 **III[B]** Wootton, 1943, pp. 358–9
4 **III[B]** Skidelsky, 1992, p. 495
5 **III[B]** Keynes, VII, 1973, p. 3
6 **III[B]** Hicks, 1937, p. 147
7 **III[B]** Keynes, VII, 1973, p. xxi
8 **III[B]** Hicks, 1937, p. 147
9 **III[B]** Johnson, 1961, p. 2
10 **III[B]** Keynes, VII, 1973, pp. 264–5
11 **III[B]** Keynes, VII, 1973, p. 245
12 **III[B]** Hicks, 1937, pp. 156–8
13 **III[B]** Keynes, VII, 1973, p. 2
14 **III[B]** Keynes, XIV, 1973, p. 81
15 **III[B]** Keynes, VII, 1973, p. xxiii
16 **III[B]** Harrod, 1937, p. 85
17 **III[B]** Hicks, 1937, p. 158
18 **III[B]** Fry, 1979, p. 82
19 **III[B]** Skidelsky, 1992, p. 574
20 **III[B]** Keynes, VII, 1973, p. 381
21 **III[B]** Keynes, IX, 1972, p. 294
22 **III[B]** Keynes, IX, 1972, p. 306
23 **I[D]** Fry, 2001, pp. 77–9
24 **III[B]** Skidelsky, 1992, p. 232
25 **III[B]** Keynes, IX, 1972, p. 307
26 **III[B]** Keynes, IX, 1972, p. 296
27 **III[B]** Keynes, IX, 1972, pp. 301–3; **III[B]** Skidelsky, 1992, pp. 231–2
28 **III[B]** Skidelsky, 1992, p. 536
29 **I[D]** Mackenzie and Mackenzie, IV, 1985, pp. 370–1
30 **III[B]** Keynes, XXI, 1982, pp. 500–3
31 **III[B]** Keynes, XXI, 1982, pp. 494–6
32 **I[D]** Mackenzie and Mackenzie, IV, 1985, p. 371
33 **III[B]** Keynes, IX, 1972, p. 285
34 **III[B]** Moggridge, 1992, p. 465
35 **I[D]** Salter, 1967, pp. 88–9
36 **III[B]** Keynes, IX, 1972, pp. 406–7
37 **III[B]** Keynes, IX, 1972, p. 377
38 **III[B]** Robbins, 1947, p. 32
39 **III[B]** Robbins, 1947, p. 35

40   **III[B]** Keynes, IX, 1972, p. 377
41   **III[B]** Harrod, 1951, pp. 493–4; **III[B]** Keynes, IX, 1972, pp. 391–6
42   **I[B]** HC Deb., 7.4.1941, cols. 1297–335; **III[A]** Cmd. 6261, 1941; **III[A]** Sayers, 1956, pp. 58–93; **III[B]** Chester, 1951, pp. 83–101
43   **III[B]** Bridges, 1950, p. 15
44   **III[B]** Feinstein, 1983, p. 13
45   **III[B]** Cairncross and Watts, 1989, pp. 70–87; **III[B]** Meade, I, 1988, p. 199–232
46   **III[B]** Peden, 1983, pp. 281–96
47   **I[A]** PRO: CAB 87/7
48   **III[B]** Keynes, XXVII, 1980, pp. 364–72
49   **III[A]** Cmd. 6527, 1944, p. 3
50   **III[B]** Moggridge, 1992, p. 709
51   **I[C]** Wilson, 1986, p. 64
52   **I[D]** Mackenzie and Mackenzie, IV, 1985, p. 491
53   **III[A]** Cmd. 6404, 1942, p. 4
54   **III[B]** Harris, 1977, p. 386
55   **I[D]** Fry, 2001, p. 201
56   **III[B]** Harris, 1977, p. 386
57   **III[A]** Cmd. 6404, 1942, p. 170
58   **III[A]** Cmd. 6404, 1942, p. 171
59   **III[B]** Harris, 1977, pp. 3, 7–43
60   **III[A]** Cmd. 6404, 1942, pp. 15–17
61   **III[A]** Cmd. 6404, 1942, p. 155
62   **III[A]** Cmd. 6404, 1942, p. 163
63   **III[A]** Cmd. 6404, 1942, p. 158
64   **III[B]** Keynes, XXVII, 1980, p. 255
65   **III[B]** Keynes, XXVII, 1980, p. 258
66   **III[A]** Cmd. 6502, 1944, p. 52
67   **III[A]** Cmd. 6550, 1944
68   **III[A]** Cmd. 6551, 1944
69   **I[C]** Pimlott, 1986, pp. 747–8
70   **III[A]** Cmd. 6404, 1942, p. 166
71   **III[B]** Shirras and Rostas, 1942, p. 72
72   **III[A]** Sayers, 1956, pp. 99–111
73   **III[A]** Sayers, 1956, pp. 74–5
74   **III[B]** Clark, 1945, p. 380
75   **III[B]** Skidelsky, 2000, p. 276
76   **III[B]** Harrod, 1951, p. 318
77   **III[B]** Keynes, VII, 1973, p. 378
78   **III[A]** Cmd. 6527, 1944, p. 28
79   **I[B]** HC Deb., 21.6.1944, cols. 212–13, 231
80   **I[D]** Mackenzie and Mackenzie, IV, 1985, p. 260
81   **III[B]** Harris, 1977, p. 331
82   **III[B]** Beveridge, 1944, p. 128
83   **III[B]** Keynes, XXVII, 1980, p. 381
84   **III[B]** Keynes, XXVII, 1980, p. 299
85   **I[B]** Keynes, XXVII, 1980, pp. 224–5
86   **I[A]** PRO: T161/1129/S48497/2

87 III[B] Keynes, XXVII, 1980, p. 225
88 III[B] Keynes, XXVII, 1980, p. 263
89 III[A] Cmd. 6404, 1942, p. 108
90 III[A] Cmd. 6404, 1942, p. 7
91 III[B] Beveridge, 1944, p. 125
92 III[B] Beveridge, 1944, p. 175
93 III[B] Beveridge, 1944, p. 174
94 III[B] Keynes, IX, 1972, p. 309
95 III[B] Barnes and Reid, 1980, p. xiii
96   I[B] HC Deb., 23.6.1944, col. 527
97 III[B] Keynes, XXVII, 1980, p. 385
98 III[B] Keynes, VII, 1973, p. 378
99 III[B] Beveridge, 1944, p. 37
100 III[B] Viner, 1936–7, p. 149
101 III[B] Skidelsky, 2000, p. 469

4   The Electoral Revolution of 1945 and the Veto

1   I[D] Young, 1980, p. 473
2   I[C] IPimlott, 1986, pp. 360–1
3   I[D] Butler, 1989, p. 8
4   I[D] Craig, 1981, pp. xv, 82
5   I[D] Craig, 1969, pp. 52, 349, 624, 660; I[D] Craig, 1981, p. 35
6   I[D] McCallum and Readman, 1947, p. 293
7   I[D] Craig, 1969, p. 592
8   I[D] McCallum and Readman, 1947, pp. 293–5
9   I[D] McCallum and Readman, 1947, p. 261
10   I[D] Craig, 1969, p. 533
11   I[D] Craig, 1969, p. 620
12   I[D] Craig, 1969, p. 440)
13   I[D] Craig, 1969, p. 23; I[D] Pritt, 1966, p. 29
14   *The Times*, 27.7.1945; I[D] McCallum and Readman, 1947, p. 261; I[D] Craig, 1969, pp. 3–63
15   I[D] McCallum and Readman, 1947, p. 247
16   I[C] Foot, 1973, p. 17
17   I[D] Sissons and French, 1963, p. 5
18   I[C] Healey, 1990, p. 68
19   I[B] HC Deb., 18.8.1945, col. 73
20   I[D] Mitchell, 1995, p. 11
21   I[D] Namier, 1952, p. 183
22   I[D] McCallum and Readman, 1947, p. 243
23   I[D] Beales, 1947, pp. 48–60
24   I[D] Williams, 1951, p. 358
25   I[D] Pritt, 1966, p. 30)
26   I[C] Shinwell, 1955, p. 171
27   *The Economist*, 7.7.1945, p. 2
28   *The Economist*, 28.7.1945, p. 105
29   I[D] Craig, 1971, p. 101
30   *The Economist*, 16.6.1945, p. 797
31   I[D] Craig, 1975, p. 127

32   I[D] Craig, 1975, p. 135
33   I[D] Craig, 1975, p. 134
34   I[D] Craig, 1975, p. 133
35   I[D] Craig, 1975, p. 134
36   I[D] Craig, 1975, p. 133
37   I[D] Craig, 1975, p. 115
38   I[D] Craig, 1975, p. 117
39   I[D] Craig, 1975, p. 118
40   I[D] Craig, 1975, p. 129
41   I[D] Craig, 1975, p. 130
42   I[D] Craig, 1975, p. 136
43   I[D] Craig, 1975, p. 130
44   I[D] Craig, 1975, p. 126
45   I[D] Craig, 1975, p. 122
46   I[D] Gallup, I, 1976, p. 108
47   I[D] Butler, 1989, p. 57
48   I[D] Gallup, I, 1976, p. 104
49   I[C] Bullock, 1967, p. 390
50   I[C] Donoughue and Jones, 1973, p. 330
51   I[C] Pimlott, 1986, p. 360
52   I[D] Colville, 1985, p. 611
53   I[D] Mitchell, 1995, p. 83
54   I[C] Shinwell, 1955, p. 169
55   I[D] Mitchell, 1995, p. 100
56   I[D] Young, 1980, p. 476
57   I[C] Lewis, 1998, p. 103
58   *The Listener*, 7.6.1945, p. 632
59   I[D] Gallup, I, 1976, p. 117
60   I[C] Hailsham, 1975, p. 157
61   I[D] Colville, 1985, p. 606
62   I[D] Young, 1980, p. 474
63   I[D] Hogg, 1947, p. 228
64   I[C] Howard, 1987, p. 148
65   I[C] Butler, 1971, p. 128
66   I[C] Macmillan, 1969, p. 32
67   I[D] Butler, 1989, p. 8
68   I[D] Gallup, I, 1976, pp. 104, 107, 110, 111
69   I[D] Gallup, I, 1976, p. 113
70   I[D] Fry, 2001, pp. 205–6
71   I[D] Gallup, I, 1976, pp. 106–7
72   I[D] Craig, 1975, p. 129
73   I[D] Gallup, I, 1976, p. 108
74   I[D] Gallup, I, 1976, p. 109
75   I[D] Pritt, 1963, p. 28
76   I[D] Pritt, 1963, p. 29
77   I[D] Barnes and Nicholson, 1988, p. 1048
78   I[D] Taylor, 1972, p. 569
79   *The Listener*, 5.7.1945, p. 17
80   I[D] Gallup, I, 1976, p. 117

81   **I[C]** Jenkins, 2001, p. 806
82   **I[D]** Craig, 1969, p. 283
83   *The Economist*, 28.7.1945, p. 105
84   **I[D]** Fry, 2001, p. 17
85   **I[C]** Winterton, 1953, pp. 206–7
86   **I[C]** Winterton, 1953, p. 314
87   **I[D]** Taylor, 1972, pp. 568–9
88   **I[D]** Butler, 1949, pp. 396–407: **I[D]** Fry, 1991, pp. 43–7
89   **I[D]** Butler and Stokes, 1969, p. 54
90   **I[D]** Manning, 1970, p. 164
91   **I[D]** McCallum and Readman, 1947, p. 30
92   **I[D]** Calder, 1969, pp. 581–2
93   **I[D]** McCallum and Readman, 1947, p. 43
94   **I[D]** Bonham, 1954, pp. pp. 129–30
95   **I[D]** Fry, 1991, p. 54
96   *The Times*, 8.5.1947
97   **I[D]** Parkin, 1967, pp. 278–90
98   **I[D]** Nordlinger, 1967; **I[D]** MacKenzie and Silver, 1968
99   *The Times*, 5.7.1948
100   **I[C]** Dalton, 1957, p. 421
101   **I[C]** Foot, 1973, p. 19
102   **I[B]** HC Deb., 2.4.1946, col. 1213
103   **I[D]** Richards, 1945, p. 352
104   **I[D]** Mellors, 1978, p. 77
105   **I[D]** Sissons and French, 1964, p. 19
106   **I[D]** Sissons and French, 1964, p. 25
107   **I[D]** Sissons and French, 1964, p. 331
108   **I[D]** Pareto, 1966, pp. 57–9, 78, 84, 256–60
109   **I[D]** Hennessy, 1993, p. 440
110   **I[B]** HL Deb., 11.5.1948, col. 757
111   **I[D]** Gallup, I, 1976, p. 174
112   **I[B]** HC Deb., 14.4.1948, cols. 984–5
113   **I[D]** Magnus, 1973, pp. 83–5, 102–3; **I[D]** Barker, 1950, pp. 154–204
114   **I[B]** HC Deb., 14.4.1948, col. 1083
115   **I[B]** HC Deb., 14.4.1948, col. 1085
116   **I[B]** HL Deb., 2.6.1948, cols. 175–8
117   **I[A]** PRO: CAB 128/12; **I[A]** PRO: CAB 128/13
118   **I[B]** HC Deb., 16.4.1948, col. 1318
119   **I[D]** Barnett, 1986, p. 304
120   **I[B]** Barnett, 1987, p. 15
121   **I[D]** Namier, 1955, pp. 13–14
122   **I[D]** Churchill, 1929, p. 33
123   *The Times*, 25.11.1918
124   **III[B]** Johnson, 1968, p. 4
125   **I[D]** Gallup, I, 1976, p. 115
126   **I[C]** Bullock, 1967, p. 388
127   **I[C]** McCallum and Readman, 1947, pp. 137–8
128   **I[D]** Gallup, I, 1976, p. 115
129   **III[B]** Winter, 1983, p. 214

5   Wheat and Tares Together Sown

1   I[C] Dalton, 1962, p. 3
2   I[C] Pimlott, 1986, p. 361
3   I[C] Chandos, 1962, p. 329
4   I[D] Sissons and French, 1964, p. 21
5   I[D] Wheeler-Bennett, 1958, pp. 638–9, 791–4
6   I[D] Hennessy, 2000, p. 153
7   I[D] Craig, 1975, p. 126
8   I[C] Williams, 1961, p. 91
9   I[D] Morrison, 1954, pp. 334–6
10   I[C] Harris, 1982, pp. 262–3
11   I[C] Bullock, 1967, pp. 392–3
12   I[D] Hennessy, 2000, p. 150
13   *The Observer*, 6.8.1967
14   II[B] Danchev and Todman, 2001, p. 580
15   II[B] Danchev and Todman, 2001, p. 671
16   II[B] Danchev and Todman, 2001, p. 715
17   I[C] Williams, 1961, p. 7
18   I[C] Williams, 1961, p. 169
19   I[C] Harris, 1982, p. 404
20   I[C] Harris, 1982, p. 405
21   I[C] Williams, 1961, p. 83
22   I[C] Dalton, 1962, p. 287
23   I[D] Bradford, 1989, p. 388
24   I[C] Williams, 1961, p. 5
25   I[C] Harris, 1982, p. 265
26   I[D] Mackenzie and Mackenzie, IV, 1985, pp. 436–7
27   I[D] Mackenzie, III, 1978, p. 460
28   I[C] Clarke, 2002, p. 80
29   I[C] Clarke, 2002, p. 8
30   I[C] Dalton, 1962, p. 239
31   I[C] Bryant, 1998, p. 451
32   I[C] Bryant, 1998, p. 457
33   I[C] Morrison, 1960, p. 271
34   I[C] Clarke, 2002, p. 72
35   I[C] Bryant, 1998, p. 186
36   I[C] Clarke, 2002, pp. 146–7
37   I[C] Clarke, 2002, pp. 67–8
38   I[C] Lysaght, 1979, pp. 280–1
39   I[C] Dalton, 1962, p. 242
40   I[C] Williams, 1961, p. 224
41   I[C] Dalton, 1962, p. 245
42   *The Economist*, 11.8.1945, pp. 179–80
43   I[C] Harris, 1982, p. 594
44   I[C] Williams, 1961, p. 82
45   I[D] Morgan, 1984, p. 55
46   I[C] Pimlott, 1986, p. 397
47   I[C] Williams, 1961, p. 81
48   I[C] Williams, 1961, p. 84

49   I[C] Shinwell, 1955, p. 218
50   I[C] Vernon, 1982, pp. 231–5
51   I[C] Vernon, 1982, p. 128
52   I[C] Donoughue and Jones, 1973, p. 392
53   I[C] Jay, 1980, p. 151
54   I[C] Harris, 1982, p. 405
55   I[C] Wilson, 1986, p. 82
56   I[C] Wilson, 1986, p. 96
57   I[C] Williams, 1979, pp. 124–5
58   I[C] Williams, 1961, p. 85
59   I[D] Morgan, 1984, pp. 54–5
60   I[C] Pimlott, 1986, pp. 417–18
61   I[C] Pimlott, 1986, p. 361
62   I[D] Hennessy, 2000, p. 171
63   I[D] Attlee, 1937, p. 199
64   I[D] Attlee, 1937, p. 226
65   I[D] Attlee, 1937, p. 269
66   I[D] Attlee, 1937, p. 225
67   I[D] Attlee, 1937, pp. 226–47
68   II[B] X, 1946–7, p. 582
69   I[C] Harris, 1982, p. 268
70   II[B] Dilks, 1971, p. 778
71   I[D] Nicolson, 1968, p. 31
72   II[B] Dilks, 1971, p. 776
73   I[C] Harris, 1982, p. 295
74   I[D] Schneer, 1988, pp. 197–226
75   I[B] HC Deb., 18.11.1946, col. 539
76   I[B] HC Deb., 18.11.1946, col. 538
77   I[C] Harris, 1982, p. 295
78   I[A] PRO: FO/800/476/ME/47/1
79   I[A] PRO: FO/800/501/SU/46/15
80   I[A] PRO: FO/800/476/ME/47/4
81   II[B] Smith and Zametica, 1985, p. 251; II[B] Montgomery, 1958, pp. 435–6
82   II[B] Acheson, 1970, p. 164
83   I[C] Williams, 1961, pp. 118–19
84   II[B] Gowing, 1974, pp. 21–2
85   I[C] Bullock, 1983, p. 352
86   II[B] Byrnes, 1947, p. 79
87   II[B} Truman, 1955, p. 324
88   II[B] Millis, 1952, p. 132
89   II[B] Henderson, 1984, p. 22
90   I[D] Williams, 1970, pp. 242–3
91   I[C] Williams, 1961, p. 170
92   I[C] Williams, 1961, p. 71
93   I[C] Bullock, 1983, p. 382
94   I[D] Nicolson, 1968, p. 54
95   I[C] Bullock, 1967, p. 384
96   I[C] Bullock, 1967, p. 385

97	**II[B]** Ovendale, 1984, pp. 28–9
98	**I[C]** Bullock, 1983, pp. 746–7
99	**I[C]** Bullock, 1983, p. 234
100	**I[C]** Bullock, 1983, pp. 359–61
101	**II[B]** Gladwyn, 1972, pp. 175–7
102	**I[C]** Dalton, 1962, p. 129
103	**I[C]** Dalton, 1962, p. 104
104	**II[B]** Gladwyn, 1972, p. 177
105	**II[B]** Barclay, 1975, pp. 83–4
106	**I[A]** PRO: CAB 134/594
107	**I[A]** PRO: FO 55581/9927
108	**II[B]** Smith, 1988, pp. 646–7
109	**II[B]** Ovendale, 1984, p. 25
110	**II[B]** Ovendale, 1984, p. 3
111	**I[D]** Taylor, 1972, p. 570
112	**II[B]** Bullock, 1982, p. 10
113	**I[D]** Nicolson, 1968, pp. 115–16
114	**II[B]** Ovendale, 1984, p. 29
115	**II[B]** Baylis, 1982, p. 245
116	**I[C]** Pimlott, 1986, p. 443
117	**II[B]** Zametica, 1990, p. 2
118	**I[A]** PRO: FO 371/62420/UE 678
119	**II[B]** FRUS 1947, V, p. 51
120	**II[B]** FRUS 1946, V, pp. 635–48
121	**II[B]** Acheson, 1970, p. 219
122	**II[B]** Merrill, 7, 1996, pp. 68–91; **II[B]** Kennan, 1967, pp. 547–59
123	**II[B]** Merrill, 7, 1996, pp. 211–95
124	**II[B]** Merrill, 8, 1996, pp. 102–3
125	**II[B]** Merrill, 8, 1996, p. 103
126	**II[B]** Merrill, 13, 1996, pp. 172–3
127	**I[C]** Williams, 1952, p. 264
128	**I[C]** Bullock, 1983, pp. 404–5
129	**II[B]** FRUS 1947, III, p. 268
130	**II[B]** FRUS 1947, III, p. 281
131	**II[B]** FRUS 1947, III, p. 276
132	**II[B]** FRUS 1947, III, p. 268
133	**II[B]** FRUS 1947, III, p. 277
134	**II[B]** FRUS 1947, III, p. 270
135	**II[B]** FRUS 1947, III, p. 277
136	**I[C]** Bullock, 1983, p. 599
137	**II[B]** Hogan, 1987, pp. 125–7
138	**II[B]** Milward, 1984, p. 465
139	**II[B]** Hogan, 1987, pp. 431–2
140	**I[B]** HC Deb., 27.1.1948, cols. 397–8
141	**II[B]** FRUS 1948, III, p. 42
142	**II[B]** FRUS 1948, III, p. 48
143	**II[B]** Duke, 1987, pp. 50–9
144	**II[B]** Acheson, 1970, pp. 276–84
145	**I[B]** HC Deb., 18.3.1949, cols. 2533–4

146   **I[B]** Acheson, 1970, pp. 569–70
147   **II[B]** Strang, 1956, p. 289
148   **I[B]** HC Deb., 17.11.1949, col. 2204
149   **I[B]** HC Deb., 22.1.1948, col. 401
150   **II[B]** Truman, 1956, p. 140
151   **I[B]** HC Deb., 13.11.1945, col. 1928
152   **I[B]** HC Deb., 13.11.1945, col. 1934
153   **I[B]** HC Deb., 13.11.1945, col. 1927
154   **I[B]** HC Deb., 18.2.1947, col. 988
155   **II[B]** Bethell, 1979, p. 347
156   **II[B]** Bethell, 1979, p. 358
157   **I[C]** Morgan, 1981, p. 326
158   **II[B]** Sykes, 1965, pp. 328, 329, 338–9, 353, 357
159   **III[B]** Skidelsky, 1983, pp. 92, 360; **III[B]** Skidelsky, 1992, pp. 238–9
160   **III[B]** Marx and Engels, III, 1975, pp. 146–74
161   **II[B]** Henderson, 1984, p. 49
162   **I[C]** Williams, 1952, p. 258
163   **I[C]** [Bullock, 1967, p. 206
164   **I[D]** Mackenzie and Mackenzie, IV, 1985, p. 484
165   **II[B]** Mansergh, I, 1970, p. 112
166   **I[C]** Bullock, 1983, p. 234
167   **I[A]** PRO: FO 800/470/IND/47/1
168   **I[A]** PRO: FO 800/470/IND/47/1
169   **II[B]** Mansergh, 1969, p. 306
170   **II[B]** Mansergh, 1969, p. 315
171   **II[B]** Ovendale, 1984, p. 91
172   **II[B]** Mansergh, 1969, p. 326
173   **II[B]** Ovendale, 1984, pp. 139–41
174   **II[B]** Wolf, 1983, p. 312
175   **I[C]** Morrison, 1960, p. 270
176   **II[B]** Ferrell, 1994, p. 328
177   **II[B]** Acheson, 1970, p. 480
178   **II[B]** FRUS 1950, VII, pp. 1361–74, 1392–408
179   **II[B]** Acheson, 1970, pp. 481–2
180   **II[B]** FRUS 1950, VII, p. 1368
181   **II[B]** FRUS 1950, VII, p. 1374
182   **II[B]** Acheson, 1970, p. 483
183   **II[B]** Ferrell, 1994, pp. 330–4
184   **II[B]** Acheson, 1970, p. 485
185   **I[B]** HC Deb., 12.12.1950, cols. 981–4, 985, 986; **I[B]** HC Deb., 14.12.1950, cols. 1350–62
186   **I[C]** Pimlott, 1986, p. 501
187   **I[C]** Williams, 1979, p. 244
188   *The Times*, 16.4.1951
189   **I[A]** PRO: FO 800/470/IND/47/1
190   **II[B]** Scott, 1993, pp. 257–8
191   **II[A]** BDEE, Series B, vol. 4, pt. 1, 1998, pp. 59; **II[A]** BDEE, Series B, vol. 5, pt. 1, pp. xxxviii–lx, 120–60; **I[C]** Bullock, 1983, pp. 253–4, 324, 472, 507

192   **II[B]** Ovendale, 1984, pp. 34–5
193   **I[C]** Bullock, 1983, p. 659
194   **I[B]** HC Deb., 28.3.1950, col. 330
195   **I[C]** Donoughue and Jones, 1973, p. 481
196   **II[B]** Ovendale, 1984, p. 35
197   **I[B]** HC Deb., 30.7.1951, col. 989
198   **II[B]** Barclay, 1975, p. 94
199   **I[C]** Donoughue and Jones, 1973, p. 507
200   **I[C]** Donoughue and Jones, 1973, p. 468
201   **I[C]** Williams, 1961, p. 243
202   **I[B]** HC Deb., 9.5.1951, cols. 1952–4
203   **II[B]** Acheson, 1970, p. 505
204   **II[B]** Barclay, 1975, p. 96
205   **I[C]** Pimlott, 1986, pp. 548–9
206   **I[C]** Attlee, 1954, p. 175
207   **II[B]** Acheson, 1970, pp. 499–511
208   **II[B]** Bill and Louis, 1988, p. 249
209   **II[B]** Cable, 1991, p. 121
210   **III[B]** Keynes, XXIV, 1979, pp. 410–11
211   **III[B]** Keynes, XXIV, 1979, p. 397
212   **III[B]** Keynes, XXIV, 1979, p. 410
213   **II[A]** DBPO, Series I, vol. III, 1986, p. 28
214   **I[C]** Dalton, 1962, p. 93
215   **I[B]** HC Deb., 9.4.1946, col. 1807
216   **I[B]** HC Deb., 13.12.1945, cols. 652–3
217   **III[A]** Cmd. 6707, 1945, pp. 3–5
218   **III[B]** Keynes, XXIV, 1979, p. 262
219   **I[C]** Dalton, 1962, p. 93
220   **II[B]** Taylor, 1993, p. 67
221   **III[B]** Zweig, 1952, pp. 182–3; q.v. **III[B]** Taylor, 1993, p. 46
222   **III[B]** Keynes, XXI, 1982, pp. 33–4
223   **I[D]** Morrison, 1954, p. 298
224   **III[B]** Dow, 1964, pp. 144–5
225   **I[D]** Morrison, 1954, p. 299
226   **III[B]** Dow, 1964, p. 146
227   **III[B]** Dow, 1964, p. 1
228   **III[B]**Tawney, 1943, pp. 1–30
229   **I[B]** HC Deb., 22.3.1951, Written Answers, col. 320
230   **I[D]** Fry, 1969, p. 252
231   **I[B]** HC Deb., 23.10.1945, col. 1886
232   **III[B]** Dow, 1964, p. 20
233   **I[B]** HC Deb., 23.10.1945, col. 1886
234   **I[C]** Dalton, 1962, p. 165
235   **III[B]** Dow, 1964, p. 19; c.f. **I[B]** HC Deb., 9.4.1946, col. 1829
236   **I[B]** HC Deb., 21.8.1945, col. 504
237   **I[B]** HC Deb., 23.10.1945, col. 1881
238   **I[C]** Dalton, 1962, pp. 30, 113, 160–5, 178–84, 231
239   **I[C]** HC Deb., 21.8.1945, col. 504
240   **I[C]** HC Deb., 23.10.1945, col. 1881

241   **III[B]** Worswick and Ady, 1952, p. 188
242   **III[B]** Dow, 1964, pp. 21–2
243   **I[C]** Dalton, 1962, p. 256
244   **III[B]** Gardner, 1980, p. 319
245   **I[C]** Dalton, 1962, p. 262
246   **I[C]** Dalton, 1962, p. 187
247   **I[C]** Jay, 1980, pp. 142–51
248   **III[B]** Robertson, 1987, p. 43
249   **I[C]** Dalton, 1962, pp. 203–4; c.f. **I[A]** PRO: CAB 128/129, CM(47) 17, 18
250   *The Economist*, 15.2.1947, pp. 266–7
251   **III[B]** Tookey, 2001, pp. 486–510
252   **III[B]** Ashworth, 1986, pp. 130–4
253   **III[B]** Robertson, 1987, pp. 158–9
254   **I[C]** Dalton, 1962, p. 205
255   **I[C]** Foot, 1962, pp. 503–4
256   **III[B]** Meade, IV, 1990, pp. 114–15
257   **III[B]** Cairncross, 1989, p. 8
258   **III[B]** Rogow and Shore, 1955, pp. 54–6
259   **III[B]** Chick, 1998, pp. 199–200
260   **III[B]** Rogow and Shore, 1955, pp. 55–6
261   **I[C]** Pimlott, 1986, p. 496
262   **I[C]** Wilson, 1986, pp. 99–102
263   **I[C]** Pimlott, 1992, pp. 111–13
264   **I[C]** Pimlott, 1986, p. 496
265   **III[B]** Worswick and Ady, 1952, pp. 399–423
266   **III[B]** Worswick and Ady, 1952, pp. 285, 292; Wilson, 1986, pp. 102–3
267   **III[B]** Rogow and Shore, 1955, p. 42
268   **III[B]** Worswick and Ady, 1952, p. 172
269   **I[B]** HC Deb., 12.11.1947, col. 391
270   **I[C]** Pimlott, 1986, p. 497
271   **I[C]** Jay, 1980, p. 178
272   **I[C]** Cooke, 1957, p. 355
273   *The Economist*, 22.1.1949, p. 130
274   **III[B]** Brittan, 1964, p. 155
275   **I[C]** Pimlott, 1986, p. 444
276   **III[B]** Cairncross, 1989, pp. 222–3
277   **III[B]** Dow, 1964, p. 35; Taylor, 1993, pp. 52–9
278   **III[B]** Dow, 1964, pp. 41–4; **III[B]** Cairncross, 1985, pp. 165–211
279   **I[C]** Williams, 1979, pp. 195–235
280   **I[C]** Williams, 1983, p. 215
281   **I[C]** Williams, 1979, p. 238
282   **I[C]** Donoughue and Jones, 1973, p. 466
283   **I[C]** Williams, 1979, p. 266
284   **I[C]** Williams, 1979, p. 249
285   **I[C]** HC Deb., 24.4.1951, col. 228
286   **I[B]** HC Deb., 15.2.1951, cols. 739–40
287   **I[B]** HC Deb., 29.1.1951, col. 583
288   **I[B]** HC Deb., 15.2.1951, col. 644
289   **I[B]** HC Deb., 24.2.1951, col. 229

290   **I[B]** HC Deb., 9.12.1949, col. 2264
291   **I[B]** HC Deb., 23.4.1951, col. 42
292   **I[D]** Hunter, 1959, p. 32
293   **I[B]** LPACR 1948, p. 122
294   **I[B]** HC Deb., 23.4.1951, col. 43
295   **I[C]** Foot, 1973, p. 371
296   **III[B]** Fry, 1994, p. 19
297   **III[A]** Chester, 1975, pp. 1008–9
298   **III[B]** Hannah, 1982, pp. 1–4; **III[B]** Hannah, 1979, pp. 329–56
299   **I[C]** Shinwell, 1955, pp. 172–3; c.f. **I[C]** Wigg, 1972, p. 125
300   **III[A]** Chester, 1975, p. 20
301   **III[A]** Chester, 1975, p. 44
302   **I[B]** HC Deb., 30.1.1946 col. 969
303   **III[B]** Robson, 1962, pp. 138–62
304   **III[B]** Chester, 1950, pp. 67–74
305   **III[B]** Foldes, 1957, p. 122
306   **I[C]** Griffiths, 1969, p. 88
307   **III[B]** Lowe, 1993, pp. 196–204
308   **III[B]** Macnicol, 1980, pp. 138–50, 176–8
309   **I[C]** Griffiths, 1969, p. 81
310   **III[B]** Stocks, 1949, p. 319
311   **I[B]** HC Deb., 12.6.1945, col. 1510
312   **III[B]** Walley, 1972, p. 85
313   **I[B]** HC Deb., 10.10.1945, col. 284
314   **I[B]** HC Deb., 6.2.1946, col. 1739
315   **I[C]** Griffiths, 1969, p. 84
316   **III[A]** Cmd. 6404, 1942, pp. 137–42
317   **I[B]** HC Deb., 30.10.1947, col. 1093
318   **III[B]** Deacon and Bradshaw, 1983, pp. 39–40
319   **I[B]** HC Deb., 6.2.1946, col. 1742
320   **III[B]** Deacon and Bradshaw, 1983, p. 45
321   **I[D]** Morgan, 1984, p. 151
322   **III[B]** Rowntree and Lavers, 1951, pp. 26–45
323   **I[C]** Foot, 1962, p. 509
324   **I[C]** Dalton, 1962, p. 358
325   **I[B]** LPACR 1947, p. 191
326   **I[B]** LPACR 1947, p. 192
327   **I[C]** Dalton, 1962, p. 358
328   **III[B]** Worswick and Ady, 1952, p. 375
329   **I[C]** Foot, 1967, p. 82
330   **III[B]** Worswick and Ady, 1952, p. 134
331   **I[C]** Foot, 1967, p. 87
332   **I[C]** Campbell, 1987, p. 154
333   **I[C]** Foot, 1967, p. 84
334   **III[A]** Cmd. 6404, 1942, p. 158
335   **III[A]** Webster, 1988, p. 22; c.f. **III[A]** Titmuss, 1950, pp. 466–505
336   **I[A]** PRO: CAB 21/2032 (CP(45)205
337   **I[A]** PRO: CAB 21/2032 (CP(45)227
338   **I[A]** PRO: CAB 21/2032 (CP(45)231

339   **III[A]** Cmd. 6761, 1946, pp. 3–4
340   **III[A]** Cmd. 6761, 1946, p. 18
341   **I[B]** HC Deb., 30.4.1946, cols. 60–1
342   **III[B]** Abel-Smith, 1964, p. 480
343   **III[B]** Abel-Smith, 1964, pp. 486–7
344   **I[C]** Hill, 1964, pp. 99–100
345   **III[B]** Rupke, 1988, p. 199
346   **I[C]** Foot, 1973, p. 195
347   **III[A]** Webster, 1988, pp. 157–66
348   **I[B]** HC Deb., 23.4.1951, cols. 38–9
349   **I[D]** Terrill, 1974, p. 230
350   **III[B]** Cairncross, 1985, p. 507
351   **I[D]** Morgan 1984, p. vii
352   *The Listener*, 8.7.1948, pp. 39–40
353   **I[C]** Foot, 1967, pp. 237–8
354   **III[B]** Worswick and Ady, 1952, pp. 159–87, 314–21
355   **III[B]** Worswick and Ady, 1952, p. 362
356   **I[D]** Barnett, 1995, pp. 397–8
357   **I[D]** Tiratsoo, 1991; **I[D]** Fielding, Thompson, and Tiratsoo, 1995
358   **I[D]** Butler, 1952, p. 251
359   **I[D]** Butler, 1951, p. 306
360   **I[D]** Butler, 1952, p. 251
361   **I[D]** Craig, 1981, p. 37

6   Fast Falls the Eventide

 1   **I[C]** Moran, 1966, pp. 348–9
 2   **I[C]** Stuart, 1967, p. 155
 3   **I[D]** Butler, 1952, p. 237
 4   **I[D]** Douglas, 1971, p. 265
 5   **I[D]** Sissons and French, 1964, pp. 306–29
 6   **I[D]** Taylor, 1972, p. 569
 7   **I[D]** Craig, 1975, pp. 171–2
 8   **I[C]** Butler, 1971, p. 155
 9   **I[D]** Craig, 1975, p. 144
10   **I[D]** Craig, 1975, p. 147
11   **I[C]** Butler, 1971, pp. 154–5; **I[B]** CPACR 1950, pp. 56–65
12   **I[D]** Skelton, 1924, p. 17; **I[D]** Eden, 1947, pp. 418–24
13   **I[C]** Gilbert, 1988, p. 312
14   **I[D]** Ramsden, 1995, p. 141
15   **I[D]** Craig, 1975, p. 170
16   **I[C]** Woolton, 1959, p. 346
17   **I[D]** Hoffman, 1964, pp. 96–7
18   **III[B]** Zweiniger-Bargielowska, 2000, pp. 263–4
19   **I[C]** Woolton, 1959, p. 367
20   **I[D]** Butler, 1952, pp. 35, 270–2
21   **I[D]** Nicholas, 1951, pp. 2–5
22   **I[D]** Butler, 1952, pp. 243, 251
23   **I[C]** Woolton, 1959, pp. 365–6
24   **I[C]** Macmillan, 1969, pp. 362–3

25   I[C] Gilbert, VIII, 1988, p. 653
26   I[C] Seldon, 1981, pp. 296–303
27   I[C] Ismay, 1960, pp. 452–3
28   *The Times*, 31.10.1951
29   I[C] Moran, 1966, p. 467
30   I[C] Chandos, 1962, pp. 342–4
31   I[C] Kilmuir, 1964, p. 193
32   I[C] Macmillan, 1969, p. 363
33   I[C] Birkenhead, 1969, p. 274
34   I[C] Macmillan, 1969, p. 364
35   I[C] Morgan, 1981, p. 30
36   I[C] Kilmuir, 1964, p. 191
37   I[D] Colville, 1985, p. 759
38   I[D] Wheeler-Bennett, 1969, pp. 111–12
39   I[D] Wheeler-Bennett, 1969, pp. 119–20
40   I[C] Avon, 1960, p. 247
41   I[C] Kilmuir, 1964, p. 193
42   III[B] Cairncross, 1989, p. 280
43   II[B] Shuckburgh, 1986, p. 18
44   I[D] Rhodes James, VIII, 1974, p. 8069
45   I[B] HC Deb., 14.7.1954, col. 498
46   II[B] Charlton, 1983, p. 151
47   I[B] HC Deb., 11.5.1953, col. 891
48   I[A] PRO: CAB 128/27 CC62(54)1; I[C] Avon, 1960, pp. 146–74; I[B] HC
      Deb., 19.10.1954, cols. 1037–44; I[B] HC Deb., 25.10.1954, cols. 1601–7;
      II[A] Cmd. 9289, 1954; II[B] Young, 1988, pp. 81–107
49   II[B] Gerson, 1967, p. 141
50   I[B] HC Deb., 17.12.1953, col. 583
51   I[C] Avon, 1960, pp. 175–88
52   I[A] PRO: FO371/103519/1053
53   II[B] Ambrose, 1984, p. 222
54   II[B] Ambrose, 1984, p. 360
55   I[D] Colville, 1985, p. 647
56   I[D] Colville, 1985, p. 658; c.f. I[D] Seldon, 1981, pp. 390–1
57   I[C] Avon, 1960, pp. 63–4, 98–9, 158–9
58   II[B] Shuckburgh, 1986, p. 23
59   II[B] LaFeber, 1989, p. 510; c.f. I[C] Moran, 1966, p. 545
60   II[B] Boyle, 1990
61   I[C] Moran, 1966, p. 438; I[D] Colville, 1985, p. 672
62   I[D] Seldon, 1981, p. 391
63   II[B] Ambrose, 1984, pp. 21–2
64   I[C] Macmillan, 1969, p. 533
65   I[C] Gilbert, VIII, 1988, p. 817
66   I[C] Gilbert, VIII, 1988, p. 923
67   I[C] Gilbert, VIII, 1988, p. 1004
68   I[D] Colville, 1985, pp. 691–3, 701–3; I[C] Macmillan, 1969, pp. 533–9;
      II[B] Shuckburgh, 1986, pp. 221–3; I[A] PRO: PREM 11/1074; I[A] PRO:
      CAB 128/27, CC(54) 47, 48, 49, 50, 52, 53; II[A] Cmd. 9418, 1955; I[B]
      HC Deb., 14.3.1955, cols. 960–3; I[B] HC Deb., 24.3.1955, cols. 2268–9

69   I[C] Gilbert, VIII, 1988, p. 1004
70   I[C] Gilbert, VIII, 1988, p. 1000
71   II[B] Shuckburgh, 1986, p. 32; c.f. II[B] FRUS 1952–4, VI, pt. 1, pp. 729–864
72   II[B] Shuckburgh, 1986, p. 63
73   I[D] Colville, 1985, p. 686
74   II[B] Bill and Louis, 1988, pp. 286–8; II[B] LaFeber, 1989, pp. 517–18; II[B] Young, 1988, pp. 164–70; II[B] Ruehsen, 1993, pp. 467–86; II[B] Heiss, 1994, pp. 511–35; II[B] Ovendale, 1996, pp. 70–4
75   II[B] Ovendale, 1996, pp. 87–8
76   I[C] Avon, 1960, p. 336
77   I[A] PRO: CAB 129/66
78   I[C] Avon, 1960, pp. 334–5
79   I[C] Avon, 1960, pp. 246–7
80   II[B] Shuckburgh, 1986, p. 75
81   I[C] Moran, 1966, p. 478
82   I[B] HC Deb., 29.7.1954, col. 750
83   II[B] Shuckburgh, 1986, p. 19
84   II[B] Young, 1988, pp. 207–31
85   II[B] Shuckburgh, 1986, p. 17
86   II[B] Shuckburgh, 1986, p. 19
87   I[D] Colville, 1985, p. 694; c.f. I[C] Moran, 1966, p. 568
88   I[A] PRO: CAB 128/26
89   II[B] FRUS 1952–4, XVI, pp. 395–1568; I[A] PRO: FO 371/112075; II[B] Gerson, 1967, pp. 167–88; I[C] Avon, 1960, pp. 107–45; II[B] Young, 1988, pp. 233–59; II[B] Shuckburgh, 1986, pp. 168–203; Ruane, 1994, pp. 153–72
90   II[B] Hinton, 1966, p. 103
91   I[B] HC Deb., 22.7.1954, col. 1572
92   I[B] Cable, 1986, p. 3
93   I[C] Moran, 1966, p. 726
94   II[B] Shuckburgh, 1986, p. 15
95   I[C] Butler, 1971, pp. 156–7
96   *The Economist*, 13.2.1954, p. 440
97   III[B] Shonfield, 1959, p. 185
98   I[A] PRO: CAB 129/48
99   I[A] PRO: T236/3245
100 III[B] Cairncross, 1989, p. 205
101 III[B] Fforde, 1992, p. 446
102 I[C] Butler, 1971, p. 156
103 I[D] Seldon, 1981, p. 167
104 I[D] Seldon, 1981, p. 167
105 I[A] PRO: T236 3240, T236 3242, T236 3243, T236 3245
106 I[D] Salter, 1967, pp. 215–24
107 I[C] Birkenhead, 1961, pp. 284–8
108 I[C] Butler, 1971, pp. 158–9
109 I[C] Butler, 1971, p. 160
110 III[B] Shonfield, 1959, p. 185
111 I[D] Barnett, 2001, pp. 404–5

112   **I[B]** HC Deb., 7.11.1951, col. 205
113   **I[B]** HC Deb., 11.3.1952, col. 1282
114   **III[A]** Cmd. 8800, 1952, p. 20
115   **I[B]** HC Deb., 14.4.1953, cols. 33–71
116   **I[B]** HC Deb., 6.4.1954, cols. 226–7
117   *The Economist*, 25.4.1953, p. 200
118   *The Economist*, 3.4.1954, p. 45
119   **I[B]** HC Deb., 6.4.1954, col. 227
120   *The Economist*, 16.4.1955, p. 178
121   **III[B]** Dow, 1964, p. 79
122   **I[B]** HC Deb., 19.4.1955, cols. 58–61
123   **III[A]** Cmd. 9412, 1955, p. 37
124   **III[B]** Dow, 1964, p. 77
125   **I[B]** HC Deb., 14.4.1953, col. 62
126   **III[B]** Dow, 1964, pp. 80, 88
127   **I[C]** Birkenhead, 1969, p. 275
128   **I[C]** Birkenhead, 1969, p. 276
129   **I[C]** Birkenhead, 1969, p. 283
130   **I[C]** Moran, 1966, pp. 394–5
131   **I[C]** Woolton, 1959, pp. 379–80
132   **I[C]** Butler, 1971, p. 164
133   **I[C]** Moran, 1966, pp. 465–6
134   **I[C]** Birkenhead, 1969, p. 302
135   **I[D]** Seldon, 1981, p. 202
136   *The Economist*, 19.12.1953, p. 864
137   **I[B]** HC Deb., 6.11.1951, col. 69
138   **I[A]** PRO: CAB 134/849, EA(53) 148; **I[A]** PRO: CAB 134/851, EA(54) 24; **I[A]** PRO: CAB 134/851, EA(54) 25; **I[D]** Barnett, 2001, p. 416
139   **III[A]** Cmd. 9352, 1955, para. 10
140   **III[B]** Fry, 1994, pp. 24–5
141   **III[B]** Brittan, 1964, pp. 223–4
142   **I[D]** Fry, 1969, pp. 257–64
143   **I[D]** Walsha, 2000, p. 191
144   **III[B]** Powell, 1953, p. 165
145   **I[C]** Fisher, 1973, p. 82
146   **I[B]** HC Deb., 27.3.1952, col. 886
147   **I[B]** HC Deb., 27.3.1952, col. 889
148   **I[B]** HC Deb., 27.3.1952, cols. 961–7; **I[C]** Foot, 1973, pp. 357–8
149   **I[B]** HC Deb., 27.3.1952, cols. 890, 893, 894
150   **III[A]** Webster, 1988, p. 202
151   **III[A]** Webster, 1988, pp. 202–11; **III[A]** Cmd. 9663, 1956, p. 268
152   **I[C]** Pimlott, 1986, p. 565
153   **I[C]** Macmillan, 1969, p. 498; **I[A]** PRO: CAB 128/25
154   **I[C]** Macmillan, 1969, p. 400
155   **I[C]** Macmillan, 1969, p. 374
156   **I[A]** PRO: CAB 128/25
157   **I[D]** Medlicott, 1967, p. 522
158   **I[D]** Seldon, 1981, p. 434
159   **I[D]** Roberts, 1994, pp. 211–41

160   **I[B]** HC Deb., 6.11.1951, col. 68
161   **I[D]** Nicolson, 1968, p. 224
162 **III[B]** Cairncross, 1989, p. 266
163   **I[D]** Churchill, 1929, p. 378
164   **I[B]** HC Deb., 6.11. 1951, col. 69
165   **I[D]** Wheeler-Bennett, 1969, p. 58
166   **I[C]** Williams, 1983, p. 307
167   **I[D]** Craig, 1971, p. 284
168   **I[C]** Butler, 1971, p. 172
169 **III[B]** Macrae, 1963, p. 41; c.f. **I[C]** Butler, 1971, p. 182
170   **I[C]** Butler, 1971, p. 173
171   **I[D]** Wheeler-Bennett, 1969, p. 59
172   **I[D]** Butler, 1955, p. 80

7   The Reckoning

1   **I[D]** Butler, 1955, p. 154
2   **I[C]** Woolton, 1959, p. 419
3   **I[B]** AP 20/1/31
4   **I[D]** Butler, 1955, p. 171
5   **I[C]** Avon, 1960, pp. 289–90
6   **I[C]** Williams, 1983, p. 411
7   **I[C]** Moran, 1966, p. 550
8   **I[C]** Horne, 1988, pp. 371–2
9   **I[C]** Howard, 1987, p. 215
10   **I[C]** Howard, 1987, pp. 218–19
11   **I[C]** Avon, 1960, pp. 323–6
12 **III[B]** Brittan, 1964, p. 181
13   **I[B]** HC Deb., 17.4.1956, cols. 879–81
14   **I[B]** HC Deb., 17.4.1956, col. 867
15   **I[C]** Avon, 1960, p. 316
16   Interview: Lord Boyle
17   **I[D]** Butler, 1955, p. 120
18   **I[D]** Butler, 1955, p. 171
19   **I[C]** Rhodes James, 1986, p. 412
20   **I[D]** Hart-Davis, 1990, p. 170
21   **I[C]** Rhodes James, 1986, pp. 425; **I[C]** Thorpe, 2003, pp. 459–60
22   **I[C]** Howard, 1987, p. 222
23   **I[C]** Avon, 1960, p. 120
24   **I[C]** Williams, 1979, pp. 332–3
25   **I[C]** Williams, 1983, p. 544
26   **I[D]** Colville, 1985, p. 171
27   **I[D]** Gallup, I, 1976, p. 350
28   **I[B]** HC Deb., 16.2.1956, cols. 2627–35
29   **I[B]** HC Deb., 16.2.1956, cols. 2556–65
30   **I[B]** HC Deb., 16.2.1956, cols. 2569–79
31   **I[A]** PRO: CAB 128/30; CAB 129/78; CAB 129/79; CAB 129/83
32   **I[C]** Butler, 1971, p. 201
33   **I[A]** PRO: PREM 11/824; CAB 128/29; CAB 129/75; CAB 129/77
34   **I[C]** Rhodes James, 1986, p. 419

35   **I[D]** Lamb, 1987, p. 32
36   **III[B]** Cmd. 9703, 1956; **I[D]** Barnett, 2001, pp. 143–4, 466, 480–1
37   **I[B]** Cmd. 9613, 1955
38   **III[B]** Williams, 1956, pp. 621–34
39   **III[B]** Wootton, 1955, pp. 161–90
40   **I[C]** Avon, 1960, pp. 286–7; **I[A]** PRO: PREM 11/1029, CAB 129/75, LAB
      10/1392
41   **I[B]** TUCACR 1956, p. 400
42   **III[A]** Cmd. 9672, 1956, paras. 372–3; **III[B]** Robson, 1962, p. 297; **III[B]**
      Fry, 1994, p. 26
43   **III[B]** Shonfield, 1959, p. 197
44   **I[C]** Avon, 1960, p. 356
45   **I[C]** Churchill, 1959, pp. 219–20; **I[C]** Rhodes James, 1986, pp. 433–7;
      I[C] Thorpe, 2003, pp. 470–2
46   **I[C]** Murphy, 1999, pp. 120–1
47   **II[B]** Charlton, 1983, pp. 194–5
48   **I[B]** HC Deb., 15.6.1955, cols. 604–5
49   **I[C]** Macmillan, 1971, p. 67
50   **I[B]** HC Deb., 26.11.1956, cols. 37–8
51   **II[B]** FRUS 1955–7, XXVII, p. 620
52   **II[B]** Duchene, 1994, pp. 288–9
53   **I[B]** HC Deb., 26.11.1956, col. 71
54   **I[C]** Avon, 1960, p. 337
55   **II[B]** Nutting, 1967, p. 18
56   **I[C]** Avon, 1960, p. 431
57   **I[B]** HC Deb. 2.8.1956, cols. 1612–13
58   **I[C]** Williams, 1983, pp. 552–3
59   **I[B]** HC Deb., 2.8.1956, col. 1617
60   **I[C]** Williams, 1983, p. 568
61   **I[C]** Williams, 1983, p. 571
62   *The Listener*, 8.11.1956, p. 738
63   **II[B]** Braddon, 1973, p. 194
64   **II[B]** Moncrieff, 1967, p. 112
65   **I[C]** Morgan, 1981, p. 550
66   **I[C]** Morgan, 1981, p. 548
67   **I[C]** Avon, 1960, p. 429
68   **I[C]** Avon, 1960, p. 430
69   **II[B]** Moncrieff, 1967, p. 44
70   **I[B]** HC Deb., 16.12.1958, cols. 1071–2
71   **I[C]** Churchill, 1959, p. 245
72   **II[B]** Ziegler, 1985, p. 541
73   **II[B]** Kyle, 1991, p. 136
74   **I[C]** Avon, 1960, p. 446
75   **II[B]** Eisenhower, 1963, p. 482
76   **II[B]** Murphy, 1964, p. 463
77   **II[B]** Murphy, 1964, p. 465
78   **II[B]** Murphy, 1964, p. 467
79   **I[B]** AP 20/1/31
80   **I[C]** Avon, 1960, p. 437; c.f. **II[B]** FRUS 1955–57, XVI, p. 98
81   **II[B]** Murphy, 1964, p. 470

82   **II[B]** Robertson, 1965, p. 118
83   **I[B]** AP 20/1/32
84   **II[B]** FRUS, 1955–7, XVI, p. 64
85   **II[B]** Eisenhower, 1966, p. 108
86   **II[B]** FRUS, 1955–7, XVI, p. 1081; c.f. **II[B]** Ambrose, 1984, p. 371
87   **II[B]** Eisenhower, 1966, p. 39
88   **II[B]** FRUS 1955–7, XI, p. 70
89   **II[B]** Eisenhower, 1966, pp. 39–40
90   **I[A]** PRO: PREM 11/1102
91   **I[B]** HC Deb., 19.12.1956, col. 1243
92   **II[B]** Kyle, 1991, p. 319
93   **II[B]** Lloyd, 1978, p. 185
94   **II[B]** Lloyd, 1978, p. 183
95   **II[B]** Robertson, 1965, pp. 157–63; Kyle, 1991, pp. 314–31
96   **I[B]** HC Deb., 31.10.1956, col. 1569
97   **I[B]** HC Deb., 20.12.1956, col. 1518
98   **II[B]** Moncrieff, 1967, p. 45
99   **I[C]** Avon, 1960, p. 574
100 **II[B]** Nutting, 1967, p. 145
101   **I[D]** Colville, 1985, p. 721
102   **I[D]** Colville, 1985, p. 725
103 **II[B]** Lloyd, 1978, p. 219
104 **II[B]** Finer, 1964, p. 454
105 **II[B]** Kyle, 1991, p. 258
106 **II[B]** Eisenhower, 1966, p. 95
107 **II[B]** Eisenhower, 1966, p. 93
108 *The Listener*, 8.11. 1956, pp. 737–8
109   **I[C]** Campbell, 1997, p. 323
110 **II[B]** Eisenhower, 1966, p. 108
111   **I[C]** Avon, 1960, p. 559
112   **I[C]** Gilbert, VIII, 1988, p. 1222
113 **II[B]** Monroe, 1981, p. 209
114 **II[B]** Shuckburgh, 1986, p. 365
115   **I[C]** Thorpe, 2003, p. 382

8   The Failure of the Middle Way

1   **I[C]** Heffer, 1998, p. 210
2   Interview: Lord Boyle
3   **I[C]** Foot, 1967, p. 535
4   **I[C]** Macmillan, 1966, p. 325
5   **I[C]** Macmillan, 1972, p. 310
6   **III[B]** Macmillan, 1938, p. 367
7   **III[B]** Brittan, 1964, p. 180
8   Interview: Lord Boyle
9   **I[C]** Macmillan, 1966, p. 325
10   Interview: Lord Boyle
11   **I[C]** Horne, 1989, p. 4
12   **I[C]** Kilmuir, 1964, pp. 288–9
13   **II[B]** Epstein, 1964, p. 152; **I[D]** Butler, 1960. p. 282
14   *The Economist*, 19.1.1957, p. 181

15   I[C] Kilmuir, 1964, p. 288
16   I[C] Horne, 1989, pp. 36–9
17   I[B] HC Deb., 13.5.1957, cols. 35–7
18   I[B] HC Deb., 13.5.1957, col. 42
19   I[B] HC Deb. 15.5.1957, cols. 436–7
20   II{A] Cmnd. 124, 1957, p. 9
21   I[C] Eden, 1960, pp. 373–4
22   II[A] Cmnd. 124, 1957, p. 7
23   II[A] Cmnd. 124, 1957, pp. 1–2
24   I[C] Avon, 1960, p. 374
25   II[A] Cmnd. 363, 1958, p. 6
26   II[B] Martin, 1962, p. 38
27   II[A] Cmnd. 124, 1957, p. 7
28   II[B] Eisenhower, 1966, p. 681
29   I[C] Macmillan, 1971, p. 195
30   II[B] FRUS 1955–7, XX, pp. 682–3
31   II[B] FRUS 1955–7, XX, pp. 704–67
32   II[B] FRUS 1955–7, XX, pp. 788–839
33   II[B] FRUS 1958–60, VII, pp. 859–65; I[C] Macmillan, 1972, pp. 251–8;
      I[C] Horne, 1989, pp. 275–7
34   I[C] Horne, 1989, p. 122
35   I[C] Macmillan, 1971, p. 630
36   I[C] Horne, 1989, p. 231; I[C] Macmillan, 1972, pp. 178–216
37   I[C] Horne, 1989, pp. 278–9; I[C] Macmillan, 1972, pp. 272–81
38   II[B] Eayrs, 1964, p. 424
39   I[C] Sampson, 1967, pp. 136–9
40   I[C] Macmillan, 1972, p. 156
41   II[B] Hunt, 1975, p. 102
42   I[C] Macmillan, 1972, pp. 118–19
43   I[C] Macmillan, 1972, p. 122
44   I[C] Horne, 1989, p. 198
45   I[C] Horne, 1989, p. 187
46   I[C] Horne, 1989, p. 188
47   I[C] Horne, 1989, p. 187
48   I[C] Horne, 1989, p. 414
49   II[B] Welensky, 1964, p. 361
50   I[B] HL Deb. 7.3.1961, col. 307
51   II[B] Wood, 1983, p. 1004
52   II[B] Alport, 1965, p. 168
53   II[B] Charlton, 1983, pp. 203–6
54   II[B] Charlton, 1983, p. 209
55   I[C] Maudling, 1978, pp. 67–73
56   I[C] Macmillan, 1971, p. 457
57   I[C] Macmillan, 1971, p. 455
58   III[B] Cairncross, 1991, p. 193
59   I[C] Horne, 1989, p. 470
60   I[C] Macmillan, 1971, p. 709
61   III[B] Cairncross, 1991, p. 179
62   III[B] Cairncross, 1991, p. 178
63   III[B] Cairncross, 1991, p. 116

64   **III[B]** Macmillan, 1971, p. 352
65   **III[A]** Cmnd. 350, 1958, p. 9
66   **III[B]** Cairncross, 1991, p. 126
67   **I[A]** PRO: PREM 11/1823
68   **III[B]** Cairncross, 1991, p. 126
69   **III[B]** Cairncross, 1991, p. 143
70   *The Economist*, 18.1.1958, pp. 187–8
71   **I[B]** HC Deb., 29.10.1957, col. 51
72   *The Times*, 25.9.1957
73   **I[C]** Macmillan, 1971, p. 372
74   **I[C]** Horne, 1989, p. 74
75   **I[B]** HC Deb., 7.4.1959, col. 46
76   **I[C]** Shepherd, 1994, p. 140
77   **I[D]** Craig, 1975, p. 214
78   *The Listener*, 3.9.1959, pp. 341–3
79   **I[D]** Butler and Rose, 1960, pp. 87–8
80   **I[C]** Macmillan, 1971, p. 350
81   **I[C]** Butler and Rose, 1960, p. 201
82   **III[B]** Worswick and Ady, 1962, pp. 268–9
83   **I[B]** HC Deb., 7.4.1959, cols. 55–8
84   **I[D]** Butler and Rose, 1960, p. 204
85   **I[D]** Butler and Rose, 1960, pp. 200–1
86   **I[C]** Jay, 1980, pp. 273–4
87   **I[B]** LPACR 1959, pp. 105–14; **I[C]** Williams, 1979, pp. 537–73
88   **I[B]** LPACR 1960, p. 201
89   **I[B]** LPACR 1961, p. 194
90   **I[C]** Jay, 1980, pp. 274–5
91   **I[D]** Douglas, 1971, pp. 271–2
92   Interview: Lord Boyle
93   **I[C]** Macmillan, 1971, p. 649
94   **I[C]** Horne, 1989, p. 280
95   **I[C]** Horne, 1989, p. 577
96   **I[C]** Butler, 1971, p. 231
97   **I[C]** Macmillan, 1973, p. 357
98   **II[B]** FRUS 1961–3, V, pp. 172–97, 206–30
99   **II[B]** FRUS 1961–3, XIV, XV
100 **II[B]** FRUS 1961–3, XI; **II[B]** Schlesinger, 1965, pp. 795–831; **II[B]** Sorenson, 1965, pp. 737–94; **II[B]** Parmet, 1984, pp. 277–300); **I[C]** Horne, 1989, pp. 361–85
101   **I[C]** Macmillan, 1973, p. 187
102 *The Times*, 6.12.1962
103   **I[C]** Macmillan, 1973, p. 339
104 **II[B]** FRUS 1961–3, XIII, pp. 1091–128; **II[B]** Schlesinger, 1965, pp. 862–5; **II[B]** Sorenson, 1965, pp. 624–8; **I[C]** Macmillan, 1973, pp. 355–63, 553–5; **I[C]** Horne, 1989, pp. 437–43
105 **II[B]** FRUS 1961–3, VII, pp. 688, 728–35, 744–76, 768–881; **II[B]** Schlesinger, 1975, pp. 902–9; **II[B]** Sorenson, 1975, pp. 811–18; **I[C]** Macmillan, 1973, pp. 475–87; **I[C]** Horne, 1989, pp. 499–526; **I[C]** Hailsham, 1975, p. 219; **II[A]** Cmnd. 2118, 1963
106   **I[C]** Macmillan, 1973, p. 339

107   **II[B]** Braddon. 1973, p. 208
108   *The Listener*, 28.7.1966, p. 116
109   **I[D]** Gallup, I, 1976, p. 610
110   **I[B]** HC Deb., 16.11.1961, col. 802
111   *The Economist*, 24.6.1961, p. 1349
112   **I[B]** HC Deb., 14.11.1961, col. 190
113   **I[C]** Williams, 1979, p. 679
114   **I[B]** HC Deb., 31.7.1961, cols. 928–31
115   **I[B]** HC Deb., 2.8.1961, col. 1491
116   **I[B]** HC Deb., 2.8.1961, cols. Cols. 1498–9
117   **I[B]** LPACR 1962, p. 159
118   **I[C]** Macmillan, 1973, pp. 16–17
119   **I[B]** HC Deb., 2.8.1961, col. 1502
120   **II[B]** Ball, 1982, pp. 217–18
121   **I[C]** Macmillan, 1973, p. 111
122   **II[B]** Ludlow, 1997, p. 120
123   **II[B]** Ball, 1982, p. 217
124   **I[A]** PRO: FO 371 158177; M1091/539
125   **II[B]** Ludlow, 1997, p. 196
126   **II[A]** Milward, 2002, pp. 463–83
127   **I[C]** Horne, 1989, p. 446; c.f. PRO: FO 371 171449; M1092/129
128   **II[B]** Moravcsik, 1998, p. 184
129   **I[C]** Horne, 1989, p. 447
130   **I[D]** Bruce–Gardyne and Lawson, 1976, pp. 10–37
131   **III[A]** Cmnd. 1432, 1961, p. 6
132   **III[B]** Francis and Zweiniger–Bargielowska, 1996, pp. 255–73
133   **III[A]** Cmnd. 1604, 1962
134   **III[A]** Cmnd, 2154, 1963, paras. 153, 465, 491, 647
135   **I[D]** Fry, 1981, pp. 59–60
136   **I[C]** Macmillan, 1969, p. 560
137   **I[C]** Macmillan, 1973, pp. 408–21; **II[A]** Cmnd. 2097, 1963; **I[D]** Fry, 1981, pp. 122–3; **II[B]** Ziegler, 1985, pp. 608–24
138   **II[A]** Cmnd. 2276, 1964; **I[D]** Fry, 1981, pp. 128–31
139   **III[A]** Cmnd. 1337, 1961; **III[B]** Fry, 1994, pp. 27–8
140   **III[A]** Beeching Report, 1963, pp. 59–60; **I[A]** PRO: CAB 128/37; **I[A]** PRO: CAB 129/113; **III[B]** Munby, 1962–3, pp. 161–82; **III[B]** Gourvish, 1986, pp. 401–7, 412–15, 425–30, 436–7
141   **I[B]** HC Deb., 25.7.1961, cols. 221–2
142   **I[B]** HC Deb., 25.7.1961, col. 220
143   **I[C]** Macmillan, 1973, p. 37
144   **III[B]** Jewkes, 1968, pp. 8–9
145   **III[B]** Macrae, 1963, p. 179
146   **I[C]** Kilmuir, 1964, p. 323
147   **I[C]** Hill, 1964, p. 248
148   **I[A]** PRO: CAB 128/35; **I[A]** PRO: PREM 11/3765; **I[C]** Thorpe, 1989, pp. 336–43
149   *The Times*, 14.7.1962
150   **I[C]** Macmillan, 1973, p. 95
151   **I[C]** Macmillan, 1973, p. 100

152   **I[D]** Hennessy, 2000, pp. 69–70, 75–6
153   **I[C]** Butler, 1971, p. 232
154   **I[C]** Horne, 1989, p. 347
155   **I[B]** HC Deb., 22.3.1963, cols. 809–10
156   **I[C]** Macmillan, 1972, p. 232
157   **I[B]** Cmnd. 2152, 1963
158   **I[C]** Macmillan, 1971, p. 350
159   **I[A]** PRO: PREM 11/2311; q.v. **I[C]** Turner, 1994, p. 240
160   **I[C]** Rodgers, 1964, p. 124
161   **I[D]** Bogdanor and Skidelsky, 1970, p. 32
162   **I[C]** Horne, 1989, p. 569
163   **I[C]** Horne, 1989, p. 554
164   **I[C]** Heath, 1998, p. 263; **I[A]** PRO: PREM 11/5154; **I[A]** PRO: CAB 128/38; **I[A]** PRO: CAB 129/117; **I[B]** HC Deb., 10.3.1964, cols. 255–380
165   **I[C]** Heath, 1998, p. 260
166   **I[C]** Boyd-Carpenter, 1980, pp. 185–6
167   **I[C]** Home, 1976, p. 215
168   **III[B]** Findlay, 2001, pp. 327–53
169   **I[C]** Thorpe, 1996, p. 344
170   **I[C]** Horne, 1989, p. 582
171   **I[D]** Butler and Rose, 1965, p. 303
172   **I[C]** Kilmuir, 1964, pp. 321–2
173   **I[C]** Horne, 1989, p. 582

9   The Wrong Revolution

1   **I[D]** Bogdanor and Skidelsky, 1970, p. 109
2   **I[C]** Newman, 1989, p. 153
3   **I[C]** Thompson, 1993, p. 219
4   **I[C]** Williams, 1979, p. 69
5   **I[D]** Crosland, 1956, p. 524
6   **I[C]** Jefferys, 1999, p. 28
7   **I[D]** Vaizey, 1983, p. 86
8   **I[C]** Williams, 1979, p. 570
9   **I[B]** LPACR 1960, p. 221
10   **I[B]** LPACR 1960, p. 12
11   **I[C]** Pearce, 1991, p. 259
12   **I[C]** Rodgers, 1964, p. 126
13   **I[C]** Pimlott, 1992, p. 256
14   **I[C]** Morgan, 1981, p. 971
15   **I[C]** Goodman, 1979, p. 346
16   **I[C]** Morgan, 1981, p. 972
17   **I[C]** Morgan, 1981, p. 986
18   **I[C]** Zeigler, 1993, p. 117
19   **I[C]** Pimlott, 1992, p. 212
20   **I[D]** Favretto, 2000, pp. 54–80
21   **I[C]** Zeigler, 1993, pp. 173–4
22   **I[B]** LPACR 1963, p. 140
23   **I[B]** LPACR 1963, p. 134
24   **I[C]** Smith, 1964, p. 193

25   I[D] Butler and King, 1966, p. 262
26   I[D] Butler and King, 1966, p. 296
27   I[D] Butler and King, 1966, p. 259
28   I[D] Craig, 1975, p. 292
29   I[D] Craig, 1975, pp. 259–63
30   I[C] Jay, 1980, p. 296
31   I[C] Castle, 1984, p. ix
32   I[C] Castle, 1984, p. xi
33   I[C] Castle, 1984, p. x
34   I[C] Castle, 1984, p. xi
35   I[C] Jenkins, 1992, p. 157
36   *The Listener*, 5.3.1964, p. 396
37   I[C] Wilson, 1971, p. 713
38   I[D] Robson, 1964, pp. 203–7
39   I[C] Wilson, 1971, p. 9
40   Interview: Lord Boyle
41   I[C] Pimlott, 1992, p. 328
42   I[C] Morgan, 1981, p. 972
43   I[C] Morgan, 1981, p. 984
44   I[C] Morgan, 1981, p. 972
45   I[C] Ziegler, 1993, p. 175
46   I[C] Castle, 1993, p. 342
47   I[D] Williams, 1972, p. 344
48   I[D] Williams, 1972, p. 359
49   I[D] Fry, 1969, pp. 361–426; I[D] Fry, 1993
50   II[A] Cmnd. 2276, 1969, pp. 2–3
51   II[A] Cmnd. 4107, 1969, p. 5
52   I[D] Fry, 1981, pp. 130–1
53   I[C] Pearce, 1991, pp. 298–9
54   I[C] Stewart, 1980, pp. 199–200
55   I[C] Brown, 1971, p. 212
56   I[C] Heath, 1998, p. 355
57   I[C] Ziegler, 1993, p. 241
58   I[D] King, 1972, p. 72
59   I[D] King, 1972, p. 95
60   I[C] Pimlott, 1992, p. 377; c.f. II[B] FRUS 1964–8, XII, p. 510
61   I[C] Elwyn Jones, 1983, pp. 208–14
62   I[C] Castle, 1984, p. 199
63   I[D] Williams, 1972, p. 272
64   II[B] Smith, 1998, pp. 9–24
65   I[C] Pimlott, 1992, p. 70
66   I[C] Ziegler, 1993, p. 22
67   I[D] Williams, 1972, p. 272
68   I[C] Healey, 1990, p. 332
69   I[C] Crossman, III, 1977, p. 422
70   I[D] King, 1972, pp. 323–4
71   I[C] Brown, 1971, p. 127
72   I[C] Healey, 1990, p. 333
73   I[C] Wilson, 1971, p. 213

74   **I[C]** Wilson, 1971, pp. 345–51, 353, 355–61
75   **II[B]** Johnson, 1971, p. 255
76   **II[B]** FRUS 1964–8, XII, pp. 511–12
77   **I[C]** Castle, 1993, p. 383
78   **I[C]** Castle, 1984, p. 46
79   **I[D]** Heren, 1970, p. 260
80   **I[D]** Heren, 1970, p. 231
81   **I[C]** Castle, 1984, p. 602
82   **I[C]** Wilson, 1971, pp. 579–80
83   **II[B]** Kissinger, 1979, pp. 59, 62, 91
84   **I[C]** Healey, 1990, pp. 324–5
85   **I[C]** Crossman, II, 1976, p. 647
86   **II[B]** Reed and Williams, 1971, p. 240
87   **II[B]** Reed and Williams, 1971, p. 246
88   **II[B]** Kitson, 1977, pp. 67–151; **II[B]** Mockaitis, 1995, pp. 14–43
89   **I[C]** Healey, 1990, p. 231
90   **I[C]** Healey, 1990, p. 282
91   **II[B]** Mockaitis, 1995, pp. 44–71; **II[A]** Cmnd. 2901, 1966, p. 8; **I[A]** PRO:
       DEFE 13/710 77705 (I owe this reference to C. Jones)
92   **I[C]** Healey, 1990, p. 284
93   **II[A]** Cmnd. 4290, 1970, p. 1
94   **I[C]** Pimlott, 1992, p. 388
95   **II[A]** Cmnd. 2901, 1966, p. 8
96   **II[A]** Cmnd. 2901, 1966, pp. 9–10
97   **I[B]** HC Deb., 22.2.1966, cols. 254–65
98   **III[B]** Brandon, 1966, p. 33
99   **I[C]** Jay, 1980, pp. 298–9; **I[A]** PRO: CAB 128/39
100   **III[B]** Beckerman, 1972, p. 61
101   **I[B]** HC Deb., 20.11.1967, cols. 946–7
102   **I[A]** PRO: CAB 128/41; **I[C]** Wilson, 1971, p. 257; **I[C]** Brown, 1971,
       pp. 114–16; **I[C]** Callaghan, 1988, pp. 195–200; **I[C]** Crossman, I, 1975,
       pp. 572–7; **I[C]** Crosland, 1982, pp. 173–5; **I[C]** Castle, 1984, pp. 145–51;
       I[C] Benn, 1988, pp. 457–8; **III[B]** Cairncross, 1997, pp. 147–54
103   **I[C]** Brown, 1971, p. 95
104   **I[C]** Wilson, 1971, p. 257
105   **I[D]** Fry, 1969, pp. 254–5
106   **III[B]** Brandon, 1966, pp. 35–6
107   **I[C]** Wilson, 1971, pp. 3–5; **I[C]** Brown, 1971, p. 97; **III[B]** Clifford,
       1997, pp. 95–7
108   **I[C]** Benn, 1987, p. 25; **III[B]** Clifford and McMillan, 1997, p. 122
109   **I[C]** Jay, 1980, p. 295
110   **I[C]** Thorpe, 1996, p. 257
111   **I[C]** Morgan, 1997, pp. 203–89
112   **I[C]** Callaghan, 1988, p. 213
113   **I[C]** Callaghan, 1988, pp. 193–4
114   **I[C]** Castle, 1984, p. 121
115   **I[B]** HC Deb., 3.5.1966, cols. 1149–298
116   **I[D]** Fry, 1981, pp. 64–5
117   **I[C]** Marsh, 1978, pp. 62–3

118   I[C] Goodman, 1979, pp. 413, 475
119   I[C] Crossman, I, 1975, p. 204
120   I[C] Wilson, 1971, p. 8
121   I[C] Goodman, 1979, pp. 495–6
122   I[C] Benn, 1988, p. 386
123   I[C] Goodman, 1979, p. 444
124   I[C] Benn, 1989, p. 203–5
125   I[C] Goodman, 1979, p. 431
126   I[D] Fry, 1981, p. 99
127   III[A] Cmnd. 3437, 1967; III[B] Fry, 1994, pp. 28–9
128   *The Economist*, 15.6.1968, pp. 16–17
129   I[C] Castle, 1984, p. 566
130   I[C] Castle, 1984, p. 415
131   I[C] Wilson, 1971, pp. 521–2
132   I[C] Castle, 1984, p. 419
133   I[C] Castle, 1984, p. 518
134   I[C] Castle, 1993, p. 413
135   I[C] Castle, 1984, p. 477
136   III[B] Jones, 1986, p. 193
137   I[C] Castle, 1984, p. 576
138   I[C] Castle, 1984, p. 585
139   III[A] Cmnd., 3888, 1969, p. 39
140   III[B] Jones, 1986, pp. 85–98, 140–54, 199–209
141   I[C] Castle, 1984, p. 560
142   I[C] Castle, 1984, p. 596
143   III[B] Jones, 1986, p. 204
144   III[B] Jenkins, 1970, pp. 75–97
145   I[C] Crossman, III, 1977, p. 526
146   I[C] Castle, 1984, p. 807
147   III[B] Jenkins, 1970, p. 140
148   I[C] Crossman, II, 1976, p. 668
149   I[C] Crossman, III, 1977, p. 21
150   I[D] Crosland, 1956, p. 518
151   I[C] Crosland, 1982, p. 148
152   I[D] Crosland, 1974, p. 206
153   III[B] Kogan, 1971, p. 193
154   I[C] Crosland, 1982, p. 159
155   I[C] Crosland, 1982, p. 147
156   I[C] Jefferys, 1999, p. 109; I[C] Hollis, 1997, pp. 297–351; I[C] Ziegler, 1993, p. 475
157   III[B] Townsend, 1975, p. 320
158   I[C] Benn, 1988, p. 513
159   I[C] Castle, 1984, p. 327
160   I[C] Benn, 1988, p. 513
161   I[C] Castle, 1984, p. 333
162   I[C] Jenkins, 1992, p. 229
163   I[C] Jenkins, 1992, pp. 246–7; I[B] H.C. Deb., 19.3.1968, cols. 251–302
164   *The Economist*, 23.3.1968, p. 13
165   *The Economist*, 19.4.1969, pp. 13–14; I[B] HC Deb., 15.4.1969, cols. 991–1043

166   **I[C]** Castle, 1984, p. 674
167   *The Economist*, 4.4.1970, p. 12
168   *The Economist*, 18.4.1970, p. 13; **I[B]** HC Deb., 14.4.1970, cols. 1212–53
169   **I[C]** Jenkins, 1992, p. 294
170   **I[C]** Castle, 1984, p. 786
171   *The Economist*, 11.4.1970, p. 11
172   **I[D]** Butler and Pinto-Duschinsky, 1971, pp. 166–7, 347
173   **III[B]** Middleton, 1996, pp. 448, 484
174   *The Economist*, 4.4.1970, p. 12
175   **I[D]** Jenkins, 1959, p. 9
176   **I[D]** Jenkins, 1959, p. 135
177   **I[D]** Crosland, 1956, p. 522
178   **I[D]** Jenkins, 1959, pp. 135–40
179   **II[B]** Lodge, 1982, p. 7
180   **I[D]** Radice, 2003, p. 144
181   **I[B]** HC Deb., 5.3.1965, col. 1734
182   **I[D]** Gallup, II, 1976, p. 788
183   **I[B]** HC Deb., 26.5.1965, cols. 529–33, 544, 566–7
184   **I[B]** HC Deb., 16.12.1969, cols. 1149–298
185   **I[D]** Gallup, II, 1976, p. 1087
186   **I[D]** Gallup, II, 1976, p. 823
187   **I[C]** Thomas, 1985, p. 91
188   **I[C]** Heffer, 1998, p. 454
189   **I[D]** Gallup, II, 1976, p. 984
190   **I[C]** Castle, 1984, p. 429
191   **I[C]** Benn, 1988, p. 60
192   **I[C]** Crossman, III, 1977, p. 29
193   **I[D]** Saggar, 1993, pp. 272–3
194   **I[C]** Heffer, 1998, pp. 559
195   **I[D]** Gilmour, 1977, p. 134
196   **I[C]** Morgan, 1981, p. 944
197   **I[D]** Gallup, II, 1976, p. 874
198   **I[D]** Abse, 1973, pp. 145–58; **I[D]** Richards, 1970, pp. 61–84; **I[D]** Davies, 1975, pp. 93–139, 206–7, 234–5
199   **I[D]** Steel, 1991, pp. 59–66; **I[C]** Jenkins, 1992, pp. 196, 208–10; **I[D]** Davies, 1975, pp. 21–7
200   **I[D]** Gallup, II, 1976, pp. 854, 910
201   **I[D]** Gallup, II, 1976, p. 965
202   **I[D]** Gallup, II, 1976, p. 930
203   **I[D]** Richards, 1970, p. 113–31
204   **I[D]** Abse, 1973, pp. 231–2
205   **I[C]** Castle, 1984, p. 153

10   The Heath Experiment

1   **I[C]** Laing, 1972, p. 9
2   **I[C]** Prior, 1986, p. 33
3   **I[D]** Proudfoot, 1974, p. 225
4   Interview: Lord Boyle
5   Interview: David Howell

6   **I[C]** Whitelaw, 1990, pp. 80–2
7   **I[D]** Butler and Pinto-Duschinsky, 1971, p. 354
8   **I[D]** Butler and Pinto-Duschinsky, 1971, p. 392
9   **I[D]** Butler and Pinto-Duschinsky, 1971, p. 346
10   **I[D]** Butler and Pinto-Duschinsky, 1971, pp. 386–7
11   *The Economist*, 20.6.1970, p. 9
12   **I[D]** Butler and Pinto-Duschinsky, 1971, p. 346
13   **I[D]** Craig, 1975, pp. 329–30, 333–9
14   **I[D]** Whitehead, 1985, p. 30
15   **I[B]** Conservative Party Archive: ACP/70/70; **I[D]** Fry, 1995, p. 25
16   Interview: Lord Cockfield; **I[D]** Fry, 1981, p. 91
17   **I[D]** Whitehead, 1985, p. 39
18   **I[D]** Whitehead, 1985, p. 33
19   **I[D]** Craig, 1975, p. 342
20   **I[B]** HL Deb., 27.7.1971, col. 278
21   **II[A]** Hannay, 2000, pp. 301–4
22   **I[D]** Gallup, II, 1976, pp. 1099, 1102, 1107–8, 1115–16, 1122, 1124, 1132–3, 1134, 1136–8, 1139–41, 1143–4, 1147–51, 1215, 1157–8, 1161, 1215; **II[B]** Lord, 1993, pp. 118–19
23   **I[D]** Hurd, 1979, p. 58
24   **II[A]** Hannay, 2000, p. 347
25   **II[B]** Charlton, 1983, p. 268
26   **II[B]** Lord, 1993, pp. 78–97
27   **II[B]** Moravcsik, 1998, p. 303
28   **II[A]** Hannay, 2000, pp. 355–60
29   **II[A]** Cmnd. 4715, 1971, p. 17
30   **II[A]** Cmnd. 4715, 1971, p. 16
31   **I[C]** Heath, 1998, p. 362
32   **I[D]** Craig, 1975, p. 325
33   *The Economist*, 23.10.1971, p. 14
34   **I[B]** HC Deb., 21.10.1971, cols. 912–1071; **I[B]** HC Deb., 22.10.1971, cols. 1094–186; **I[B]** HC Deb., 25.10.1971, cols. 1234–437; **I[B]** HC Deb., 26.10.1971, cols. 1480–686; **I[B]** HC Deb., 27.10.1971, cols. 1732–2033; **I[B]** HC Deb., 28.10.1971, cols. 2076–218
35   **I[B]** HC Deb., 17.2.1971, cols 752–9
36   **I[B]** HC Deb., 28.10.1971, col. 2211
37   **I[C]** Heath, 1998, p. 395
38   **I[B]** CPACR 1970, p. 130
39   **I[B]** CPACR 1970, p. 129
40   **I[B]** CPACR 1970, p. 132
41   **I[D]** Hurd, 1979, pp. 138–9
42   **I[C]** Campbell, 1993, p. 310
43   **I[C]** Prior, 1986, p. 71
44   **I[C]** Heath, 1998, p. 409
45   **III[B]** Heath, 1971, pp. 90–108
46   **III[B]** Thomson and Engleman, 1975, pp. 22–4
47   **I[C]** Heath, 1998, p. 408
48   **I[C]** Prior, 1986, p. 72

49   **I[B]** Cmnd. 4506, 1970, pp. 2–3
50   **I[B]** Cmnd. 4506, 1970, pp. 13–14
51   **I[C]** Prior, 1986, p. 76
52   **I[C]** Thorpe, 1996, pp. 404, 414–18
53   Interview: Lord Boyle
54   **I[C]** Maudling, 1978, pp. 193–205
55   **I[C]** Maudling, 1978, p. 161
56   **I[C]** Prior, 1986, p. 77
57   **I[B]** HC Deb., 4.11.1970, cols. 1211–12
58   **I[B]** HC Deb., 4.2.1971, col. 1922
59   **I[D]** Holmes, 1982, pp. 40–1
60   **I[D]** Holmes, 1982, pp. 42–4
61   **I[C]** Prior, 1986, p. 74
62   **I[D]** Hurd, 1979, p. 103
63   **I[D]** Craig, 1981, p. 66
64   **I[D]** Norton, 1978
65   *The Economist*, 25.3.1971, p. 17
66   **I[D]** Whitehead, 1985, p. 83
67   **I[B]** HC Deb., 27.10.1970, col. 51
68   **I[B]** HC Deb., 30.3.1971, col. 1397
69   **I[D]** Gallup, II, 1976, pp. 1142, 1144, 1151, 1154, 1159, 1163, 1166, 1171, 1176
70   **I[C]** Prior, 1986, p. 73
71   **I[B]** HC Deb, 21.3.1972, col. 1390
72   **I[D]** Holmes, 1982, pp. 128–9
73   **I[B]** HC Deb. 22.3.1972, cols. 1555–6
74   **I[D]** Whitehead, 1985, p. 83
75   **I[C]** Heath, 1998, p. 400
76   *The Economist*, 13.5.1972, p. 104
77   **I[C]** Prior, 1986, p. 72
78   **I[C]** Heath, 1998, pp. 411–15
79   **I[C]** Prior, 1986, p. 75
80   **I[C]** Carrington, 1988, p. 265
81   **I[D]** Butler and Kavanagh, 1974, pp. 275–6
82   **I[D]** Butler and Kavanagh, 1974, p. 260
83   **I[C]** Campbell, 1988, p. 23
84   **I[D]** Kandiah, 1995, p. 217
85   **I[C]** Heath, 1998, p. 401
86   **I[C]** Heath, 1998, p. 418
87   **III[A]** Cmnd. 4018, 1969
88   **III[B]** Fry, 1994, p. 29
89   **I[C]** Heath, 1998, p. 409
90   **I[D]** Jeffery and Hennessy, 1983, p. 233
91   **I[D]** Ball and Seldon, 1996, p. 191
92   **I[C]** Tebbit, 1989, p. 164
93   **I[B]** HC Deb., 6.11.1972, col. 631
94   **I[D]** Butler and Kavanagh, 1975, pp. 280, 294

11   The Last Act

1   I[C] Wilson, 1979, p. 17
2   I[C] Jenkins, 1992, p. 373
3   I[C] Jenkins, 1992, p. 376
4   I[D] Donoughue, 2002, 154–5
5   I[D] Donoughue, 2002, pp. 127, 228
6   I[D] Donoughue, 2002, pp. 191–229; c.f. I[D] Haines, 1977, pp. 198–222
7   III[B] Dell, 1991, p. 12
8   I[D] Hatfield, 1978, p. 17
9   I[C] Jenkins, 1992, p. 341
10   I[D] Hatfield, 1978, pp. 165–6
11   I[D] Whitehead, 1985, pp. 121–2
12   I[D] Butler and Kavanagh, 1974, p. 276
13   I[D] Butler and Kavanagh, 1975, pp. 293–4
14   III[B] Dell, 1991, p. 19
15   I[C] Castle, 1980, pp. 37–8
16   I[C] Healey, 1990, p. 394; I[B] H.C. Deb., 15.4.1975, cols. 280–1
17   III[B] Dell, 1991, p. 15
18   I[C] Castle, 1980, p. 181
19   I[C] Healey, 1990, p. 394; c.f. I[B] LPACR 1973, p. 129
20   I[D] Hatfield, 1978, p. 161; III[B] Wickham-Jones, 1996, pp. 53–84
21   I[D] Hatfield, 1978, p. 235
22   III[B] Dell, 1991, p. 26
23   I[C] Castle, 1980, p. 417
24   I[C] Castle, 1980, p. 448
25   III[B] Dell, 1991, p. 175
26   I[C] Castle, 1980, p. 723
27   I[C] Jenkins, 1992, p. 441
28   I[D] Whitehead, 1985, p. 181–2
29   I[C] Callaghan, 1988, p. 415
30   I[C] Callaghan, 1988, p. 418
31   I[C] Callaghan, 1988, p. 414
32   I[B] LPACR 1976, p. 319; I[C] Healey, 1990, p. 429
33   I[C] Callaghan, 1988, pp. 430–44; I[C] Morgan, 1997, pp. 537–9, 541–52; I[C] Benn, 1990, pp. 649, 661–79; 682–6; I[C] Crosland, 1982, pp. 375–82; I[D] Holmes, 1985, pp. 80–102; I[D] Whitehead, 1985, pp. 190–201; III[B] Artis and Cobham, 1991, pp. 12–13, 23, 33, 78; III[B] Burk and Cairncross, 1992, pp. 75–110, 229–36; I[D] Donoughue, 1987, pp. 79–100; I[D] Donoughue, 2001, pp. 243–8; I[D] Seldon and Hickson, 2004, pp. 41–7
34   I[C] Healey, 1990, p. 431
35   I[C] Healey, 1990, p. 433
36   III[B] Burk and Cairncross, 1992, p. 225
37   *The Economist*, 19.4.1975, p. 90
38   I[D] Whitehead, 1985, p. 187
39   I[D] Whitehead, 1985, p. 189
40   III[B] Burk and Cairncross, 1992, p. xiv
41   I[B] LPACR 1976, p. 188

42 **I[D]** Whitehead, 1985, pp. 196–7
43 **I[D]** Whitehead, 1985, p. 199
44 **I[C]** Benn, 1990, p. 62
45 **III[B]** Burk and Cairncross, 1992, p. 14
46 **I[B]** LPACR 1976, p. 188

Bibliography

I Political and constitutional history

[A] Public Record Office documents (PRO)
All Public Record Office documents cited are listed under the individual references.

[B] Parliamentary and private papers and party archive materials
Official Reports of House of Commons Debates [HC Deb]
Official Reports of House of Lords Debates [HL Deb]
Private Papers of Lord Avon [Avon Papers] (University Library, Birmingham)
Private Papers of Lord Boyle [Boyle Papers] (Brotherton Library, University of Leeds)
Conservative Party Archive (Bodleian Library, Oxford) [Conservative Party Annual Conference Reports (CPACR) and Conservative Research Department (CRD) Reports]
Labour Party Archive and Study Centre (John Rylands University Library, Victoria University of Manchester) Labour Party Annual Conference Reports (LPACR) and National Executive Minutes, and Trades Union Council Annual Conference Reports (TUCACR)
Cmd. 7326 [1948] *British Nationality Bill, Summary of Main Provisions*
Cmd. 7616 [1949] *Report of the* (Lynskey) *Tribunal appointed to inquire into Allegations reflecting on the Official Conduct of Ministers of the Crown and other Public Servants*
Cmd. 9613 (1955) *Report of the* (Priestley) *Royal Commission on the Civil Service*
Cmnd. 2152 [1963] *Lord Denning's Report*
Cmnd. 3638 [1968] *Report of the* (Fulton) *Committee on the Civil Service*
Cmnd. 4040 [1969] *Report of the* (Redcliffe-Maud) *Royal Commission on Local Government in England*
Cmnd. 4150 [1969] *Report of the* (Wheatley) *Royal Commission on Local Government in Scotland*
Cmnd. 4506 [1970] *The Reorganization of Central Government*
Cmnd. 4583 [1971] *Reform of Local Government in Scotland*
Cmnd. 4584 [1971] *Local Government in England, Government Proposals for Reorganization*
Cmnd. 5460 [1973] *Report of the* (Crowther-Kilbrandon) *Royal Commission on the Constitution*

[C] Political memoirs and biographies
Attlee, C.R., *As It Happened* (London, Heinemann, 1954)
Avon, Lord, *Full Circle* (London, Cassell, 1960)
Avon, Lord, *Facing the Dictators* (London, Cassell, 1962)
Avon, Lord, *The Reckoning* (London, Cassell,1965)
Avon, Lord, *Another World: 1897–1917* (London, Allen Lane, 1976)

Benn, T., *Out of the Wilderness. Diaries 1963–67* (London, Arrow, 1988)

Benn, T., *Office Without Power. Diaries 1968–72* (London, Arrow, 1989)

Benn, T., *Against The Tide. Diaries 1973–76* (London, Arrow, 1990)

Bevins, R., *The Greasy Pole* (London, Houghton & Stoughton, 1965)

Birkenhead, Lord, *The Prof in Two Worlds* (London, Collins, 1961)

Birkenhead, Lord, *Walter Monckton* (London, Weidenfeld & Nicolson, 1969)

Blake, R. and Louis, W.R., eds, *Churchill* (Oxford, Oxford University Press, 1993)

Boyd-Carpenter, J., *Way of Life* (London, Sidgwick & Jackson, 1980)

Brown, G., *In My Way* (London, Gollancz, 1971)

Brivati, B., *Hugh Gaitskell* (London, Cohen, 1996)

Bryant, C., *Stafford Cripps, The First Modern Chancellor* (London, Hodder & Stoughton, 1997)

Bullock, A., *The Life and Times of Ernest Bevin*, II: *Minister of Labour 1940–1945* (London, Heinemann, 1967)

Bullock, A., *The Life and Times of Ernest Bevin*, III: *Foreign Secretary 1945–1951* (London, Heinemann, 1983)

Butler, Lord, *The Art of the Possible* (London, Hamish Hamilton, 1971)

Callaghan J, *Time and Chance* (London, Collins, 1987)

Campbell, J., *Nye Bevan* (London Hodder & Stoughton, 1987)

Campbell, J., *Edward Heath* (London, Cape, 1993)

Carlton, D., *Anthony Eden* (London, Allen Lane, 1981)

Carrington, Lord, *Reflect on Things Past* (London, Collins, 1988)

Castle, B., *The Castle Diaries 1964–70* (London, Weidenfeld & Nicolson, 1984)

Castle, B., *The Castle Diaries 1974–76* (London, Weidenfeld & Nicolson, 1980)

Castle, B., *Fighting All The Way* (London, Macmillan, 1993)

Chandos, Lord, *Memoirs* (London, Bodley Head, 1962)

Churchill, R., *The Rise and Fall of Sir Anthony Eden* (London, MacGibbon & Kee, 1959)

Churchill, W.S., *The Second World War*, I: *The Gathering Storm* (London, Cassell, 1948)

Churchill, W.S., *The Second World War*, VI: *Triumph and Tragedy* (London, Cassell, 1954)

Clarke, P., *The Cripps Version. The Life of Sir Stafford Cripps 1889–1952* (London, Allen Lane, 2002)

Cooke, C., *The Life of Richard Stafford Cripps* (London, Hodder & Stoughton, 1957)

Crosland, S., *Tony Crosland* (London, Cape, 1982)

Crossman, R.H.S., *The Diaries of a Cabinet Minister*, 3 vols (London, Hamish Hamilton and Jonathan Cape, 1975–1977)

Dalton, H., *The Fateful Years. Memoirs 1931–1945* (London, Muller, 1957)

Dalton, H., *High Tide and After. Memoirs 1945–1960* ((London, Muller, 1962)

Donoughue, B. and Jones, G.W., *Herbert Morrison. Portrait of a Politician* (London, Weidenfeld & Nicolson, 1973)

Dutton, D., *Anthony Eden. A Life and Reputation* (London, Arnold, 1997)

Elwyn Jones, Lord, *In My Time* (London, Weidenfeld & Nicolson, 1983)

Estorick, E., *Stafford Cripps* (Heinemann, Melbourne, 1949)

Fisher, N., *Iain Macleod* (London, Deutsch, 1973)

Foot, M.M., *Aneurin Bevan 1897–1945* (London, MacGibbon & Kee, 1962)

Foot, M.M., *Aneurin Bevan 1945–1960* (London, Davis–Poynter, 1973)

Gilbert, M., *Winston S. Churchill*, VIII: *Never Despair 1945–1965* (London, Heinemann, 1988)

Griffiths, J., *Pages From Memory* (London, Dent, 1969)

Goodman, G., *The Awkward Warrior. Frank Cousins: His Life and Times* (London, Davis–Poynter, 1979)

Hailsham, Lord, *The Door Wherein I Went* (London, Collins, 1975)

Harris, K., *Attlee* (London, Weidenfeld & Nicolson, 1982)

Healey, D., *The Time of My Life* (Harmondsworth, Penguin, 1990)

Heath, E., *The Course of My Life* (London, Hodder & Stoughton, 1998)

Heffer, S., *Like The Roman. The Life of Enoch Powell* (London, Weidenfeld & Nicolson, 1998)

Hill, Lord, *Both Sides of the Hill* (London, Heinemann, 1964)

Hollis, P., *Jennie Lee* (Oxford, Oxford University Press, 1997)

Home, Lord, *The Way The Wind Blows* (London, Collins, 1976)

Horne, A., *Macmillan 1894–1956* (London, Macmillan, 1988)

Horne, A., *Macmillan 1957–1986* (London, Macmillan, 1989)

Howard, A., *RAB. The Life of R.A. Butler* (London, Cape, 1987)

Ismay, Lord, *Memoirs* (London, Heinemann, 1960)

Jay, D., *Change and Fortune* (London, Hutchinson, 1980)

Jefferys, K., *Anthony Crosland* (London, Richard Cohen, 1999)

Jenkins, R., *A Life At The Centre* (London, Pan, 1992)

Jenkins, R., *Churchill* (Basingstoke, Macmillan, 2001)

Kilmuir, Lord, *Political Adventure* (London, Weidenfeld & Nicolson, 1964)

Laing, M., *Edward Heath. Prime Minister* (London, Sidgwick & Jackson, 1972)

Lewis, G., *Lord Hailsham* (London, Pimlico, 1998)

Lysaght, C.E., *Brendan Bracken* (London, Allen Lane, 1979)

Macmillan, H., *Winds of Change 1914–1939* (London, Macmillan, 1966)

Macmillan, H., *The Blast of War 1939–1945* (London, Macmillan, 1967)

Macmillan, H., *Tides of Fortune 1945–1955* (London, Macmillan, 1969)

Macmillan, H., *Riding The Storm 1956–1959* (London, Macmillan, 1971)

Macmillan, H., *Pointing The Way 1959–1961*(London, Macmillan, 1972)

Macmillan, H., *At The End Of The Day 1961–1963* (London, Macmillan, 1973)

Marsh, R., *Off The Rails* (London, Weidenfeld & Nicolson, 1978)

Maudling, R., *Memoirs* (London, Sidgwick & Jackson, 1978)

Morgan, J., ed., *The Backbench Diaries of Richard Crossman* (London, Hamilton and Cape, 1981)

Morgan, K.O., *Callaghan* (Oxford, Oxford University Press, 1997)

Morrison, Lord, *Herbert Morrison. An Autobiography* (London, Odhams, 1960)

Moran, Lord, *Winston Churchill. The Struggle for Survival 1940–1965* (London, Constable, 1966)

Murphy, P., *Alan Lennox–Boyd* (London, Tauris, 1999)

Newman, M., *John Strachey* (Manchester, Manchester University Press, 1989)

Pearce, R., ed., *Patrick Gordon Walker. Political Diaries 1932–1971* (London, Historians' Press, 1991)

Pelling, H., *Winston Churchill* (London, Macmillan, 1974)

Pimlott, B., *Hugh Dalton* (London, Cape, 1985)

Pimlott, B., ed., *The Political Diary of Hugh Dalton 1918–40, 1945–60* (London, Cape, 1986)

Pimlott, B., ed., *The Second World War Diary of Hugh Dalton 1940–1945* (London, Cape, 1986)

Pimlott, B., *Harold Wilson* (London, HarperCollins, 1992)

Prior, J., *A Balance of Power* (London, Hamish Hamilton, 1986)
Reed, B., and Williams, G., *Denis Healey and the Politics of Power* (London, Sidgwick & Jackson, 1971)
Rhodes James, R., *Anthony Eden* (London, Weidenfeld & Nicolson, 1986)
Rodgers, W.T., ed., *Hugh Gaitskell 1906–1963* (London, Thames and Hudson, 1964)
Shepherd, R., *Iain Macleod* (London, Hutchinson, 1994)
Sampson, A., *Macmillan. A Study in Ambiguity* (London, Allen Lane, 1967)
Shinwell, E., *Conflict Without Malice* (London, Odhams, 1955)
Smith, L., *Harold Wilson* (London, Hodder & Stoughton, 1964)
Stewart, M., *Life and Labour* (London, Sidgwick & Jackson, 1980)
Stuart, Lord, *Within The Fringe* (London, Bodley Head, 1967)
Slowe, P., *Manny Shinwell* (London, Pluto Press, 1993)
Tebbit, N., *Upwardly Mobile* (London, Futura, 1989)
Thomas, H., *John Strachey* (London, Eyre Methuen, 1973)
Thompson, N., *John Strachey. An Intellectual Biography* (Basingstoke, Macmillan 1993)
Thorpe, D.R., *Selwyn Lloyd* (London, Cape, 1989)
Thorpe, D.R., *Alec Douglas-Home* (London, Sinclair-Stevenson, 1996)
Thorpe, D.R., *Eden. The Life and Times of Anthony Eden* (London, Chatto & Windus, 2003)
Turner, J., *Macmillan* (London, Longman, 1994)
Vernon, B.D., *Ellen Wilkinson 1891–1947* (London, Croom Helm, 1982)
Whitelaw, Lord, *The Whitelaw Memoirs* (London, Headline, 1990)
Wigg, Lord, *George Wigg* (London, Michael Joseph, 1972)
Williams, F., *A Prime Minister Remembers* (London, Heinemann, 1961)
Williams, F., *Ernest Bevin* (London, Odhams, 1952)
Williams, P.M., *Hugh Gaitskell. A Political Biography* (London, Cape, 1979)
Williams, P.M., ed., *The Diaries of Hugh Gaitskell 1945–1960* (London, Cape, 1983)
Wilson, H., *The Labour Government 1964–1970. A Personal Record* (London, Weidenfeld & Nicolson and Michael Joseph, 1971)
Wilson, H., *Final Term. The Labour Government 1974–1976* (London, Weidenfeld & Nicolson and Michael Joseph, 1979)
Wilson, H., *Memoirs. The Making of a Prime Minister 1916–1964* (London, Weidenfeld & Nicolson and Michael Joseph, 1986)
Winterton, Lord, *Orders Of The Day* (London, Cassell, 1953)
Woolton, Lord, *Memoirs* (London, Cassell, 1959)
Zeigler, P., *Wilson* (London, Weidenfeld & Nicolson, 1993)

[D] Further sources

Abrams, P. and Rose, R., *Must Labour Lose?* (Harmondsworth, Penguin, 1960)
Abse, L., *Private Member* (London, Macdonald, 1973)
Addison, P., *The Road to 1945. British Politics and the Second World War* (London, Cape, 1975)
Attlee, C.R., *The Labour Party in Perspective* (London, Gollancz, 1937)
Annan, N., *Our Age. Portrait of a Generation* (London, Weidenfeld & Nicolson, 1990)
Bagehot, W., *The English Constitution* [1867] (London, Oxford University Press, 1928)

Ball, S. and Seldon, A., eds, *The Heath Government 1970–74* (London, Longman, 1996)

Balneil, Lord et al, *The Responsible Society* (London, Conservative Political Centre, 1959)

Barker, Sir E., *Essays on Government* (Oxford, Clarendon Press, 1950)

Barnes, J., and Nicholson, D., eds, *The Empire At Bay. The Leo Amery Diaries 1929–1945* (London, Hutchinson, 1988)

Barnett, C., *The Collapse of British Power* (Gloucester, Sutton, 1984)

Barnett, C., *The Audit of War. The Illusion and Reality of Britain as a Great Nation* (London, Macmillan, 1986)

Barnett, C., *The Lost Victory. British Dreams, British Realities 1945–1950* (London, Macmillan, 1995)

Barnett, C., *The Verdict of Peace. Britain Between Her Yesterday and the Future* (London, Macmillan, 2001)

Beales, H.L., 'Has Labour Come To Stay?' *Political Quarterly*, XVIII (1947): pp. 48–60.

Bevan, A. [Celticus], *Why Not Trust The Tories?* (London, Gollancz, 1944)

Bevan A., *In Place of Fear* (London, Heinemann, 1952)

Bonham, J., *The Middle Class Vote* (London, Faber & Faber, 1954)

Bradford, S., *King George VI* (London, Weidenfeld & Nicolson, 1989)

Bruce–Gardyne, J., *Whatever Happened to the Quiet Revolution?* (London, Knight, 1974)

Bruce–Gardyne, J., and Lawson, N., *The Power Game* (London, Macmillan, 1976)

Butler, D.E., 'Trends in British By-Elections', *Journal of Politics*, IX (1949): pp. 396–407)

Butler, D.E., *The British General Election of 1950* (London, Macmillan, 1951)

Butler, D.E., *The British General Election of 1951* (London, Macmillan, 1952)

Butler, D.E., *The British General Election of 1955* (London, Macmillan, 1955)

Butler, D.E., *The Electoral System in Britain Since 1918* (Oxford, Clarendon Press, 1963)

Butler, D.E., *British General Elections since 1945* (Oxford, Blackwell,1989)

Butler, D.E. and Rose, R., *The British General Election of 1959* (London, Macmillan, 1960)

Butler, D.E. and King, A., *The British General Election of 1964* (London, Macmillan, 1965)

Butler, D.E. and King, A., *The British General Election of 1966* (London, Macmillan, 1966)

Butler, D.E. and Stokes, D., *Political Change in Britain* (London, Macmillan, 1969)

Butler, D.E. and Pinto-Duschinsky, M., *The British General Election of 1970* (London, Macmillan, 1971)

Butler, D.E. and Kavanagh, D., *The British General Election of February 1974* (London, Macmillan, 1974)

Butler, D.E. and Kavanagh, D., *The British General Election of October 1974* (London, Macmillan, 1975)

Butler, D.E. and Kitzinger, U., *The 1975 Referendum* (London, Macmillan, 1976)

Calder, A., *The People's War. Britain 1939–1945* (London, Cape, 1969)

Churchill, W.S., *The World Crisis. The Aftermath* (London, Thornton Butterworth, 1929)

Clark, A., *The Tories. The Conservatives and The Nation State 1922–1997* (London, Phoenix, 1999)

Colville, J., *Footprints In Time* (London, Collins, 1976)

Colville, Sir J., *The Churchillians* (London, Weidenfeld & Nicolson, 1981)

Colville, Sir J., *The Fringes of Power. Downing Street Diaries 1939–1955* (London, Hodder & Stoughton, 1985)

Coopey, R., Fielding, S., and Tiratsoo, N., eds, *The Wilson Governments 1964–1970* (New York, Pinter, 1993)

Craig, F.W.S., ed., *British Parliamentary Election Results 1918–1949* (Glasgow, Political Reference Publications 1969)

Craig, F.W.S., ed., *British Parliamentary Election Results 1950–1970* (Chichester, Political Reference Publications, 1971)

Craig, F.W.S., ed., *British General Election Manifestos 1900–1974* (London, Macmillan, 1975)

Craig, F.W.S., ed., *British Electoral Facts 1832–1980* (Chichester, Parliamentary Research Services,1981)

Christoph, J.B., *Capital Punishment and British Politics* (London, Allen & Unwin, 1962)

Crosland, C.A.R., *The Future of Socialism* (London, Cape, 1956)

Crosland, C.A.R., *The Conservative Enemy* (London, Cape, 1962)

Crosland, C.A.R., *Socialism Now* (London, Cape, 1974)

Cudlipp, H., *Publish and be Damned! The Astonishing Story of the Daily Mirror* (London, Dakers, 1953)

Davies, J.C.H., *Permissive Britain* (London, Pitman, 1975)

Donoughue, B., *Prime Minister. The Conduct of Policy under Harold Wilson and James Callaghan* (London, Cape, 1987)

Donoughue, B., *The Heat of the Kitchen* (London, Politico's, 2002)

Douglas, R., *The History of the Liberal Party 1895–1970* (London, Sidgwick & Jackson, 1971)

Eden, Sir A., *Freedom and Order. Selected Speeches 1939–1946* (London, Faber & Faber, 1947)

Favretto, I., 'Wilsonism reconsidered: Labour Party revisionism 1952–1964', *Contemporary British History*, 14 (2000): pp. 54–80

Fielding, S., 'What did "The People" want?: the meaning of the 1945 General Election', *Historical Journal*, 35 (1992): pp. 623–9

Fielding, S., Thompson, P., and Tiratsoo, N., *'England Arise!' The Labour Party and Popular Politics in 1940s Britain* (Manchester, Manchester University Press, 1995)

Findlay, R., 'The Conservative Party and Defeat: The Significance of Resale Price Maintenance for the Election of 1964', *Twentieth Century British History*, 12 (200!): pp. 327–63

Foot, M.M. and Jones, M., *Guilty Men 1957* (London, Gollancz, 1957)

Foot, P., *The Politics of Harold Wilson* (Harmondsworth, Penguin, 1968)

Francis, M. and Zweiniger–Bargielowska, I., eds, *The Conservatives and Modern Society 1880–1990* (Cardiff, University of Wales Press, 1996)

Fry, G.K., *Statesmen In Disguise. The Changing Role of the Administrative Class of the British Home Civil Service 1853–1966* (London, Macmillan, 1969)

Fry, G.K., *The Administrative 'Revolution' in Whitehall. A Study of the Politics of Administrative Change in British Central Government since the 1950s* (London, Croom Helm, 1981)

Fry, G.K., 'A Reconsideration of the British General Election of 1935 and the Electoral Revolution of 1945', *History*, 76 (1991): pp. 43–55

Fry, G.K., *Policy and Management in the British Civil Service* (London, Prentice Hall, 1995)

Fry, G.K., *The Politics of Crisis. An Interpretation of British Politics 1931–1945* (Basingstoke, Palgrave, 2001)

Gallup, G.H., ed., *The Gallup International Public Opinion Polls. Great Britain 1937–1975*, 2 vols (New York, Random House, 1976)

Gilmour, Sir I., *Inside Right. A Study of Conservatism* (London, Hutchinson, 1977)

Goldthorpe, J.H., Lockwood, D., Bechhofer, F., and Platt, J., *The Affluent Worker: Political Attitudes and Behaviour* (Cambridge, Cambridge University Press, 1968)

Haines, J., *The Politics of Power* (London, Cape, 1977)

Hart–Davis, D., *The House the Berrys Built* (London, Hodder & Stoughton, 1990)

Hatfield, M., *The House the Left Built. Inside Labour Policy Making 1970–75* (London, Gollancz, 1978)

Hayek, F.A., *The Road to Serfdom* (London, Routledge, 1944)

Hennessy, P., *Never Again. Britain 1945–1951* (London, Vintage, 1993)

Hennessy, P., *The Prime Minister. The Office and its Holders since 1945* (London, Allen Lane, 2000)

Hoffman, J.D., *The Conservative Party in Opposition 1945–51* (London, MacGibbon & Kee, 1964)

Hogg, Q., *The Case for Conservatism* (West Drayton, Penguin, 1947)

Holmes, M., *Political Pressure and Economic Policy. British Government 1970–1974* (London, Butterworths, 1982)

Holmes, M., *The Labour Government 1974–79. Political Aims and Economic Reality* (London, Macmillan, 1985)

Hunter, L., *The Road to Brighton Pier* (London, Arthur Barker, 1959)

Hurd, D., *An End to Promises. Sketch of a Government 1970–74* (London, Collins, 1979)

Jenkins, P., *The Battle of Downing Street* (London, Knight, 1970)

Jenkins, R., *The Labour Case* (Harmondsworth, Penguin, 1959)

Jeffery, and Hennessy, P., *States of Emergency* (London, Routledge and Kegan Paul, 1983)

Kandiah, M.D., ed., 'Witness Seminar: The Heath Government', *Journal of Contemporary British History*, 9 (1995): pp. 188–219

King, Lord, *The Cecil King Diary 1965–1970* (London, Cape, 1972)

Kinnear, M., *The British Voter. An Atlas and Survey since 1885* (London, Batsford, 1968)

Lamb, R., *The Failure of the Eden Government* (London, Sidgwick & Jackson, 1987)

Lamb, R., *The Macmillan Years 1957–1963* (London, Murray, 1995)

Lively, J., ed., *The Works of Joseph de Maistre* (London, Allen & Unwin, 1965)

McCallum, R.B. and Readman, A., *The British General Election of 1945* (London, Oxford University Press, 1947)

MacKenzie, N. and Mackenzie, J., eds, *The Diary of Beatrice Webb*, IV: *1924–1943* (London, Virago, 1985)

MacKenzie, N., ed., *The Letters of Sidney and Beatrice Webb. III. Pilgrimage 1912–1947* (Cambridge, Cambridge University Press, 1978)

McKenzie, R., and Silver, A., *Angels in Marble. Working Class Conservatives in Urban England* (London Heinemann, 1968)

Macleod, I. and Maude, A., eds, *One Nation: A Tory Approach to Social Problems* (London, Conservative Political Centre, 1950)

Magnus, Sir P., *Edmund Burke. A Life* (New York, Russell and Russell, 1973)

Manning, L., *A Life For Education* (London, Gollancz, 1970)

Marx, K., and Engels, F., *Collected Works*, III (London, Lawrence & Wishart, 1975)

Medlicott, W.N., *Contemporary England 1914–1964* (London, Longmans, 1967)

Mellors, C., *The British M.P.* (Farnborough, Saxon House, 1978)

Mitchell, A., *Election '45. Reflections on the Revolution in Britain* (London, Bellew, 1995)

Moore, G.E., *Principia Ethica* (Cambridge, Cambridge University Press, 1903)

Morgan, K.O., *Labour In Power 1945–1951* (Oxford, Clarendon Press, 1984)

Morrison, H, *Government and Parliament. A Survey From The Inside* (London, Oxford University Press, 1954)

Namier, Sir L., *Avenues of History* (London, Hamilton, 1952)

Namier, Sir L., *Personalities and Powers* (London, Hamilton, 1955)

Nicholas, H.G., *The British General Election of 1950* (London, Macmillan, 1951)

Nicolson, H., *Diaries and Letters 1945–1962* (London, Collins, 1968)

Nordlinger, E.A., *The Working Class Tories* (London, MacGibbon & Kee, 1967)

Norton, P., *Conservative Dissidents. Dissent within the Parliamentary Conservative Party 1970–74* (London, Temple Smith, 1978)

Pareto, V., *Sociological Writings* (London, Pall Mall, 1966)

Parkin, F., 'Working Class Conservatives: A Theory of Political Deviance', *British Journal of Sociology*, 18 (1967): pp. 278–90

Pelling, H., 'The 1945 General Election Reconsidered', *Historical Journal*, 23 (1980): pp. 399–414

Ponting, C., *Breach of Promise. Labour in Power 1964–1970* (London, Hamish Hamilton, 1989)

Powell, J.E. and Maude, A., eds, *Change is Our Ally* (London, Conservative Centre, 1954)

Pritt, D.N., *The Labour Government 1945–51* (London, Lawrence & Wishart, 1963)

Pritt, D.N., *Brasshats and Bureaucrats* (London, Lawrence & Wishart, 1966)

Proudfoot, M., *British Politics and Government 1951–1970* (London, Faber & Faber, 1974)

Radice, G., *Friends and Rivals. Crosland, Jenkins and Healey* (London, Abacus, 2003)

Ramsden, J., *The Age of Churchill and Eden* (London, Longman, 1995)

Rhodes James, R., ed., *Winston S. Churchill. His Complete Speeches 1887–1963*, VII: *1943–1949* (London, Chelsea House, 1974)

Richards, P.G., 'The Political Temper', *Political Quarterly*, XVI (1945): pp. 57–66

Richards, P.G., 'The Labour Victory: Election Figures', *Political Quarterly*, XVI (1945): pp. 350–56

Richards, P.G., *Parliament and Conscience* (London, Allen & Unwin, 1970)

Roberts, A., *'The Holy Fox.' A Biography of Lord Halifax* (London, Weidenfeld & Nicolson, 1991)

Roberts, A., *Eminent Churchillians* (London, Weidenfeld & Nicolson, 1994)

Roberts, A., *Salisbury: Victorian Titan* (London, Weidenfeld & Nicolson, 1999)

Robson, W.A., 'The Reform of Government', *Political Quarterly* 35 (1964): pp. 193–211

Russell, Lord, *The Autobiography of Bertrand Russell*, 3 vols (London, Allen & Unwin, 1967–1970)

Saggar, S., 'Re-examining the 1964–70 Labour Government's Race Relations Strategy', *Contemporary Record*, 7 (1993): pp. 253–81

Salter, Lord, *Slave of the Lamp* (London, Weidenfeld & Nicolson, 1967)

Schneer, J., *Labour's Conscience: The Labour Left 1945–1951* (London, Unwin Hyman, 1988)

Seldon, A., *Churchill's Indian Summer. The Conservative Government 1951–1955* (London, Hodder & Stoughton, 1981)

Seldon, A. and Hickson, K., eds, *New Labour, Old Labour. The Wilson and Callaghan Governments 1974–79* (London, Routledge, 2004)

Sissons, M. and French, P., eds, *Age of Austerity 1945–1951* (Harmondsworth, Penguin, 1963)

Skelton, A., *Constructive Conservation* (London, Blackwood,1924)

Somervell, D.C., *British Politics Since 1900* (London, Dakers, 1950)

Steel, D., *Against Goliath* (London, Pan, 1991)

Strachey, J., *Contemporary Capitalism* (London, Gollancz, 1956)

Taylor, A.J.P., *English History 1914–1945* (Oxford, Oxford University Press, 1965)

Taylor, A.J.P., *Beaverbrook* (London, Hamish Hamilton, 1972)

Terrill, R., *R.H. Tawney and His Times* (London, Deutsch, 1974)

The Times, House of Commons 1945 (*The Times*, London, 1945)

Tiratsoo, N., ed., *The Attlee Years* (London, Pinter, 1991)

Tracey, M., *A Variety of Lives. A Biography of Sir Hugh Greene* (London, The Bodley Head, 1983)

Vaizey, J., *In Breach of Promise. Five Men Who Shaped A Generation* (London, Weidenfeld & Nicolson, 1983)

Walsha, R., 'The One Nation Group: A Tory Approach to Backbench Politics and Organization 1950–1955', *Twentieth Century British History*, 11 (2000): pp 183–214

Wheeler–Bennett, Sir J., *King George VI: His Life and Reign* (London, Macmillan, 1958)

Wheeler–Bennett, Sir J., ed., *Action This day. Working with Churchill* (London, Macmillan, 1969)

Whitehead, P., *The Writing on the Wall* (London, Joseph, 1985)

Williams, F., *Fifty Years March. The Rise of the Labour Party* (London, Odhams, 1951)

Williams, F., *Dangerous Estate. The Anatomy of Newspapers* (London, Longmans, Green, 1957)

Williams, F., *Nothing So Strange* (London, Cassell, 1970)

Williams, M., *Inside Number 10* (London, Weidenfeld & Nicolson, 1972)

Winter, J., ed., *The Working Class in Modern British History* (Cambridge, Cambridge University Press, 1983)

Young, K., ed., *The Diaries of Sir Robert Bruce Lockhart*, II: *1939–1965* (London, Macmillan, 1980)

II   Diplomatic and military history

[A] Government publications [London: HMSO]

Documents on British Policy Overseas [DPBO] Series I
Documents on British Policy Overseas [DPBO] Series II

British Documents on the End of Empire [BDEE] Series A
British Documents on the End of Empire [BDEE] Series B
Constitutional Relations Between Britain and India. The Transfer of Power 1942–47 (ed. Mansergh, N), 12 vols [1970–1983]
Cmd. 6743 [1946] *Statement Relating to Defence, 1946*
Cmd. 7042 [1947] *Statement Relating to Defence, 1947*
Cmd. 7327 [1948] *Statement Relating to Defence, 1948*
Cmd. 7631 [1949] *Statement on Defence, 1949*
Cmd. 7789 [1949] *North Atlantic Treaty*
Cmd. 7895 [1950] *Statement on Defence, 1950*
Cmd. 8146 [1951] *Defence Programme*
Cmd. 8475 [1952] *Statement on Defence, 1952*
Cmd. 8768 [1953] *Statement on Defence, 1953*
Cmd. 9075 [1954] *Statement on Defence, 1954*
Cmd. 9186 [1954] *Documents relating to the Discussion of Korea and Indo–China at the Geneva Conference*
Cmd. 9288 [1954] *Memorandum of Understanding between the Governments of the United Kingdom of Great Britain and Northern Ireland, Italy, the United States of America, and Yugoslavia regarding the Free Territory of Trieste*
Cmd. 9289 [1954] *Nine Power Conference. Final Act of the Nine Power Conference held in London Sept. 28 to Oct 3 1954*
Cmd. 9391 [1955] *Statement on Defence, 1955*
Cmd. 9418 [1955] *Exchange of Letters between Winston Churchill and Mr Molotov, the Soviet Foreign Minister about the Prime Minister's Proposal for a Two Power Meeting between the United Kingdom and the Union of Soviet Socialist Republics*
Cmnd. 124 [1957] *Defence: Outline of Future Policy*
Cmnd. 363 [1958] *Report on Defence. Britain's Contribution to Peace and Security*
Cmnd. 476 [1958] *Central Organization for Defence*
Cmnd. 662 [1959] *Defence Plan. Progress of the Five Year Defence Plan*
Cmnd. 952 [1960] *Report on Defence 1960*
Cmnd. 1288 [1961] *Report on Defence 1961*
Cmnd. 1639 [1962] *Statement on Defence. The Next Five Years*
Cmnd. 1936 [1963] *Statement on Defence 1963*
Cmnd. 2097 [1963] *Central Organization for Defence*
Cmnd. 2118 (1963) *Nuclear Weapon Tests. Draft Treaty Banning Nuclear Weapon Tests in the Atmosphere, in Outer Space, and Under Water*
Cmnd. 2270 [1964] *Statement on Defence 1964*
Cmnd. 2276 [1964] *Report of the* [Plowden] *Committee on Representational Services Overseas*
Cmnd. 2592 [1965] *Statement on the Defence Estimates 1965*
Cmnd. 2901[1966] *Statement on the Defence Estimates 1966*, Part I: *The Defence Review*
Cmnd. 3203 [1967] *Statement on the Defence Estimates 1967*
Cmnd. 3357 [1967] *Supplementary Statement on Defence Policy 1967*
Cmnd. 3540 [1968] *Statement on the Defence Estimates 1968*
Cmnd. 3701 [1968] *Supplementary Statement on Defence Policy 1968*
Cmnd. 3927 [1969] *Statement on the Defence Estimates 1969*
Cmnd. 4107 [1969] *Report of the* (Duncan) *Review Committee on Overseas Representation*

Cmnd. 4290 [1970] *Statement on the Defence Estimates 1970*

Cmnd. 4401 [1970] *The United Kingdom and the European Communities: A Statement on behalf of H.M. Government at Luxembourg on 30 June 1970*

Cmnd. 4521 [1970] *Supplementary Statement on Defence Policy 1970*

Cmnd. 4592 [1971] *Statement on the Defence Estimates 1971*

Cmnd. 4715 [1971] *The United Kingdom and the European Communities*

Cmnd. 4891 [1972] *Statement on the Defence Estimates 1972*

Cmnd. 5231 [1973] *Statement on the Defence Estimates 1973*

Cmnd. 5593 [1974] *European Communities no. 8 (1974). Renegotiation of the Terms of Entry into the European Economic Community*

Cmnd. 5976 [1975] *Statement on the Defence Estimates 1975*

Cmnd. 6003 [1975] *Membership of the European Community: Report on Renegotiation*

Cmnd. 6432 [1976] *Statement on the Defence Estimates 1976*

Hannay, Sir D., ed., *Britain's Entry into the European Community Report by Sir Con O'Neill on the Negotiations of 1970–1972* (London, Whitehall History Publishing and Frank Cass, 2000)

Millward, A.S., *The U.K. and the European Communities. I. The Rise and Fall of a National Strategy* (London, Whitehall History Publishing and Frank Cass, 2002)

[B] Further sources

Acheson, D., *Present At The Creation. My Years in the State Department* (London, Hamish Hamilton, 1970)

Allen, C., *The Savage Wars of Peace. Soldiers' Voices 1945–1989* (London, Michael Joseph, 199)

Alport, Lord, *Sudden Assignment* (London, Hodder & Stoughton, 1965)

Ambrose, S.E., *Eisenhower*, I: *Soldier. General of the Army. President-Elect* (London, Allen & Unwin, 1984)

Ambrose, S.E., *Eisenhower*, II: *The President 1952–1969* (London, Allen & Unwin, 1984)

Ambrose, S.E., *Nixon. Triumph of a Politician 1962–1972* (New York, Simon & Schuster, 1989)

Anderson, T.H., *The United States, Great Britain, and the Cold War 1944–1947* (Columbia, University of Missouri Press, 1981)

Andrew, C. and Mitrokhin, V., *The Mitrokhin Archive. The KGB in Europe and the West* (Harmondsworth, Penguin, 2000)

Balfour-Paul, G., *The End of Empire in the Middle East. Britain's Relinquishment of Power in Her Last Three Arab Dependencies* (Cambridge, Cambridge University Press, 1991

Ball, G.W., *The Past Has Another Pattern* (New York, Norton, 1982)

Bannister, R.C., ed., *On Liberty, Society, and Politics. The Essential Essays of William Graham Sumner* (Indianapolis, Liberty Fund, 1992)

Barclay, Sir R., *Ernest Bevin and the Foreign Office 1932–1969* (London, Privately Published, 1975)

Baylis, J, 'Britain and the Dunkirk Treaty: The Origins of NATO', *The Journal of Strategic Studies*, 5 (1982): pp. 236–47

Bethell, N., *The Palestine Triangle. The Struggle between the British, the Jews and the Arabs 1935–48* (London, Deutsch, 1979)

Bevin, E., 'The North Atlantic Pact', *The Listener*, 23.3.1949, 471–2

Bill, J.A. and Louis, W.R., eds, *Musaddiq, Iranian Nationalism, and Oil* (London, Tauris, 1988)

Blum, J.M., ed., *The Price of Vision. The Diary of Henry A. Wallace 1942–1946* (Boston, Houghton Miffin, 1973)

Braddon, R., *Suez: Splitting of a Nation* (London, Collins, 1973)

Boyle, P.G., *The Churchill–Eisenhower Correspondence 1953–1955* (Chapel Hill, University of North Carolina Press, 1990)

Bullock, A., 'Bevin provided the Basis for Western Security', *The Listener*, 14.10.1982, pp. 10–13

Byrnes, J., *Speaking Frankly* (London, Heinemann, 1947)

Cable, J., *The Geneva Conference of 1954 on Indo–China* (Basingstoke, Macmillan, 1986)

Cable, J., *Intervention at Abadan: Plan Buccaneer* (Basingstoke, Macmillan, 1991)

Camps, M., *Britain and the European Community 1955–1963* (Princeton, N.J., Princeton University Press, 1964)

Carr, R., *Spain 1808–1975* (Oxford, Clarendon Press, 1982)

Charlton, M., *The Price of Victory* (London, BBC, 1983)

Churchill, W.S., *The World Crisis*, V: *The Aftermath* (London, Butterworth, 1929)

Churchill, W.S., *A History of the English Speaking Peoples*, 4 vols (London, Cassell, 1956–1958)

Collier, P. and Horowitz, D., *The Kennedys* (London, Pan Books, 1985)

Crossman, R.H.S., *Palestine Mission* (London, Hamilton, 1947)

Daddow, O.J., ed., *Harold Wilson and European Integration. Britain's Second Application to join the E.E.C.* (London, Cass, 2003)

Dallek, R., *Flawed Giant. Lyndon Johnson and His Times 1961–1973* (New York, Oxford University Press, 1998)

Danchev, A. and Todman, D., eds, *War Diaries 1939–1945. Lord Alanbrooke* (London, Weidenfeld & Nicolson, 2001)

Daniels, J., *The Man of Independence* (London, Gollancz, 1951)

Dawson, R.H., *The Decision To Aid Russia 1941* (Chapel Hill, University of North Carolina Press, 1959)

Deane, J.R., *The Strange Alliance. The Story of American Efforts at Wartime Co-operation with Russia* (London, John Murray, 1947)

Dilks, D.N., ed., *The Diaries of Sir Alexander Cadogan 1938–1945* (London, Cassell, 1971)

Dixon, P., *Double Diploma* (London, Hutchinson, 1968)

Dockrill, S., *Britain's Policy for West German Rearmament 1950–1955* (Cambridge, Cambridge University Press, 199!)

Dockrill, S., 'Britain's Power and Influence: Dealing with Three Roles and the Wilson Government's Defence Debate at Chequers in November 1964', *Diplomacy and Statecraft*, 11, no. 1 (2000): pp. 211–40

Dockrill, M. and Young, J.W., eds, *British Foreign Policy 1945–1956* (Basingstoke, Macmillan, 1989)

Duchene, F., *Jean Monnet* (New York, Norton, 1994)

Duke, S., *U.S. Defence Bases in the United Kingdom* (Basingstoke, Macmillan, 1987)

Eayrs, J., ed., *The Commonwealth and Suez. A Documentary Survey* (Toronto, Oxford University Press, 1964)

Eban, A., *An Autobiography* (New York, Random House,1977)

Eisenhower, D.D., *Mandate for Change 1953–1956* (London, Heinemann, 1963)

Eisenhower, D.D., *Waging Peace 1956–1961* London, Heinemann, 1966)

Epstein, L., British Politics in the Suez Crisis (London, Pall Mall Press, 1964)

Ferguson, N., *The Pity of War* (London, Allen Lane, 1998)

Ferrell, R.H., *Off The Record. The Private Papers of Harry S. Truman* (Harmondsworth, Penguin Books, 1982)

Ferrell, R.H., *Harry S. Truman. A Life* (Columbia, Missouri, University of Missouri Press, 1994)

Finer, H., *Dulles Over Suez* (London, Heinemann, 1964)

Foreign Relations of the United States, Annual Volumes

Gerson, L.L., *John Foster Dulles* (Cooper Square, New York, 1967)

Gimbel, J., *The Origins of the Marshall Plan* (Stanford, Stanford University Press, 1976)

Gladwyn, Lord, *Memoirs* (London, Weidenfeld & Nicolson, 1972)

Gowing, M.M., *Independence and Deterrence. Britain and Atomic Energy 1945–1952*, 2 vols (London, Macmillan, 1974)

Haynes, J.E. and Kiehr, H., *Venona. Decoding Soviet Espionage in America* (New Haven, Yale University Press, 1999)

Heikal, H.M., *Cutting The Lion's Tale. Suez through Egyptian Eyes* (London, Corgi, 1988)

Heiss, M.A., 'The United States, Great Britain, and the Creation of the Anglo-Iranian Oil Consortium', *International History Review*, 16 (1994): pp. 511–35

Henderson, N., *The Private Office* (London, Weidenfeld & Nicolson, 1984)

Heren, L., *No Hail, No Farewell* (London, Weidenfeld & Nicolson, 1970)

Herring, G.C., *Aid To Russia 1941–1946. Strategy, Diplomacy, the Origins of the Cold War* (New York, Columbia University Press, 1973)

Hinton, H.C., *Communist China in World Politics* (London, Macmillan, 1966)

Hogan, M.J., *The Marshall Plan. America, Britain, and the Reconstruction of Western Europe 1947–1952* (Cambridge, Cambridge University Press, 1987)

Hoopes, T., *The Devil and John Foster Dulles* (London, Deutsch, 1974)

Hull, C., *The Memoirs of Cordell Hull*, 2 vols (London, Hodder & Stoughton, 1948)

Hunt, Sir D., *On the Spot* (London, Peter Davies, 1975)

Johnson, L.B., *The Vantage Point. Perspectives of the Presidency 1963–1969* (New York, Holt, Rinehart and Winston, 1971)

Johnson, P., *The Suez War* (London, MacGibbon & Kee, 1957)

Kant, I., *Perpetual Peace* [1795] (London, Allen & Unwin, 1903)

Kennan, G., *Memoirs 1925–1950* (Boston, Little, 1967)

Kissinger, H., *The White House Years* (London, Weidenfeld & Nicolson, and Joseph, 1979)

Kitson, F., *Bunch of Five* (London, Faber & Faber, 1977)

Kyle, K., *Suez* (London, Weidenfeld & Nicolson, 1991)

LaFeber, W., *The American Age. United States Foreign Policy at Home and Abroad since 1750* (New York, Norton, 1989)

Liberman, P., *Does Conquest Pay? The Exploitation of Occupied Industrial Societies* (Princeton, N.J., Princeton Unversity Press, 1996)

Lloyd, S., *Suez 1956* (London, Cape, 1978)

Lodge, D., *Ginger, You're Barmy* (London, Secker & Warburg, 1982)

Lord, C., *British Entry to the European Community under the Heath Government of 1970–74* (Aldershot, Dartmouth, 1993)

Lord, C., *Absent At The Creation. Britain and the Formation of the European Community 1950–1952* (Aldershot, Gower, 1996)

Louis, W.R., *Imperialism At Bay 1941–1945. The United States and the Decolonization of the British Empire* (Oxford, Clarendon Press, 1977)

Louis, W.R., *The British Empire in the Middle East 1945–1951* (Oxford, Clarendon Press, 1984)

Louis, W.R. and Stookey, R.W., *The End of the Palestine Mandate* (London, Tauris, 1986)

Louis, W.R. and Bull, H., eds, *The 'Special Relationship': Anglo-American Relations since 1945* (Oxford, Oxford University Press, 1989)

Louis, W.R. and Owen, R., eds, *Suez 1956. The Crisis and its Consequences* (Oxford University Press, 1989)

Lowell, A.L. *Governments and Parties in Continental Europe*, 2 vols (London, Longmans, Green 1896)

Ludlow, N.P., *Dealing With Britain: The Six and the First U.K. Application to join the E.E.C.* (Cambridge, Cambridge University Press, 1997)

McKenzie, F., *Redefining the Bonds of Commonwealth 1939–1948* (Basingstoke, Palgrave Macmillan, 2002)

Mansergh, N., *The Commonwealth Experience* (London, Weidenfeld & Nicolson, 1969)

Martin, L.W., 'The Market for Strategic Ideas in Britain; The Sandys Era', *American Political Science Review*, LVI (1962): pp. 23–41

Matthew, H.C.G., *The Liberal Imperialists* (Oxford, Oxford University Press, 1973)

Merrill, D., ed., *Documentary History of the Truman Presidency*, 20 vols (University Publications of America, 1996)

Miller, M., *Plain Speaking. An Oral Biography of Harry S. Truman* (London, Coronet, 1978)

Millis, W., ed., *The Forrestal Diaries* (London, Cassell, 1952)

Milward, A.S., *The Reconstruction of Western Europe 1945–1951* (London, Methuen, 1984)

Milward, A.S., *The European Rescue of the Nation State* (London, Routledge, 1994)

Mockaitis, T.R. *British Counter Insurgency in the Post-Imperial Era* (Manchester, Manchester University Press, 1995)

Moncrieff, A., ed., *Suez Ten Years After* (London, BBC, 1967)

Montgomery, Lord, *Memoirs* (London, Collins, 1958)

Moravcsik, A., *The Choice for Europe. Social Purpose and State Power from Messina to Maastricht* (London, UCL Press, 1998)

Muller, J.W., ed., *Churchill as Peacemaker* (Cambridge, Cambridge University Press, 1997)

Murphy, R., *Diplomat Among Warriors* (London, Collins, 1964)

Nixon, R.M., *Memoirs* (New York, Grosset and Dunlap, 1978)

Nutting, A., *No End of a Lesson* (London, Constable, 1967)

Ovendale, R., ed., *The Foreign Policy of the British Labour Governments 1945–1951* (Leicester, Leicester University Press, 1984)

Ovendale, R., *British Defence Policy since 1945* (Manchester, Manchester University Press, 1994)

Ovendale, R., *The Origins of the Arab-Israeli Wars* (Harlow, Pearson Education, 1999)

Ovendale, R., *Britain, The United States, and the Transfer of Power in the Middle East 1945–1962* (Leicester, Leicester University Press, 1996

Parmet, H.S., *JFK The Presidency of John F. Kennedy* (Harmondsworth, Penguin, 1984)

Petersen, T.T., 'Anglo-American Rivalry in the Middle East: The Struggle for the Buraimi Oasis 1952–1957', *International History Review*, 14 (1992): pp. 71–91)

Rees, D., *Harry Dexter White. A Study in Paradox* (London, Macmillan, 1973)

Rothwell, V., *Britain and the Cold War 1941–1947* (London, Cape, 1982)

Reiss, H.S., *Political Writings of Kant* (Cambridge, Cambridge University Press, 1991)

Ridley, N., ed., *One Europe* (London, Conservative Political Centre, 1965)

Robertson, T., *Crisis. The Inside Story of the Suez Conspiracy* (London, Hutchinson, 1965)

Rosecrance, R.N. *Defense of the Realm. British Strategy in the Nuclear Epoch* (New York, Columbia Press, 1968)

Ruane, K., 'Anthony Eden, British Diplomacy, and the Origins of the Geneva Conference of 1954', *Historical Journal*, 37 (1994): pp. 153–72

Ruehsen, M. de M., 'Operation Ajax Revisited: Iran 1953', *Middle Eastern Studies*, 29 (1993): pp. 467–486

Scott, L.V., *The Politics and Policy of National Service* (Oxford, Clarendon Press, 1993)

Schlesinger, A.M., *A Thousand Days. John F. Kennedy at the White House* (Boston, Houghton Miffin, 1965)

Shuckburgh, E., *Descent to Suez. Diaries 1951–1956* (London, Weidenfeld & Nicolson, 1986)

Small, M., *The Presidency of Richard Nixon* (Lawrence, University Press of Kansas, 1999)

Smith, I., *The Great Betrayal* (London, Blake, 1997)

Smith, R., 'A Climate of Opinion: British Officials and the Development of British Soviet Policy 1945–1947', *International Affairs*, 64 (1988): pp. 631–47

Smith, R. and Zametica, J., 'The Cold Warrior: Clement Attlee Reconsidered', *International Affairs*, 61 (1985): pp. 237–52

Sorensen, T.C., *Kennedy* (New York, Harper and Row, 1965)

Strang, Lord, *Home and Abroad* (London, Deutsch, 1956)

Sykes, C., *Cross Roads to Israel* (London, Collins, 1965)

Thorne, C., *Border Crossings* (Oxford, Blackwell, 1988)

Troen, S.I. and Shemesh, M., eds, *The Suez–Sinai Crisis 1956* (London, Cass, 1990)

Truman, H.S., *Year of Decisions 1945* (London, Hodder & Stoughton, 1955)

Truman, H.S., *Years of Trial and Hope 1946–1953* (London, Hodder & Stoughton, 1956)

Weinstein, A., and Vassiliev, A., *The Haunted Wood. Soviet Espionage in America – the Stalin Era* (New York, Random House,1999)

Welensky, Sir R., *4000 Days* (London, Collins, 1964)

West, N., *Venona. The Greatest Secret of the Cold War* (London, HarperCollins, 1999)

Wilson, W., *The State. Elements of Historical and Practical Politics* (London, Heath, 1919)

Wolf, D.C., '"To Secure a Convenience": Britain Recognizes China – 1950', *Journal of Contemporary History*, 18 (1983): pp. 299–326

Wood, J.R.T., *The Welensky Papers* (Durban, Graham, 1983)
X [Kennan, G.], 'The Sources of Soviet Conduct', *Foreign Affairs*, 25 (1946–47): pp. 566–82
Young, J.W., *Britain, France and the Unity of Europe 1945–1951* (Leicester, Leicester University Press, 1984)
Young, J.W., ed., *The Foreign Policy of Churchill's Peacetime Government 1951–1955* (Leicester, Leicester University Press, 1988)
Zametica, J., ed., *British Officials and British Foreign Policy 1945–1950* (Leicester, Leicester University Press, 1990)
Zeigler, P., *Mountbatten* (London, Collins, 1985)

III   Economic and social history

[A] Government publications [London: HMSO]

Ministry of Transport, *Report of the* (McGowan) *Committee on Electricity Distribution* [1936]
Cmd 6261 [1941] *Sources of War Finance. An Analysis and an Estimate of the National Income and Expenditure in 1938 and 1940*
Cmd 6265 [1941] *Determination of Needs Act 1941*
Cmd 6404 [1942] *Social Insurance and Allied Services. Report by Sir William Beveridge*
Cmd 6458 [1942] *Educational Reconstruction*
Cmd 6502 [1944] *A National Health Service*
Cmd 6527 [1944] *Employment Policy*
Cmd 6550 [1944] *Social Insurance. Part I*
Cmd 6551[1944] *Social Insurance. Part II. Workmen's Compensation. Proposals for an Industrial Injury Scheme*
Cmd 6610 [1945] *Report of the* (Reid) *Technical Advisory Committee on Coal Mining*
Cmd 6699 [1945] *Report of the* (Heyworth) *Committee of Inquiry into the Gas Industry*
Cmd 6707 [1945] *Washington Negotiations. Statistical Material presented during the Negotiations*
Cmd 6761 [1946] *National Health Service Bill. Summary of the Proposed New Service*
Cmd 7046 [1947] *Economic Survey for 1947*
Cmd 7321 [1948] *Statement on Personal Incomes, Costs and Prices*
Cmd 7344 [1948] *Economic Survey for 1948*
Cmd 7419 [1948] *Capital Punishment*
Cmd 7647 [1949] *Economic Survey for 1949*
Hancock, W.K. and Gowing, M.M., *British War Economy* [1949]
Titmuss, R.M., *Problems of Social Policy* [1950]
Cmd *7915 [1950] Economic Survey for 1950*
Cmd *8195 [1951] Economic Survey, 1951*
Cmd 8509 [1952] *Economic Survey for 1952*
Cmd 8800 [1953] *Economic Survey for 1953*
Cmd 8932 [1953] *Report of the* (Gowers) *Royal Commission on Capital Punishment*
Cmd *9108 [1954] Economic Survey, 1954*
Cmd *9352 [1955]* (Cameron) *Interim Report of a Court of Inquiry into the Dispute between the British Transport Commission and the National Union of Railwaymen*

Cmd *9412 [1955] Economic Survey, 1955*
Cmd *9663 [1956] Report of the* (Guillebaud) *Committee of Enquiry into the Cost of the National Health Service.*
Cmd *9672 [1956] Report of the* (Herbert) *Committee of Inquiry into the Electricity Industry*
Cmd 9703 [1956] *Technical Education*
Cmd *9725 [1956] Economic Implications of Full Employment*
Cmd *9728 [1956] Economic Survey, 1956*
Sayers, R.S., *Financial Policy 1939–45 [1956]*
Cmnd 113 [1957] *Economic Survey, 1957*
Cmnd 350 [1958] *Bank Rate. Report of the* (Parker) *Tribunal*
Cmnd 394 [1958] *Economic Survey, 1958*
Cmnd 708 [1959] *Economic Survey, 1959*
15 to 18. A Report of the (Crowther) *Central Advisory Council for Education (England) 1959*
Cmnd 976 [1960] *Economic Survey, 1960*
Cmnd 1334 [1961] *Economic Survey, 1961*
Cmnd 1337 [1961] *The Financial and Economic Obligations of the Nationalized Industries*
Cmnd 1432 [1961] *Control of Public Expenditure*
Cmnd 1604 [1962] *A Hospital Plan for England and Wales*
Cmnd 1678 [1962] *Economic Survey, 1962*
Cmnd 2154 [1963] *Report of the* (Robbins) *Committee on Higher Education*
British Railways Board, *The Reshaping of British Railways* [1963]
National Economic Development Council, *Conditions Favourable to Faster Growth* [1963]
National Economic Development Council, *Growth of the U.K. Economy to 1966* [1963]
Cmnd 2577 [1965] *Machinery of Prices and Incomes Policy*
Cmnd 2639 [1965] *Prices and Incomes Policy*
Cmnd 2764 [1965] *The National Plan*
Cmnd 2808 [1965] *Prices and Incomes Policy: An 'Early Warning System'*
Cmnd 2922 [1966] *University of the Air*
Cmnd 3006 [1966] *A Plan for Polytechnics and Other Colleges*
Cmnd 3150 [1966] *Prices and Incomes Standstill: Period of Severe Restraint*
Cmnd 3235 [1967] *Prices and Incomes Policy after 30 June 1967*
Cmnd 3437 [1967] *Nationalized Industries. A Review of Economic and Financial Obligations*
Cmnd 3590 [1968] *Productivity, Prices and Incomes in 1968 and 1969*
Cmnd 3623 [1968] *Report of the* (Donovan) *Royal Commission on Trade Unions and Employers' Associations*
Cmnd 3883 [1969] *National Superannuation and Social Insurance: Proposals for Earnings Related Social Security*
Cmnd 3888 [1969] *In Place of Strife. A Policy for Industrial Relations*
Cmnd 4237 [1969] *Productivity, Prices and Incomes Policy after 1969*
Cmnd 4515 [1970] *New Policies for Public Spending*
Cmnd 4860 [1972] *Rolls Royce and the RB211 Aero Engine*
Cmnd 4918 [1972] *Shipbuilding on the Upper Clyde*
Cmnd 4942 [1972] *Industrial and Regional Development*

Cmnd 5055 [1972] *National Health Service Reorganization: England*
Cmnd 5125 [1972] *A Programme for Controlling Inflation. The First Stage*
Cmnd 5267 [1973] *Counter Inflation Programme: Operation of Stage 2*
Cmnd 5446 [1973] *The Counter Inflation Policy: Stage 3*
Cmnd 5710 [1974] *The Regeneration of British Industry*
Cmnd 6315 [1975] *An Approach to Industrial Strategy*
Chester, Sir D.N., *The Nationalization of British Industry 1945–1951*[1975]
Cmnd 6151 [1975] *The Attack on Inflation*
Cmnd 6440 [1976] *Cash Limits on Public Expenditure*
Webster, C., *The Health Services Since The War*, I: *Problems of Health Care. The National Health Service Before 1957* [1988]
Webster, C., *The Health Services Since The War*, II: *Government and Health Care. The National Health Service 1958–1979* [1996]

[B] Further sources

Abel-Smith, B., *The Hospitals 1800–1948* (London, Heinemann, 1964)
Artis, M. and Cobham, D., eds, *Labour's Economic Policies 1974–1979* (Manchester, Manchester University Press, 1991)
Ashworth, W., *The History of the British Coal Industry*, V: *1946–1982: The Nationalized Industry* (Oxford, Clarendon Press, 1986)
Barnes, D., and Reid, E., *Government and Trade Unions: The British Experience 1964–1979* (London, Heinemann, 1980)
Barnett, C., 'The Wartime Roots of Britain's Post-War Industrial "Decline"', *Contemporary Record*, I, no. 2 (Summer 1987): pp. 11–15
Barnett, M.J., *The Politics of Legislation. The Rent Act of 1957* (London, Weidenfeld & Nicolson, 1969)
Beckerman, W., ed., *The Labour Government's Economic Record 1964–1970* (London, Duckworth, 1972)
Beveridge, Sir W., *Full Employment in a Free Society* (London, Allen & Unwin, 1944)
Beveridge, Lord, *Voluntary Action* (London, Allen & Unwin, 1948)
Beveridge, Lord, *Power and Influence* (London, Hodder & Stoughton, 1953)
Bridges, Sir E.E., *Treasury Control* (London, Athlone Press, 1950)
Brandon, H., *Into The Red. The Struggle for Sterling 1964–1966* (London, Deutsch, 1966)
Briggs, A., 'The Welfare State in Historical Perspective', *Archives Européennes de Sociologie*, II (1961): pp. 221–58
Brittan, S., *The Treasury under the Tories 1951–1964* (Harmondsworth, Penguin, 1964)
Burk, K. and Cairncross, A., 'Goodbye Great Britain.' The 1976 IMF Crisis (New Haven, Yale University Press, 1992)
Cairncross, A., *Years of Recovery. British Economic Policy 1945–1951* (London, Methuen, 1985)
Cairncross, A., ed., *The Robert Hall Diaries 1947–1953* (London, Unwin Hyman,1989)
Cairncross, A. and Watts, N., *The Economic Section 1939–1961* (London, Routledge, 1989)
Cairncross, A., ed., *The Robert Hall Diaries 1954–1961* (London, Unwin Hyman, 1991)

Cairncross, A., *The Wilson Years. Treasury Diary 1964–1969* (London, The Historians' Press, 1997)

Clark, C., 'Public Finance and Changes in the Value of Money', *Economic Journal*, LV (1945): pp. 371–89)

Chester, D.N., *Lessons of the British War Economy* (Cambridge, Cambridge University Press, 1951)

Chick, M., *Industrial Policy in Britain 1945–1951* (Cambridge, Cambridge University Press, 1998)

Clifford, C., 'The Rise and Fall of the Department of Economic Affairs 1964–69: British Government and Indicative Planning', *Contemporary British History*, 11 (1997): pp. 94–116

Clifford, C. and McMillan, A., eds, 'Witness Seminar: The Department of Economic Affairs', *Contemporary British History*, 11 (1997): pp. 117–42

Collins, C.D.E., *The European Communities. The Social Policy of the First Phase*, 2 vols (London, Martin Robertson, 1975)

Deacon, A.J. and Bradshaw, J., *Reserved For The Poor. The Means Test in Social Policy* (Oxford, Martin Robertson, 1983)

Dell, E., *A Hard Pounding. Politics and Economic Crisis 1974–76* (Oxford, Oxford University Press, 1991)

Dow, J.C.R., *The Management of the British Economy 1945–1960* (Cambridge, Cambridge University Press, 1964)

Eckstein, H., *Pressure Group Politics. The Case of the British Medical Association* (London, Allen & Unwin, 1960)

Eckstein, H., *The English Health Service. Its Origins, Structure, and Achievements* (Cambridge Mass., Harvard University Press, 1964)

Engerman, S.L. and Gallman, R.E., eds, *The Cambridge Economic History of the United States*, III: *The Twentieth Century* (Cambridge University Press, 2000)

Feinstein, C., ed., *The Managed Economy. Essays in British Economic Performance since 1929* (Oxford, Oxford University Press, 1983)

Fforde, J., *The Bank of England and Public Policy 1941–1958* (Cambridge, Cambridge University Press, 1992)

Foldes, L., 'Control of Nationalized Industries', *Public Law*, 2 (1957): pp. 122–38

Fry, G.K., *The Growth of Government. The Development of Ideas about the Role of the State and the Machinery and Functions of Government in Britain since 1780* (London, Cass, 1979)

Fry, G.K., 'The Path to the Privatization of Public Enterprises in Britain: A Public Policy Analysis', *Public Policy and Administration*, 9 (1994): pp. 19–32

Galbraith, J.K., *The Affluent Society* (New York, New American Library, 1958)

Gardner, R.N., *Sterling-Dollar Diplomacy in Current Perspective. The Origins and the Prospects of Our International Economic Order* (New York, Columbia University Press, 1980)

Gourvish, T., *British Railways 1948–1973. A Business History* (Cambridge, Cambridge University Press, 1986)

Hannah, L., *Electricity Before Nationalization. A Study of the Development of the Electricity Supply Industry in Britain to 1948* (London, Macmillan, 1979)

Hannah, L., *Engineers, Managers and Politicians. The First Fifteen Years of Nationalized Electricity Supply in Britain* (London, Macmillan, 1982)

Harris, J., *William Beveridge. A Biography* (Oxford, Clarendon Press, 1977)

Harrod, R.F., 'Mr Keynes and Traditional Theory', *Econometrica*, 5 (1937): pp. 74–86

Harrod, R.F., *The Life of John Maynard Keynes* (London, Macmillan, 1951)

Heath, C.G., *A Guide to the Industrial Relations Act 1971* (London, Sweet & Maxwell, 1971)

Hicks, J.R., 'Mr Keynes and the "Classics"; A Suggested Interpretation', *Econometrica*, 5 (1937): pp. 147–59

Jewkes, J., *New Ordeal By Planning. The Experience of the Forties and the Sixties* (London, Macmillan, 1968)

Johnson, H.G., 'The *General Theory* After Twenty Five Years', *American Economic Review. Papers and Proceeding of the Seventy Third Annual Meeting of the American Economic Association*, LI (1961): pp. 1–17

Johnson, P.B., *Land Fit For Heroes* (Chicago, University of Chicago Press, 1968)

Jones, J., *Union Man* (London, Collins, 1986)

Keegan, W. and Pennant-Rea, R., *Who Runs The Economy?* (London, Temple Smith, 1979)

Keynes, J.M., *The Collected Writings of John Maynard Keynes*, 30 vols (London, Macmillan, 1971–1989)

Kindleberger, C.P., *A Financial History of Western Europe* (London, Allen & Unwin, 1984)

Kogan M., *The Politics of Education. Edward Boyle and Anthony Crosland* (Harmondsworth, Penguin, 1971).

Lowe, R., 'The Second World War, Consensus, and the Foundation of the Welfare State', *Twentieth Century British History*, 1 (1990): pp. 152–82

Lowe, R., *The Welfare State in Britain since 1945* (Basingstoke, Macmillan, 1993)

Macmillan, H., *The Middle Way* (London, Macmillan, 1938).

Macrae, N., *Sunshades in October* (London, Allen & Unwin, 1963)

Macnicol, J., *The Movement for Family Allowances 1918–1945* (London, Heinemann, 1980)

Meade, J., *The Collected Papers of James Meade*, 4 vols (London, Unwin Hyman, 1988–1990)

Mercer, H., Rollings, N., and Tomlinson, J.D., eds, *Labour Governments and Private Industry: Experience of 1945–1951* (Edinburgh, Edinburgh University Press, 1992)

Middleton, R., *Government Versus The Market* (Cheltenham Elgar, 1996)

Moggridge, D.M., *Maynard Keynes: An Economist's Biography* (London, Routledge, 1992)

Morrison, H., *Socialization and Transport* (London, Constable, 1933)

Munby, D.L., 'The Reshaping of British Railways', *Journal of Industrial Economics*, XI (1962–63): pp. 161–82

Owen, G., *From Empire to Europe. The Decline and Revival of British Industry Since the Second World War* (London, HarperCollins, 1999)

Peden, G.C., 'Sir Richard Hopkins and the 'Keynesian Revolution' in Employment Policy', *Economic History Review*, 36 (1983): pp. 281–96

Political and Economic Planning, *Government and Industry* (London, Political and Economic Planning, 1952)

Powell, J.E., 'Conservatives and Social Services', *Political Quarterly*, 24 (1953): pp. 156–66

Robertson, A.J., *The Bleak Midwinter 1947* (Manchester, Manchester University Press, 1987)

Robbins, L.C., *The Economic Problem in Peace and War* (London, Macmillan, 1947)

Robbins, Lord, *Autobiography of an Economist* (London, Macmillan, 1971)

Robson, W.A., *Nationalized Industry and Public Ownership* (London, Allen & Unwin, 1962)

Rogow, A.A., and Shore, P., *The Labour Government and British Industry 1945–1951* (Oxford, Blackwell, 1955)

Rowntree, B.S. and Lavers, G.R., *Poverty and The Welfare State. A Third Social Survey of York dealing only with Economic Questions* (London, Longmans, Green, 1951)

Rupke, N.A., ed., *Science, Politics and The Public Good* (Basingstoke, Macmillan, 1988)

Shanks, M., *The Stagnant Society: A Warning* (Harmondsworth, Penguin, 1961)

Shirras, G.F. and Rostas, L., *The Burden of British Taxation* (Cambridge, Cambridge Press, 1942)

Shonfield, A., *British Economic Policy Since The War* (Harmondsworth, Penguin, 1959)

Skidelsky, R., *John Maynard Keynes*, I: *Hopes Betrayed 1883–1920* (London, Macmillan, 1983)

Skidelsky, R., *John Maynard Keynes*, II: *The Economist as Saviour 1920–1937* (London, Macmillan, 1992)

Skidelsky, R., *John Maynard Keynes*, III: *Fighting For Britain 1937–1946* (London, Macmillan, 2000)

Stevens, R., *Medical Practice in Modern England. The Impact of Specialization and State Medicine* (New Haven, Yale University Press, 1966)

Stocks, M., *Eleanor Rathbone* (London, Gollancz, 1949)

Tawney, R.H., 'The Abolition of Economic Controls 1918–1921', *Economic History Review*, XIII (1943): pp. 1–30

Taylor, R., *The Trade Union Question in British Politics. Government and Unions Since 1945* (Oxford, Blackwell, 1993)

Thomson, A.W.J. and Engleman, S.R., *The Industrial Relations Act. A Review and Analysis* (London, Martin Robertson, 1975)

Timmins, N., *The Five Giants. A Biography of the Welfare State* (London, Fontana Press, 1996)

Tookey, M., 'Three's a Crowd?: Government, Owners, and Workers during the Nationalization of the British Coal Mining Industry 1945–47', *Twentieth Century British History*, 12 (2001): pp. 486–510

Townsend, P., *Sociology and Social Policy* (London, Allen Lane, 1975)

Viner, J., 'Mr Keynes on the Causes of Unemployment', *Quarterly Journal of Economics*, 51 (1936–37): pp. 147–67

Walley, Sir J., *Social Security. Another British Failure?* (London, Knight, 1972)

Webster, C., 'Conflict and Consensus: Explaining the British Health Service', *Twentieth Century British History*, 1 (1990): pp. 115–51

Wickham–Jones, M., *Economic Strategy and the Labour Party. Politics and Policy Making 1970–83* (Basingstoke, Macmillan, 1996)

Williams, G., 'The Myth of "Fair" Wages', *Economic Journal*, 66 (1956): pp. 621–34

Winter, J.D., ed., *The Working Class in Modern British History* (Cambridge, Cambridge University Press, 1983)

Wood, A., *The Groundnuts Affair* (London, Bodley Head, 1950)

Wootton, B., 'Before and After Beveridge', *Political Quarterly*, XIV (1943): pp. 357–63

Wootton, B., *The Social Foundations of Wage Policy* (London, Allen & Unwin, 1955)

Worswick, G.D.N., and Ady, P.H., eds, *The British Economy 1945–1950* (Oxford, Clarendon Press, 1952)

Worswick, G.D.N., and Ady, P.H., eds, *The British Economy in the Nineteen Fifties* (Oxford, Clarendon Press,1962)

Zweig, F., *The British Worker* (Harmondsworth, Penguin, 1952)

Zweiniger–Bargielowska, I., *Austerity in Britain. Rationing, Controls, and Consumption 1939–1955* (Oxford, Oxford University Press, 2000)

Index